STAR-LORD GAMORA ROCKET RACCOON GROOT DRAX IRON MAN

GN BEN

GUARDIANS OF THE GALAXY

ANGELA

WRITER: **BRIAN MICHAEL BENDIS** CONSULTANT: **NEIL GAIMAN**

ARTISTS, #4-7: **SARA PICHELLI**

WITH **OLIVIER COIPEL & MARK MORALES** (#6, PP. 3-8)

AND **VALERIO SCHITI** (#7, PP. 8-13, 20)

ART & COLOR, #8-9: **FRANCESCO FRANCAVILLA**

ARTIST, #10: **KEVIN MAGUIRE**

COLORISTS, #4-7 & #10: **JUSTIN PONSOR** WITH **IVE SVORCINA** (#6, PP. 3-8)

COVER ART: **SARA PICHELLI & JUSTIN PONSOR** (#4-7),

FRANCESCO FRANCAVILLA (#8-9) AND **KEVIN MAGUIRE & EDGAR DELGADO** (#10)

LETTERER: **VC'S CORY PETIT**

ASSISTANT EDITOR: **ELLIE PYLE** EDITOR: **STEPHEN WACKER**

ANGELA CO-CREATED BY **TODD McFARLANE & NEIL GAIMAN**

COLLECTION EDITOR: **JENNIFER GRÜNWALD** ASSISTANT EDITORS: **ALEX STARBUCK & NELSON RIBEIRO**
EDITOR, SPECIAL PROJECTS: **MARK D. BEAZLEY** SENIOR EDITOR, SPECIAL PROJECTS: **JEFF YOUNGQUIST**
SVP OF PRINT & DIGITAL PUBLISHING SALES: DAVID GABRIEL BOOK DESIGNER: **RODOLFO MURAGUCHI**

EDITOR IN CHIEF: **AXEL ALONSO** CHIEF CREATIVE OFFICER: **JOE QUESADA**
PUBLISHER: **DAN BUCKLEY** EXECUTIVE PRODUCER: **ALAN FINE**

GUARDIANS OF THE GALAXY VOL. 2: ANGELA. Contains material originally published in magazine form as GUARDIANS OF THE GALAXY #4-10. First printing 2013. ISBN# 978-0-7851-6829-4. Published by MARVEL WORLDWIDE, INC., a subsidiary of MARVEL ENTERTAINMENT, LLC. OFFICE OF PUBLICATION: 135 West 50th Street, New York, NY 10020. Copyright © 2013 Marvel Characters, Inc. All rights reserved. All characters featured in this issue and the distinctive names and likenesses thereof, and all related indicia are trademarks of Marvel Characters, Inc. No similarity between any of the names, characters, persons, and/or institutions in this magazine with those of any living or dead person or institution is intended, and any such similarity which may exist is purely coincidental. **Printed in the U.S.A.** ALAN FINE, EVP - Office of the President, Marvel Worldwide, Inc. and EVP & CMO Marvel Characters B.V.; DAN BUCKLEY, Publisher & President - Print, Animation & Digital Divisions; JOE QUESADA, Chief Creative Officer; TOM BREVOORT, SVP of Publishing; DAVID BOGART, SVP of Operations & Procurement, Publishing; C.B. CEBULSKI, SVP of Creator & Content Development; DAVID GABRIEL, SVP of Print & Digital Publishing Sales; JIM O'KEEFE, VP of Operations & Logistics; DAN CARR, Executive Director of Publishing Technology; SUSAN CRESPI, Editorial Operations Manager; ALEX MORALES, Publishing Operations Manager; STAN LEE, Chairman Emeritus. For information regarding advertising in Marvel Comics or on Marvel.com, please contact Niza Disla, Director of Marvel Partnerships, at ndisla@marvel.com. For Marvel subscription inquiries, please call 800-217-9158. Manufactured between 10/18/2013 and 12/2/2013 by R.R. DONNELLEY, INC., SALEM, VA, USA.

LEGO and the Minifigure figurine are trademarks or copyrights of the LEGO Group of Companies. ©2013 The LEGO Group. Characters featured in particular decorations are not commercial products and might not be available for purchase.

10 9 8 7 6 5 4 3 2 1

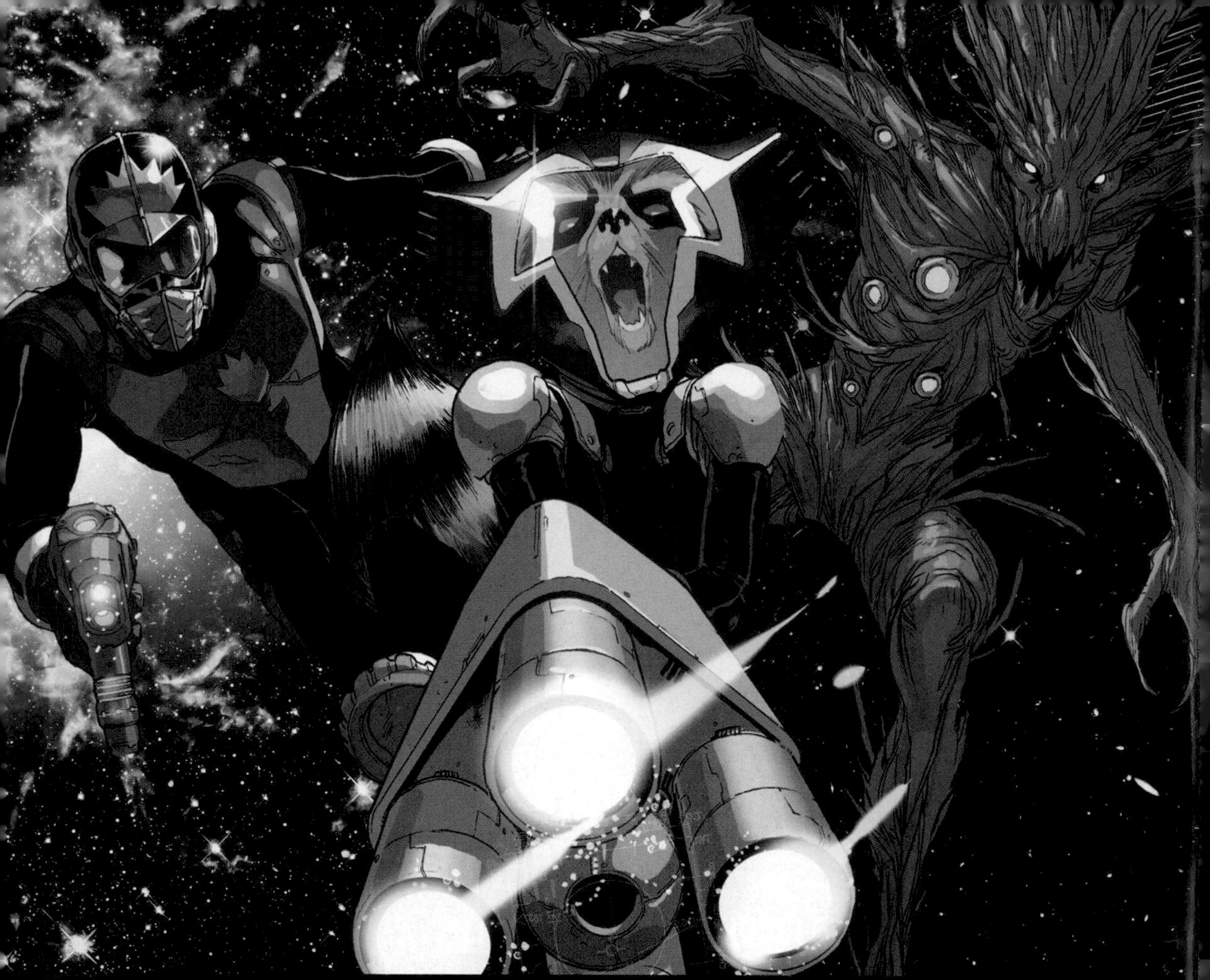

PREVIOUSLY...

LEGENDARY AVENGER IRON MAN HAS TAKEN A LEAVE OF ABSENCE FROM THE PLANET EARTH TO DISCOVER WHAT ELSE THE UNIVERSE HAS TO OFFER.

PETER QUILL'S ESTRANGED FATHER, THE KING OF SPARTAX, TRIED TO CAPTURE THE GUARDIANS FOR DISOBEYING HIS NEW RULE THAT NO ALIEN HAND MAY TOUCH THE PLANET EARTH.

THE GUARDIANS BARELY ESCAPED HIS GRASP BUT NOT BEFORE PETER PUBLICLY ACCUSED HIS FATHER OF TRYING TO TAKE THE EARTH FOR HIMSELF.

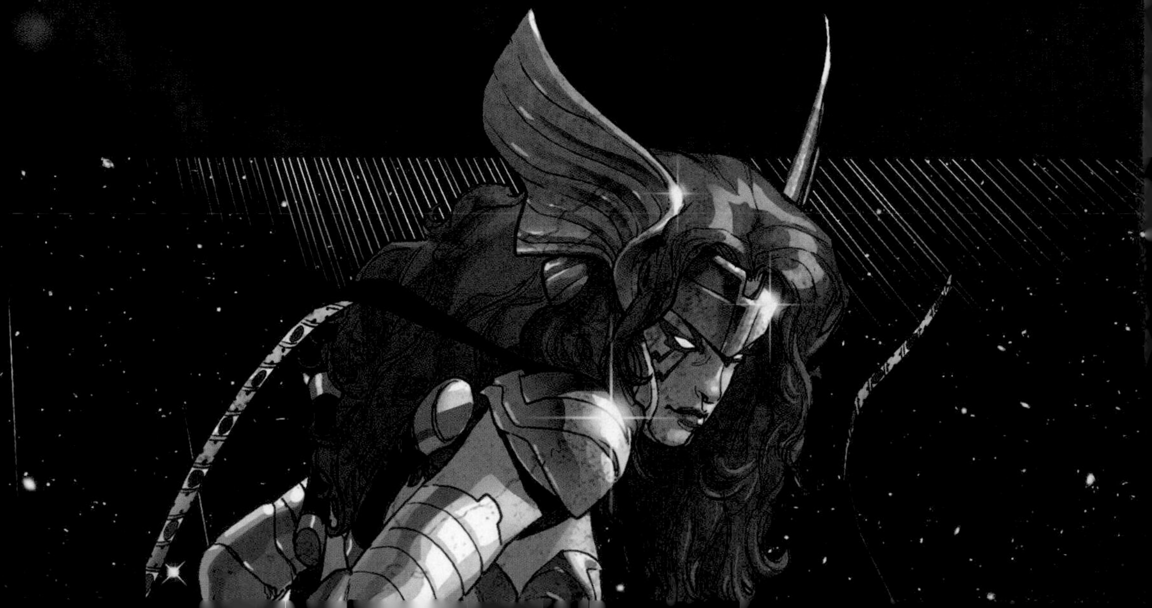

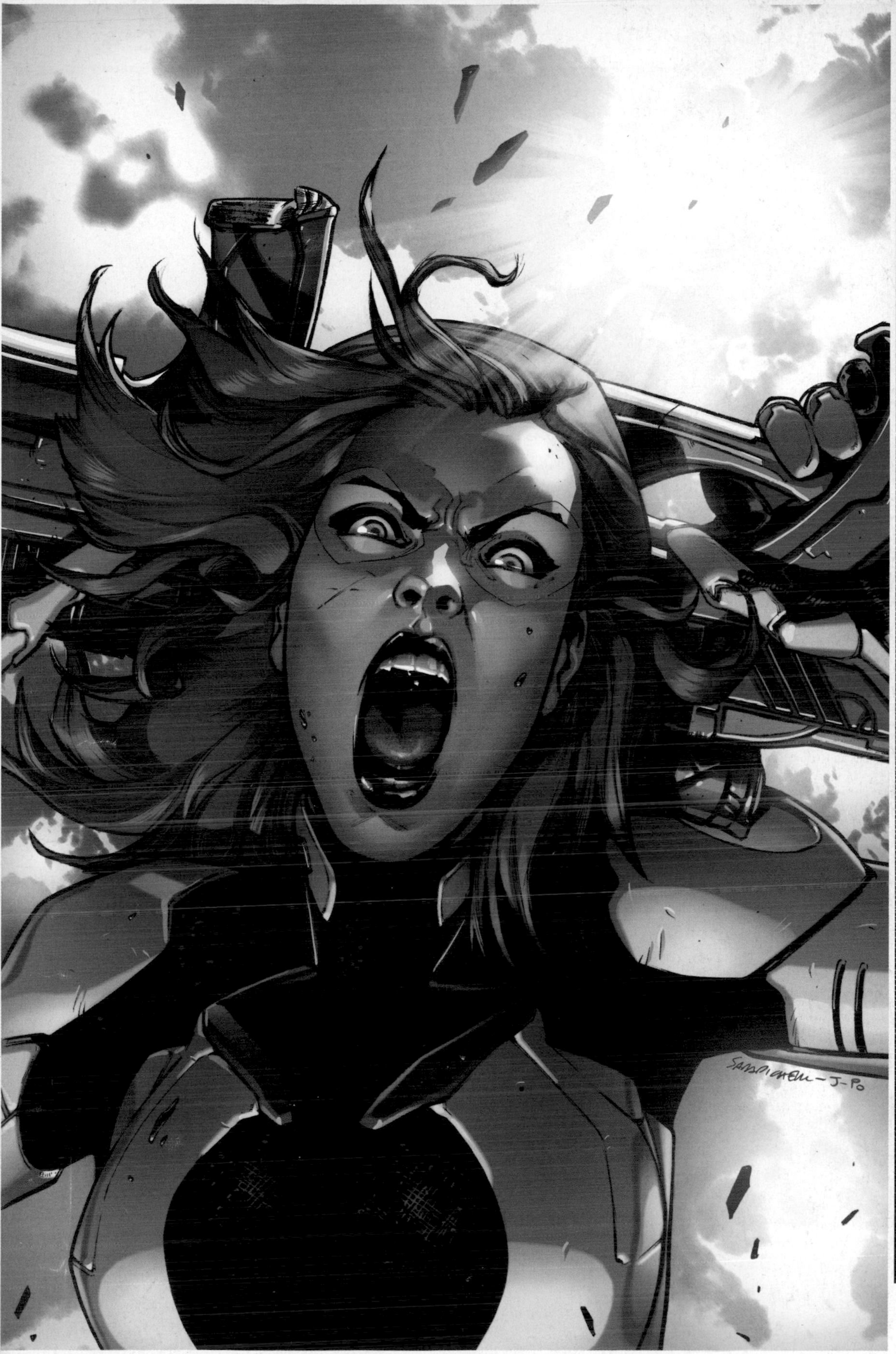

4

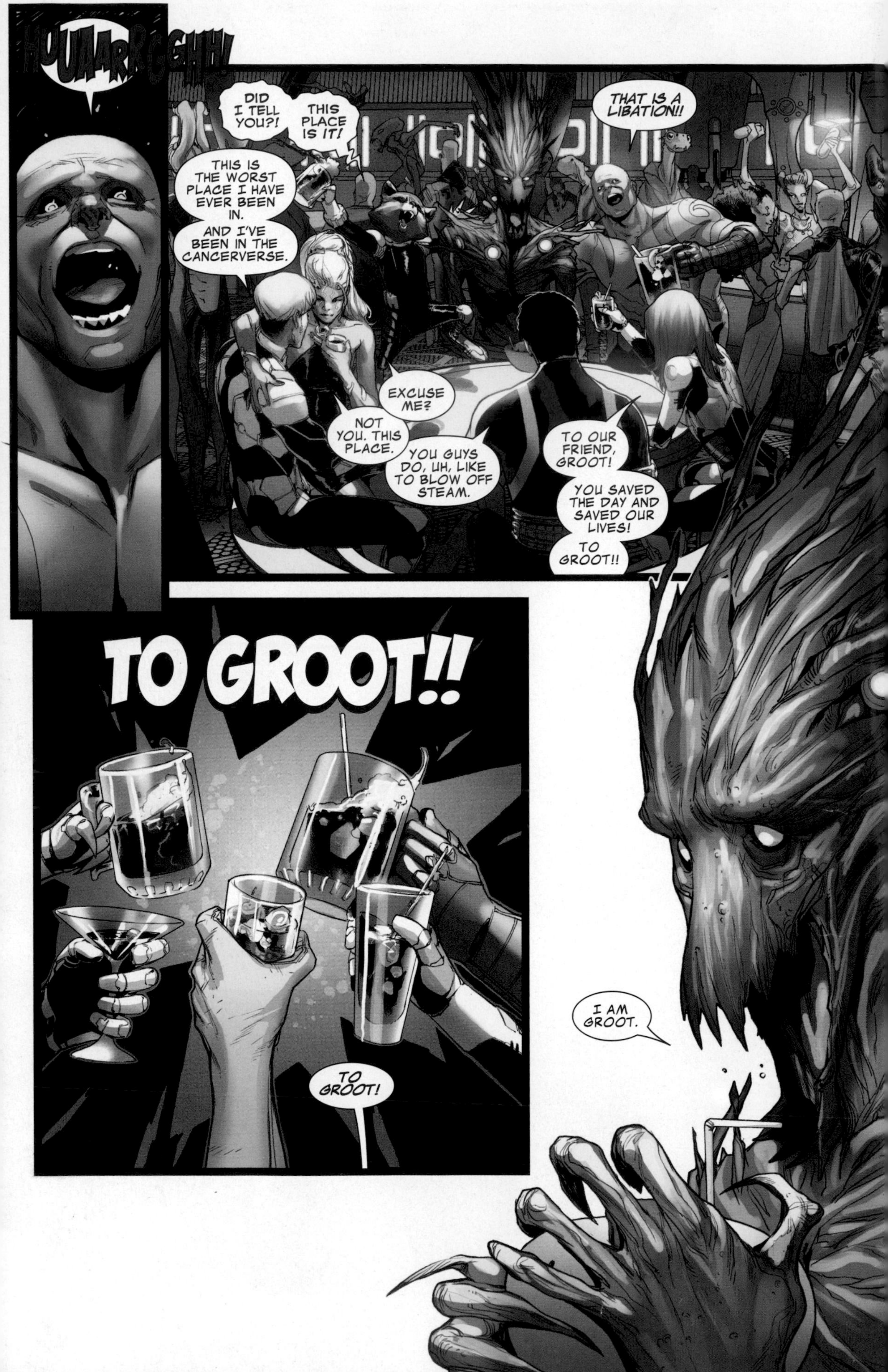
HOUAARRGGHH!
DID I TELL YOU?!
THIS PLACE IS IT!
THIS IS THE WORST PLACE I HAVE EVER BEEN IN.
AND I'VE BEEN IN THE CANCERVERSE.
THAT IS A LIBATION!!
EXCUSE ME?
NOT YOU. THIS PLACE.
YOU GUYS DO, UH, LIKE TO BLOW OFF STEAM.
TO OUR FRIEND, GROOT!
YOU SAVED THE DAY AND SAVED OUR LIVES!
TO GROOT!!
TO GROOT!!
TO GROOT!
I AM GROOT.

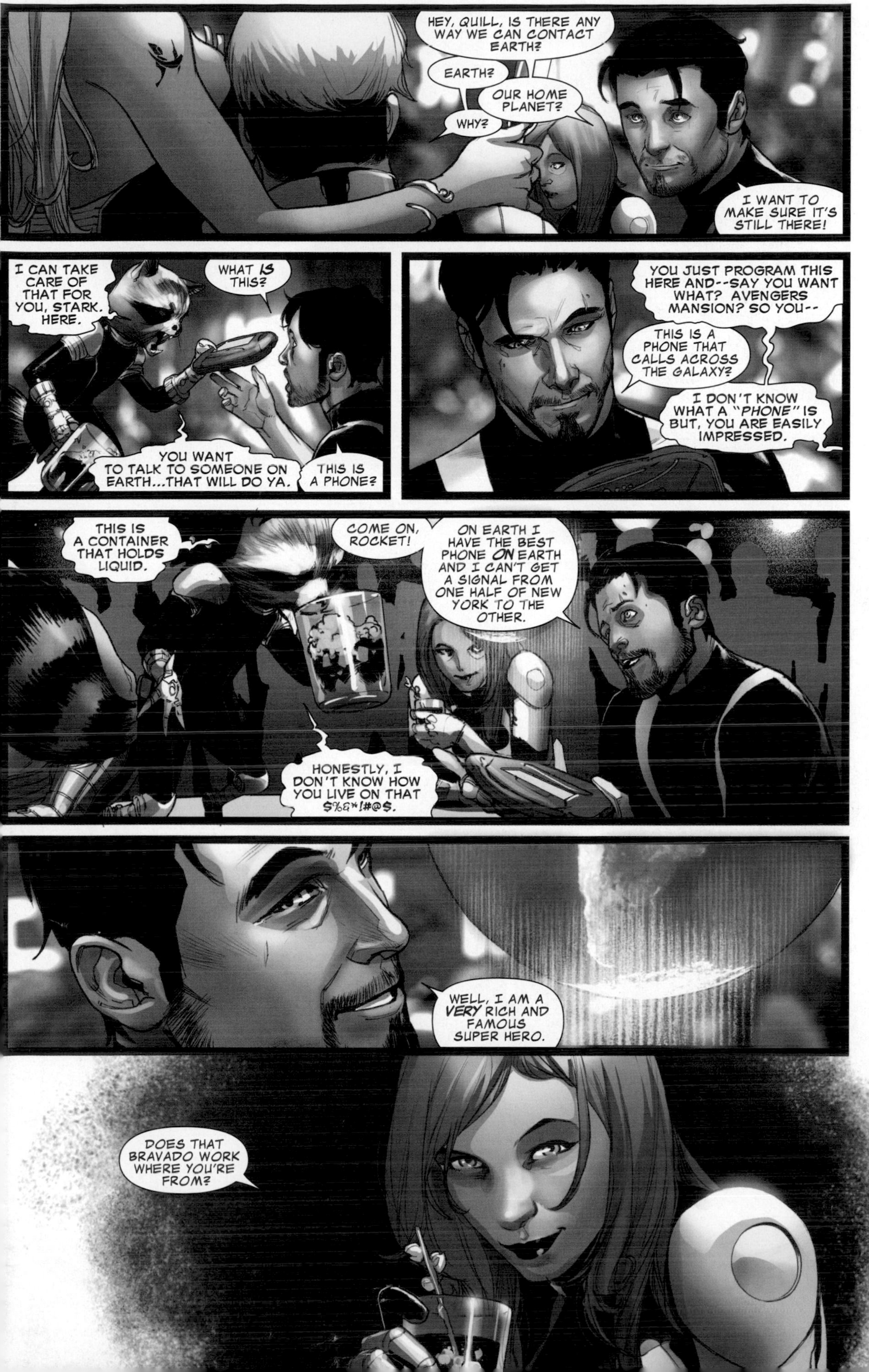
HEY, QUILL, IS THERE ANY WAY WE CAN CONTACT EARTH?
EARTH?
OUR HOME PLANET?
WHY?
I WANT TO MAKE SURE IT'S STILL THERE!
I CAN TAKE CARE OF THAT FOR YOU, STARK. HERE.
WHAT IS THIS?
YOU WANT TO TALK TO SOMEONE ON EARTH...THAT WILL DO YA.
THIS IS A PHONE?
YOU JUST PROGRAM THIS HERE AND--SAY YOU WANT WHAT? AVENGERS MANSION? SO YOU--
THIS IS A PHONE THAT CALLS ACROSS THE GALAXY?
I DON'T KNOW WHAT A "PHONE" IS BUT, YOU ARE EASILY IMPRESSED.
THIS IS A CONTAINER THAT HOLDS LIQUID.
COME ON, ROCKET!
ON EARTH I HAVE THE BEST PHONE ON EARTH AND I CAN'T GET A SIGNAL FROM ONE HALF OF NEW YORK TO THE OTHER.
HONESTLY, I DON'T KNOW HOW YOU LIVE ON THAT $%&*!#@$.
WELL, I AM A VERY RICH AND FAMOUS SUPER HERO.
DOES THAT BRAVADO WORK WHERE YOU'RE FROM?

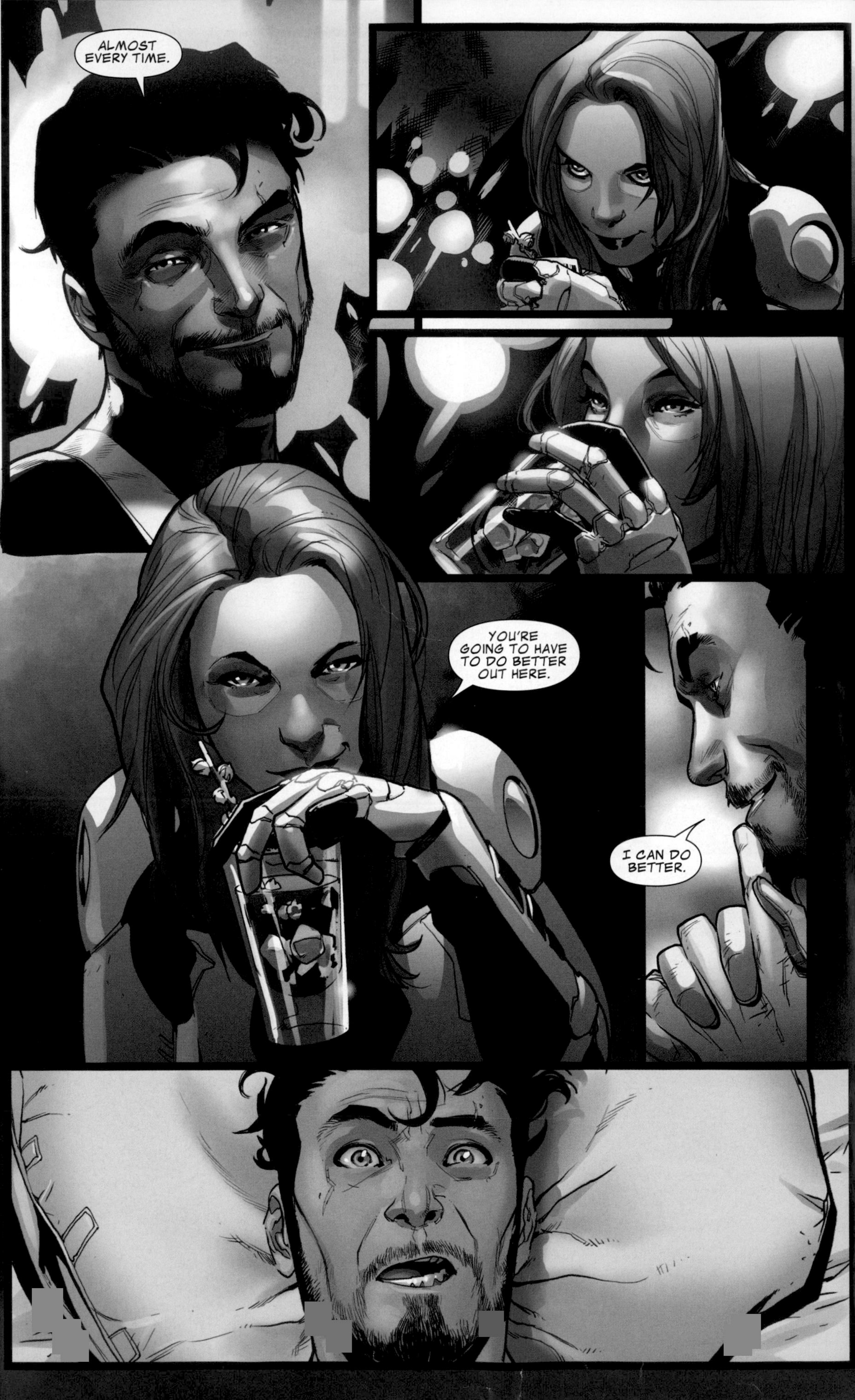
ALMOST EVERY TIME.
YOU'RE GOING TO HAVE TO DO BETTER OUT HERE.
I CAN DO BETTER.

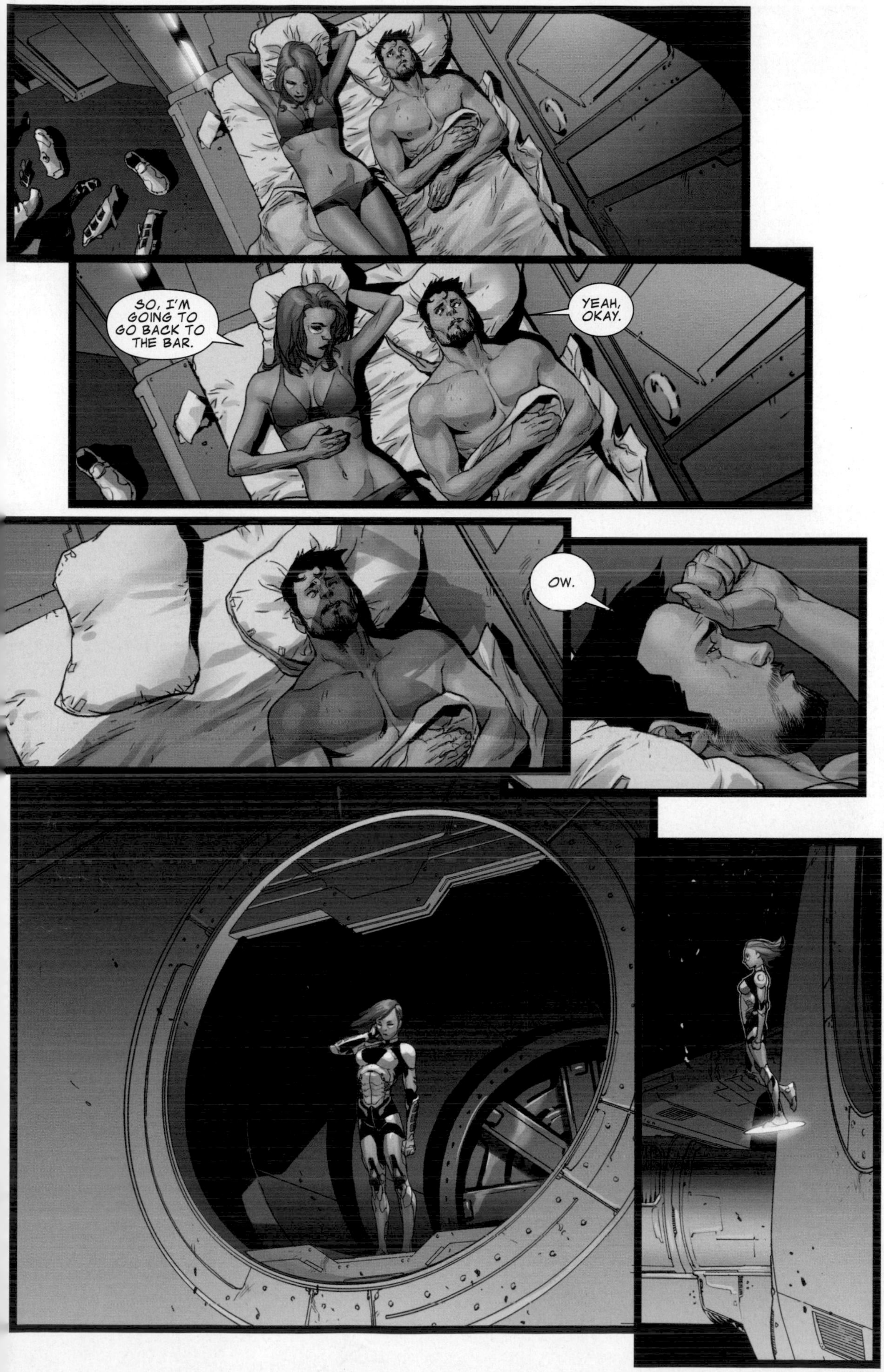
SO, I'M GOING TO GO BACK TO THE BAR.
YEAH, OKAY.
OW.

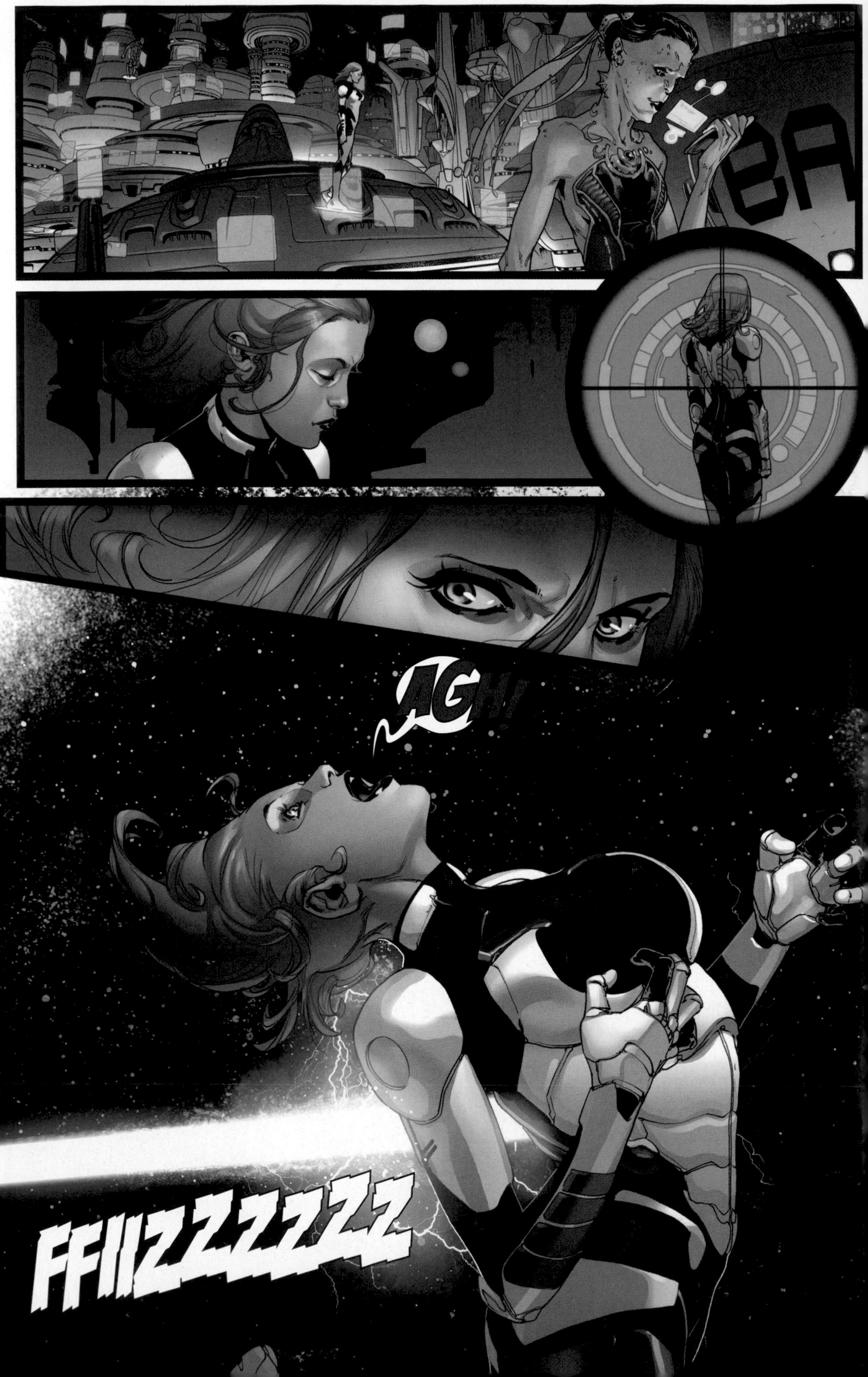
AGH!
FFIIZZZZZZ

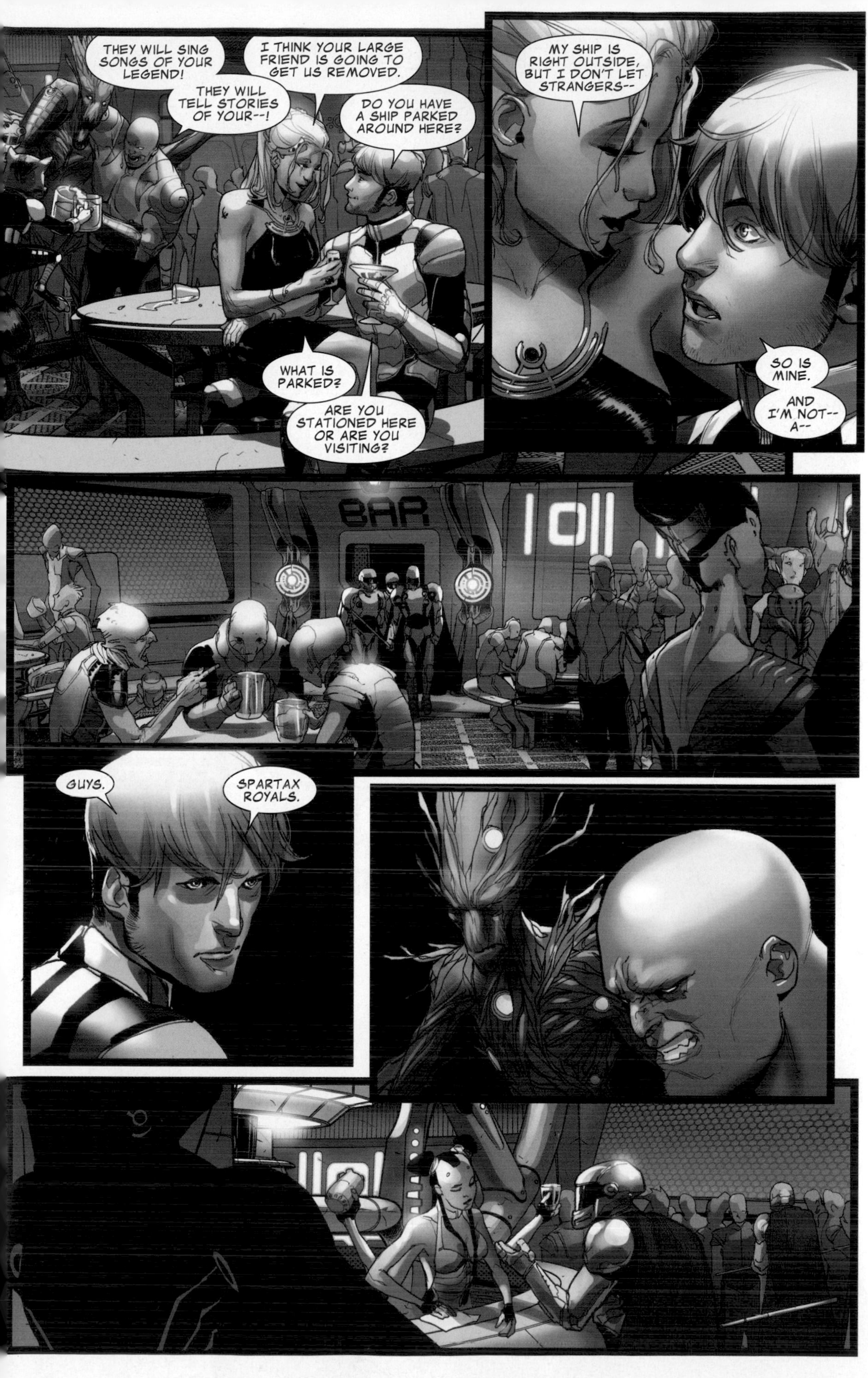
THEY WILL SING SONGS OF YOUR LEGEND!
THEY WILL TELL STORIES OF YOUR--!
I THINK YOUR LARGE FRIEND IS GOING TO GET US REMOVED.
DO YOU HAVE A SHIP PARKED AROUND HERE?
WHAT IS PARKED?
ARE YOU STATIONED HERE OR ARE YOU VISITING?
MY SHIP IS RIGHT OUTSIDE, BUT I DON'T LET STRANGERS--
SO IS MINE.
AND I'M NOT-- A--
BAR
GUYS.
SPARTAX ROYALS.

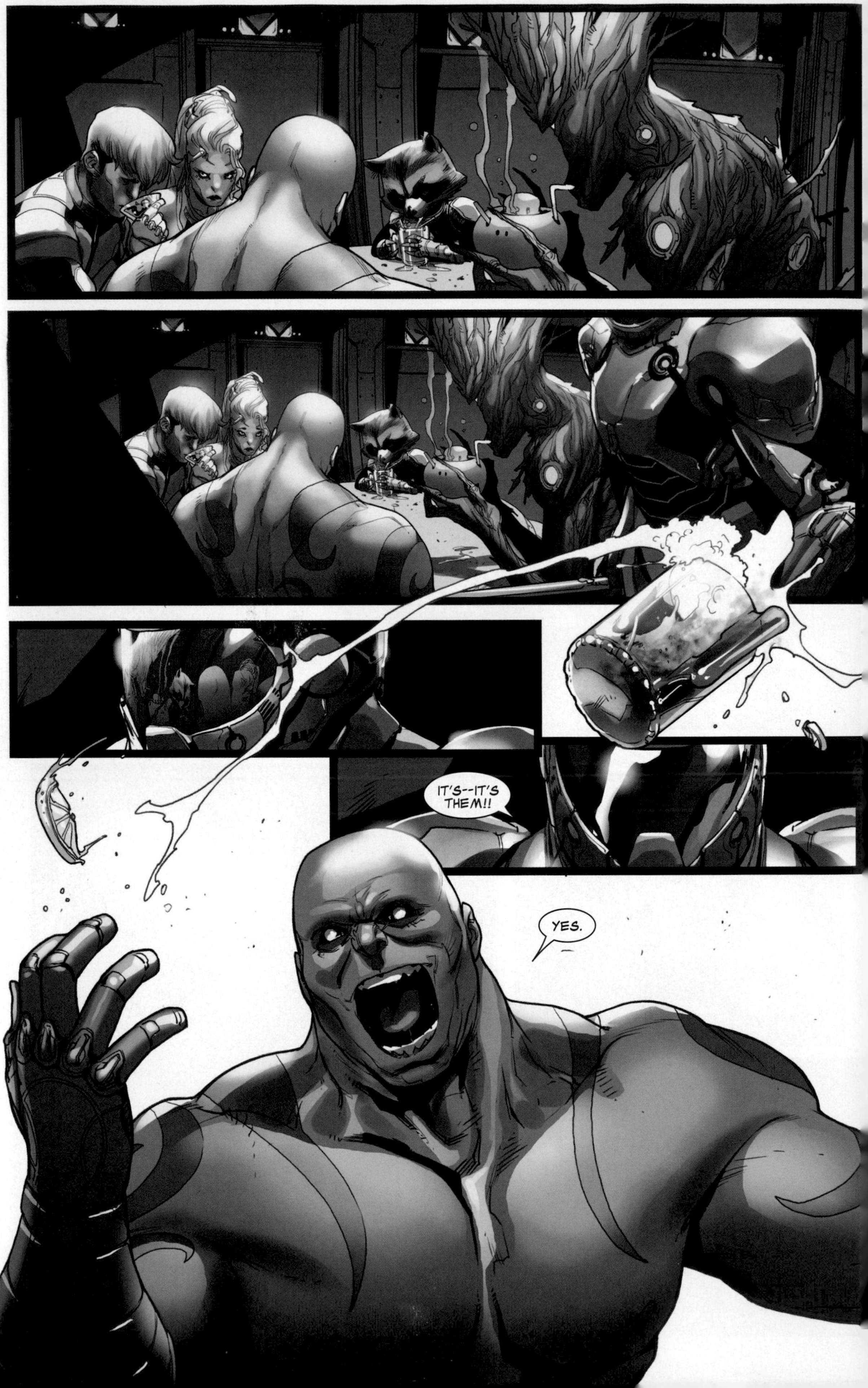
IT'S--IT'S THEM!!
YES.

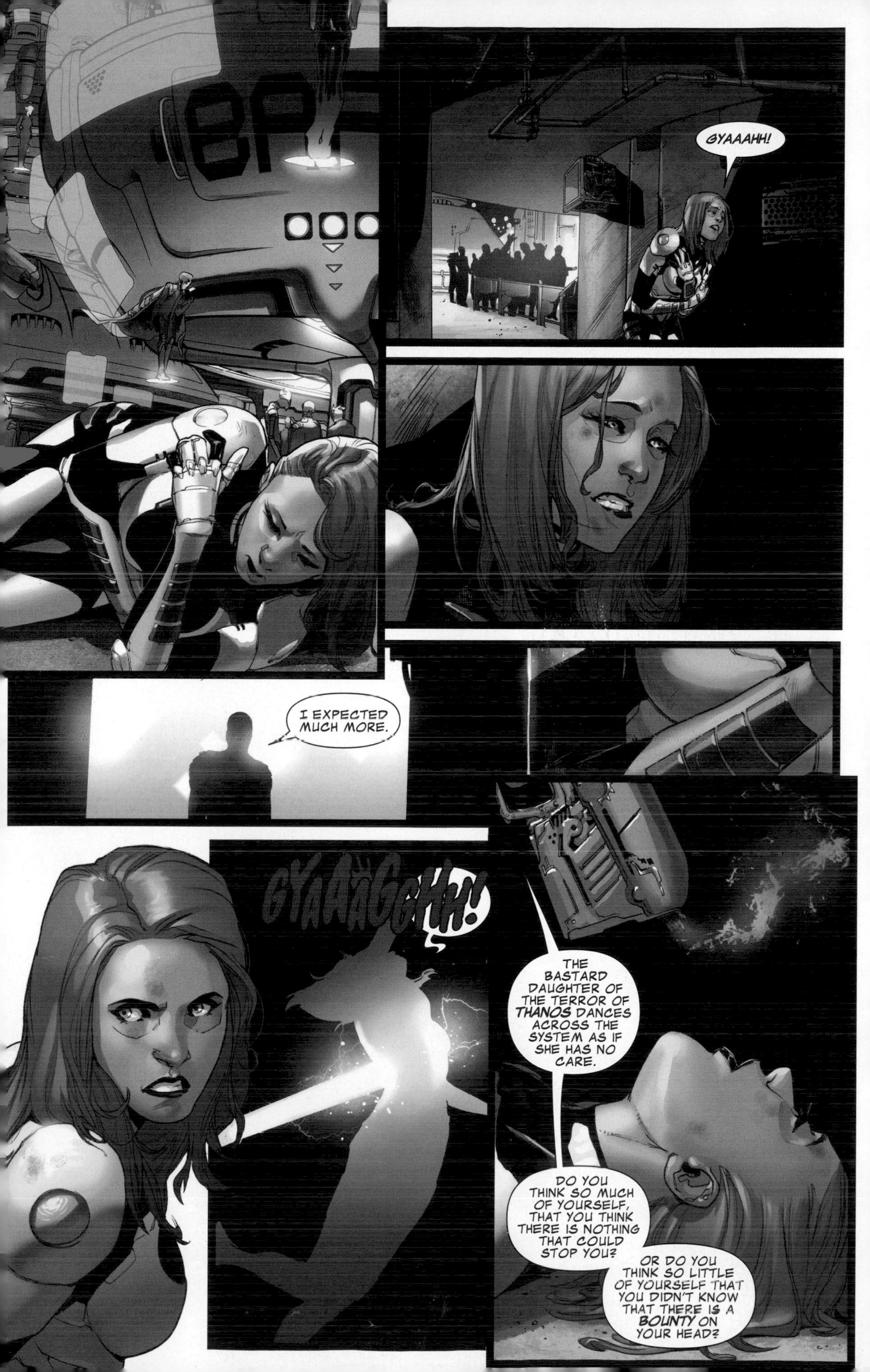
GYAAAHH!
I EXPECTED MUCH MORE.
GYAAAGGHH!
THE BASTARD DAUGHTER OF THE TERROR OF THANOS DANCES ACROSS THE SYSTEM AS IF SHE HAS NO CARE.
DO YOU THINK SO MUCH OF YOURSELF, THAT YOU THINK THERE IS NOTHING THAT COULD STOP YOU?
OR DO YOU THINK SO LITTLE OF YOURSELF THAT YOU DIDN'T KNOW THAT THERE IS A BOUNTY ON YOUR HEAD?

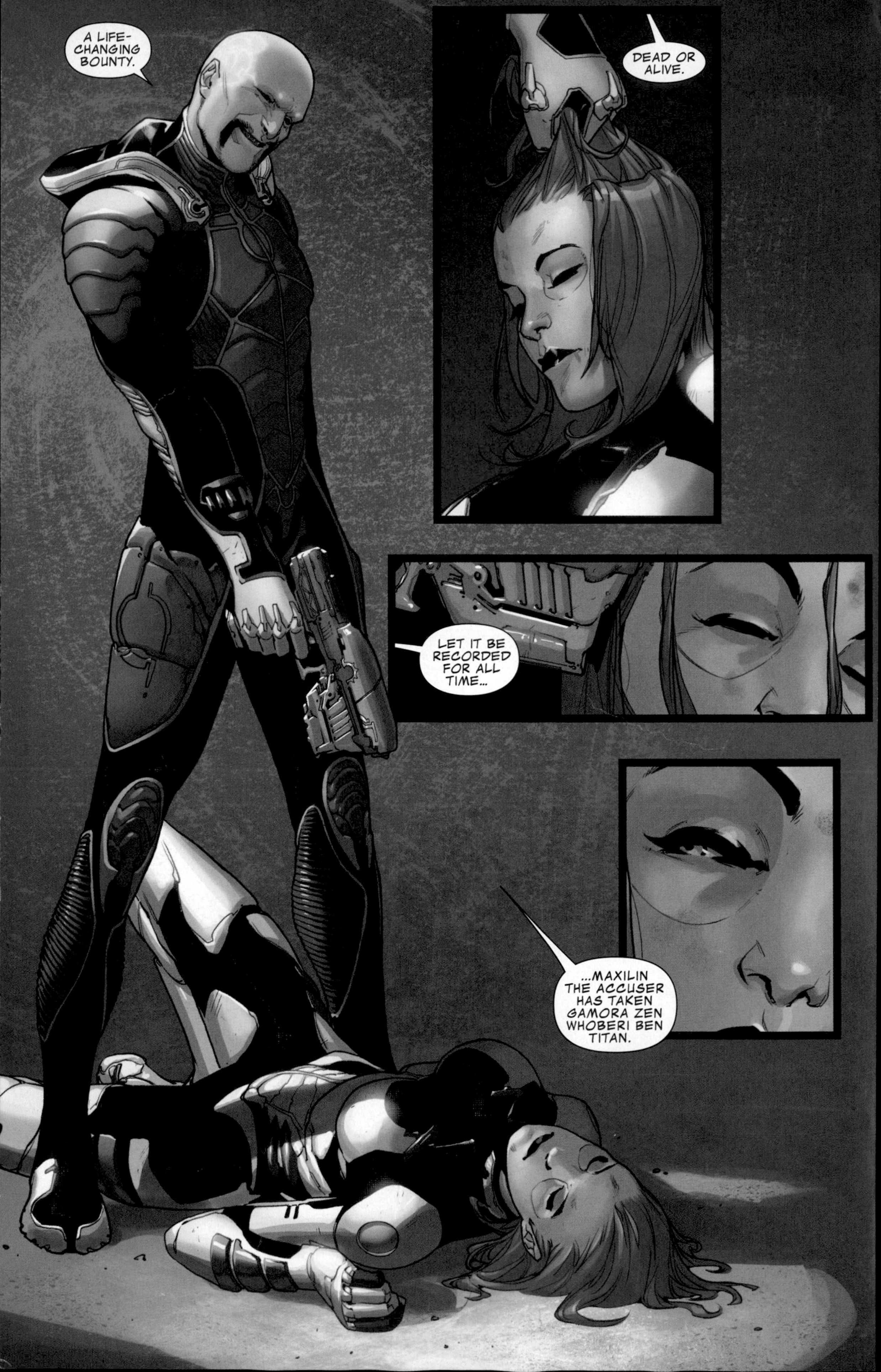
A LIFE-CHANGING BOUNTY.
DEAD OR ALIVE.
LET IT BE RECORDED FOR ALL TIME...
...MAXILIN THE ACCUSER HAS TAKEN GAMORA ZEN WHOBERI BEN TITAN.

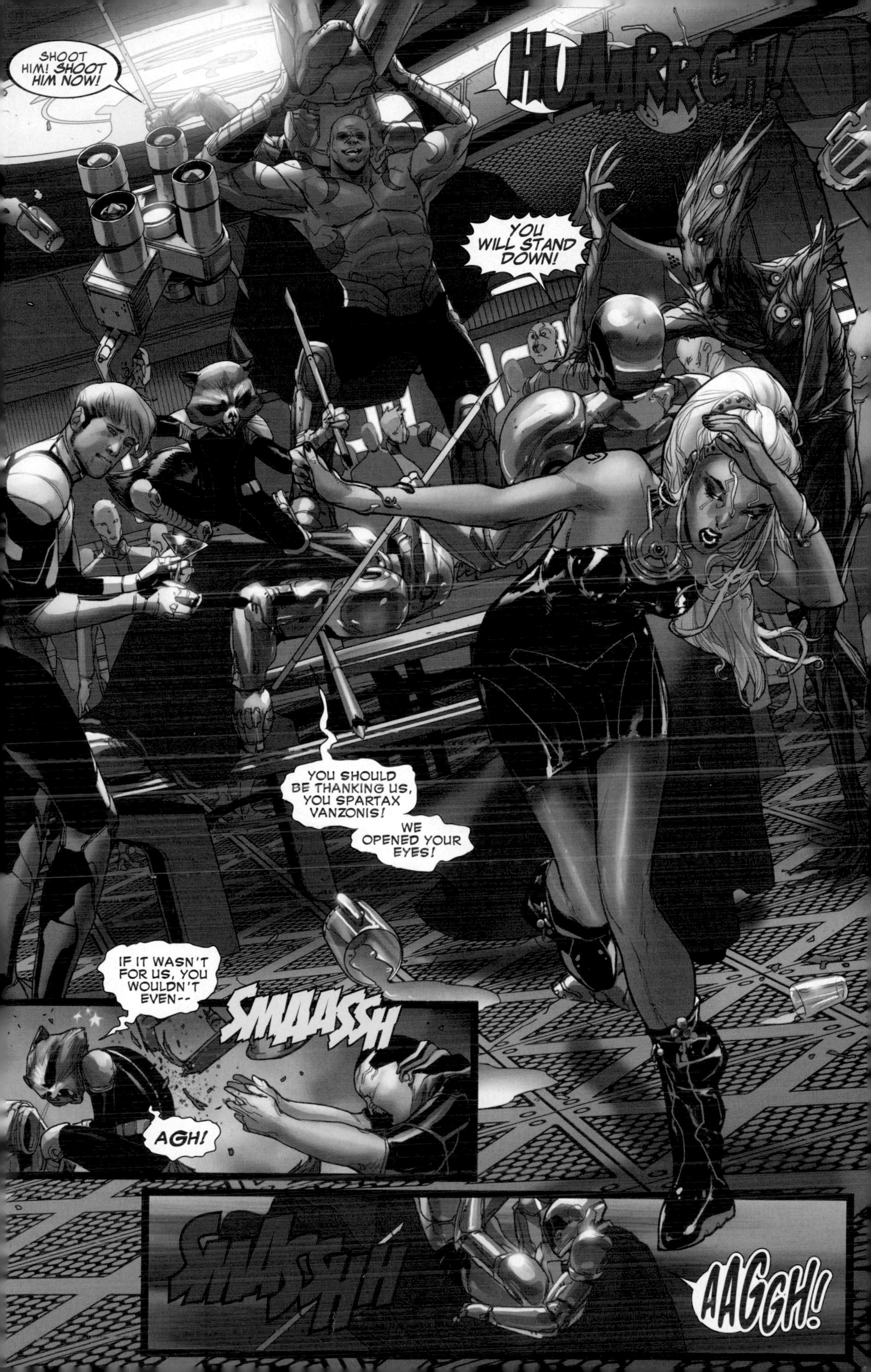
SHOOT HIM! SHOOT HIM NOW!
HUAARRGH!
YOU WILL STAND DOWN!
YOU SHOULD BE THANKING US, YOU SPARTAX VANZONIS!
WE OPENED YOUR EYES!
IF IT WASN'T FOR US, YOU WOULDN'T EVEN--
SMAASSH
AGH!
SMASSH
AAGGH!

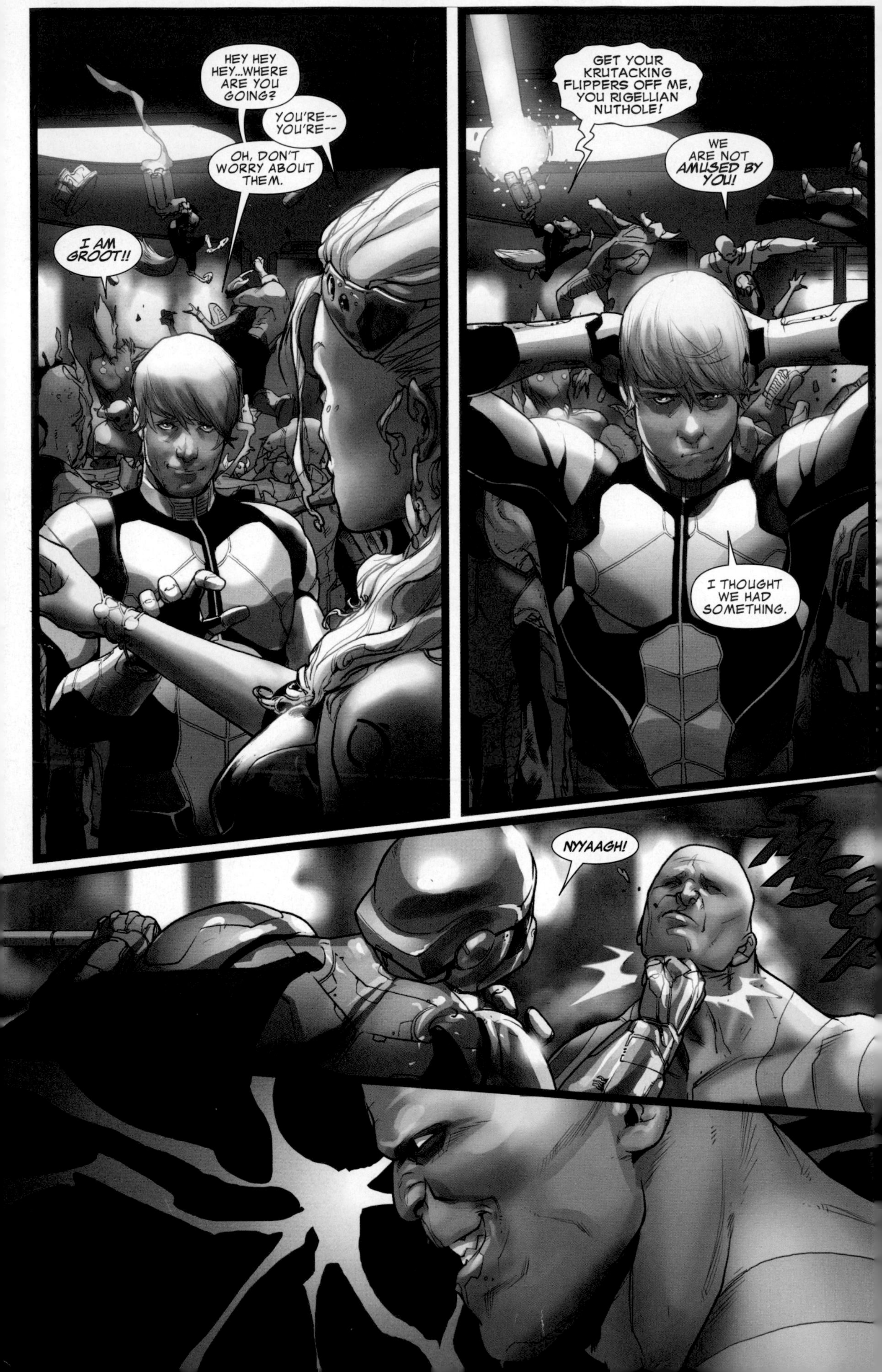
HEY HEY HEY...WHERE ARE YOU GOING?
YOU'RE-- YOU'RE--
OH, DON'T WORRY ABOUT THEM.
I AM GROOT!!
GET YOUR KRUTACKING FLIPPERS OFF ME, YOU RIGELLIAN NUTHOLE!
WE ARE NOT AMUSED BY YOU!
I THOUGHT WE HAD SOMETHING.
NYYAAGH!

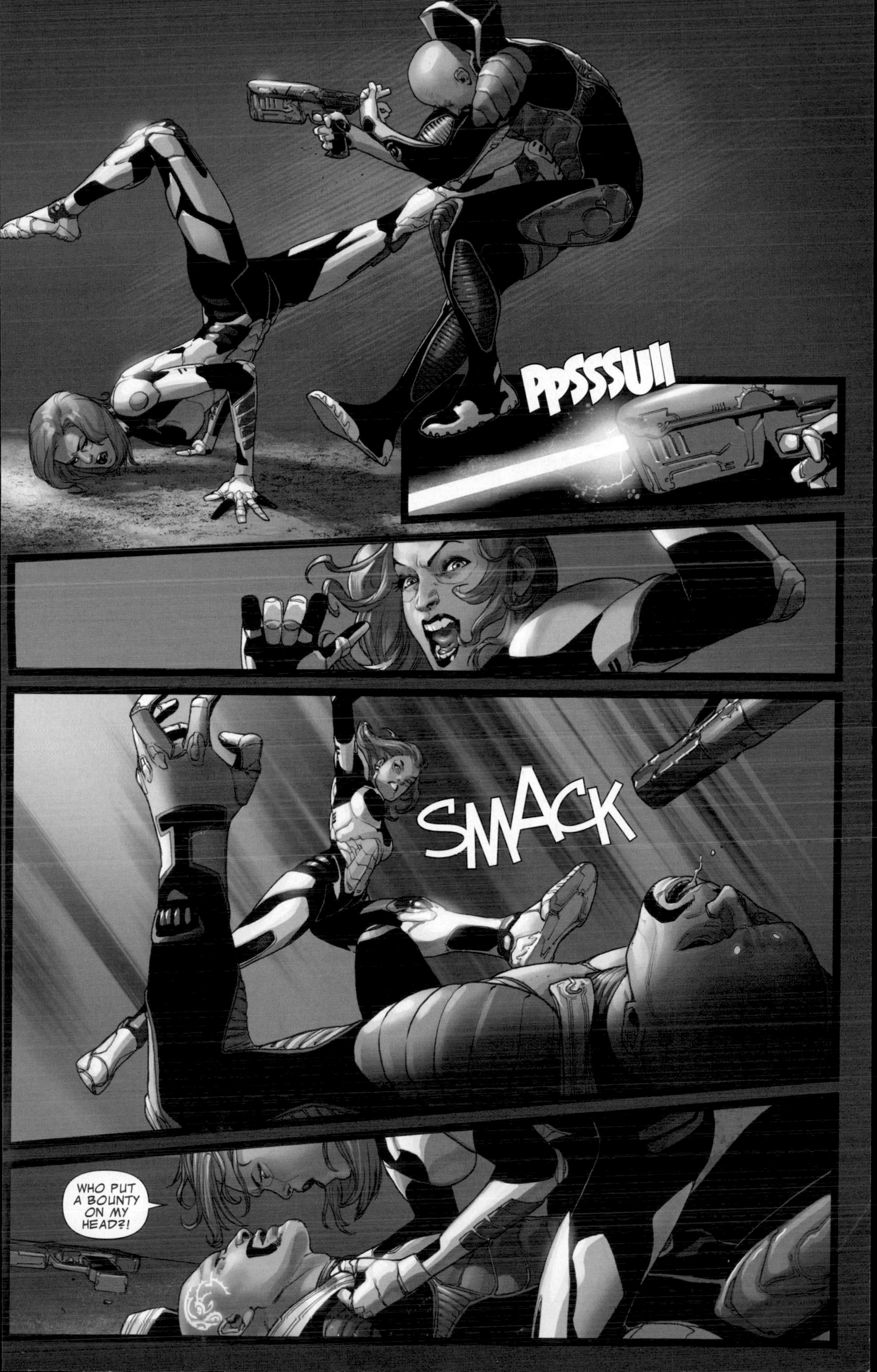
PPSSSUII
SMACK
WHO PUT A BOUNTY ON MY HEAD?!

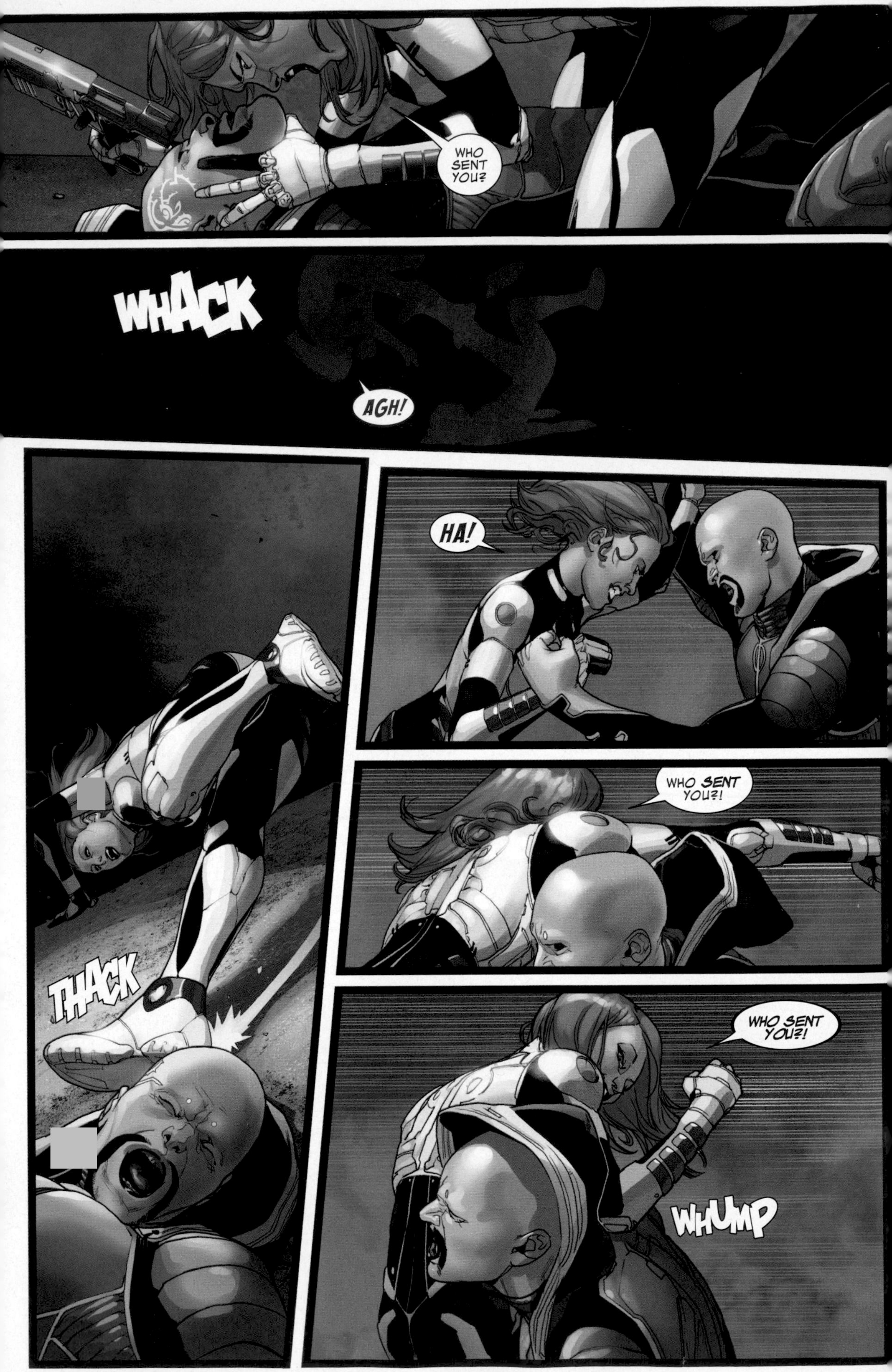
WHO SENT YOU?
WHACK
AGH!
HA!
THACK
WHO SENT YOU?!
WHO SENT YOU?!
WHUMP

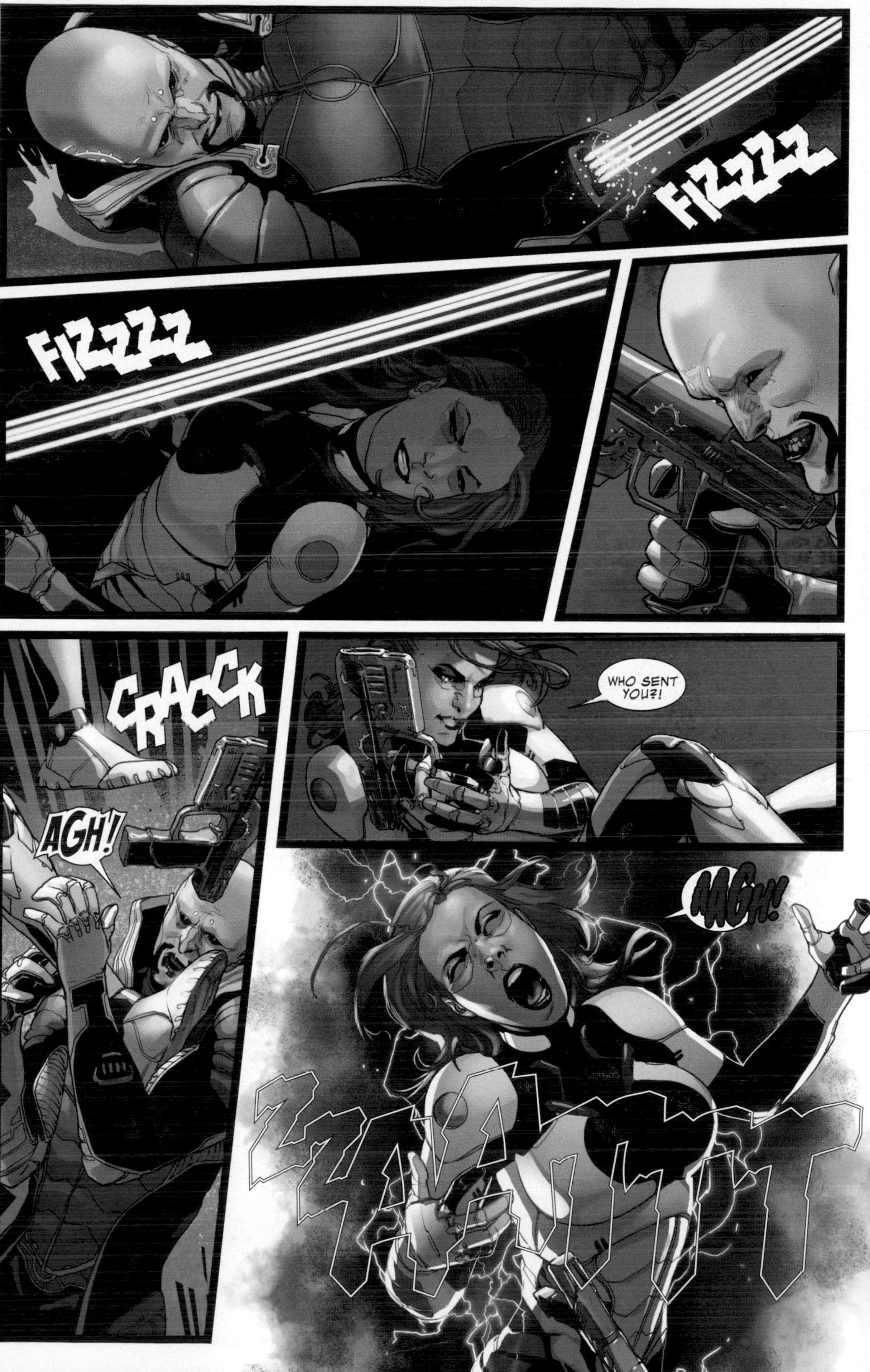
FIZZZZ
FIZZZZ
CRACCK
AGH!
WHO SENT YOU?!
AAGH!

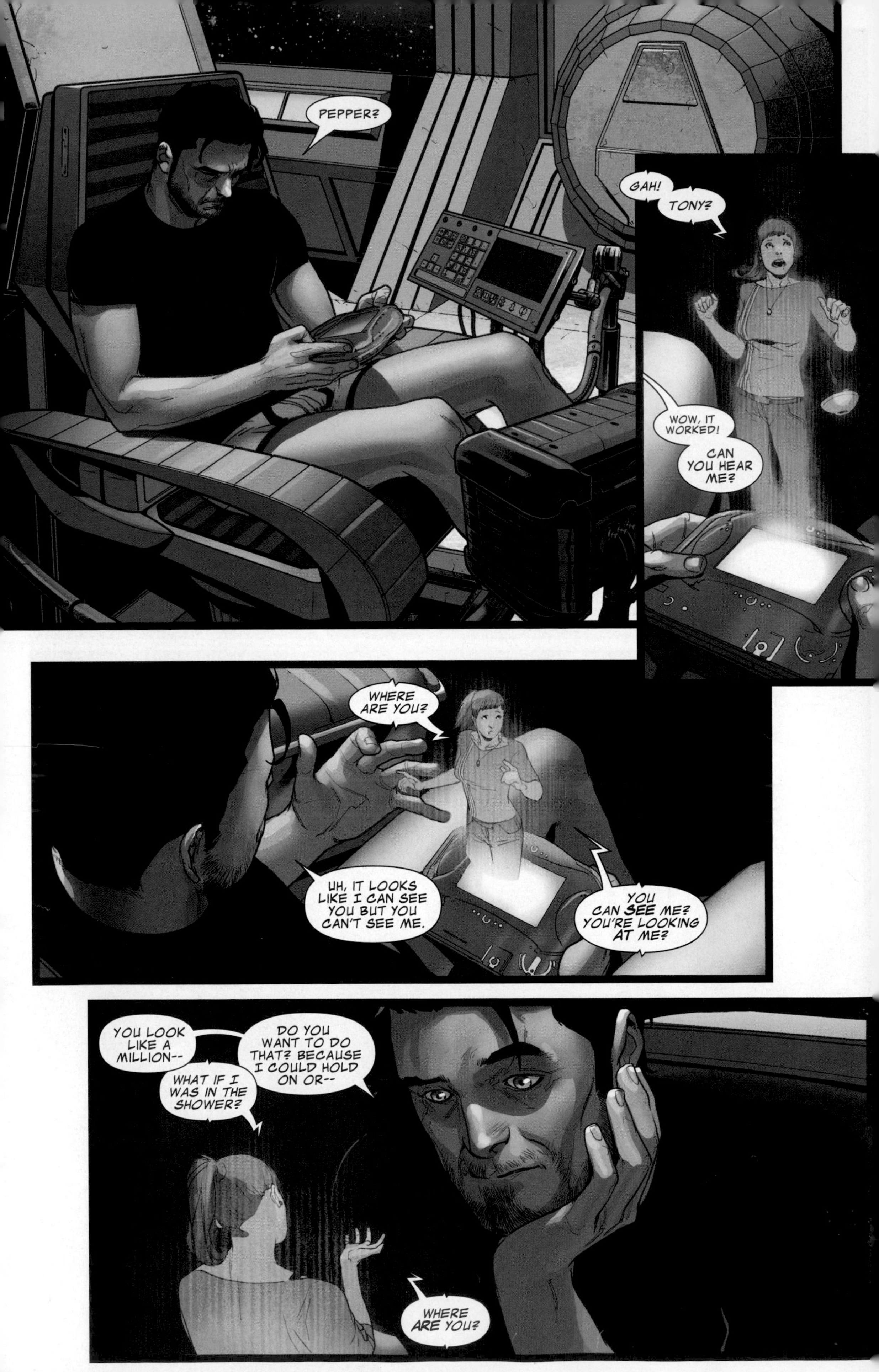
PEPPER?
GAH!
TONY?
WOW, IT WORKED!
CAN YOU HEAR ME?
WHERE ARE YOU?
UH, IT LOOKS LIKE I CAN SEE YOU BUT YOU CAN'T SEE ME.
YOU CAN SEE ME? YOU'RE LOOKING AT ME?
YOU LOOK LIKE A MILLION--
WHAT IF I WAS IN THE SHOWER?
DO YOU WANT TO DO THAT? BECAUSE I COULD HOLD ON OR--
WHERE ARE YOU?

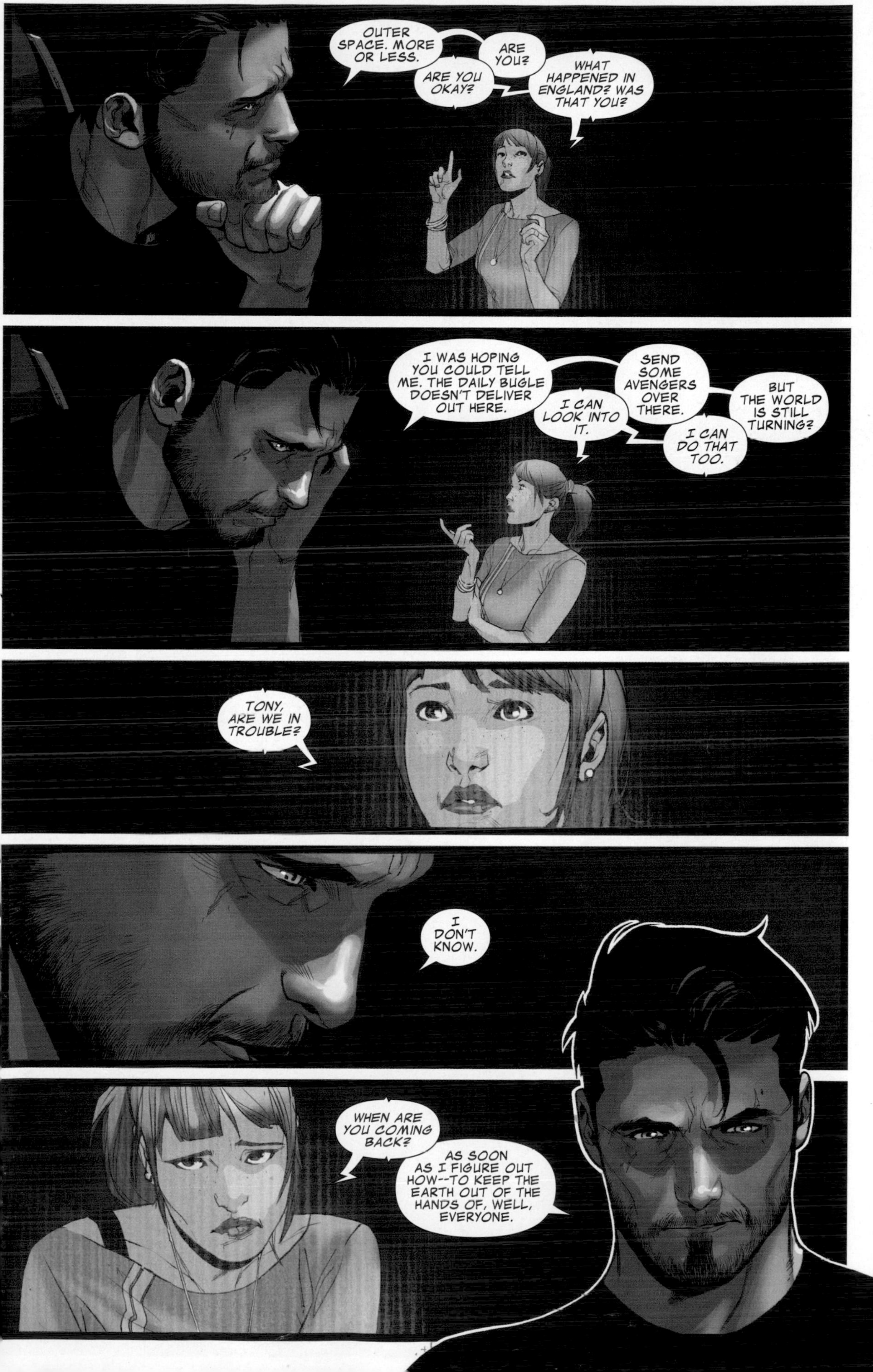
OUTER SPACE. MORE OR LESS.
ARE YOU?
ARE YOU OKAY?
WHAT HAPPENED IN ENGLAND? WAS THAT YOU?
I WAS HOPING YOU COULD TELL ME. THE DAILY BUGLE DOESN'T DELIVER OUT HERE.
I CAN LOOK INTO IT.
SEND SOME AVENGERS OVER THERE.
I CAN DO THAT TOO.
BUT THE WORLD IS STILL TURNING?
TONY, ARE WE IN TROUBLE?
I DON'T KNOW.
WHEN ARE YOU COMING BACK?
AS SOON AS I FIGURE OUT HOW--TO KEEP THE EARTH OUT OF THE HANDS OF, WELL, EVERYONE.

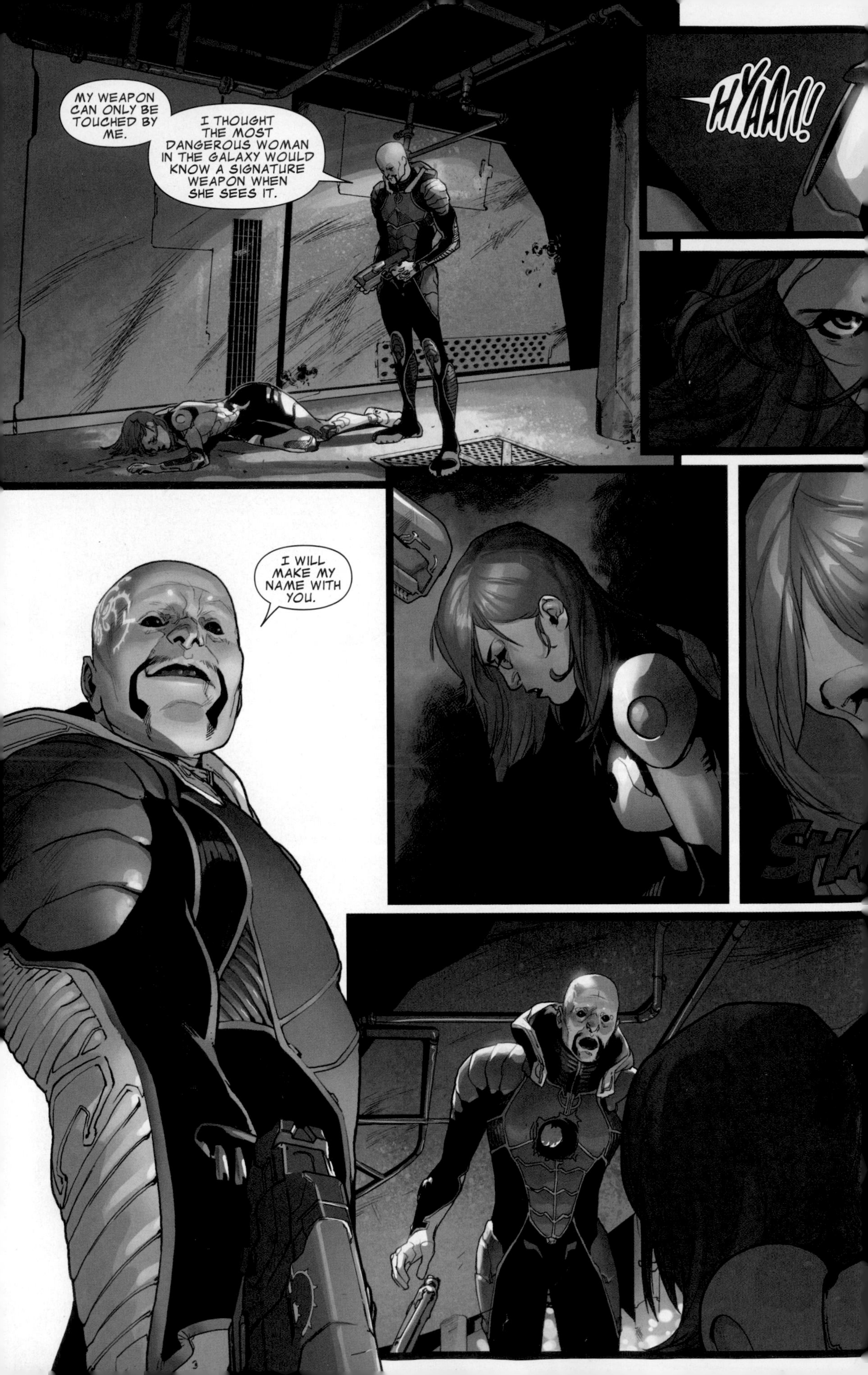
MY WEAPON CAN ONLY BE TOUCHED BY ME.
I THOUGHT THE MOST DANGEROUS WOMAN IN THE GALAXY WOULD KNOW A SIGNATURE WEAPON WHEN SHE SEES IT.
HYAAA!!
I WILL MAKE MY NAME WITH YOU.

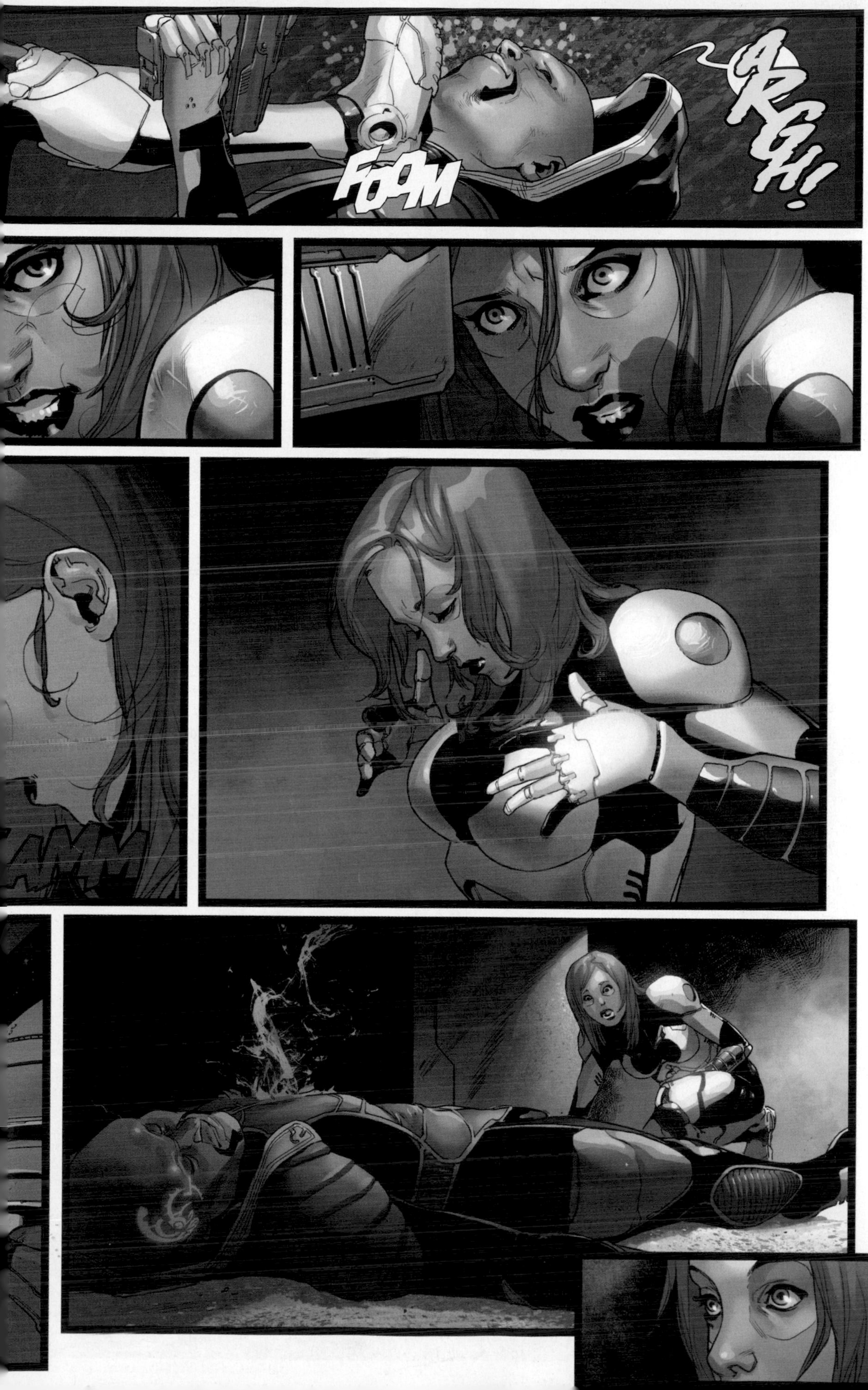
FOOM
ARGH!
AMM

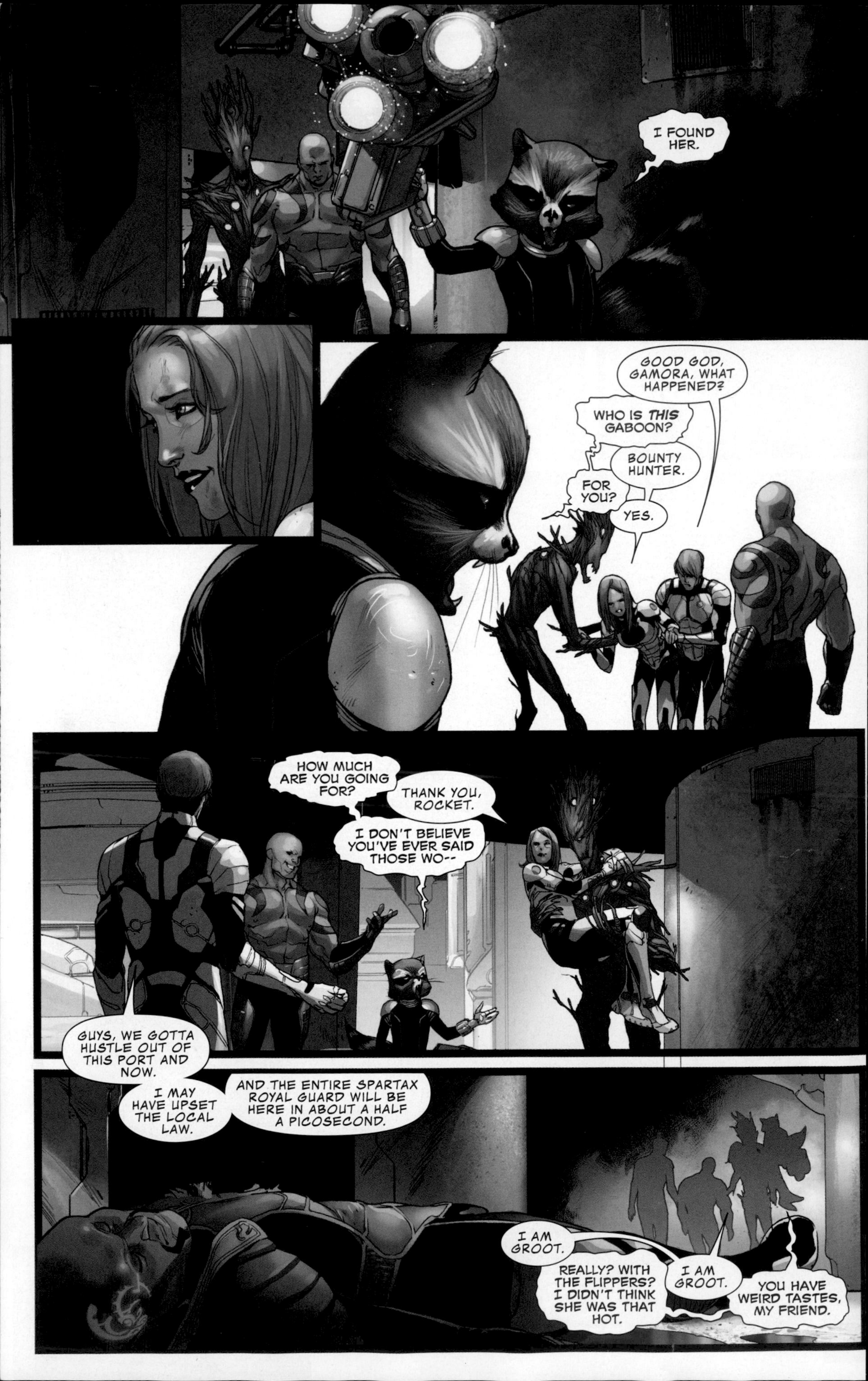
I FOUND HER.
GOOD GOD, GAMORA, WHAT HAPPENED?
WHO IS *THIS* GABOON?
BOUNTY HUNTER.
FOR YOU?
YES.
HOW MUCH ARE YOU GOING FOR?
THANK YOU, ROCKET.
I DON'T BELIEVE YOU'VE EVER SAID THOSE WO--
GUYS, WE GOTTA HUSTLE OUT OF THIS PORT AND NOW.
I MAY HAVE UPSET THE LOCAL LAW.
AND THE ENTIRE SPARTAX ROYAL GUARD WILL BE HERE IN ABOUT A HALF A PICOSECOND.
I AM GROOT.
REALLY? WITH THE FLIPPERS? I DIDN'T THINK SHE WAS THAT HOT.
I AM GROOT.
YOU HAVE WEIRD TASTES, MY FRIEND.

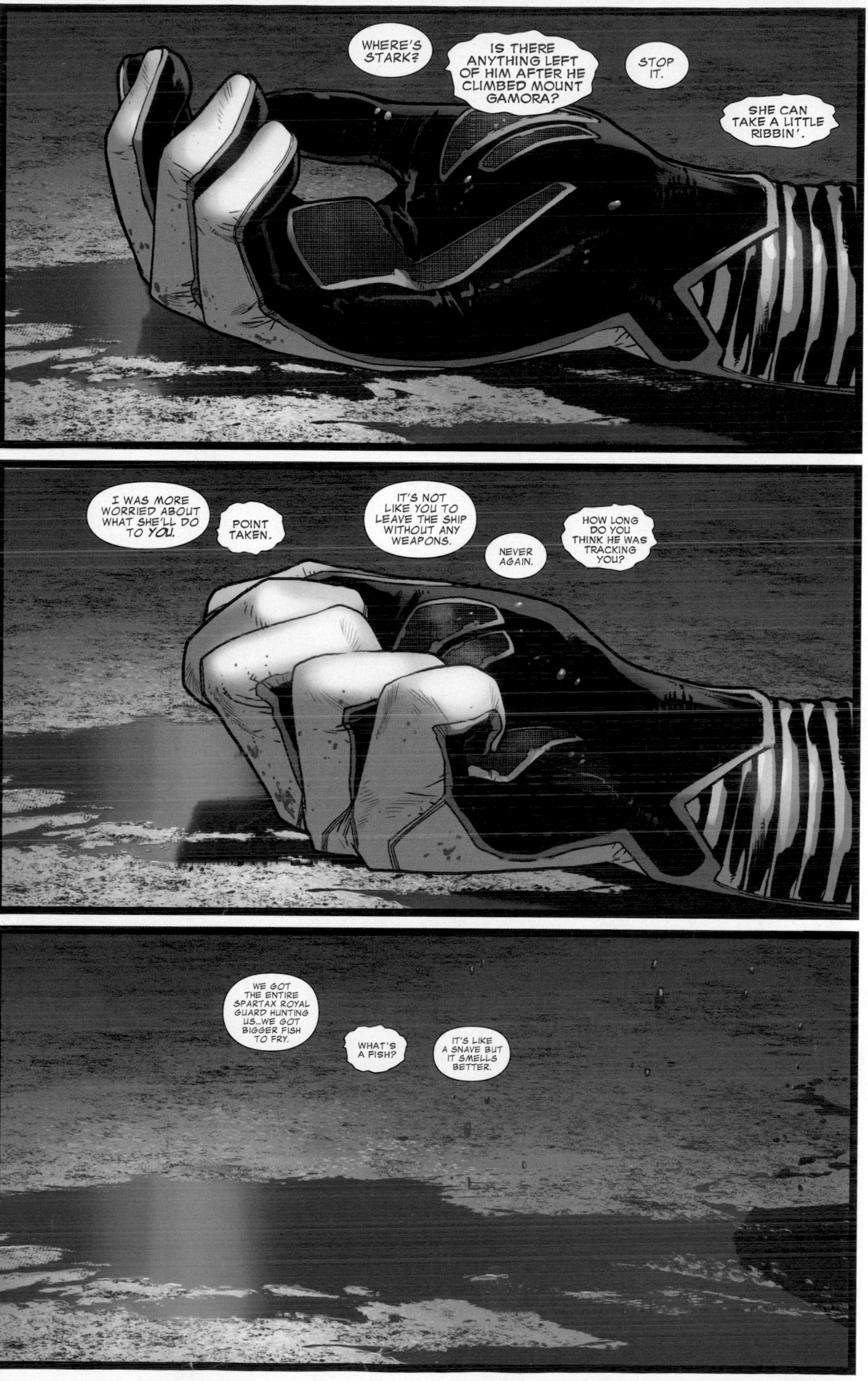
WHERE'S STARK?
IS THERE ANYTHING LEFT OF HIM AFTER HE CLIMBED MOUNT GAMORA?
STOP IT.
SHE CAN TAKE A LITTLE RIBBIN'.
I WAS MORE WORRIED ABOUT WHAT SHE'LL DO TO *YOU*.
POINT TAKEN.
IT'S NOT LIKE YOU TO LEAVE THE SHIP WITHOUT ANY WEAPONS.
NEVER AGAIN.
HOW LONG DO YOU THINK HE WAS TRACKING YOU?
WE GOT THE ENTIRE SPARTAX ROYAL GUARD HUNTING US...WE GOT BIGGER FISH TO FRY.
WHAT'S A FISH?
IT'S LIKE A SNAVE BUT IT SMELLS BETTER.

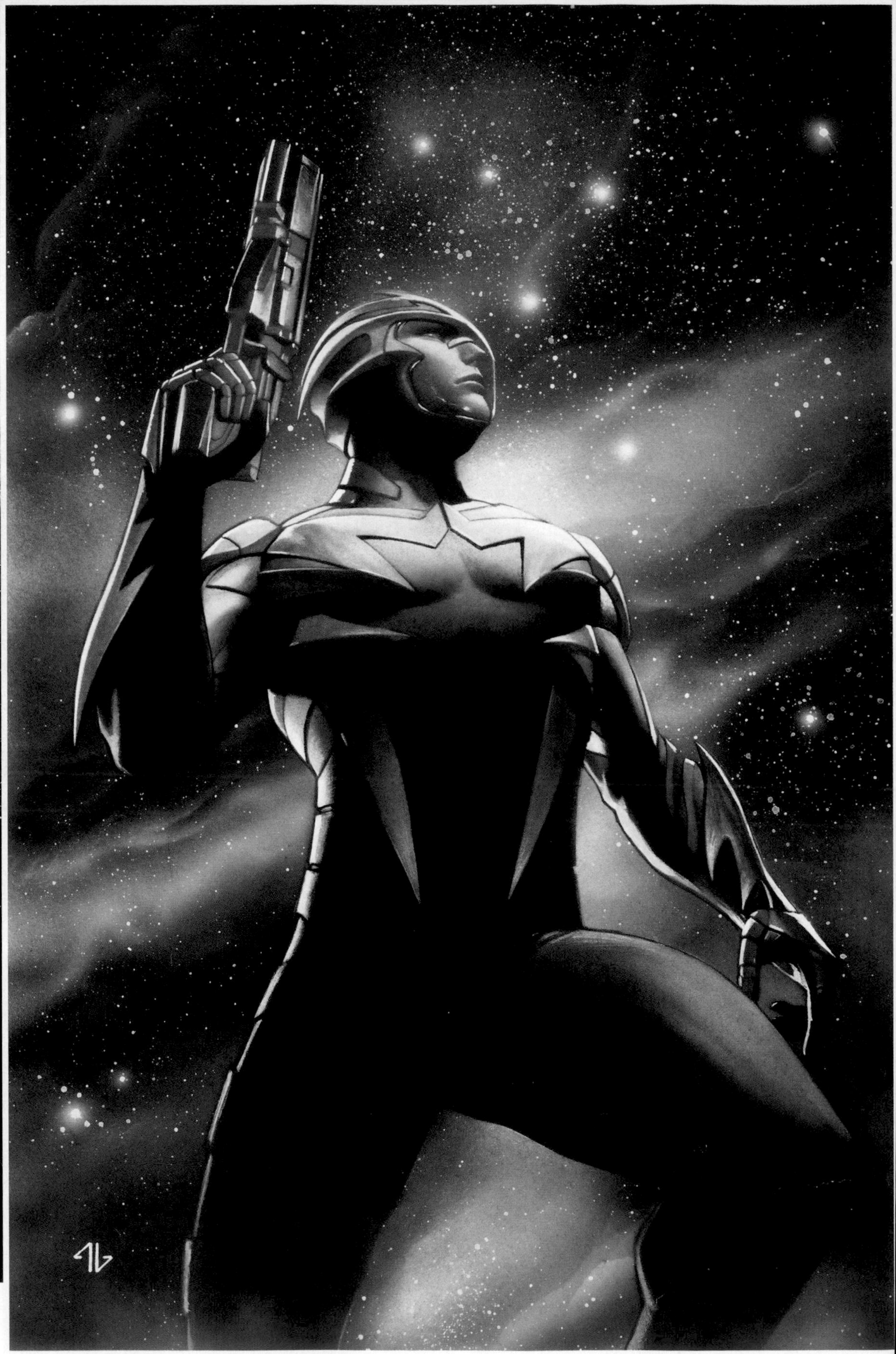

#4 VARIANT BY ADI GRANOV

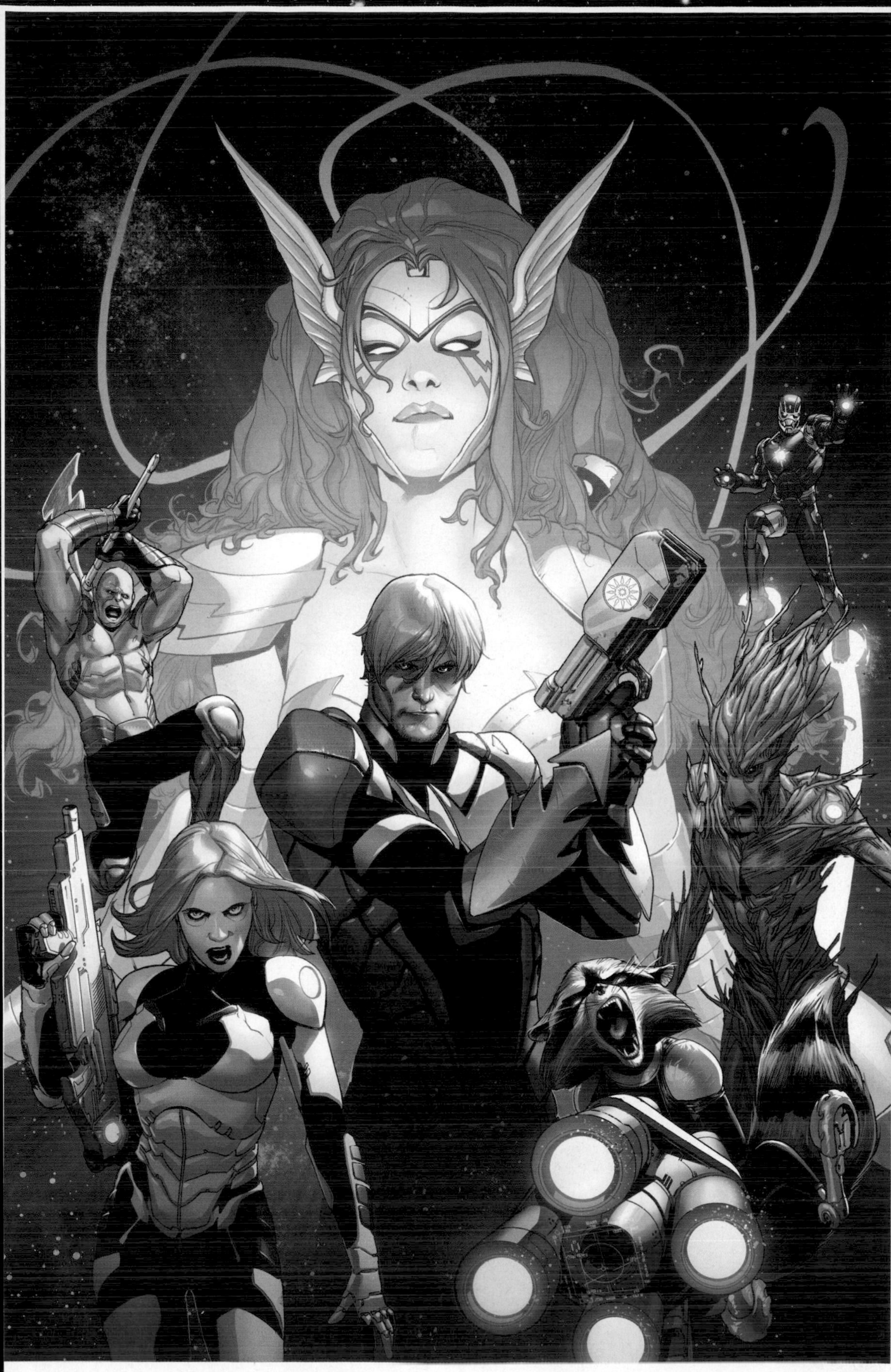

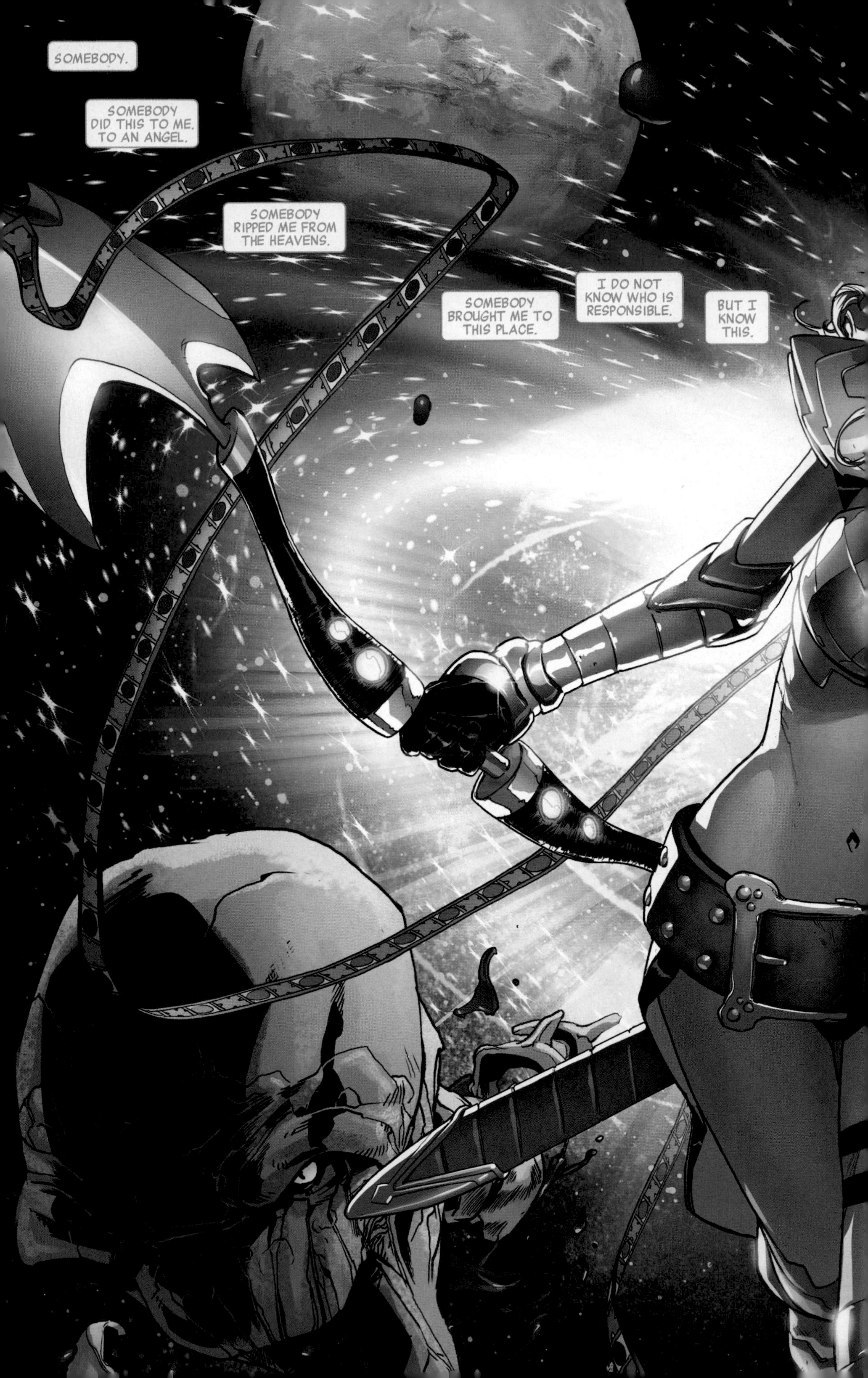
SOMEBODY.
SOMEBODY DID THIS TO ME. TO AN ANGEL.
SOMEBODY RIPPED ME FROM THE HEAVENS.
SOMEBODY BROUGHT ME TO THIS PLACE.
I DO NOT KNOW WHO IS RESPONSIBLE.
BUT I KNOW THIS.

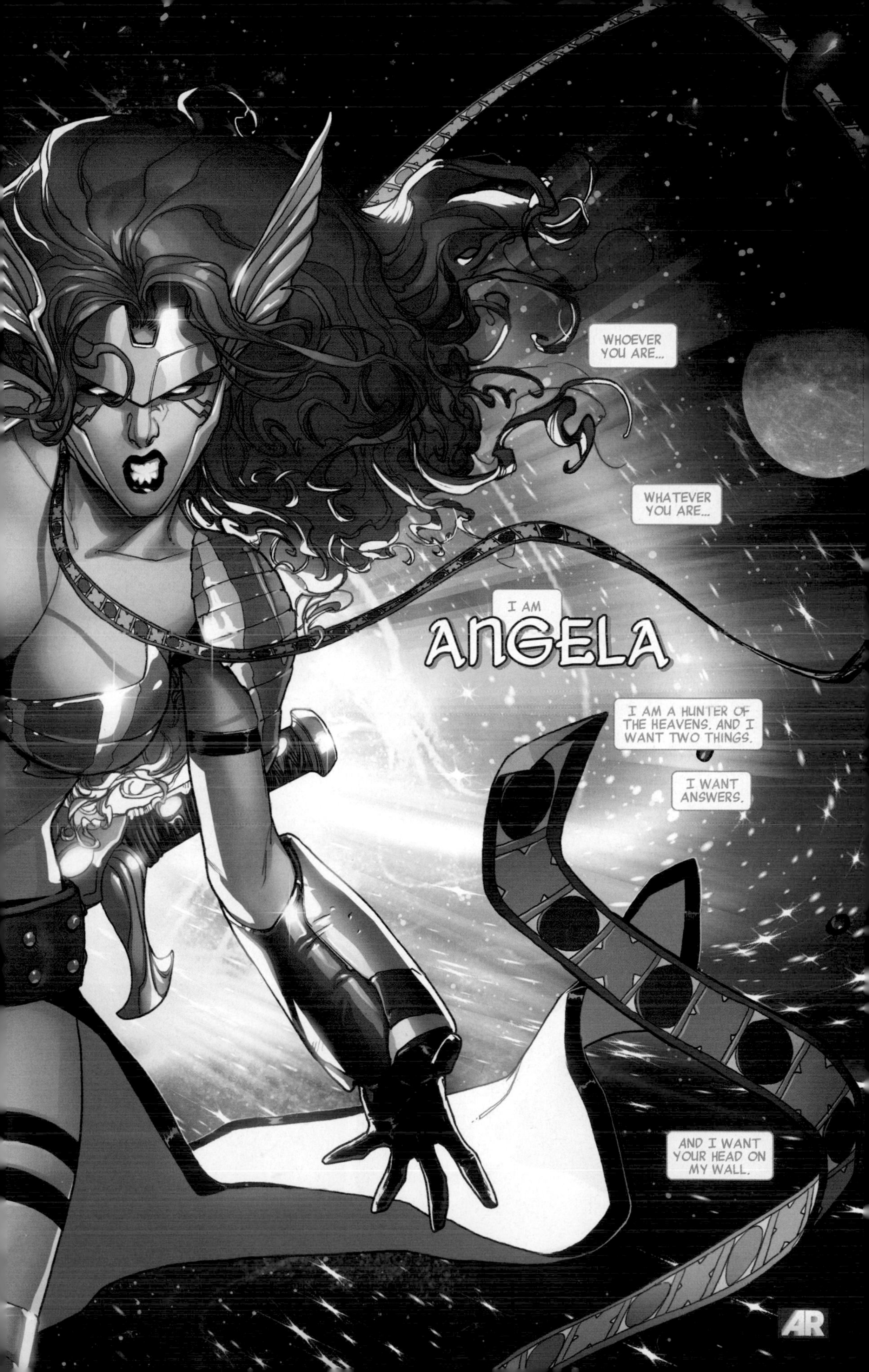
WHOEVER YOU ARE...
WHATEVER YOU ARE...
I AM
ANGELA
I AM A HUNTER OF THE HEAVENS. AND I WANT TWO THINGS.
I WANT ANSWERS.
AND I WANT YOUR HEAD ON MY WALL.
AR

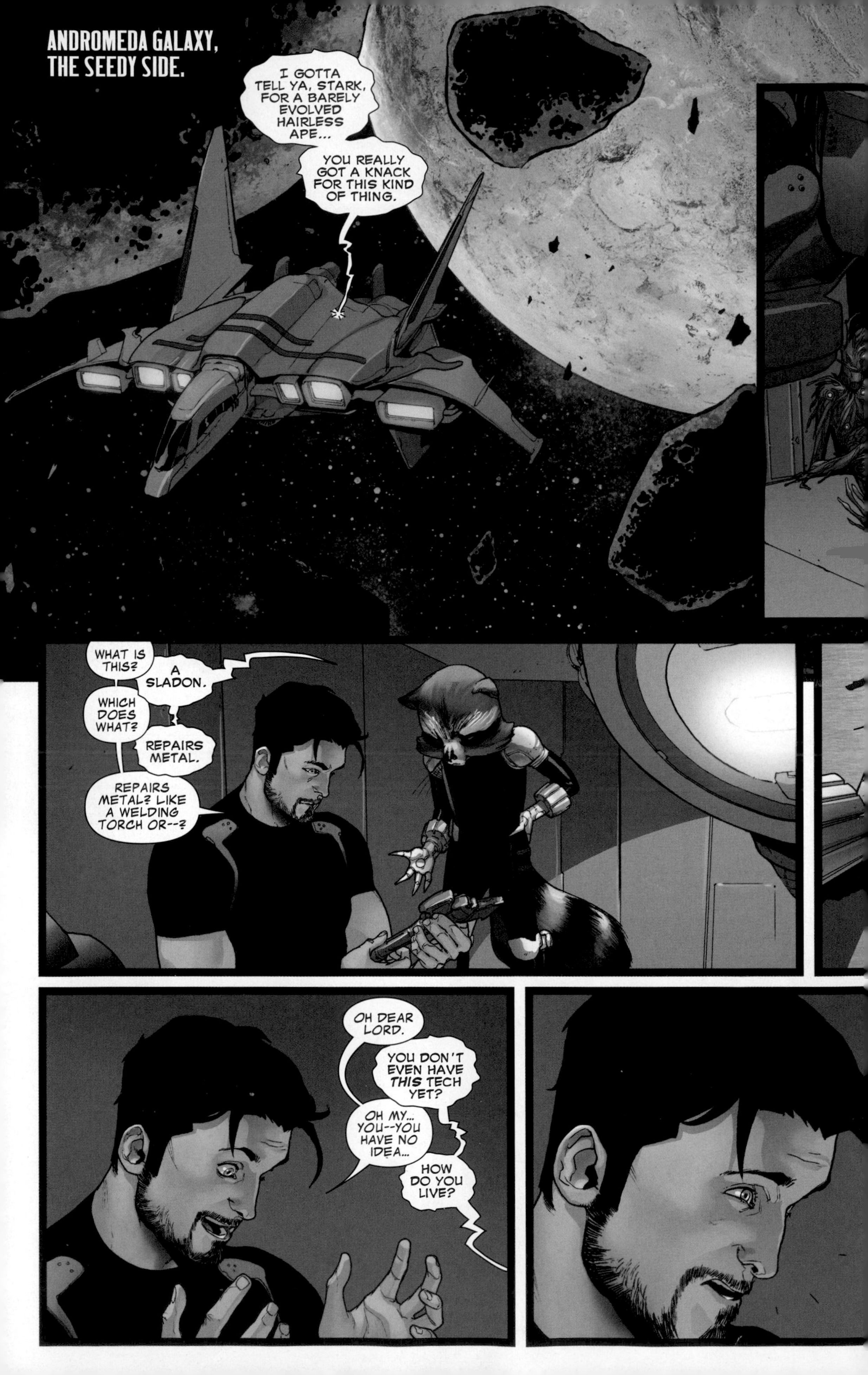
ANDROMEDA GALAXY, THE SEEDY SIDE.
I GOTTA TELL YA, STARK, FOR A BARELY EVOLVED HAIRLESS APE...
YOU REALLY GOT A KNACK FOR THIS KIND OF THING.
WHAT IS THIS?
A SLADON.
WHICH DOES WHAT?
REPAIRS METAL.
REPAIRS METAL? LIKE A WELDING TORCH OR--?
OH DEAR LORD.
YOU DON'T EVEN HAVE THIS TECH YET?
OH MY... YOU--YOU HAVE NO IDEA...
HOW DO YOU LIVE?

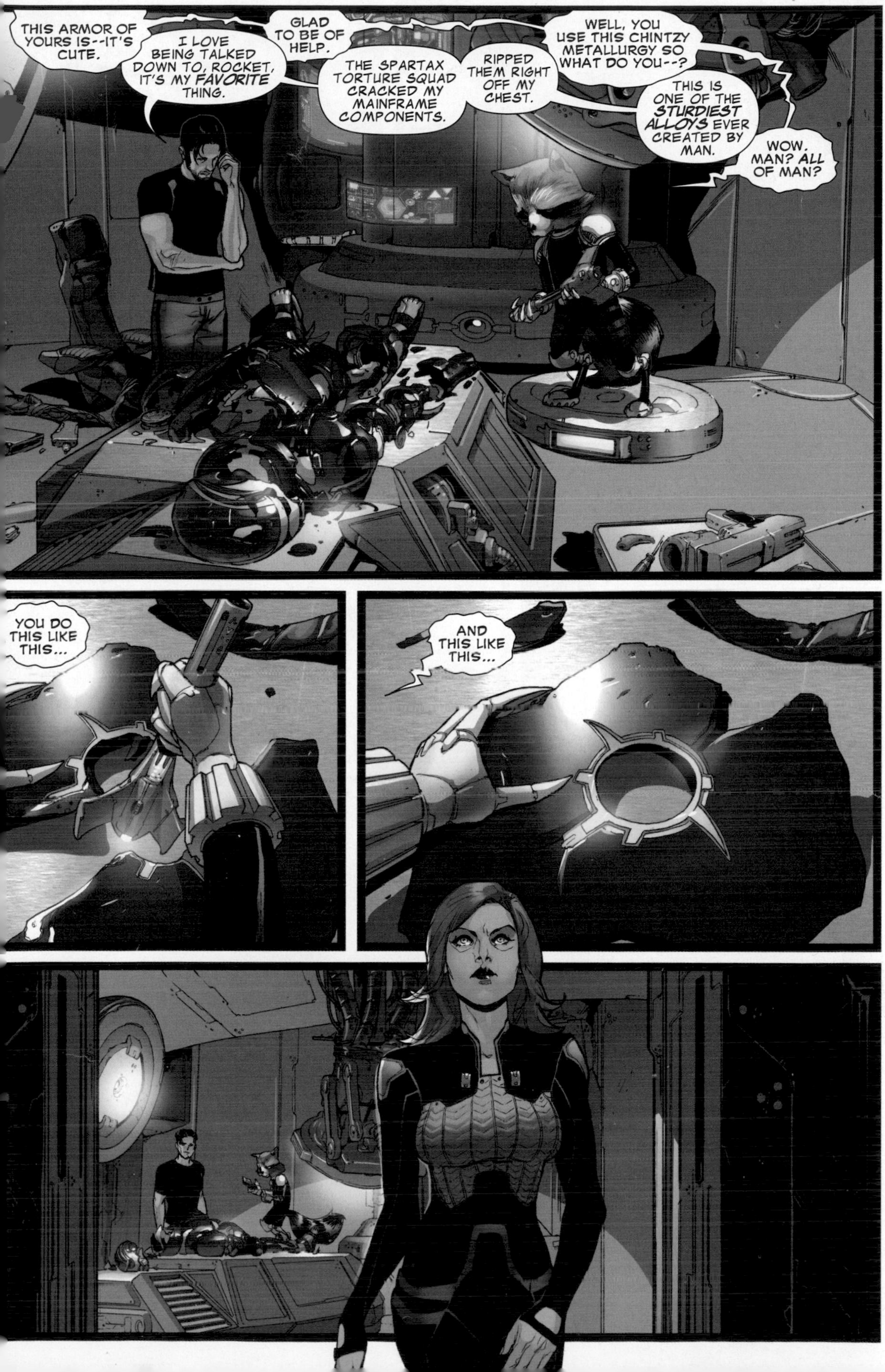
THIS ARMOR OF YOURS IS--IT'S CUTE.
I LOVE BEING TALKED DOWN TO, ROCKET, IT'S MY FAVORITE THING.
GLAD TO BE OF HELP.
THE SPARTAX TORTURE SQUAD CRACKED MY MAINFRAME COMPONENTS.
RIPPED THEM RIGHT OFF MY CHEST.
WELL, YOU USE THIS CHINTZY METALLURGY SO WHAT DO YOU--?
THIS IS ONE OF THE STURDIEST ALLOYS EVER CREATED BY MAN.
WOW. MAN? ALL OF MAN?
YOU DO THIS LIKE THIS...
AND THIS LIKE THIS...

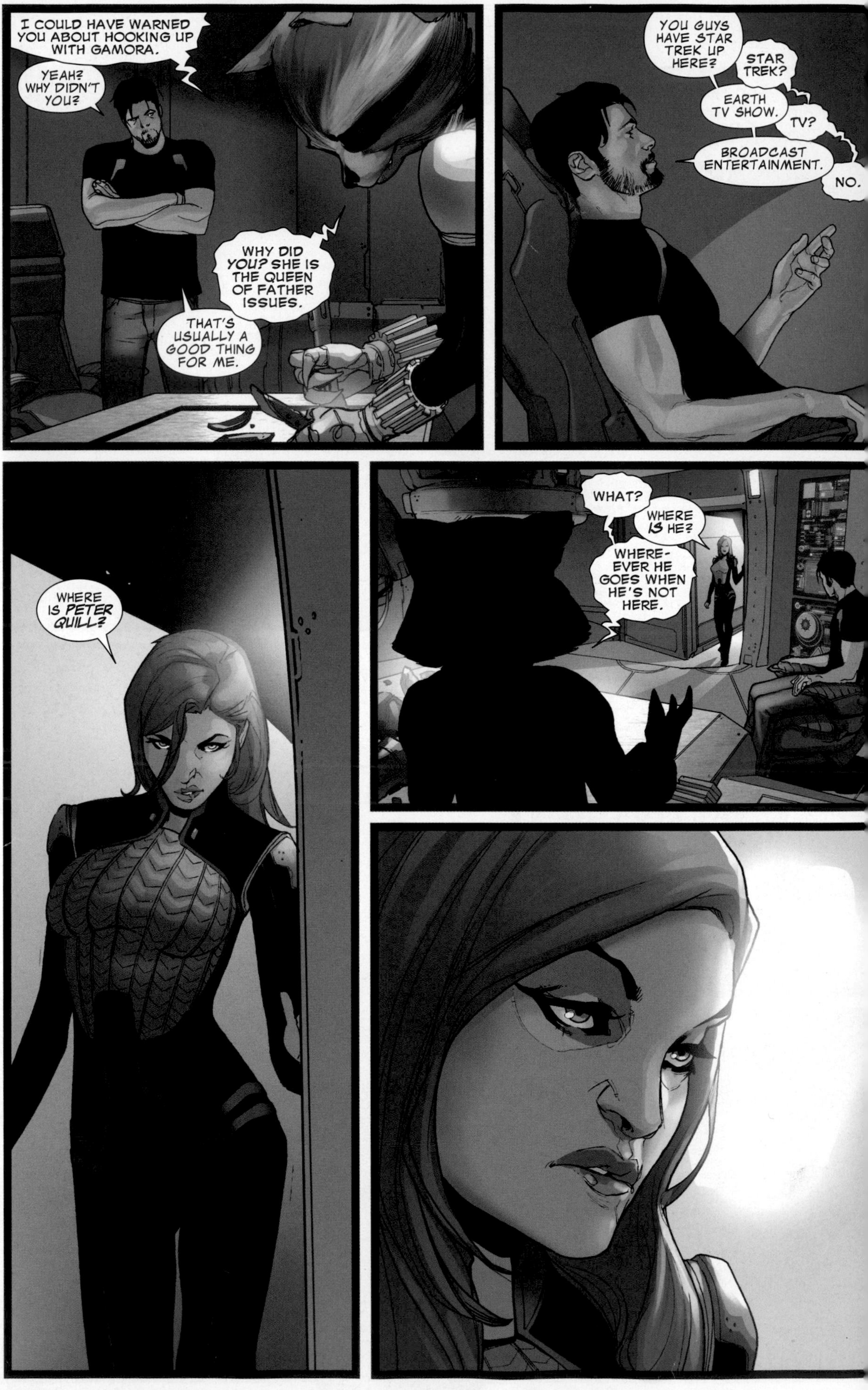

I COULD HAVE WARNED YOU ABOUT HOOKING UP WITH GAMORA.
YEAH? WHY DIDN'T YOU?
WHY DID YOU? SHE IS THE QUEEN OF FATHER ISSUES.
THAT'S USUALLY A GOOD THING FOR ME.
YOU GUYS HAVE STAR TREK UP HERE?
STAR TREK?
EARTH TV SHOW.
TV?
BROADCAST ENTERTAINMENT.
NO.
WHERE IS PETER QUILL?
WHAT?
WHERE IS HE?
WHERE-EVER HE GOES WHEN HE'S NOT HERE.

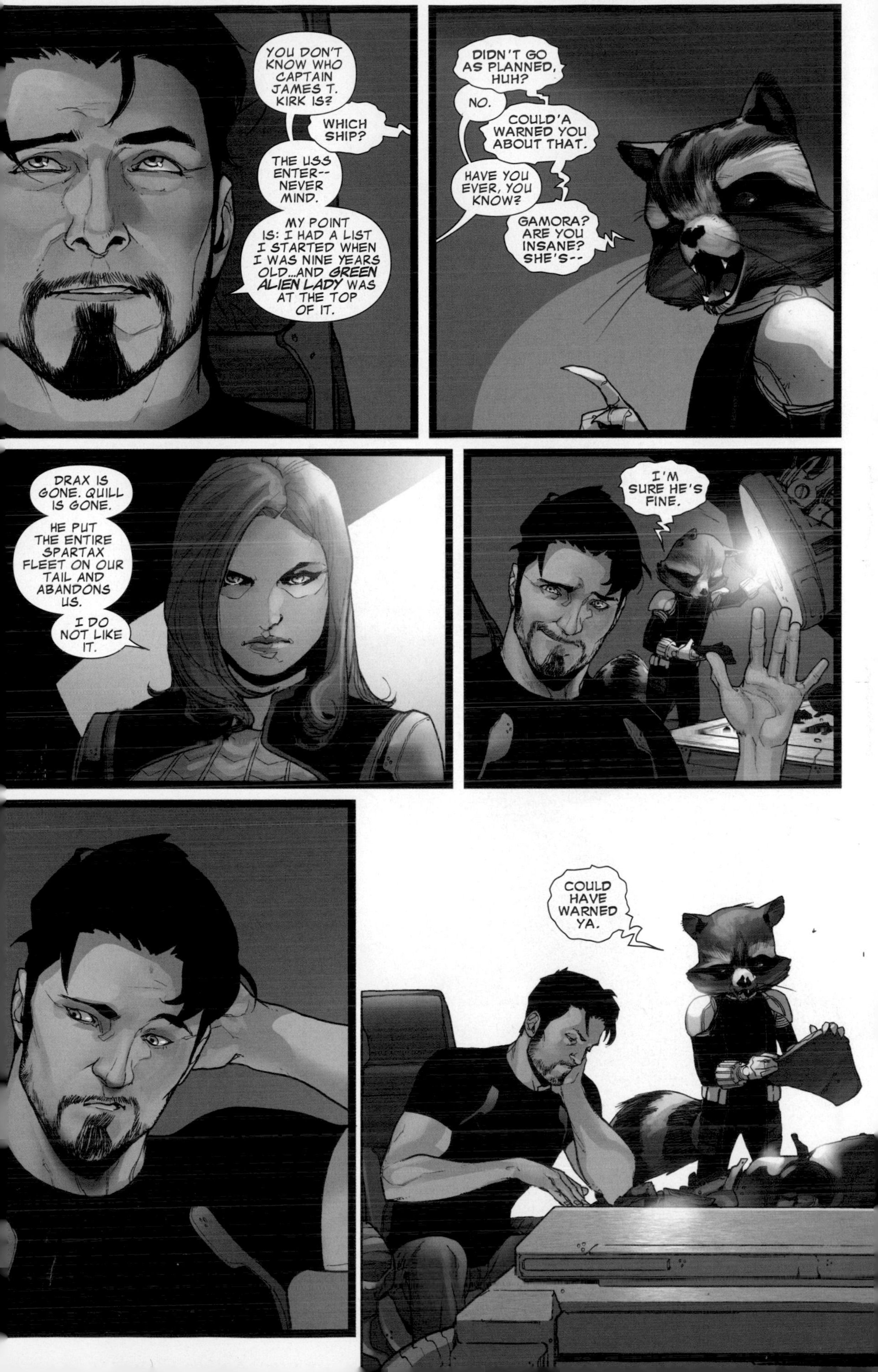
YOU DON'T KNOW WHO CAPTAIN JAMES T. KIRK IS?
WHICH SHIP?
THE USS ENTER-- NEVER MIND.
MY POINT IS: I HAD A LIST I STARTED WHEN I WAS NINE YEARS OLD...AND GREEN ALIEN LADY WAS AT THE TOP OF IT.
DIDN'T GO AS PLANNED, HUH?
NO.
COULD'A WARNED YOU ABOUT THAT.
HAVE YOU EVER, YOU KNOW?
GAMORA? ARE YOU INSANE? SHE'S--
DRAX IS GONE. QUILL IS GONE.
HE PUT THE ENTIRE SPARTAX FLEET ON OUR TAIL AND ABANDONS US.
I DO NOT LIKE IT.
I'M SURE HE'S FINE.
COULD HAVE WARNED YA.

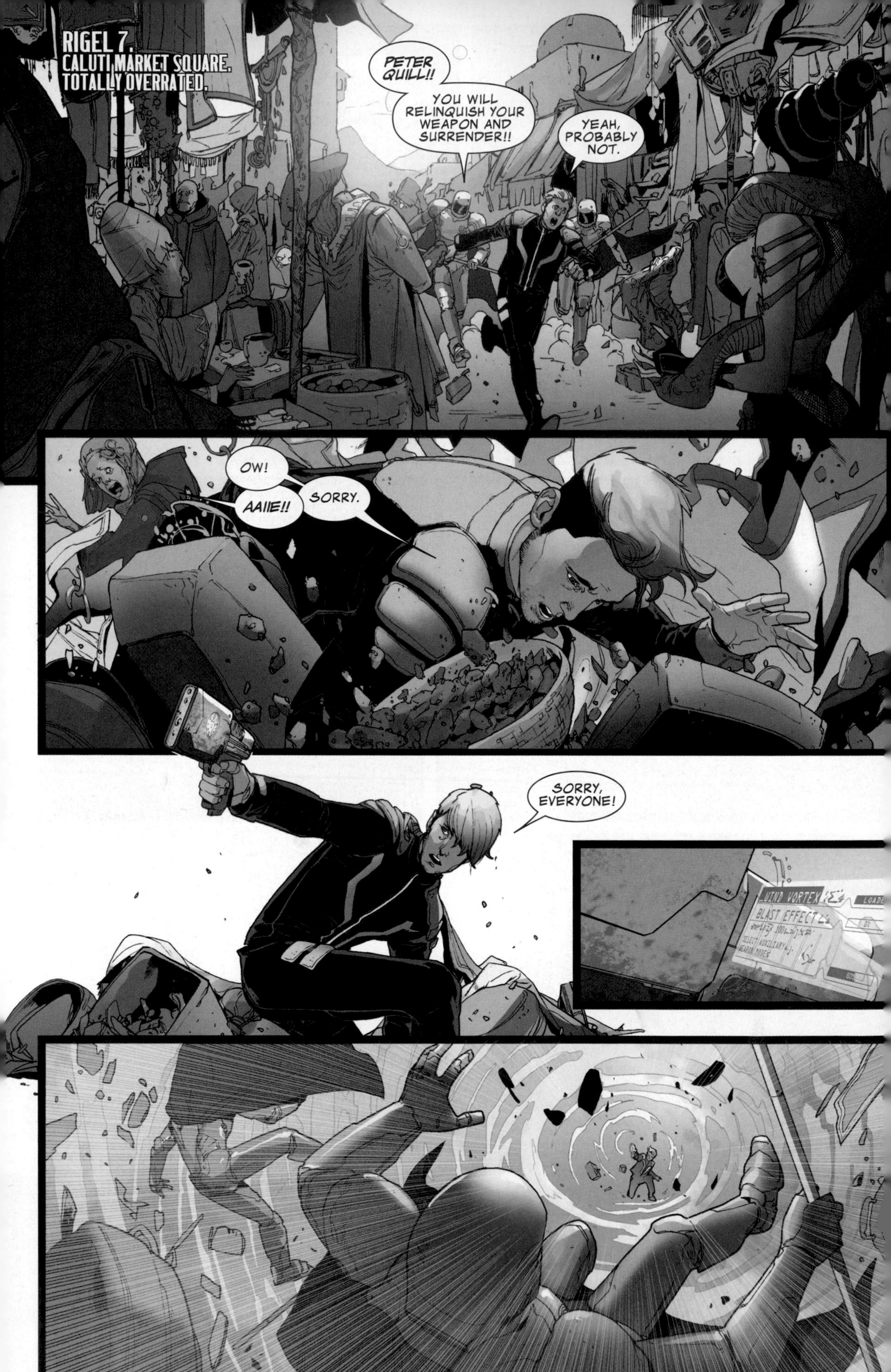
RIGEL 7. CALUTI MARKET SQUARE. TOTALLY OVERRATED.
PETER QUILL!!
YOU WILL RELINQUISH YOUR WEAPON AND SURRENDER!!
YEAH, PROBABLY NOT.
OW!
AAIIE!!
SORRY.
SORRY, EVERYONE!
WIND VORTEX
BLAST EFFECT
SELECT AUXILIARY WEAPON MODE

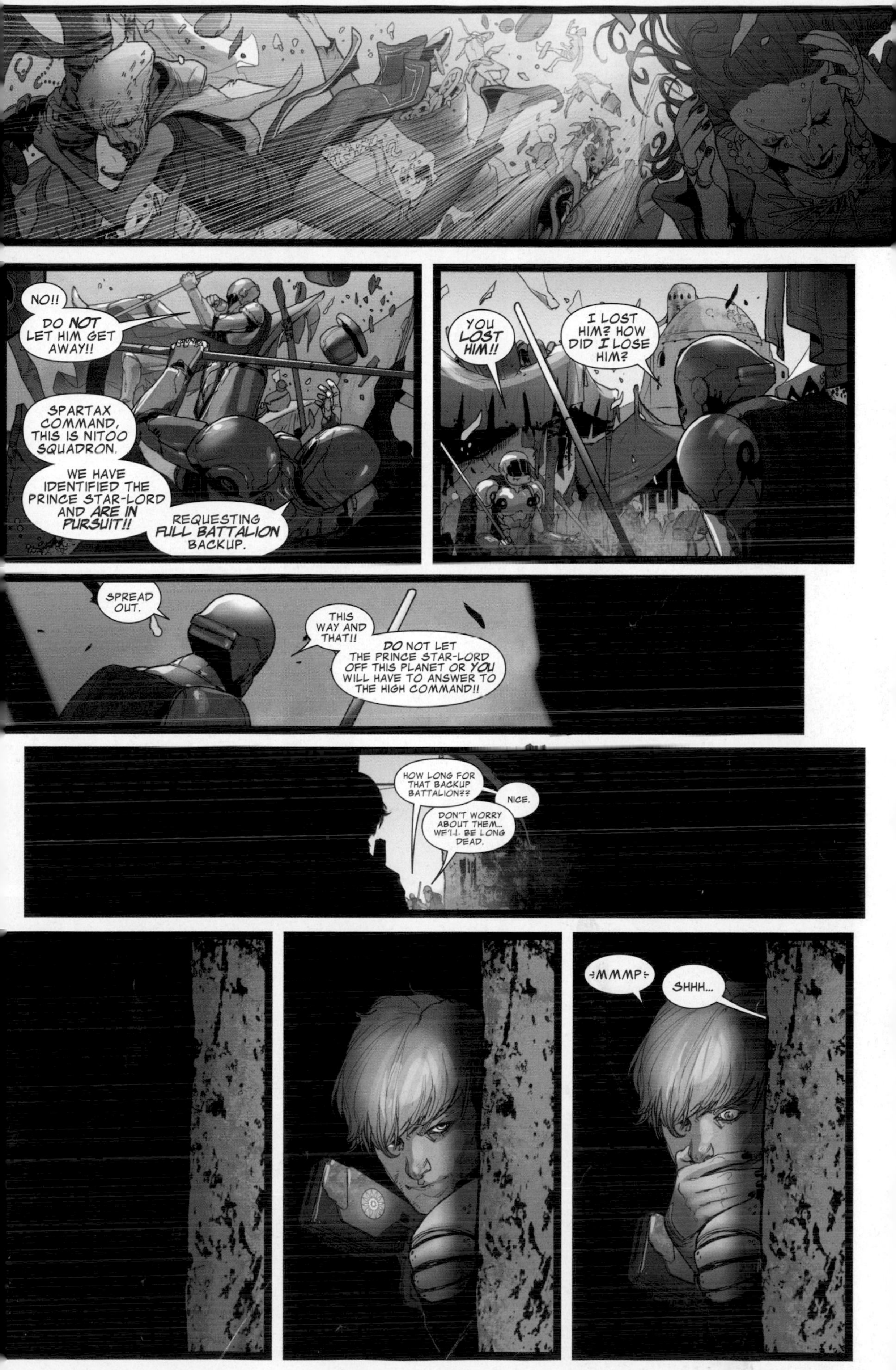
NO!!
DO NOT LET HIM GET AWAY!!
SPARTAX COMMAND, THIS IS NITOO SQUADRON.
WE HAVE IDENTIFIED THE PRINCE STAR-LORD AND ARE IN PURSUIT!!
REQUESTING FULL BATTALION BACKUP.
YOU LOST HIM!!
I LOST HIM? HOW DID I LOSE HIM?
SPREAD OUT.
THIS WAY AND THAT!!
DO NOT LET THE PRINCE STAR-LORD OFF THIS PLANET OR YOU WILL HAVE TO ANSWER TO THE HIGH COMMAND!!
HOW LONG FOR THAT BACKUP BATTALION??
NICE.
DON'T WORRY ABOUT THEM... WE'LL BE LONG DEAD.
MMMP
SHHH...

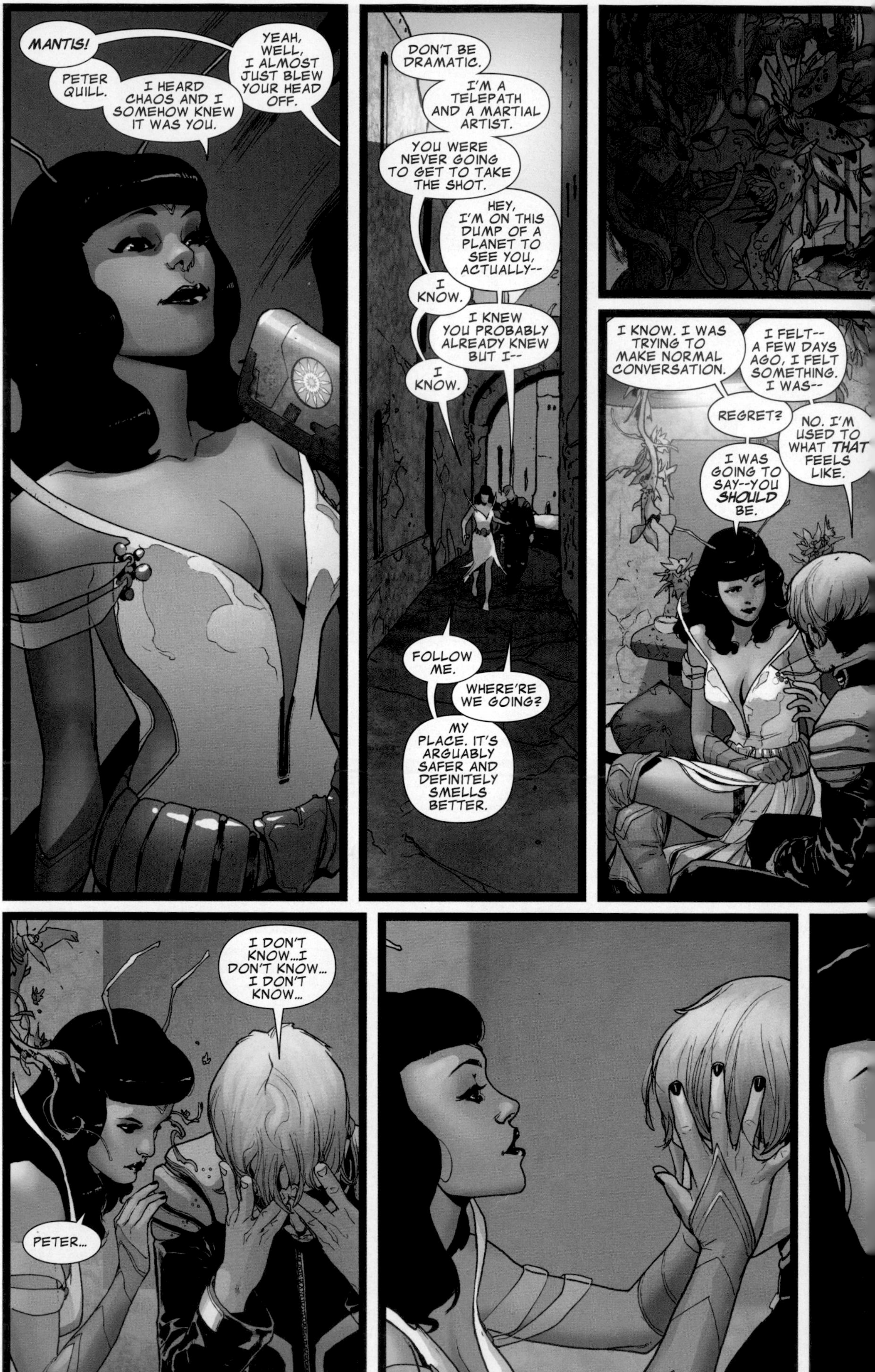
MANTIS!
PETER QUILL.
YEAH, WELL, I ALMOST JUST BLEW YOUR HEAD OFF.
I HEARD CHAOS AND I SOMEHOW KNEW IT WAS YOU.
DON'T BE DRAMATIC.
I'M A TELEPATH AND A MARTIAL ARTIST.
YOU WERE NEVER GOING TO GET TO TAKE THE SHOT.
HEY, I'M ON THIS DUMP OF A PLANET TO SEE YOU, ACTUALLY--
I KNOW.
I KNEW YOU PROBABLY ALREADY KNEW BUT I--
I KNOW.
FOLLOW ME.
WHERE'RE WE GOING?
MY PLACE. IT'S ARGUABLY SAFER AND DEFINITELY SMELLS BETTER.
I KNOW. I WAS TRYING TO MAKE NORMAL CONVERSATION.
I FELT-- A FEW DAYS AGO, I FELT SOMETHING. I WAS--
REGRET?
NO. I'M USED TO WHAT THAT FEELS LIKE.
I WAS GOING TO SAY--YOU SHOULD BE.
I DON'T KNOW...I DON'T KNOW... I DON'T KNOW...
PETER...

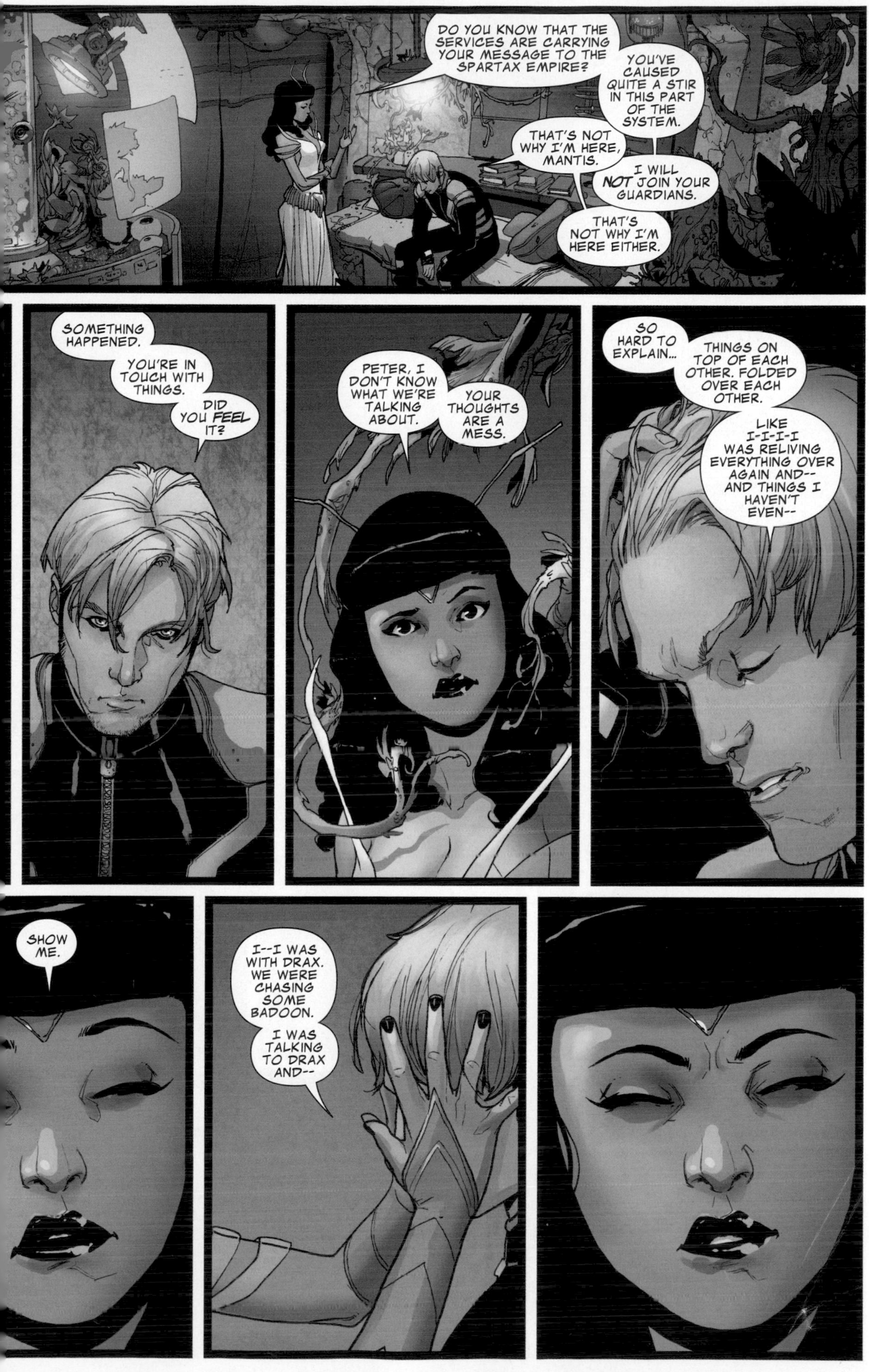
DO YOU KNOW THAT THE SERVICES ARE CARRYING YOUR MESSAGE TO THE SPARTAX EMPIRE?
YOU'VE CAUSED QUITE A STIR IN THIS PART OF THE SYSTEM.
THAT'S NOT WHY I'M HERE, MANTIS.
I WILL NOT JOIN YOUR GUARDIANS.
THAT'S NOT WHY I'M HERE EITHER.
SOMETHING HAPPENED.
YOU'RE IN TOUCH WITH THINGS.
DID YOU FEEL IT?
PETER, I DON'T KNOW WHAT WE'RE TALKING ABOUT.
YOUR THOUGHTS ARE A MESS.
SO HARD TO EXPLAIN...
THINGS ON TOP OF EACH OTHER. FOLDED OVER EACH OTHER.
LIKE I-I-I-I WAS RELIVING EVERYTHING OVER AGAIN AND-- AND THINGS I HAVEN'T EVEN--
SHOW ME.
I--I WAS WITH DRAX. WE WERE CHASING SOME BADOON.
I WAS TALKING TO DRAX AND--

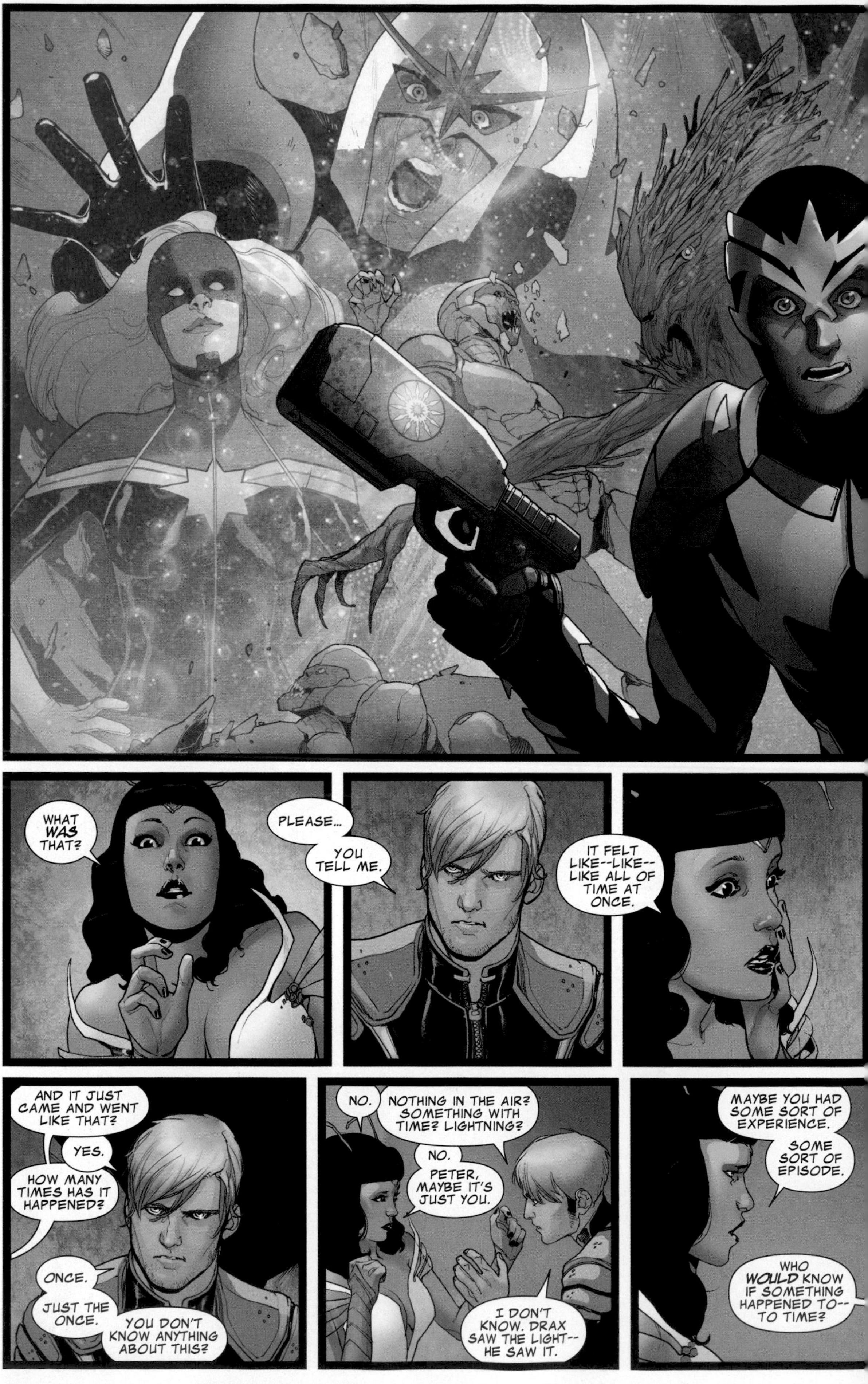
WHAT WAS THAT?
PLEASE...
YOU TELL ME.
IT FELT LIKE--LIKE--LIKE ALL OF TIME AT ONCE.
AND IT JUST CAME AND WENT LIKE THAT?
YES.
HOW MANY TIMES HAS IT HAPPENED?
ONCE.
JUST THE ONCE.
YOU DON'T KNOW ANYTHING ABOUT THIS?
NO.
NOTHING IN THE AIR? SOMETHING WITH TIME? LIGHTNING?
NO.
PETER, MAYBE IT'S JUST YOU.
I DON'T KNOW. DRAX SAW THE LIGHT--HE SAW IT.
MAYBE YOU HAD SOME SORT OF EXPERIENCE.
SOME SORT OF EPISODE.
WHO WOULD KNOW IF SOMETHING HAPPENED TO--TO TIME?

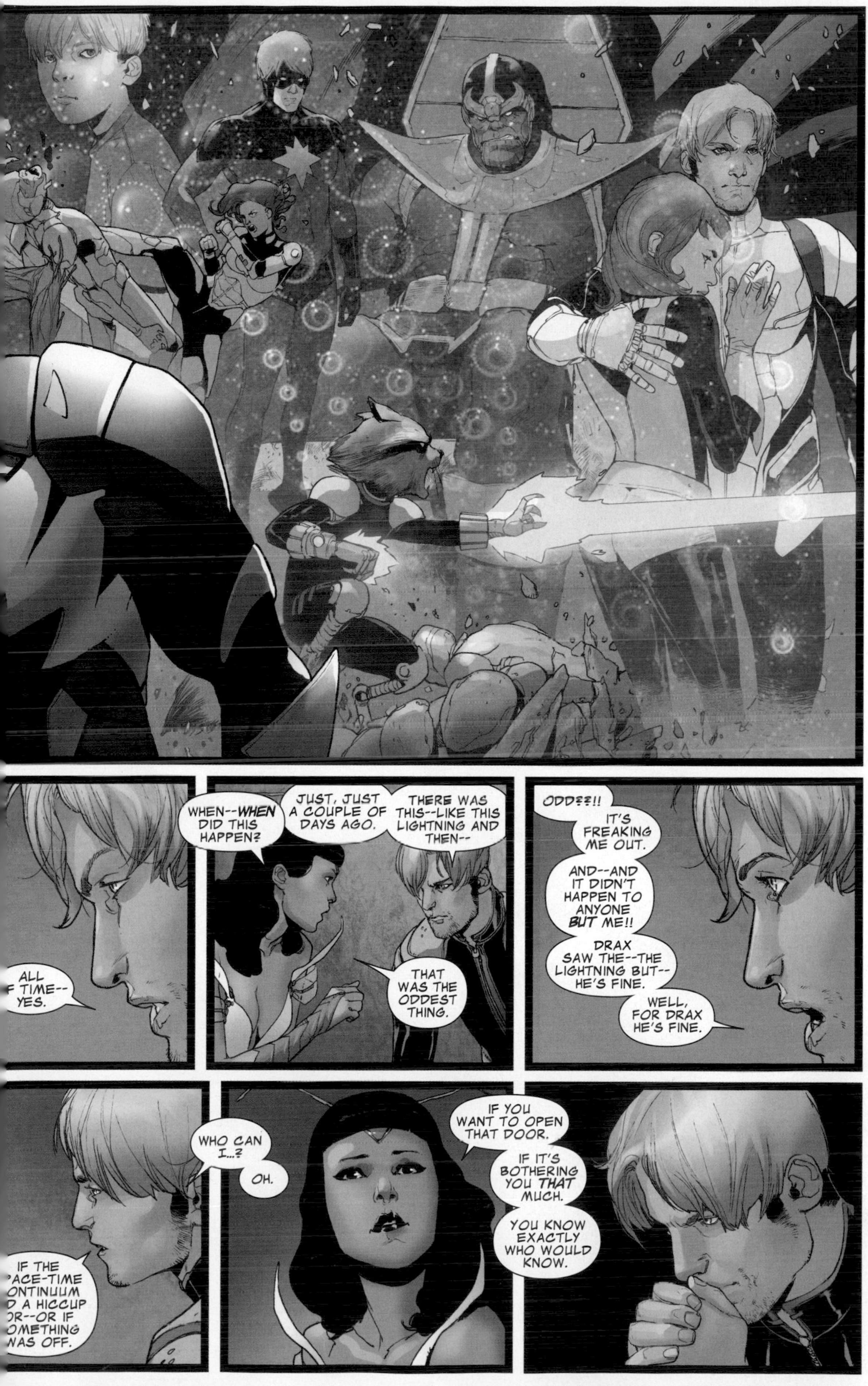
ALL
F TIME--
YES.
WHEN--WHEN DID THIS HAPPEN?
JUST, JUST A COUPLE OF DAYS AGO.
THERE WAS THIS--LIKE THIS LIGHTNING AND THEN--
THAT WAS THE ODDEST THING.
ODD???!!
IT'S FREAKING ME OUT.
AND--AND IT DIDN'T HAPPEN TO ANYONE BUT ME!!
DRAX SAW THE--THE LIGHTNING BUT--HE'S FINE.
WELL, FOR DRAX HE'S FINE.
IF THE
PACE-TIME
ONTINUUM
D A HICCUP
OR--OR IF
OMETHING
WAS OFF.
WHO CAN I...?
OH.
IF YOU WANT TO OPEN THAT DOOR.
IF IT'S BOTHERING YOU THAT MUCH.
YOU KNOW EXACTLY WHO WOULD KNOW.

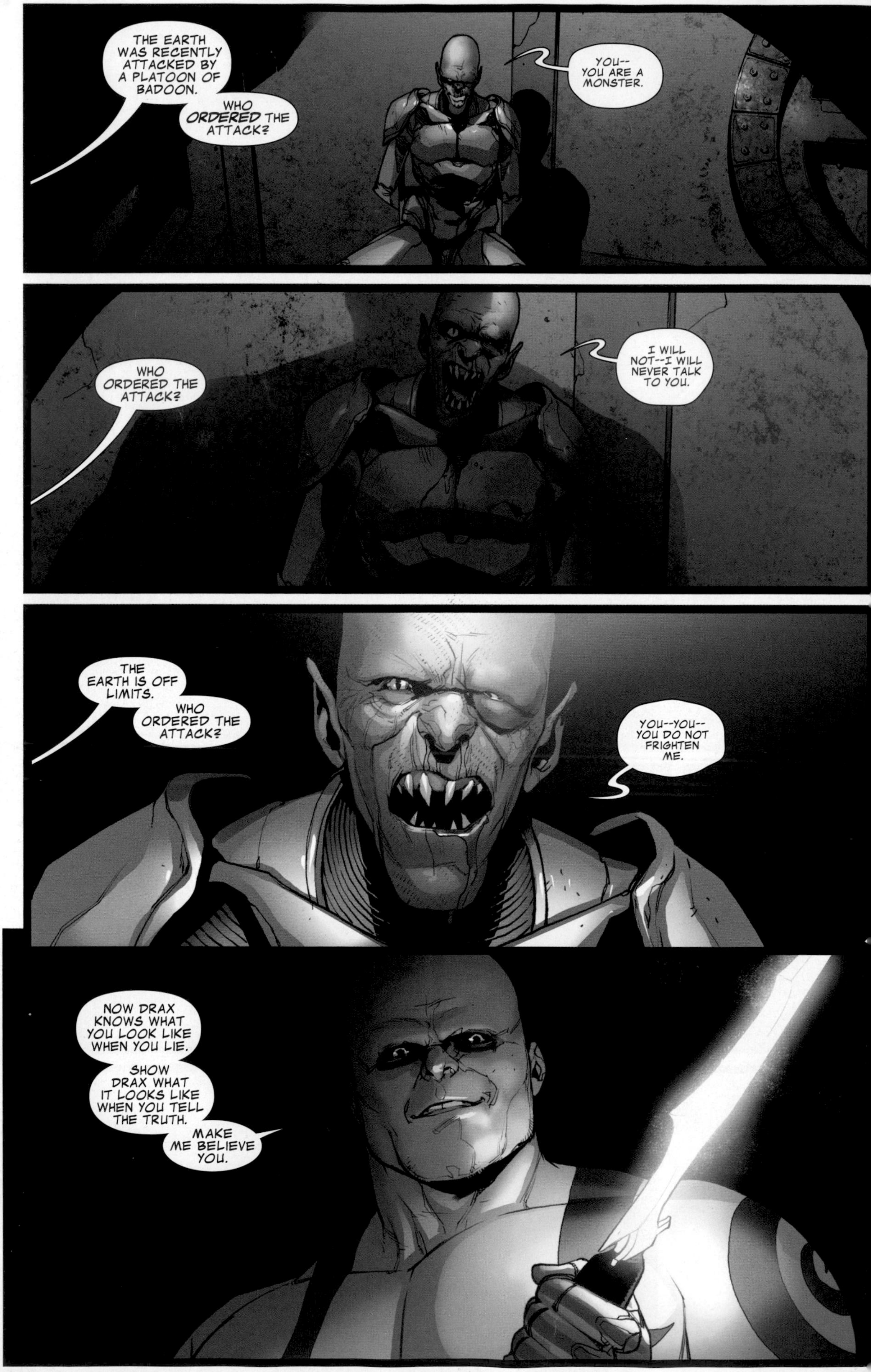
THE EARTH WAS RECENTLY ATTACKED BY A PLATOON OF BADOON.
WHO ORDERED THE ATTACK?
YOU-- YOU ARE A MONSTER.
WHO ORDERED THE ATTACK?
I WILL NOT--I WILL NEVER TALK TO YOU.
THE EARTH IS OFF LIMITS.
WHO ORDERED THE ATTACK?
YOU--YOU-- YOU DO NOT FRIGHTEN ME.
NOW DRAX KNOWS WHAT YOU LOOK LIKE WHEN YOU LIE.
SHOW DRAX WHAT IT LOOKS LIKE WHEN YOU TELL THE TRUTH.
MAKE ME BELIEVE YOU.

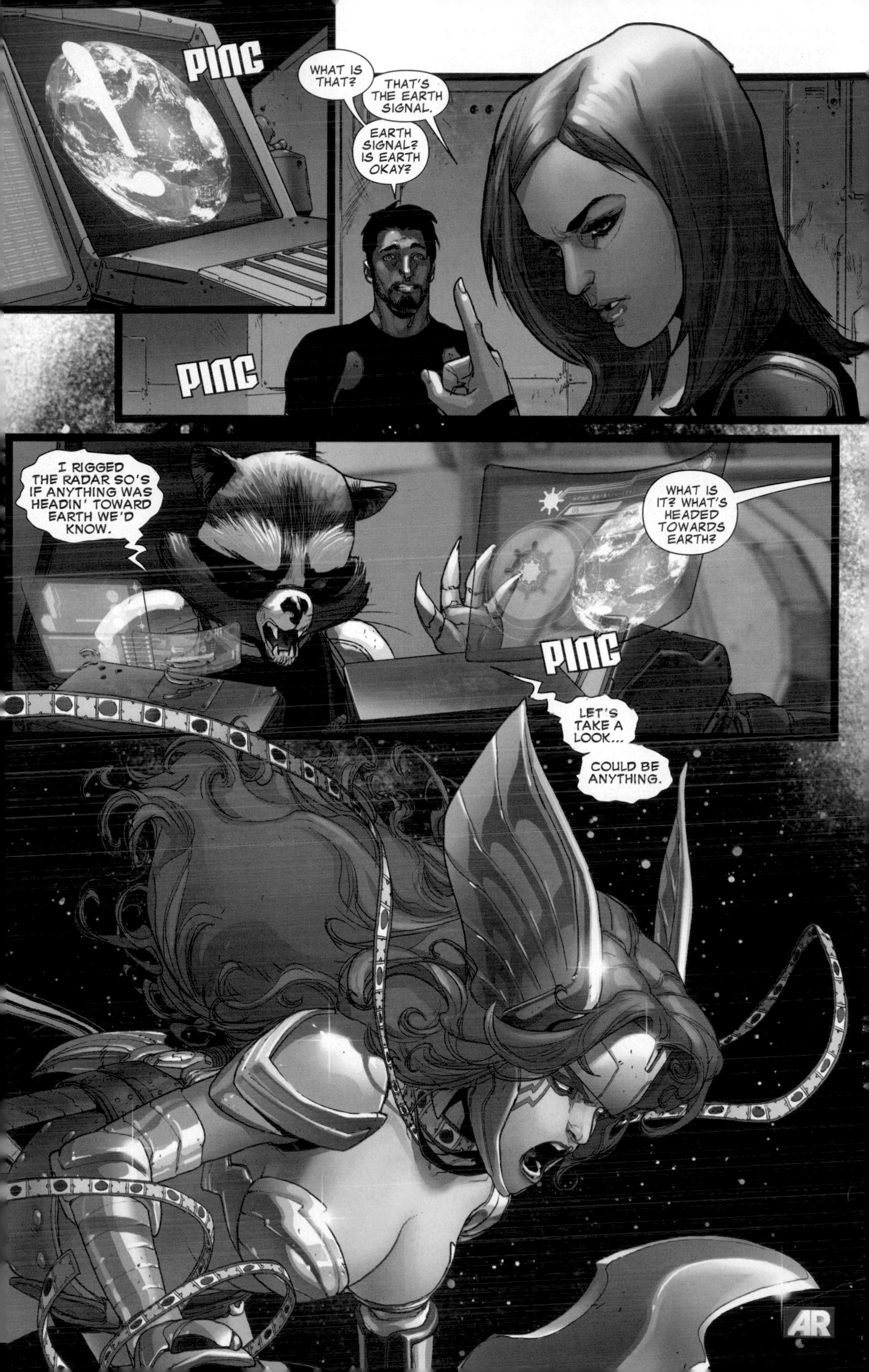
PING
WHAT IS THAT?
THAT'S THE EARTH SIGNAL.
EARTH SIGNAL? IS EARTH OKAY?
PING
I RIGGED THE RADAR SO'S IF ANYTHING WAS HEADIN' TOWARD EARTH WE'D KNOW.
WHAT IS IT? WHAT'S HEADED TOWARDS EARTH?
PING
LET'S TAKE A LOOK...
COULD BE ANYTHING.
AR

GIVE ME THAT LONG RANGE COMMUNICATION THINGY OF YOURS, I'LL CALL THE AVENGERS.

WHAT THE HELL ARE THEY GONNA DO?

WE GOT THIS.

GOT THIS? WE'RE HALF A GALAXY AWAY!

YOU'RE FUNNY. BUCKLE UP, BUTTERCUP.

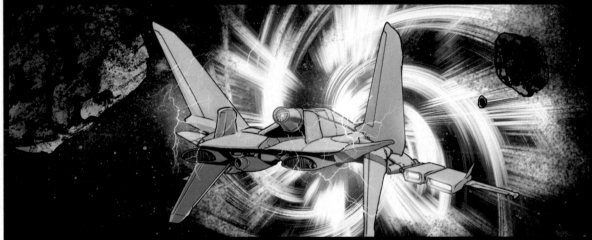

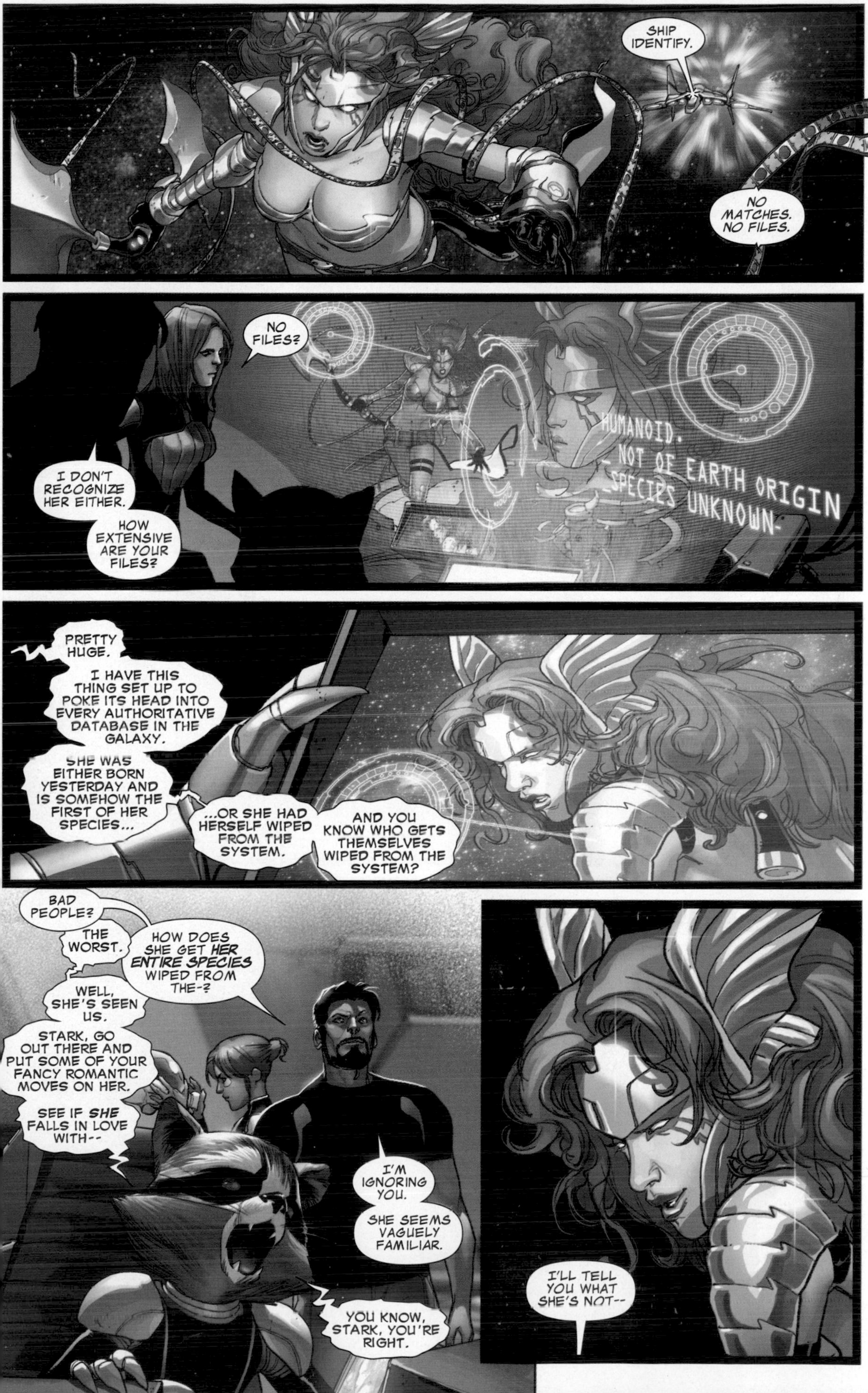
SHIP IDENTIFY.
NO MATCHES. NO FILES.
NO FILES?
HUMANOID.
- NOT OF EARTH ORIGIN
- SPECIES UNKNOWN-
I DON'T RECOGNIZE HER EITHER.
HOW EXTENSIVE ARE YOUR FILES?
PRETTY HUGE.
I HAVE THIS THING SET UP TO POKE ITS HEAD INTO EVERY AUTHORITATIVE DATABASE IN THE GALAXY.
SHE WAS EITHER BORN YESTERDAY AND IS SOMEHOW THE FIRST OF HER SPECIES...
...OR SHE HAD HERSELF WIPED FROM THE SYSTEM.
AND YOU KNOW WHO GETS THEMSELVES WIPED FROM THE SYSTEM?
BAD PEOPLE?
THE WORST.
HOW DOES SHE GET HER ENTIRE SPECIES WIPED FROM THE-?
WELL, SHE'S SEEN US.
STARK, GO OUT THERE AND PUT SOME OF YOUR FANCY ROMANTIC MOVES ON HER.
SEE IF SHE FALLS IN LOVE WITH--
I'M IGNORING YOU.
SHE SEEMS VAGUELY FAMILIAR.
YOU KNOW, STARK, YOU'RE RIGHT.
I'LL TELL YOU WHAT SHE'S NOT--

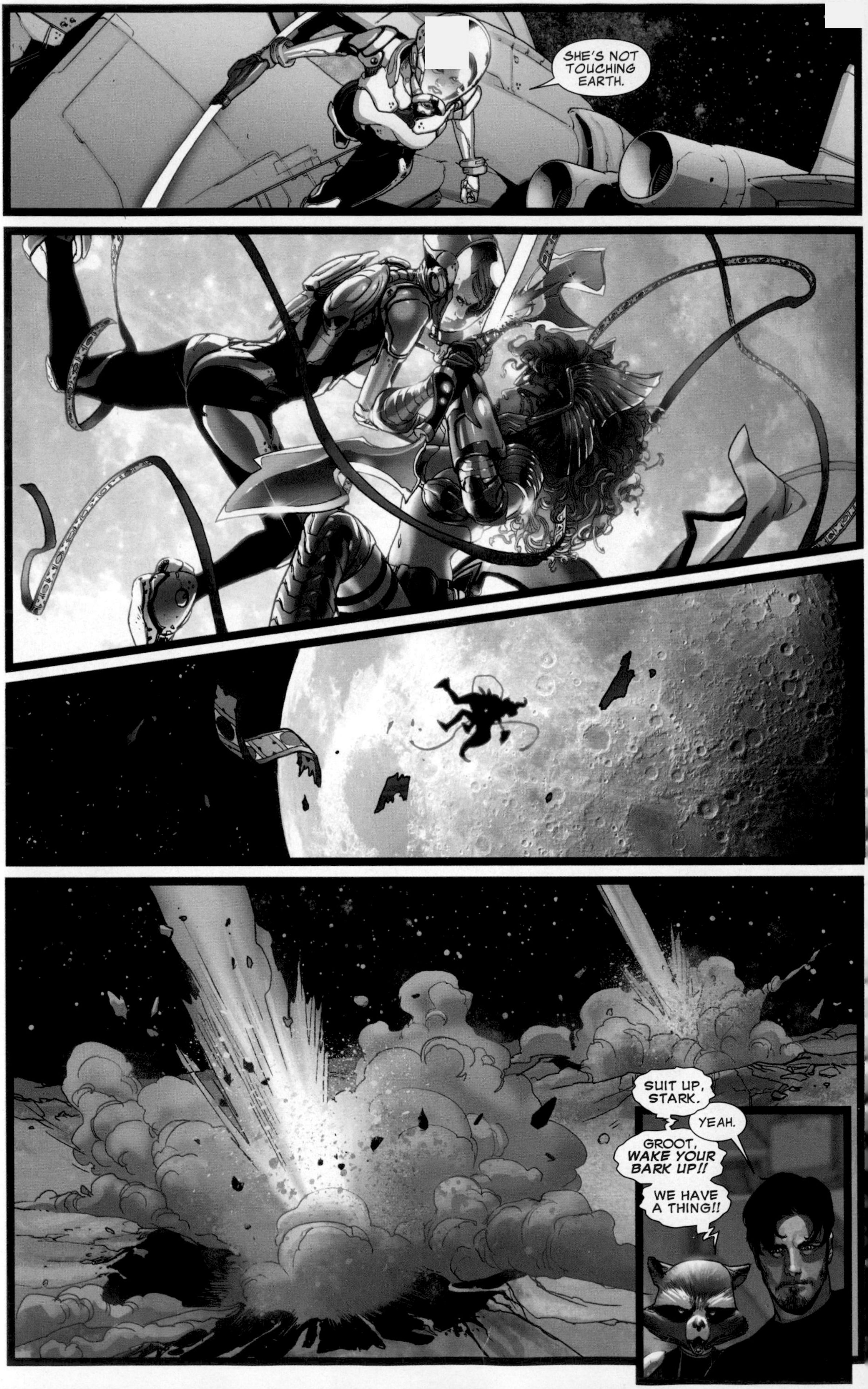
SHE'S NOT TOUCHING EARTH.
SUIT UP, STARK.
YEAH.
GROOT, WAKE YOUR BARK UP!!
WE HAVE A THING!!

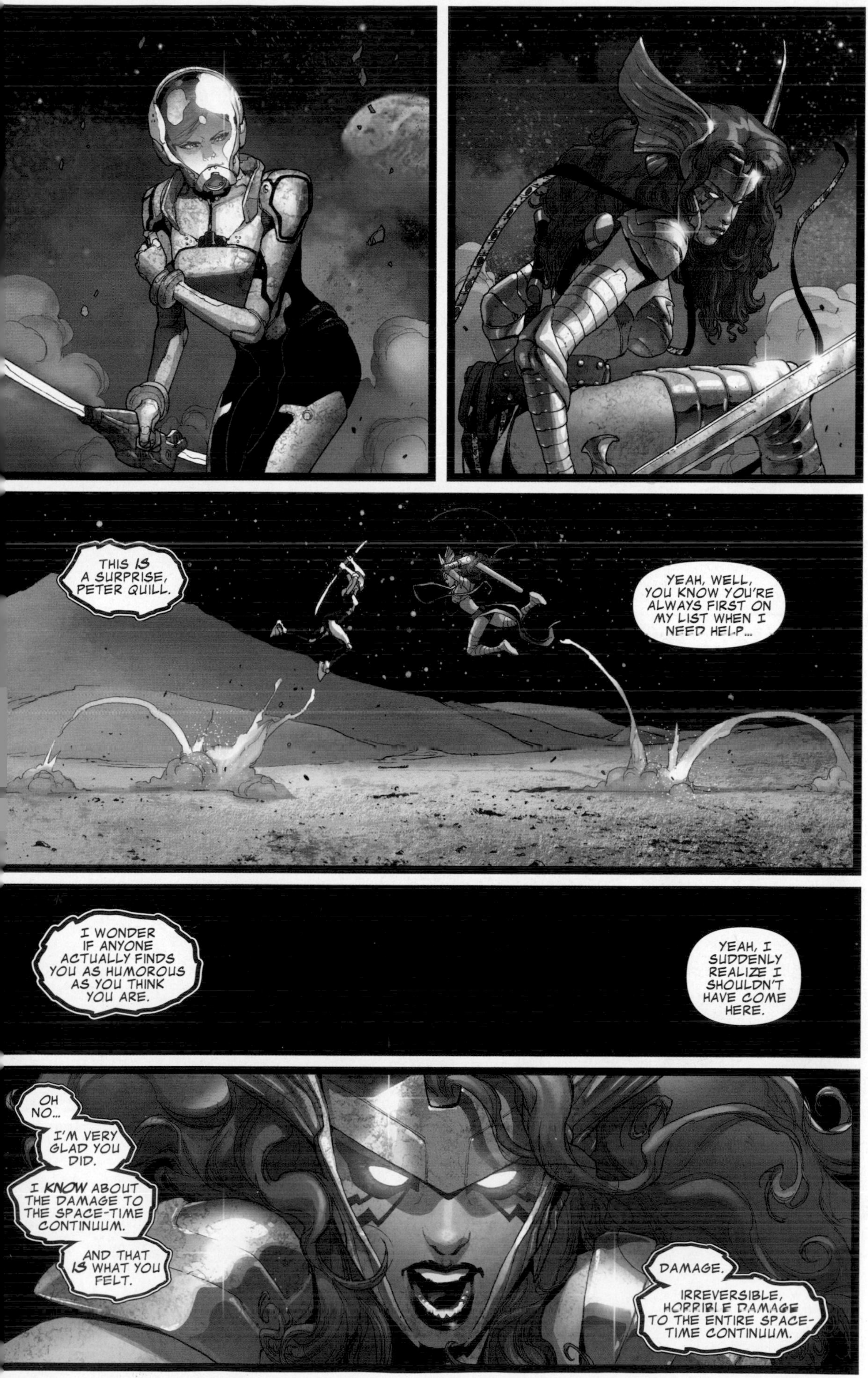

THIS IS A SURPRISE, PETER QUILL.
YEAH, WELL, YOU KNOW YOU'RE ALWAYS FIRST ON MY LIST WHEN I NEED HELP...
I WONDER IF ANYONE ACTUALLY FINDS YOU AS HUMOROUS AS YOU THINK YOU ARE.
YEAH, I SUDDENLY REALIZE I SHOULDN'T HAVE COME HERE.
OH NO...
I'M VERY GLAD YOU DID.
I KNOW ABOUT THE DAMAGE TO THE SPACE-TIME CONTINUUM.
AND THAT IS WHAT YOU FELT.
DAMAGE.
IRREVERSIBLE, HORRIBLE DAMAGE TO THE ENTIRE SPACE-TIME CONTINUUM.

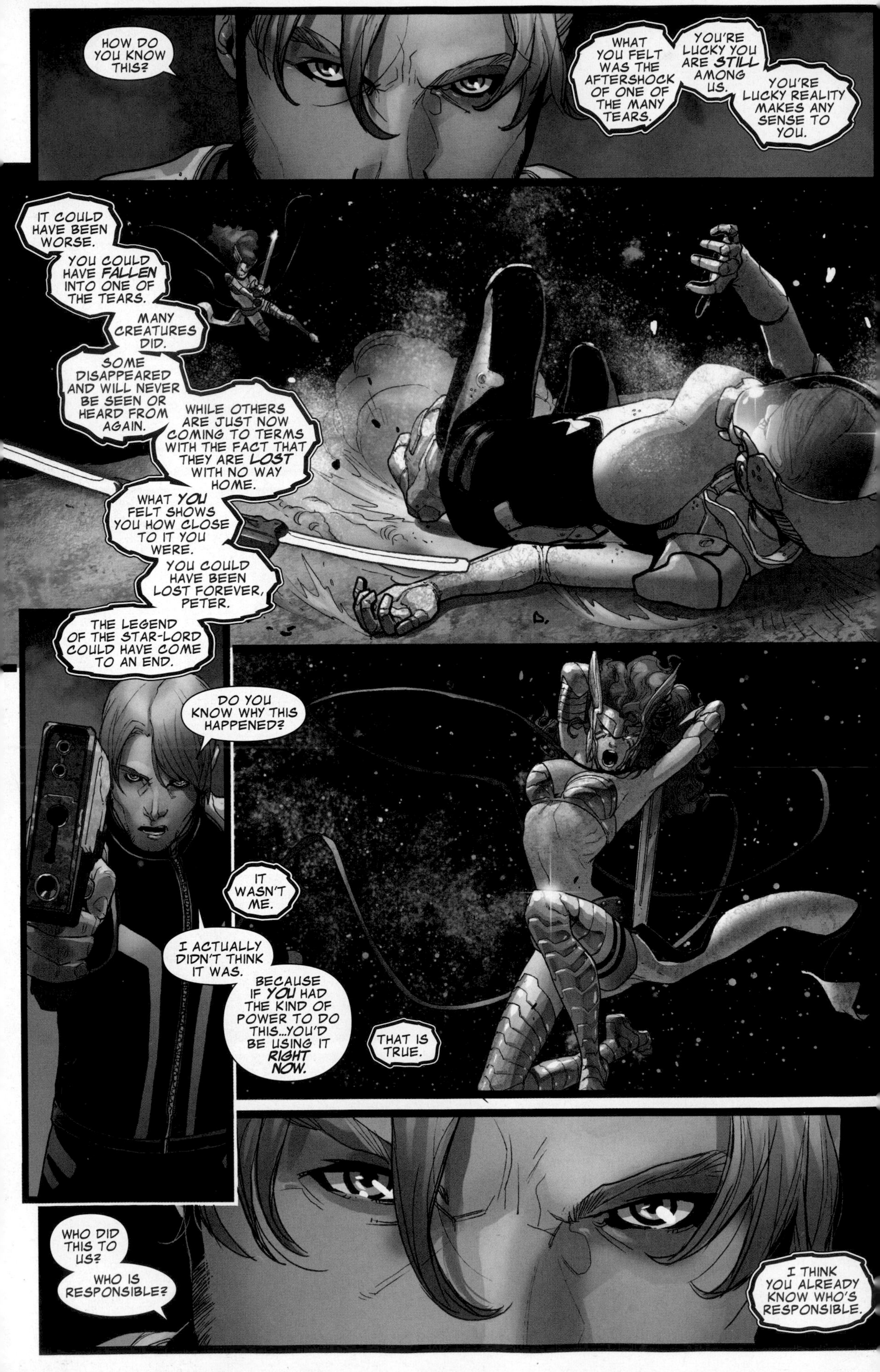

HOW DO YOU KNOW THIS?
WHAT YOU FELT WAS THE AFTERSHOCK OF ONE OF THE MANY TEARS.
YOU'RE LUCKY YOU ARE STILL AMONG US.
YOU'RE LUCKY REALITY MAKES ANY SENSE TO YOU.
IT COULD HAVE BEEN WORSE.
YOU COULD HAVE FALLEN INTO ONE OF THE TEARS.
MANY CREATURES DID.
SOME DISAPPEARED AND WILL NEVER BE SEEN OR HEARD FROM AGAIN.
WHILE OTHERS ARE JUST NOW COMING TO TERMS WITH THE FACT THAT THEY ARE LOST WITH NO WAY HOME.
WHAT YOU FELT SHOWS YOU HOW CLOSE TO IT YOU WERE.
YOU COULD HAVE BEEN LOST FOREVER, PETER.
THE LEGEND OF THE STAR-LORD COULD HAVE COME TO AN END.
DO YOU KNOW WHY THIS HAPPENED?
IT WASN'T ME.
I ACTUALLY DIDN'T THINK IT WAS.
BECAUSE IF YOU HAD THE KIND OF POWER TO DO THIS...YOU'D BE USING IT RIGHT NOW.
THAT IS TRUE.
WHO DID THIS TO US?
WHO IS RESPONSIBLE?
I THINK YOU ALREADY KNOW WHO'S RESPONSIBLE.

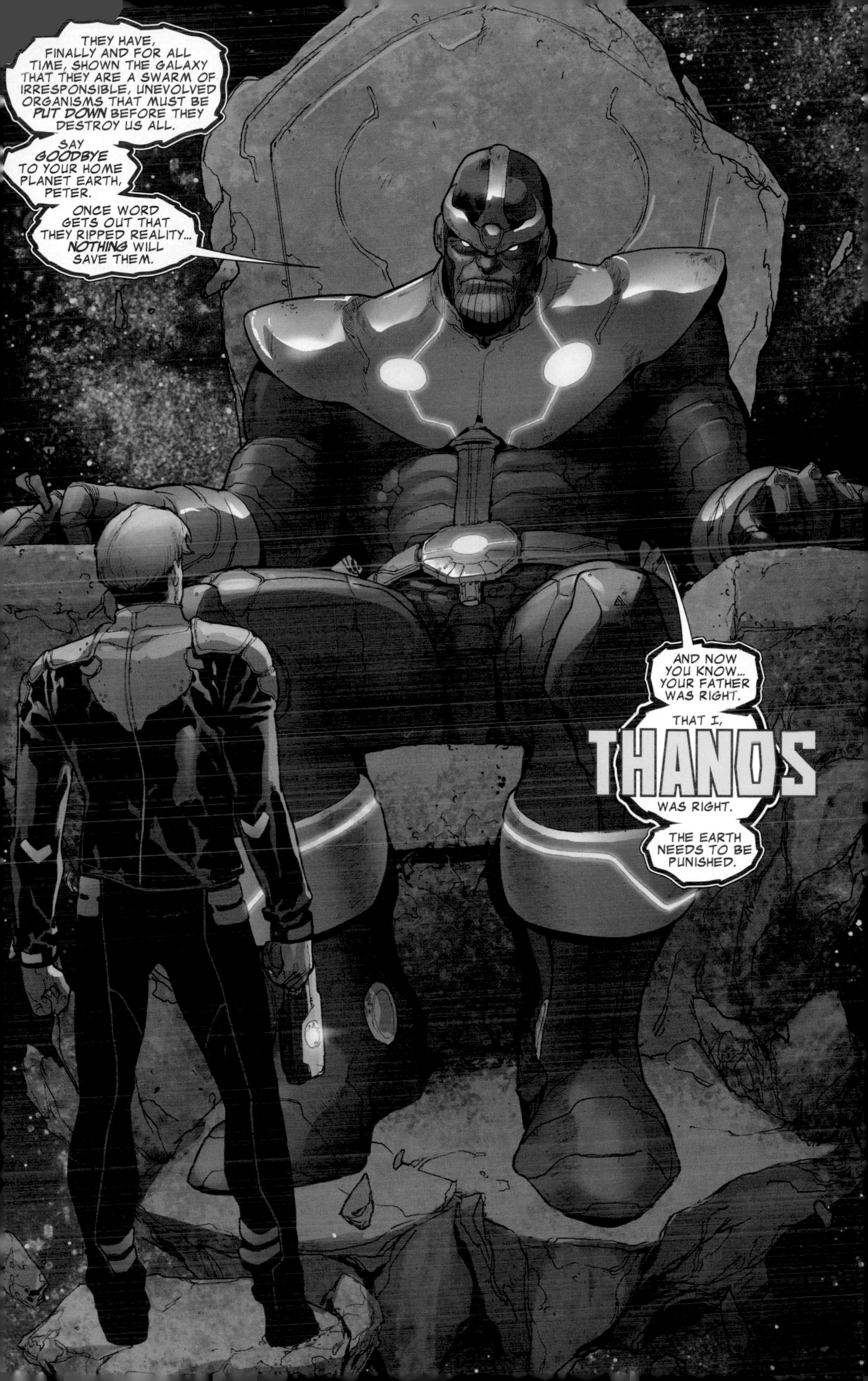
THEY HAVE, FINALLY AND FOR ALL TIME, SHOWN THE GALAXY THAT THEY ARE A SWARM OF IRRESPONSIBLE, UNEVOLVED ORGANISMS THAT MUST BE PUT DOWN BEFORE THEY DESTROY US ALL.
SAY GOODBYE TO YOUR HOME PLANET EARTH, PETER.
ONCE WORD GETS OUT THAT THEY RIPPED REALITY... NOTHING WILL SAVE THEM.
AND NOW YOU KNOW... YOUR FATHER WAS RIGHT.
THAT I, THANOS WAS RIGHT.
THE EARTH NEEDS TO BE PUNISHED.

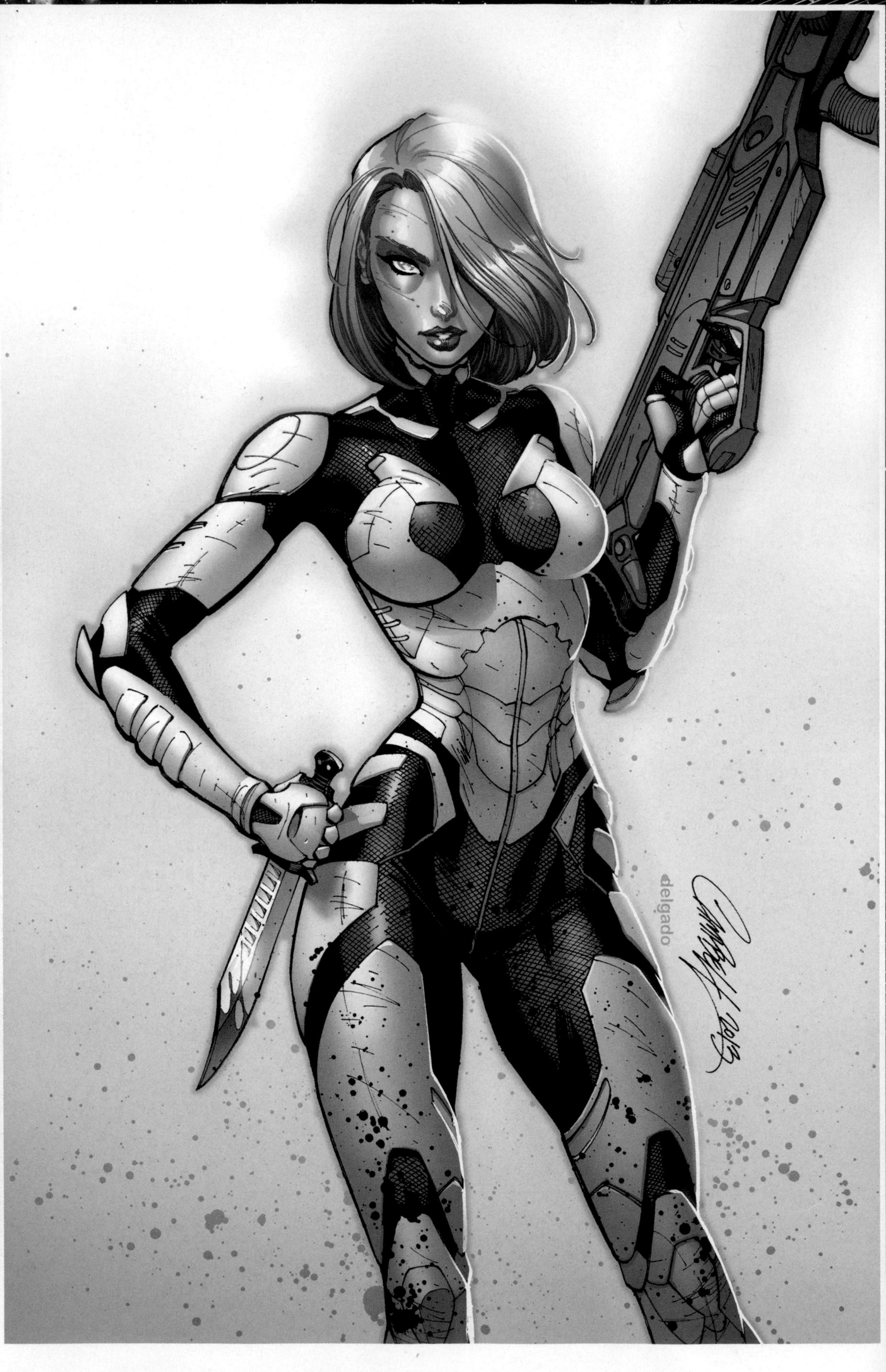
delgado

#4 VARIANT BY J. SCOTT CAMPBELL & EDGAR DELGADO

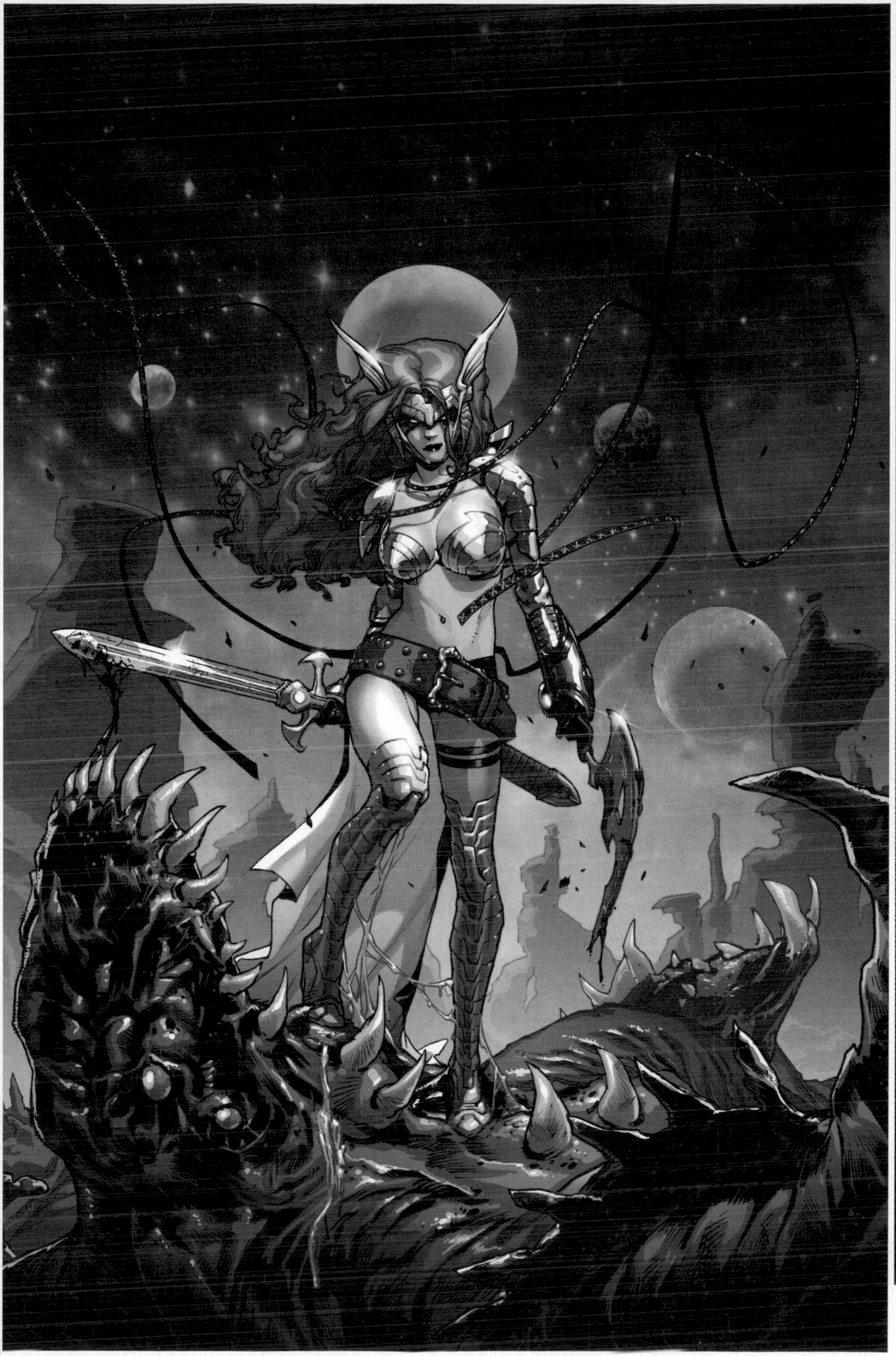

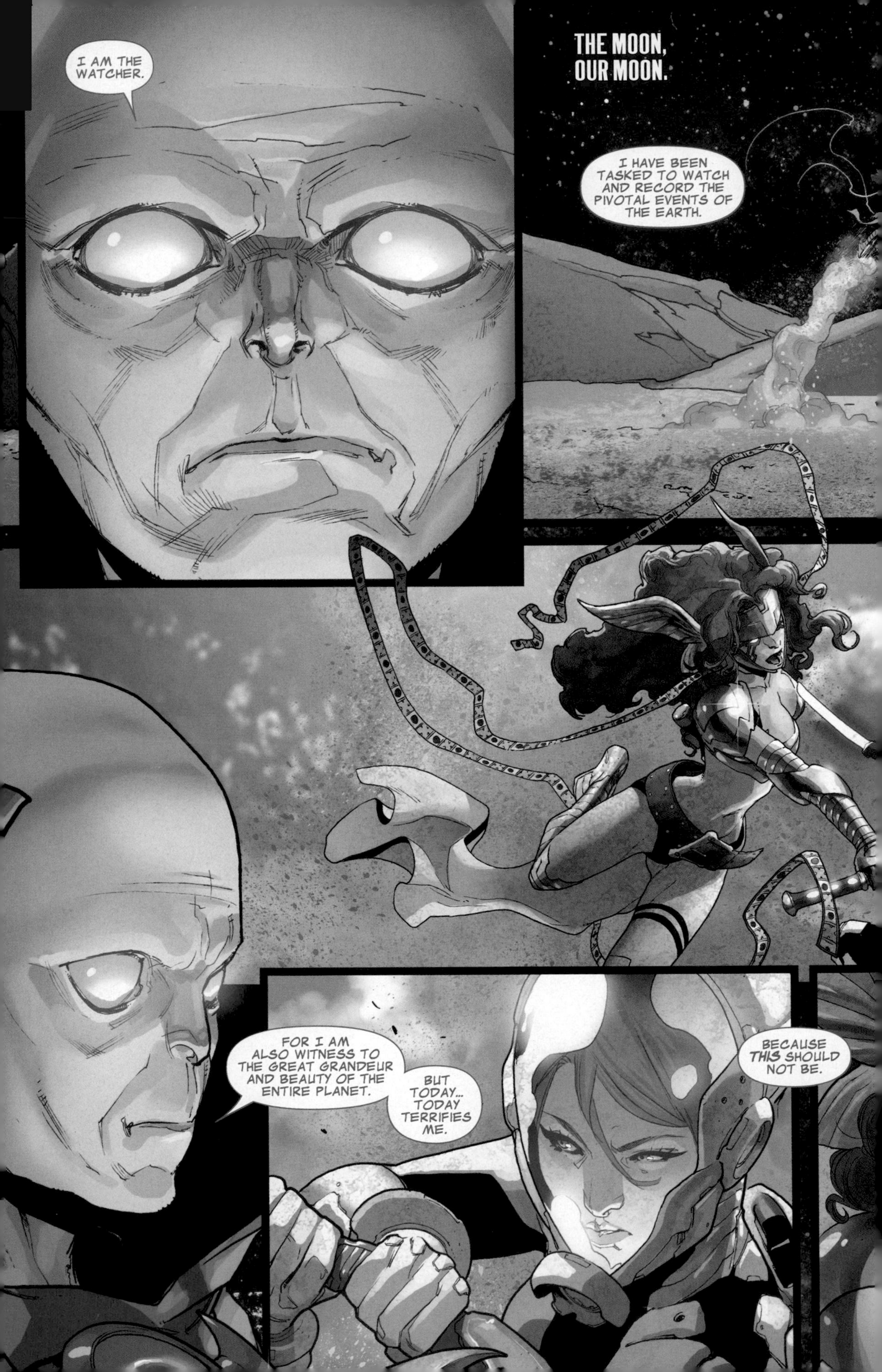
I AM THE WATCHER.
THE MOON, OUR MOON.
I HAVE BEEN TASKED TO WATCH AND RECORD THE PIVOTAL EVENTS OF THE EARTH.
FOR I AM ALSO WITNESS TO THE GREAT GRANDEUR AND BEAUTY OF THE ENTIRE PLANET.
BUT TODAY... TODAY TERRIFIES ME.
BECAUSE THIS SHOULD NOT BE.

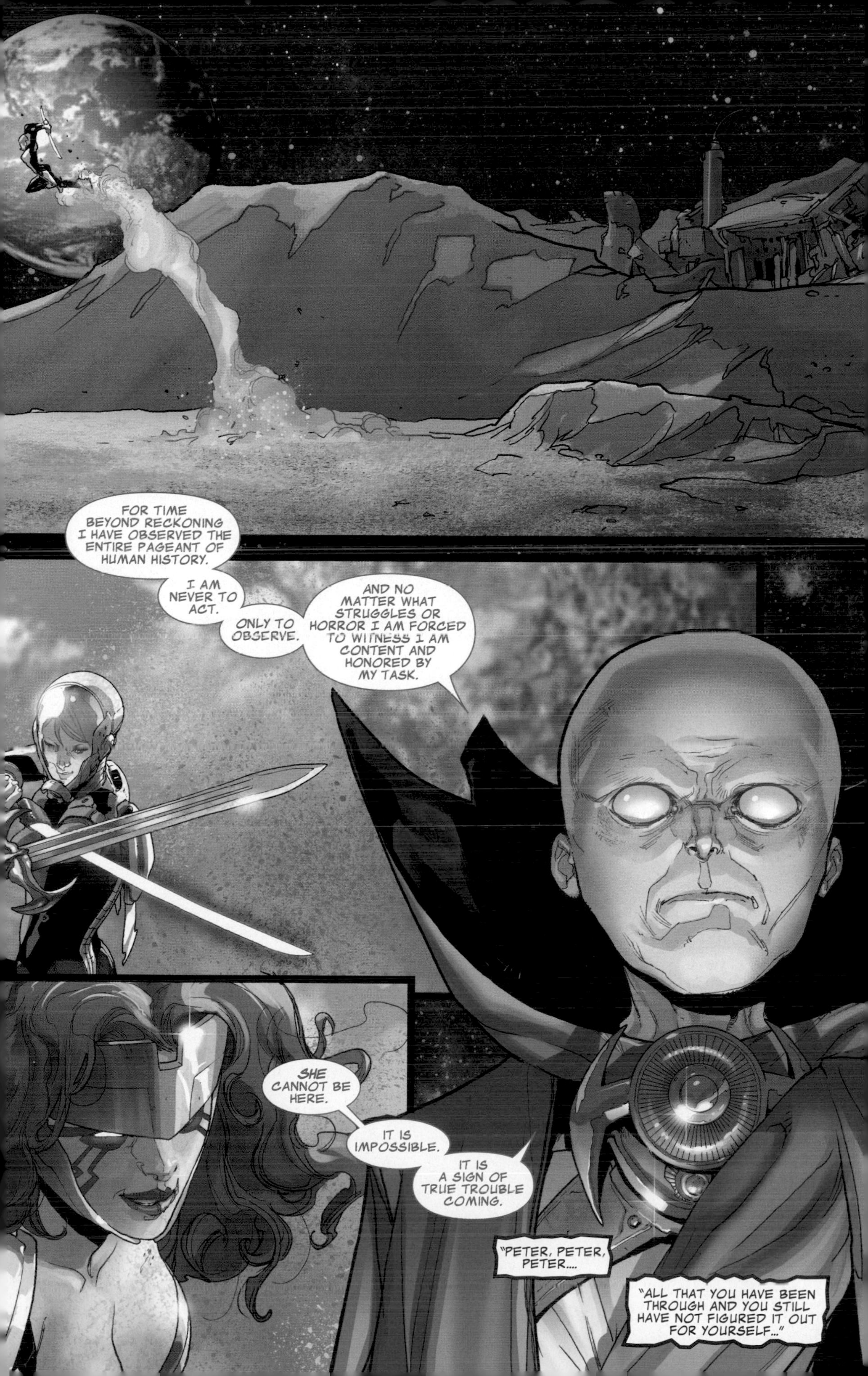
FOR TIME BEYOND RECKONING I HAVE OBSERVED THE ENTIRE PAGEANT OF HUMAN HISTORY.
I AM NEVER TO ACT.
ONLY TO OBSERVE.
AND NO MATTER WHAT STRUGGLES OR HORROR I AM FORCED TO WITNESS I AM CONTENT AND HONORED BY MY TASK.
SHE CANNOT BE HERE.
IT IS IMPOSSIBLE.
IT IS A SIGN OF TRUE TROUBLE COMING.
"PETER, PETER, PETER....
"ALL THAT YOU HAVE BEEN THROUGH AND YOU STILL HAVE NOT FIGURED IT OUT FOR YOURSELF..."

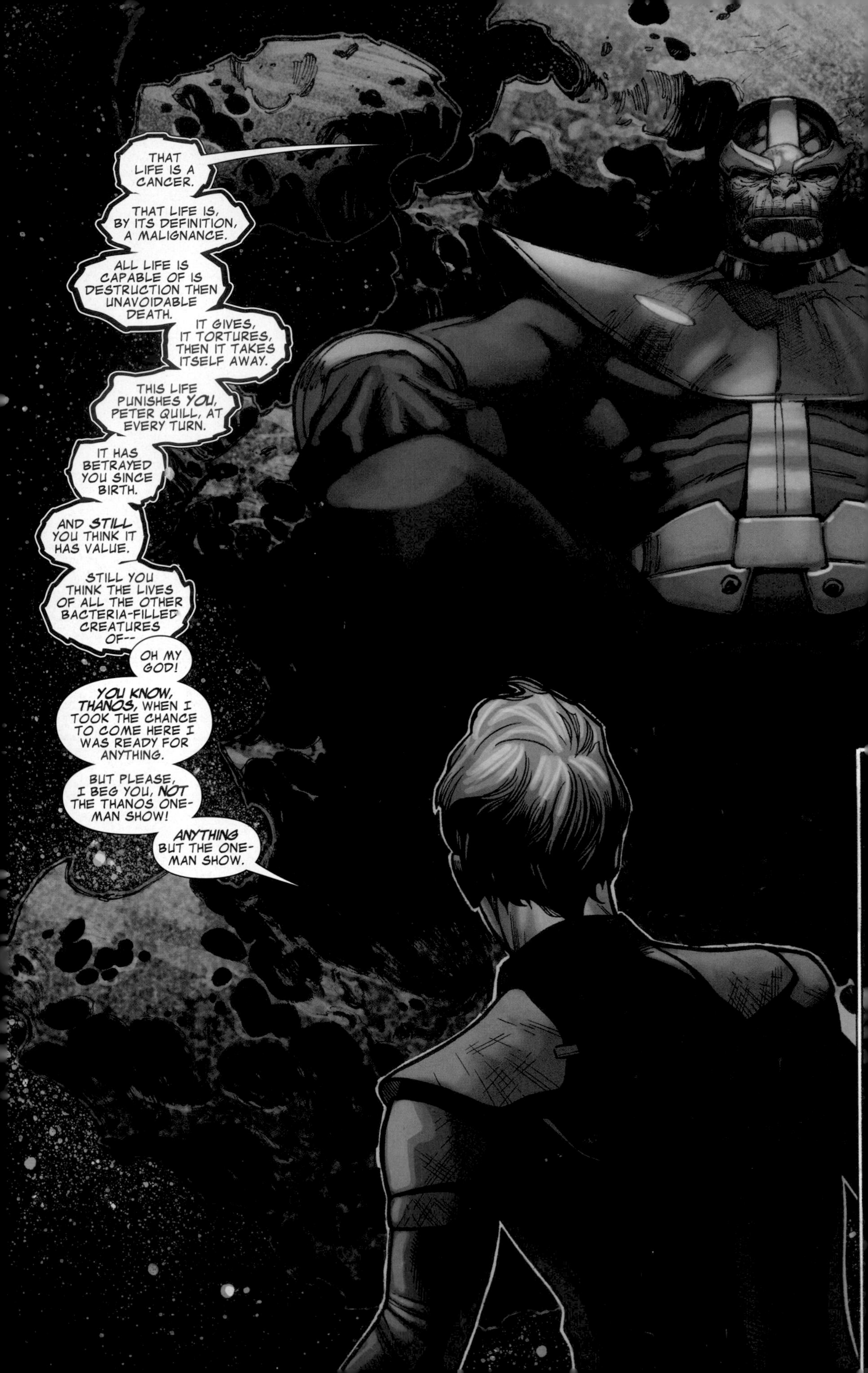
THAT LIFE IS A CANCER.
THAT LIFE IS, BY ITS DEFINITION, A MALIGNANCE.
ALL LIFE IS CAPABLE OF IS DESTRUCTION THEN UNAVOIDABLE DEATH.
IT GIVES, IT TORTURES, THEN IT TAKES ITSELF AWAY.
THIS LIFE PUNISHES YOU, PETER QUILL, AT EVERY TURN.
IT HAS BETRAYED YOU SINCE BIRTH.
AND STILL YOU THINK IT HAS VALUE.
STILL YOU THINK THE LIVES OF ALL THE OTHER BACTERIA-FILLED CREATURES OF--
OH MY GOD!
YOU KNOW, THANOS, WHEN I TOOK THE CHANCE TO COME HERE I WAS READY FOR ANYTHING.
BUT PLEASE, I BEG YOU, NOT THE THANOS ONE-MAN SHOW!
ANYTHING BUT THE ONE-MAN SHOW.

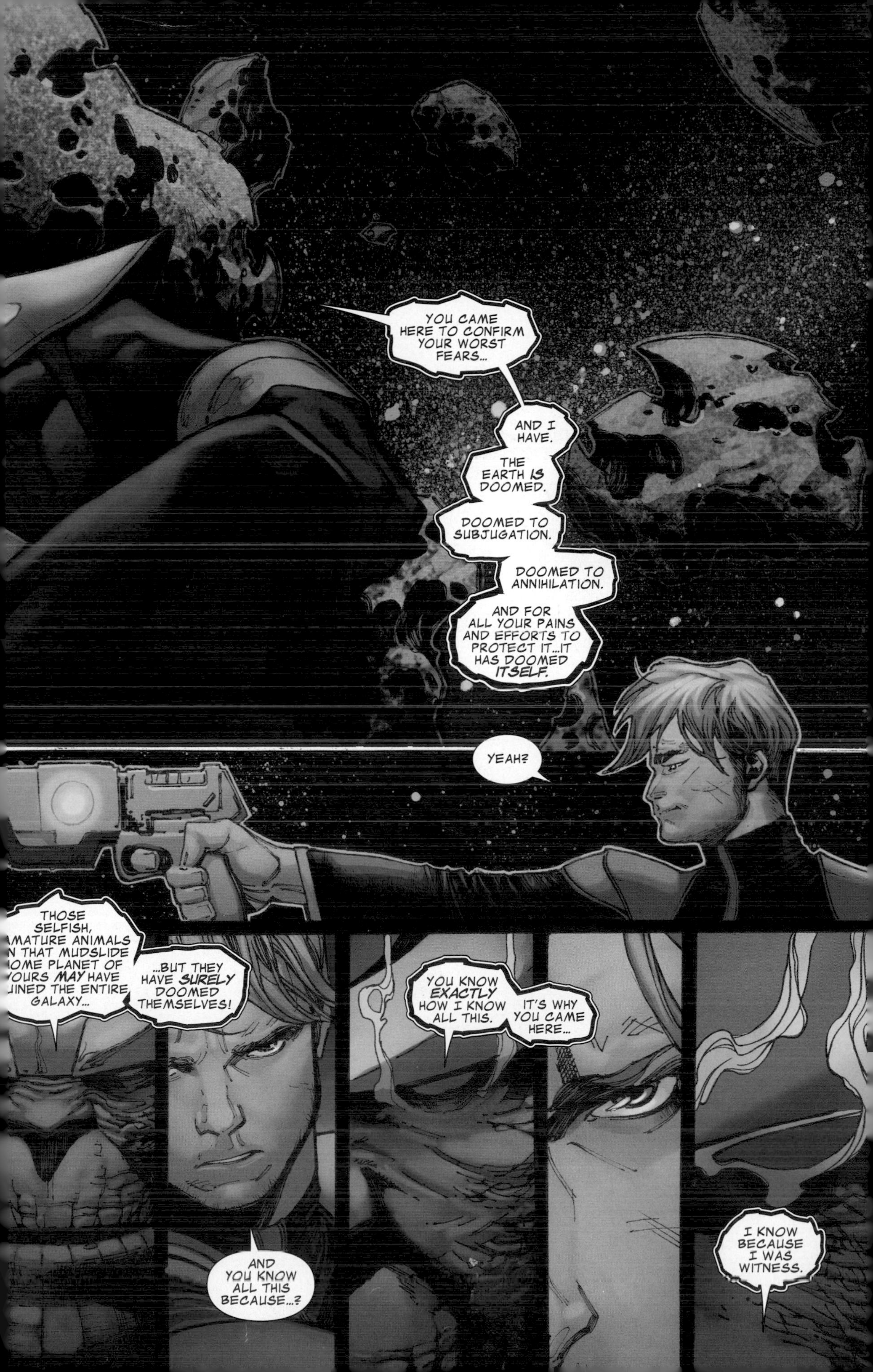
YOU CAME HERE TO CONFIRM YOUR WORST FEARS...
AND I HAVE.
THE EARTH IS DOOMED.
DOOMED TO SUBJUGATION.
DOOMED TO ANNIHILATION.
AND FOR ALL YOUR PAINS AND EFFORTS TO PROTECT IT...IT HAS DOOMED ITSELF.
YEAH?
THOSE SELFISH, IMMATURE ANIMALS ON THAT MUDSLIDE HOME PLANET OF YOURS MAY HAVE RUINED THE ENTIRE GALAXY...
...BUT THEY HAVE SURELY DOOMED THEMSELVES!
AND YOU KNOW ALL THIS BECAUSE...?
YOU KNOW EXACTLY HOW I KNOW ALL THIS.
IT'S WHY YOU CAME HERE...
I KNOW BECAUSE I WAS WITNESS.

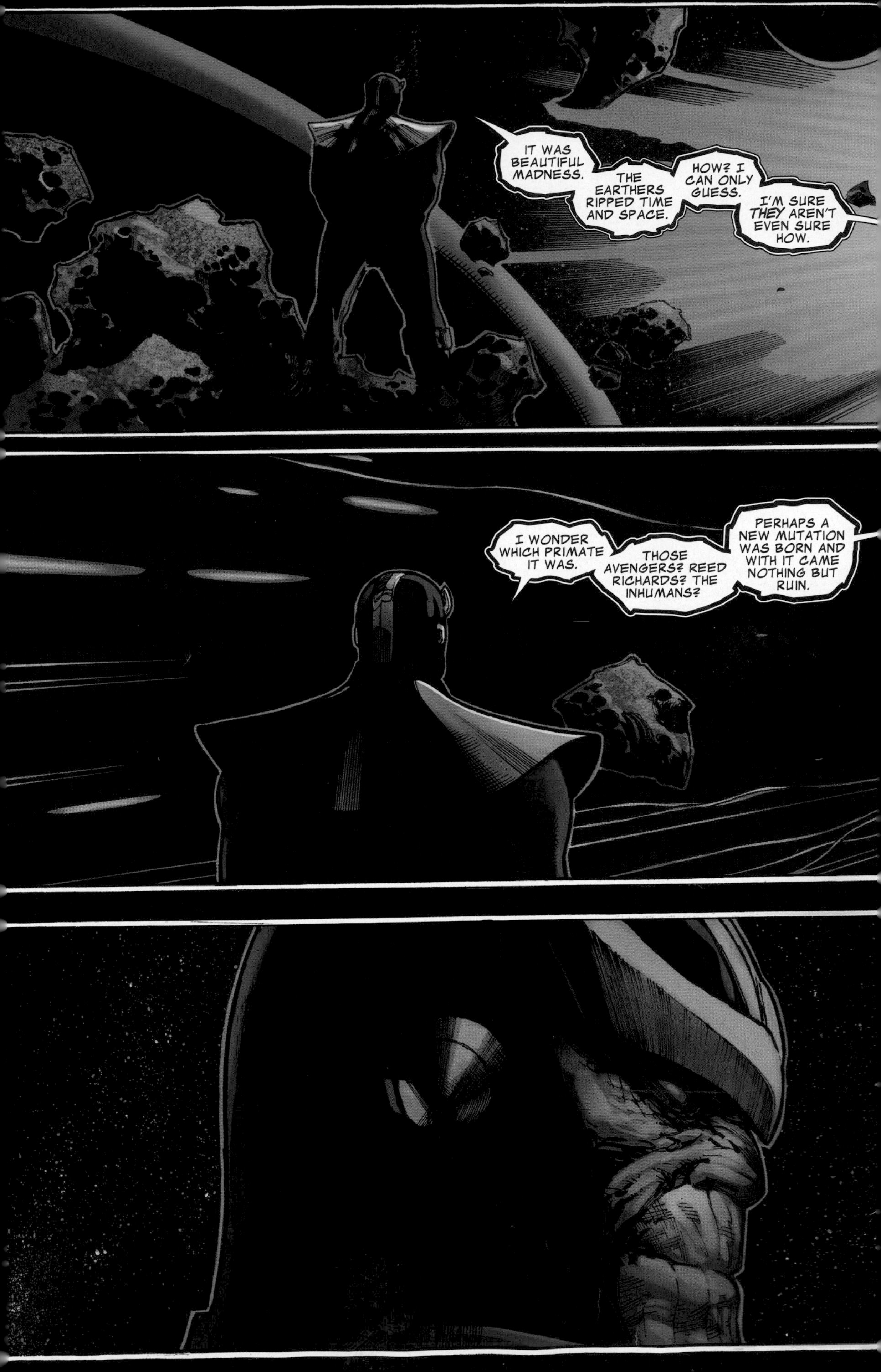
IT WAS BEAUTIFUL MADNESS.
THE EARTHERS RIPPED TIME AND SPACE.
HOW? I CAN ONLY GUESS.
I'M SURE THEY AREN'T EVEN SURE HOW.
I WONDER WHICH PRIMATE IT WAS.
THOSE AVENGERS? REED RICHARDS? THE INHUMANS?
PERHAPS A NEW MUTATION WAS BORN AND WITH IT CAME NOTHING BUT RUIN.

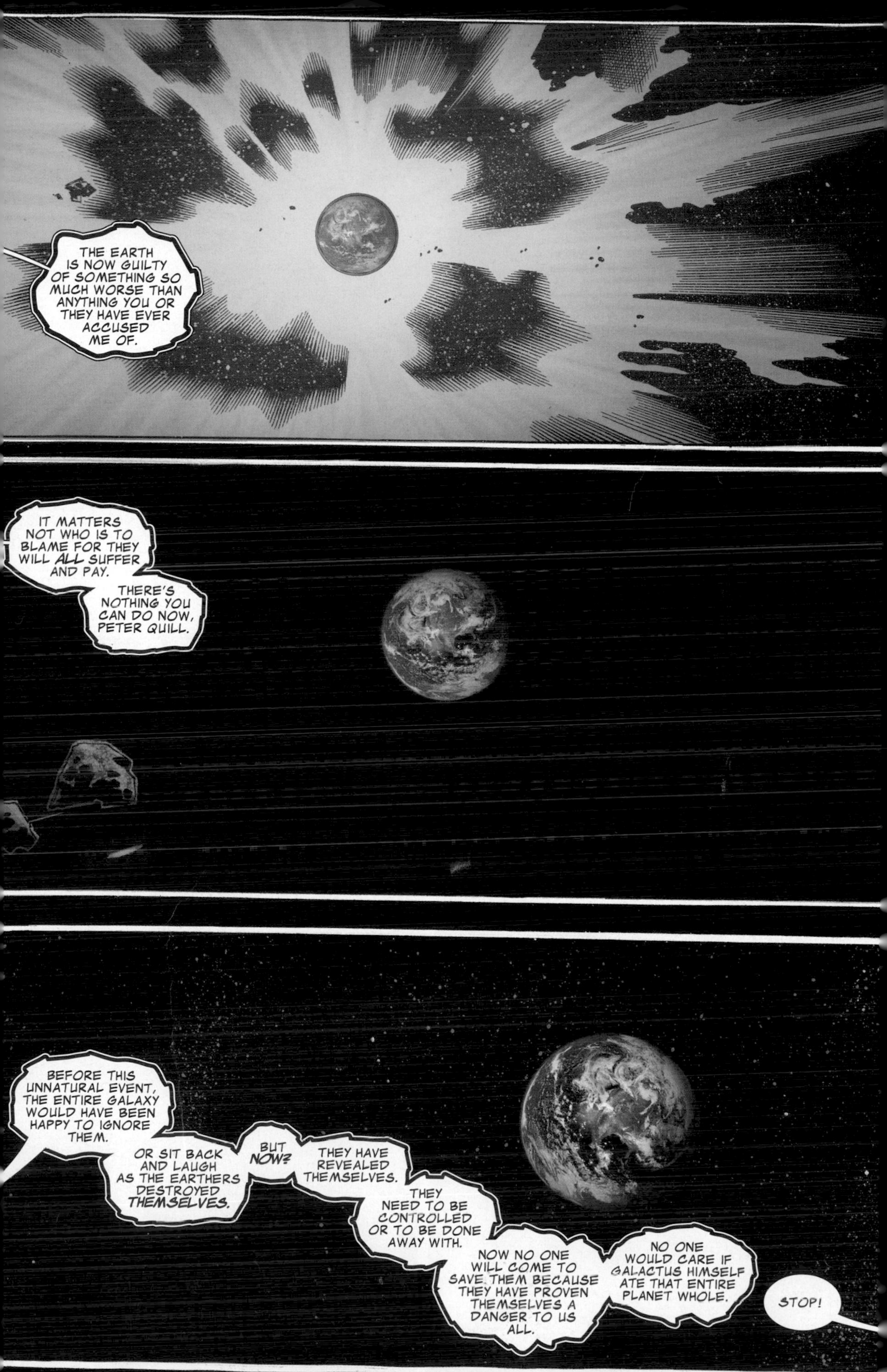
THE EARTH IS NOW GUILTY OF SOMETHING SO MUCH WORSE THAN ANYTHING YOU OR THEY HAVE EVER ACCUSED ME OF.
IT MATTERS NOT WHO IS TO BLAME FOR THEY WILL ALL SUFFER AND PAY.
THERE'S NOTHING YOU CAN DO NOW, PETER QUILL.
BEFORE THIS UNNATURAL EVENT, THE ENTIRE GALAXY WOULD HAVE BEEN HAPPY TO IGNORE THEM.
OR SIT BACK AND LAUGH AS THE EARTHERS DESTROYED THEMSELVES.
BUT NOW?
THEY HAVE REVEALED THEMSELVES.
THEY NEED TO BE CONTROLLED OR TO BE DONE AWAY WITH.
NOW NO ONE WILL COME TO SAVE THEM BECAUSE THEY HAVE PROVEN THEMSELVES A DANGER TO US ALL.
NO ONE WOULD CARE IF GALACTUS HIMSELF ATE THAT ENTIRE PLANET WHOLE.
STOP!

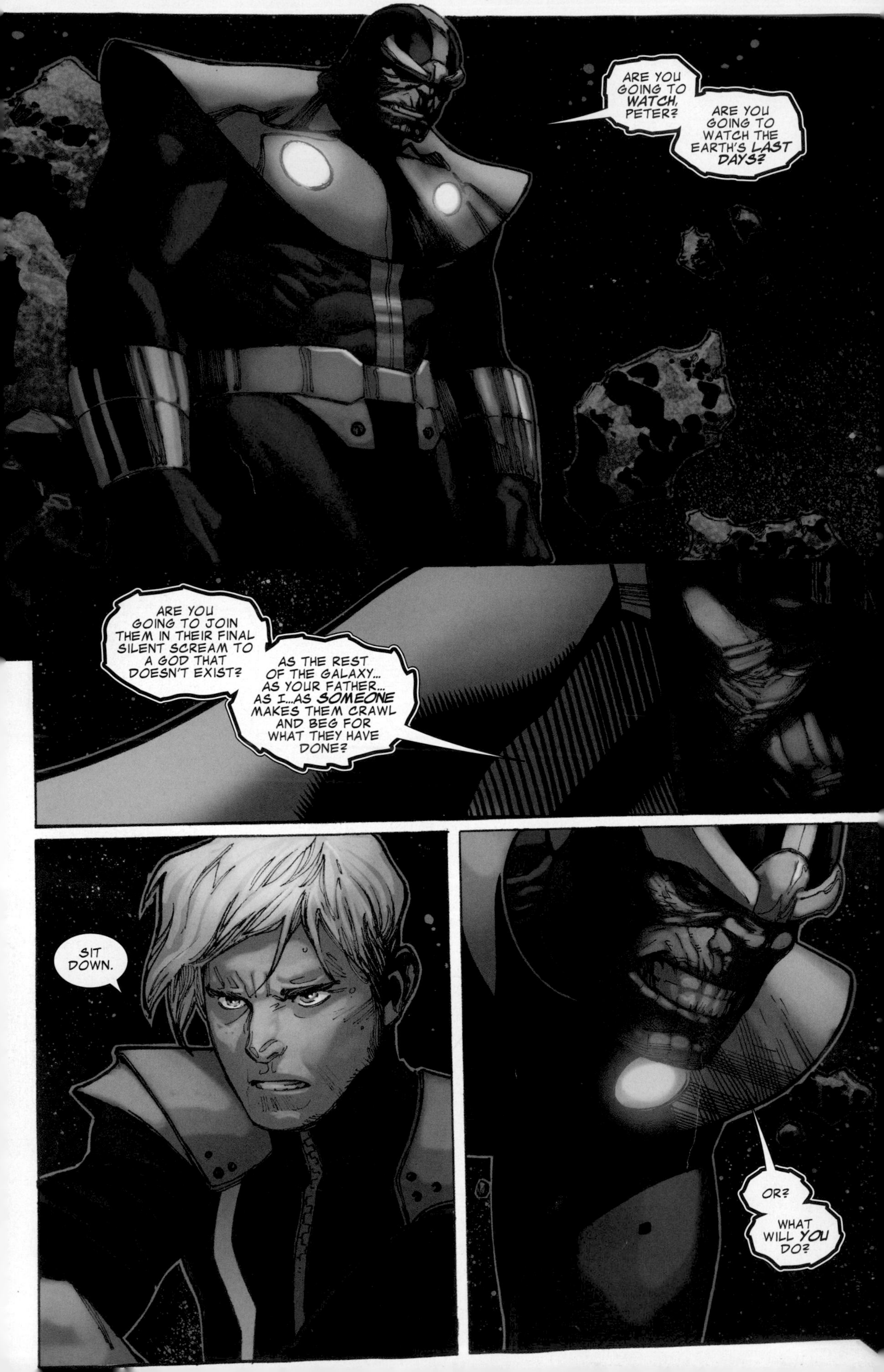
ARE YOU GOING TO WATCH, PETER?
ARE YOU GOING TO WATCH THE EARTH'S LAST DAYS?
ARE YOU GOING TO JOIN THEM IN THEIR FINAL SILENT SCREAM TO A GOD THAT DOESN'T EXIST?
AS THE REST OF THE GALAXY... AS YOUR FATHER... AS I...AS SOMEONE MAKES THEM CRAWL AND BEG FOR WHAT THEY HAVE DONE?
SIT DOWN.
OR?
WHAT WILL YOU DO?

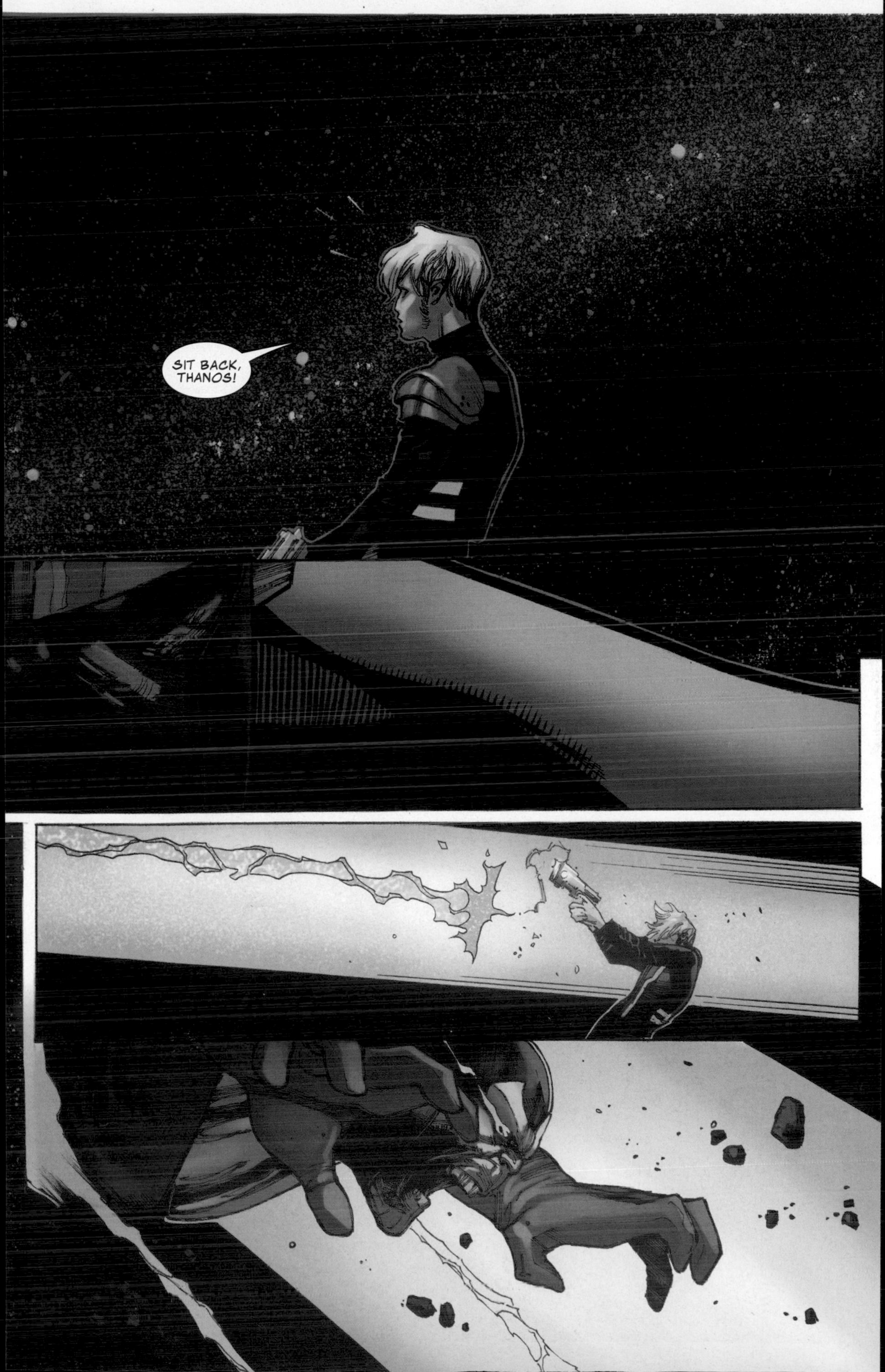
SIT BACK, THANOS!

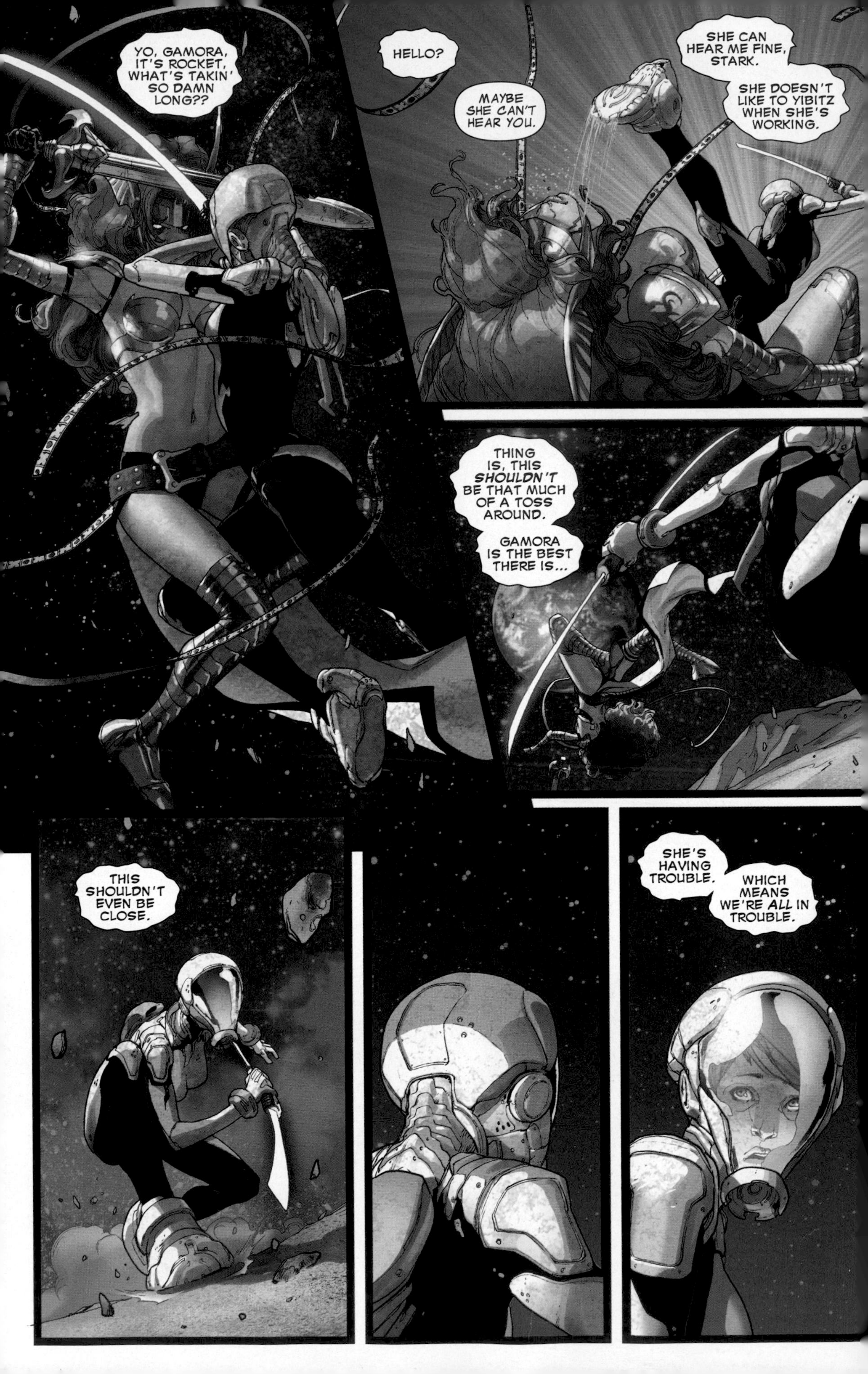
YO, GAMORA, IT'S ROCKET, WHAT'S TAKIN' SO DAMN LONG??
HELLO?
MAYBE SHE CAN'T HEAR YOU.
SHE CAN HEAR ME FINE, STARK.
SHE DOESN'T LIKE TO YIBITZ WHEN SHE'S WORKING.
THING IS, THIS SHOULDN'T BE THAT MUCH OF A TOSS AROUND.
GAMORA IS THE BEST THERE IS...
THIS SHOULDN'T EVEN BE CLOSE.
SHE'S HAVING TROUBLE.
WHICH MEANS WE'RE ALL IN TROUBLE.

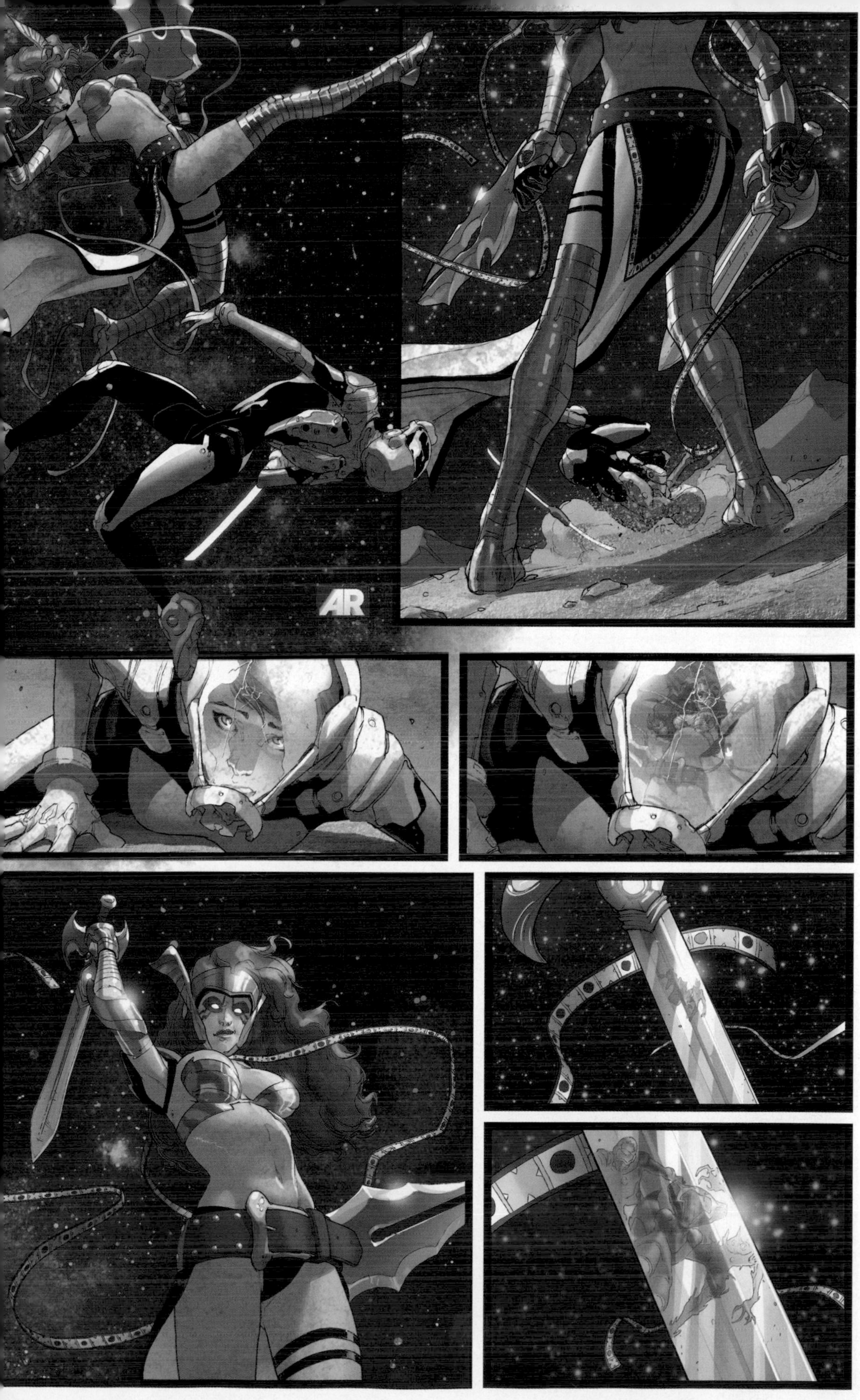

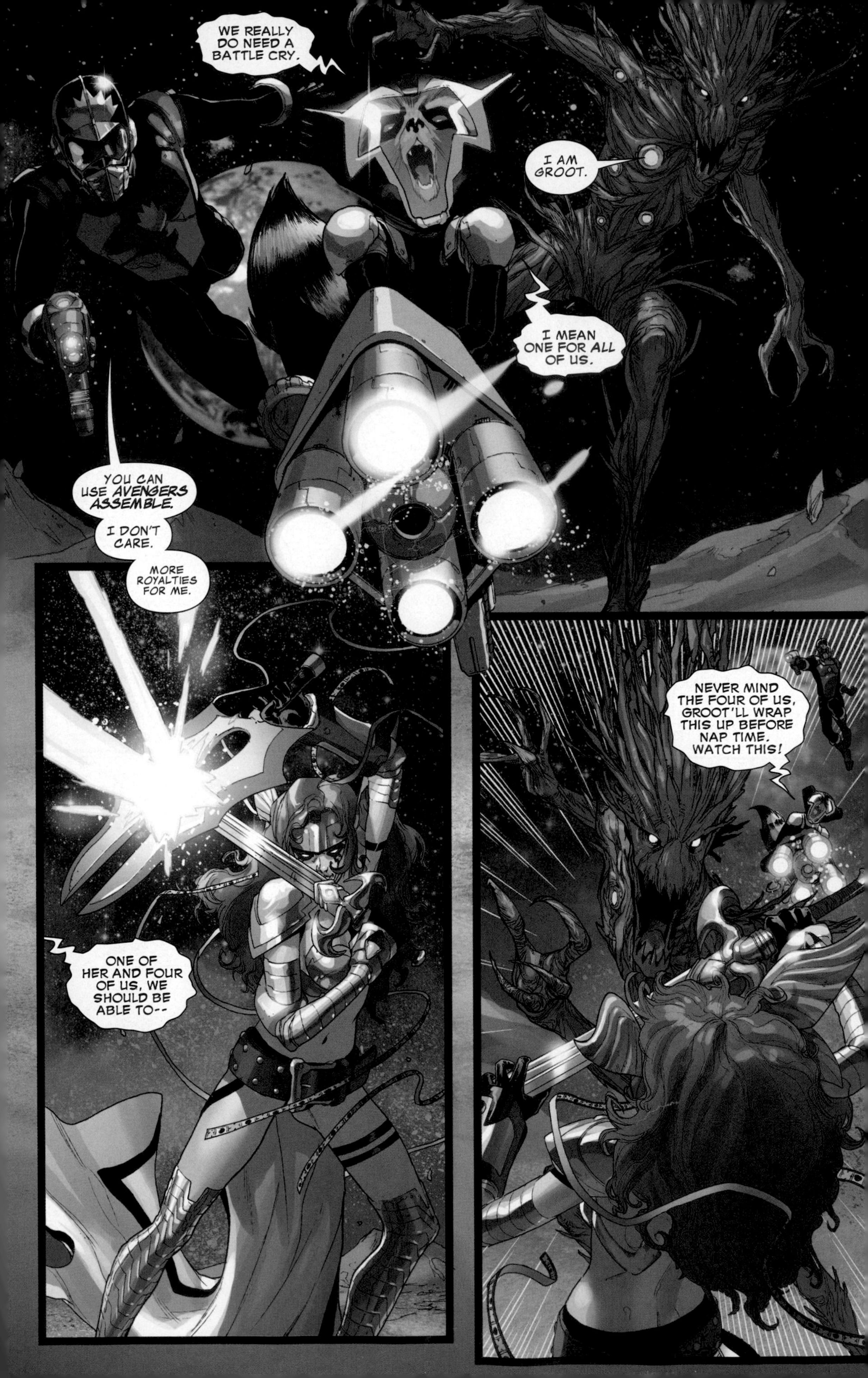
WE REALLY DO NEED A BATTLE CRY.
I AM GROOT.
I MEAN ONE FOR ALL OF US.
YOU CAN USE AVENGERS ASSEMBLE.
I DON'T CARE.
MORE ROYALTIES FOR ME.
ONE OF HER AND FOUR OF US, WE SHOULD BE ABLE TO--
NEVER MIND THE FOUR OF US, GROOT'LL WRAP THIS UP BEFORE NAP TIME. WATCH THIS!

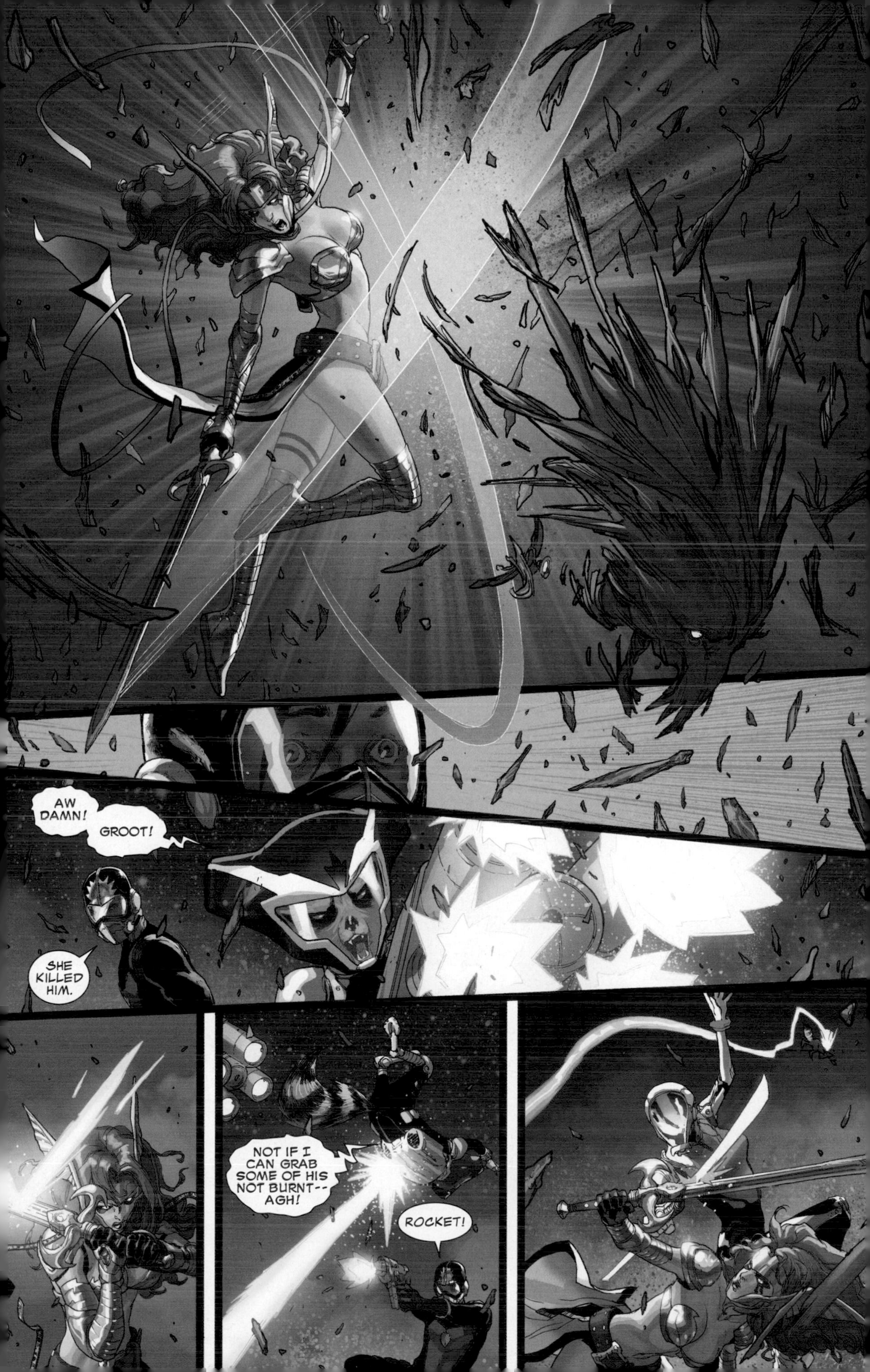
AW DAMN!
GROOT!
SHE KILLED HIM.
NOT IF I CAN GRAB SOME OF HIS NOT BURNT-- AGH!
ROCKET!

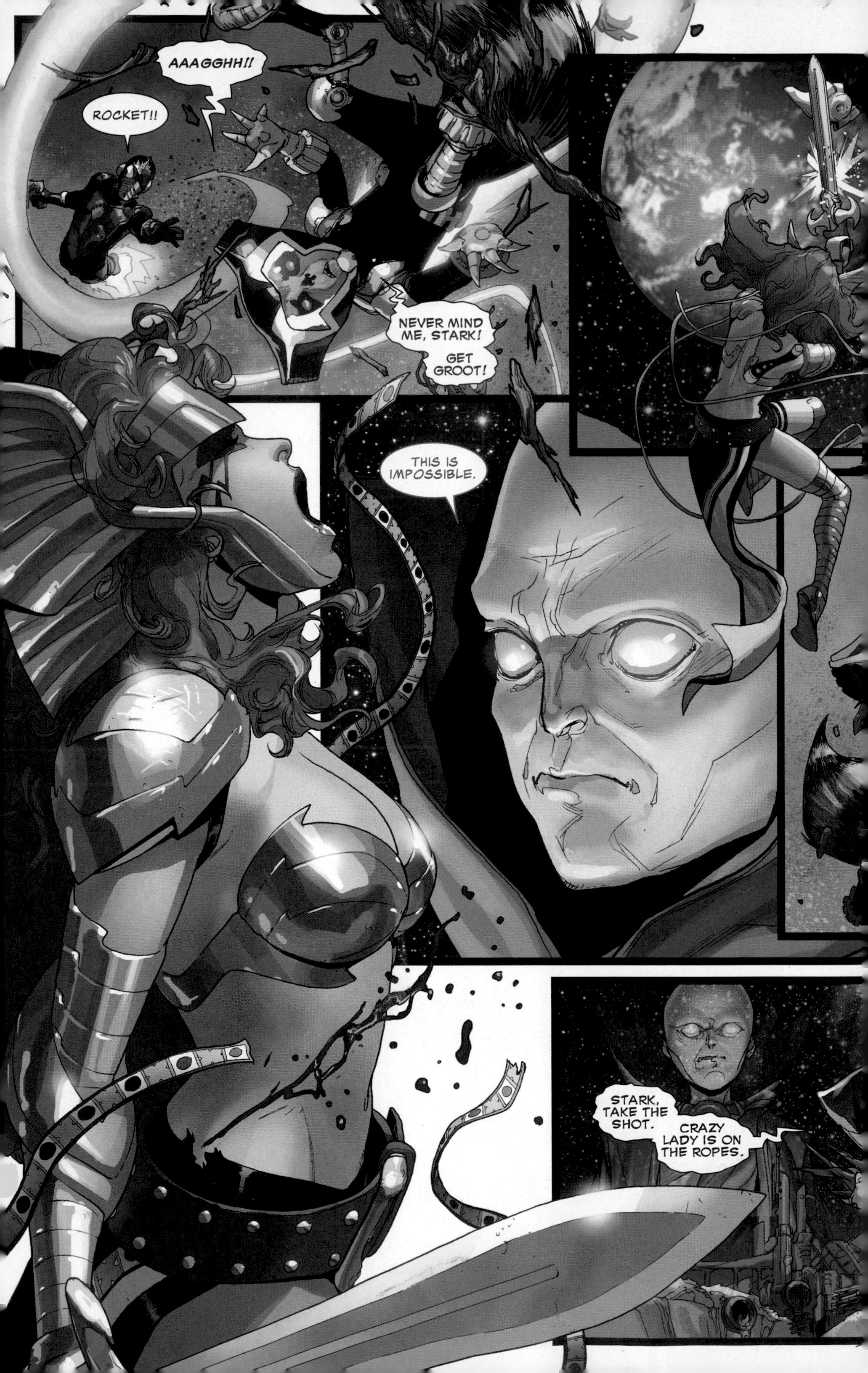
AAAGGHH!!
ROCKET!!
NEVER MIND ME, STARK!
GET GROOT!
THIS IS IMPOSSIBLE.
STARK, TAKE THE SHOT.
CRAZY LADY IS ON THE ROPES.

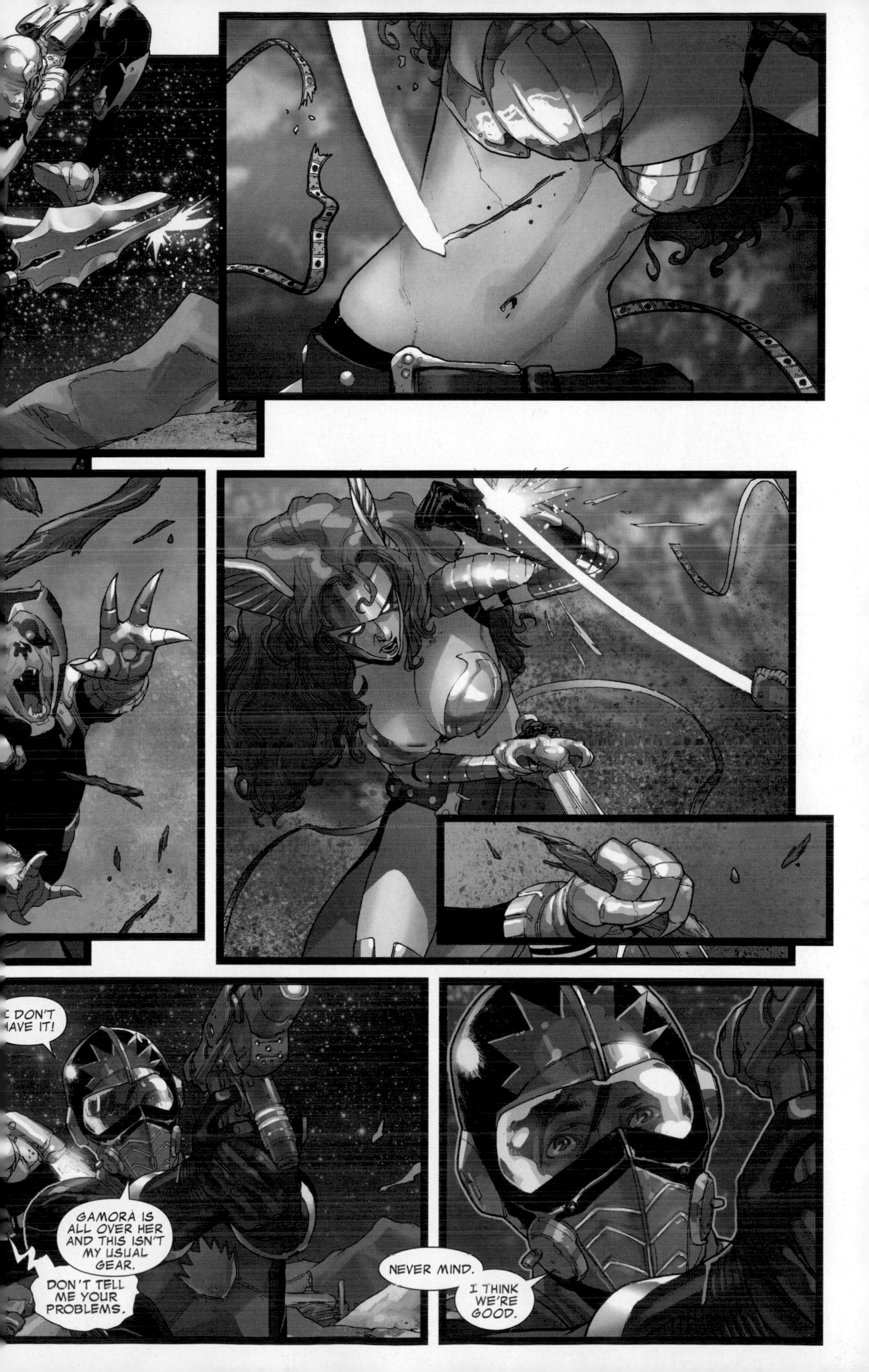
I DON'T HAVE IT!
GAMORA IS ALL OVER HER AND THIS ISN'T MY USUAL GEAR.
DON'T TELL ME YOUR PROBLEMS.
NEVER MIND.
I THINK WE'RE GOOD.

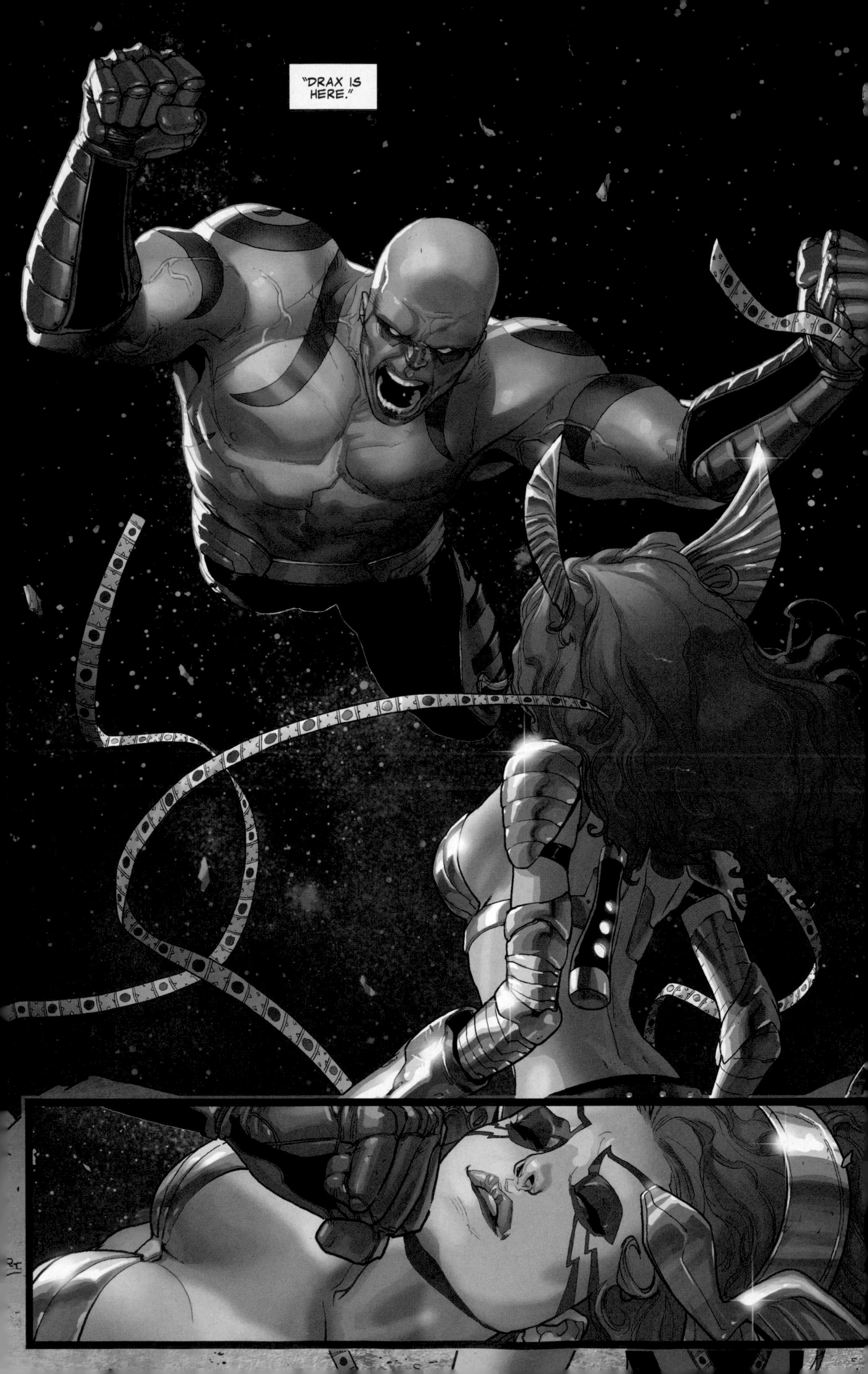
"DRAX IS HERE."

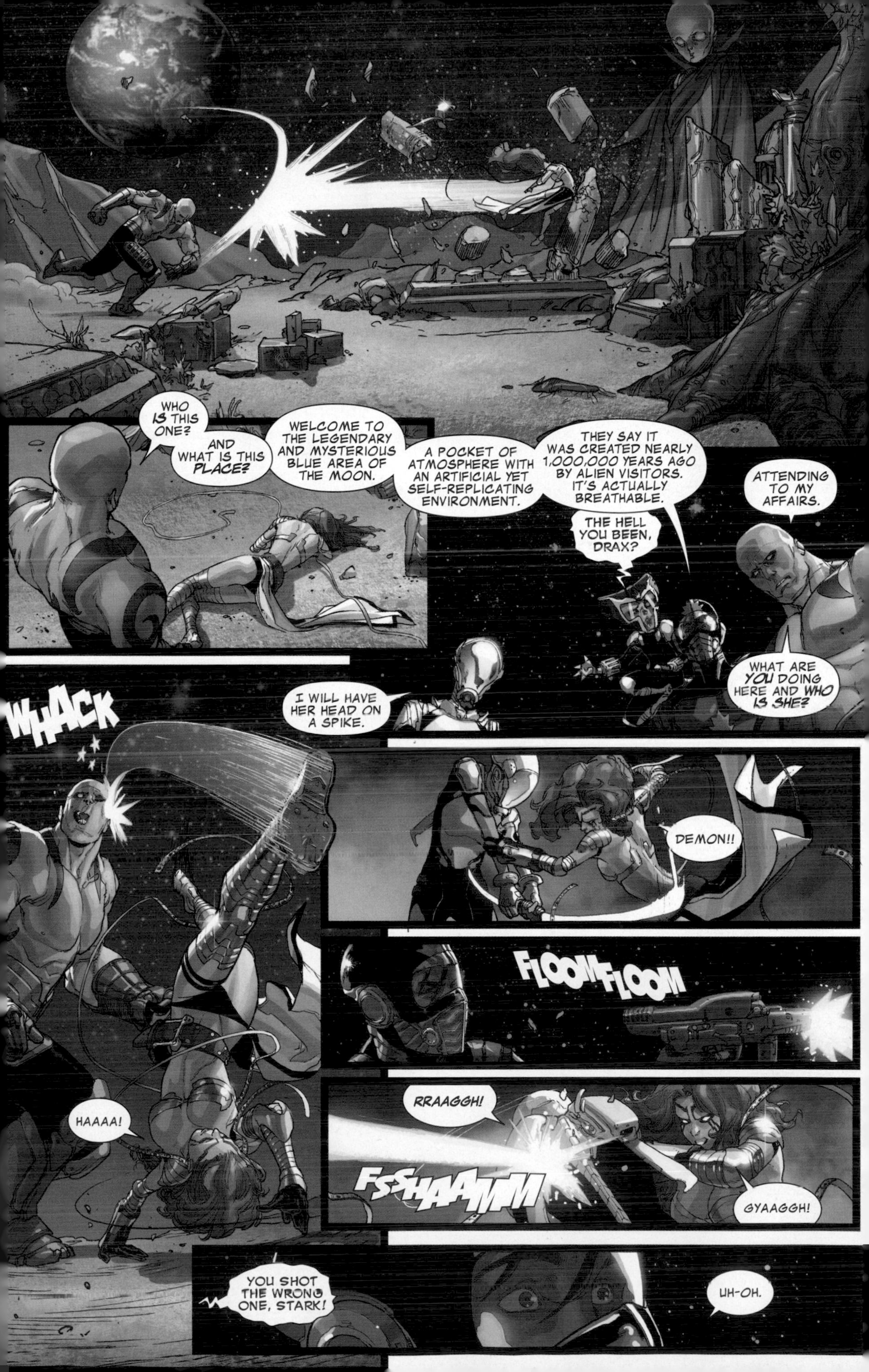
WHO IS THIS ONE?
AND WHAT IS THIS PLACE?
WELCOME TO THE LEGENDARY AND MYSTERIOUS BLUE AREA OF THE MOON.
A POCKET OF ATMOSPHERE WITH AN ARTIFICIAL YET SELF-REPLICATING ENVIRONMENT.
THEY SAY IT WAS CREATED NEARLY 1,000,000 YEARS AGO BY ALIEN VISITORS. IT'S ACTUALLY BREATHABLE.
THE HELL YOU BEEN, DRAX?
ATTENDING TO MY AFFAIRS.
WHAT ARE YOU DOING HERE AND WHO IS SHE?
I WILL HAVE HER HEAD ON A SPIKE.
WHACK
DEMON!!
HAAAA!
FLOOM FLOOM
RRAAGGH!
FSSHAAMM
GYAAGGH!
YOU SHOT THE WRONG ONE, STARK!
UH-OH.

VIXEN!

WHACK

BLAM

GRAAGGHH!

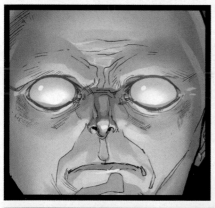

OKAY, THAT'S ENOUGH.

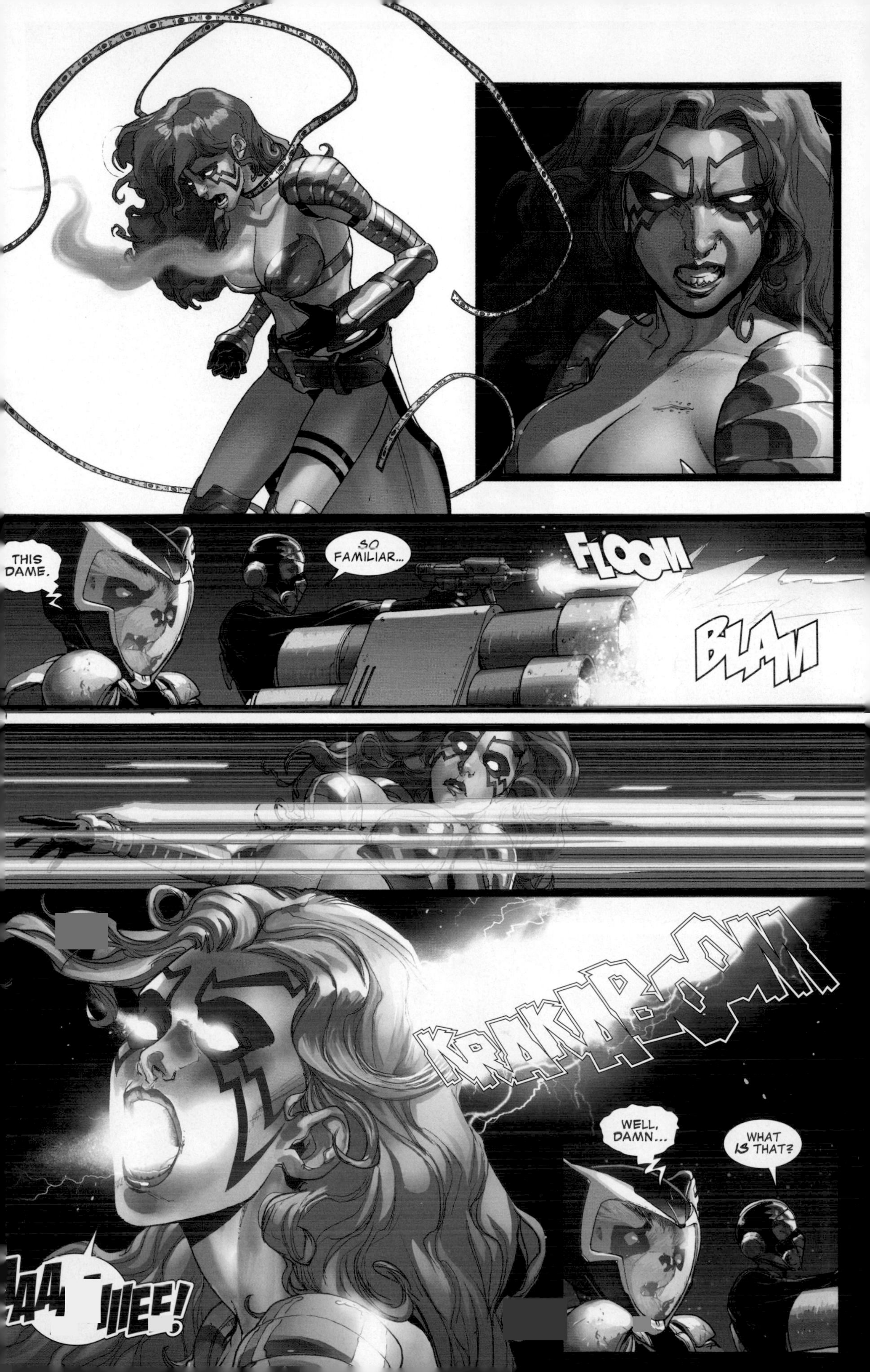
THIS DAME.
SO FAMILIAR...
FLOOM
BLAM
WELL, DAMN...
WHAT IS THAT?

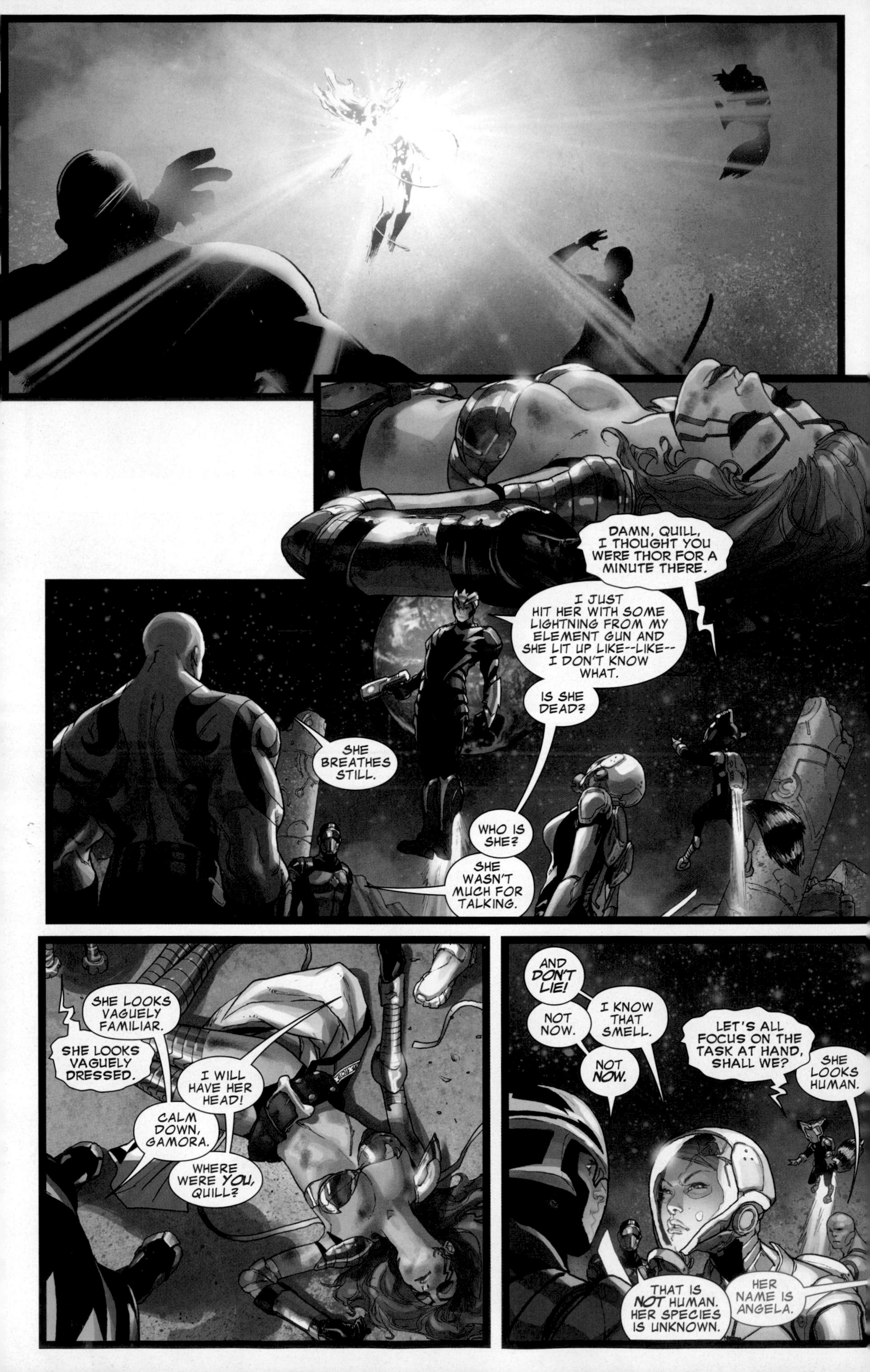
DAMN, QUILL, I THOUGHT YOU WERE THOR FOR A MINUTE THERE.
I JUST HIT HER WITH SOME LIGHTNING FROM MY ELEMENT GUN AND SHE LIT UP LIKE--LIKE-- I DON'T KNOW WHAT.
IS SHE DEAD?
SHE BREATHES STILL.
WHO IS SHE?
SHE WASN'T MUCH FOR TALKING.
SHE LOOKS VAGUELY FAMILIAR.
SHE LOOKS VAGUELY DRESSED.
I WILL HAVE HER HEAD!
CALM DOWN, GAMORA.
WHERE WERE YOU, QUILL?
AND DON'T LIE!
NOT NOW.
I KNOW THAT SMELL.
NOT NOW.
LET'S ALL FOCUS ON THE TASK AT HAND, SHALL WE?
SHE LOOKS HUMAN.
THAT IS NOT HUMAN. HER SPECIES IS UNKNOWN.
HER NAME IS ANGELA.

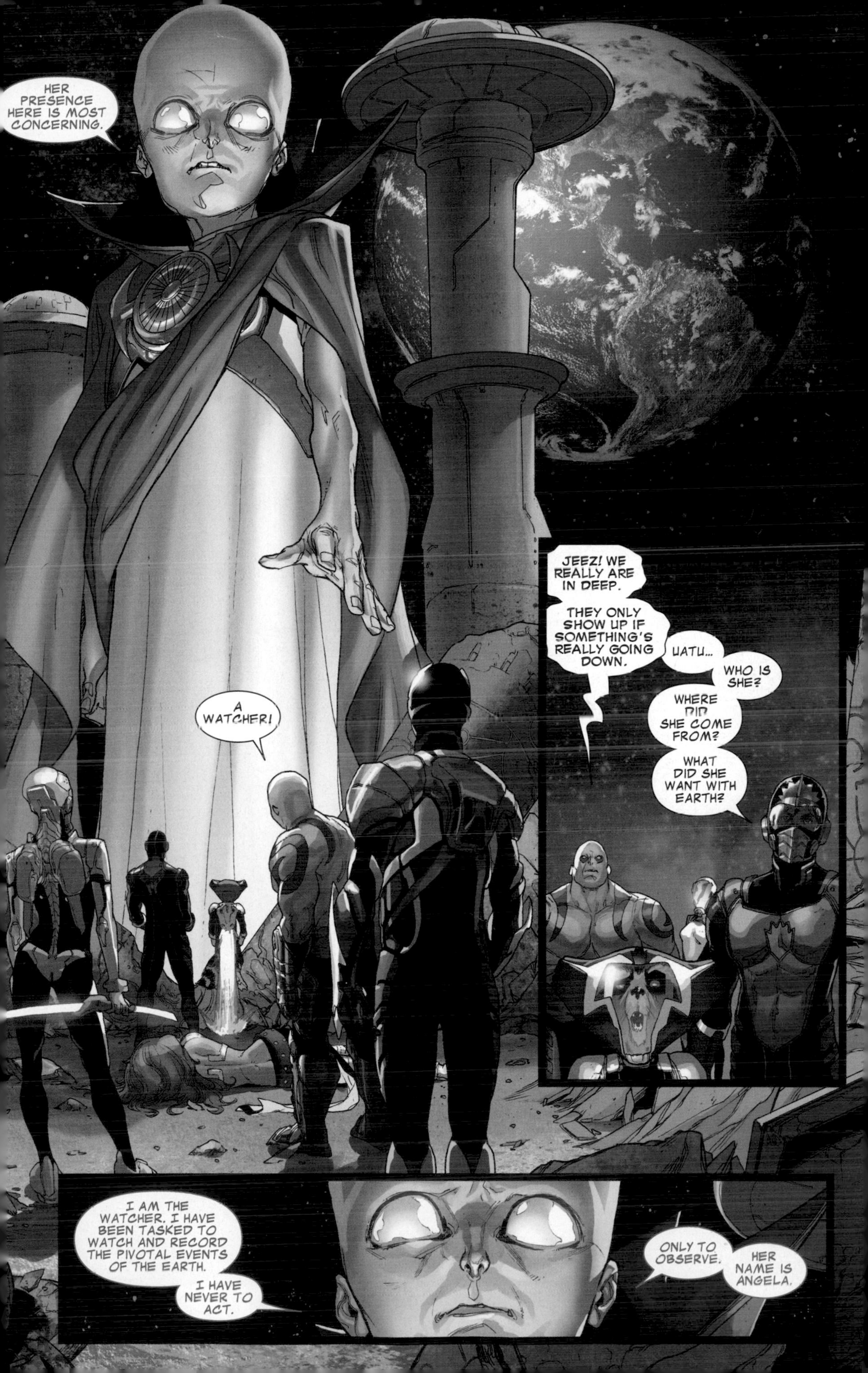
HER PRESENCE HERE IS MOST CONCERNING.
A WATCHER!
JEEZ! WE REALLY ARE IN DEEP.
THEY ONLY SHOW UP IF SOMETHING'S REALLY GOING DOWN.
UATU...
WHO IS SHE?
WHERE DID SHE COME FROM?
WHAT DID SHE WANT WITH EARTH?
I AM THE WATCHER. I HAVE BEEN TASKED TO WATCH AND RECORD THE PIVOTAL EVENTS OF THE EARTH.
I HAVE NEVER TO ACT.
ONLY TO OBSERVE.
HER NAME IS ANGELA.

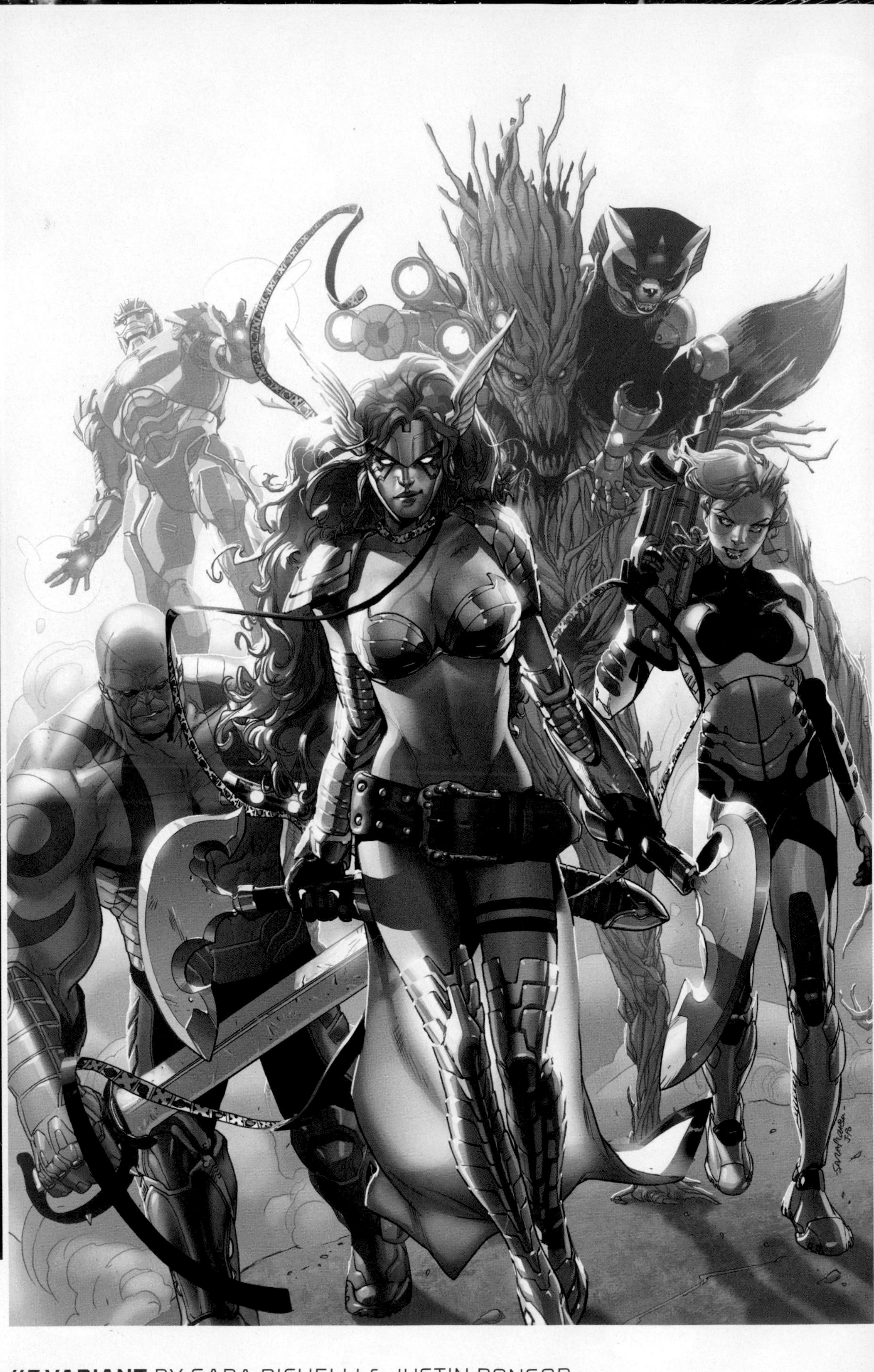

#7 VARIANT BY SARA PICHELLI & JUSTIN PONSOR

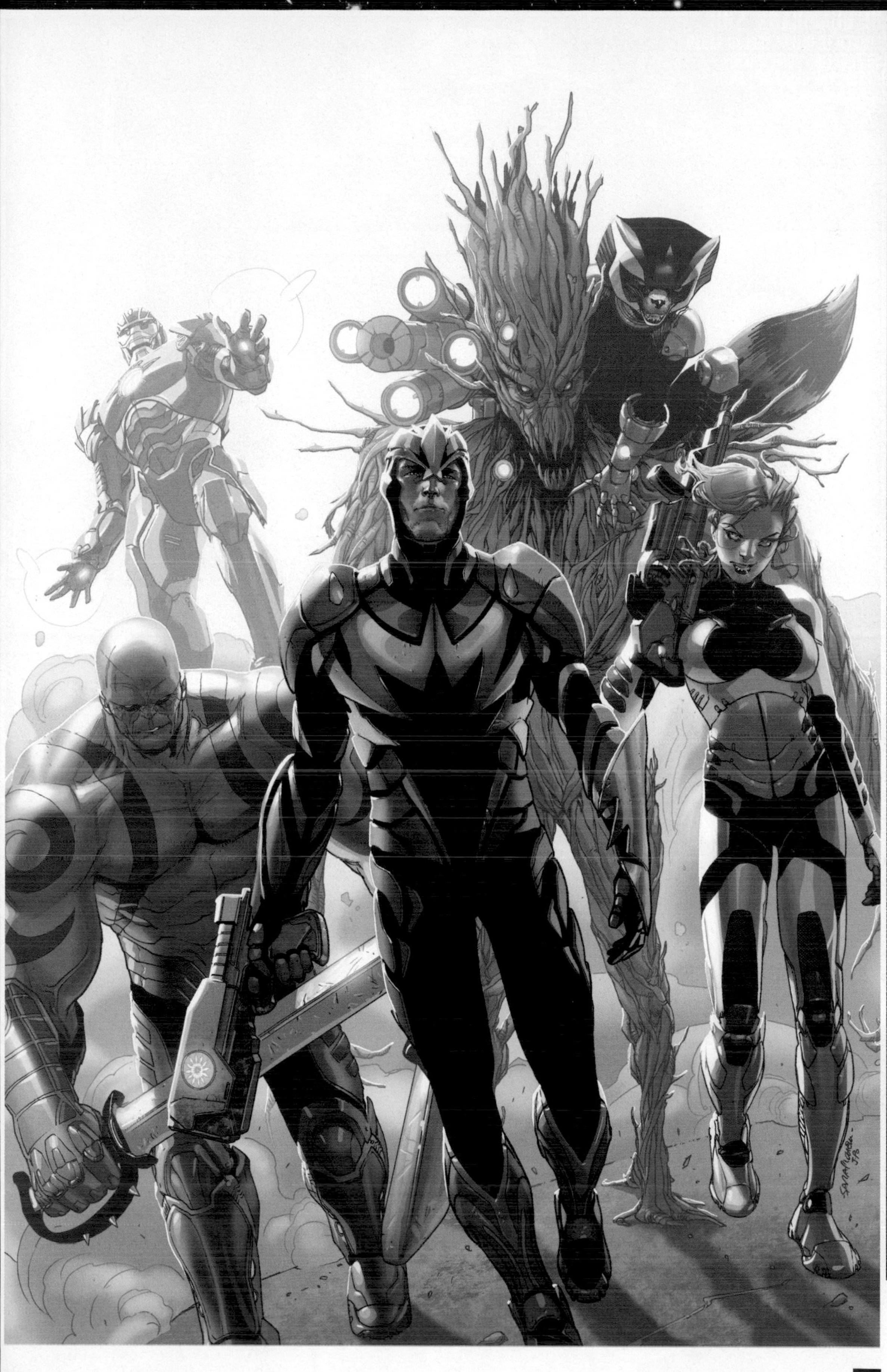

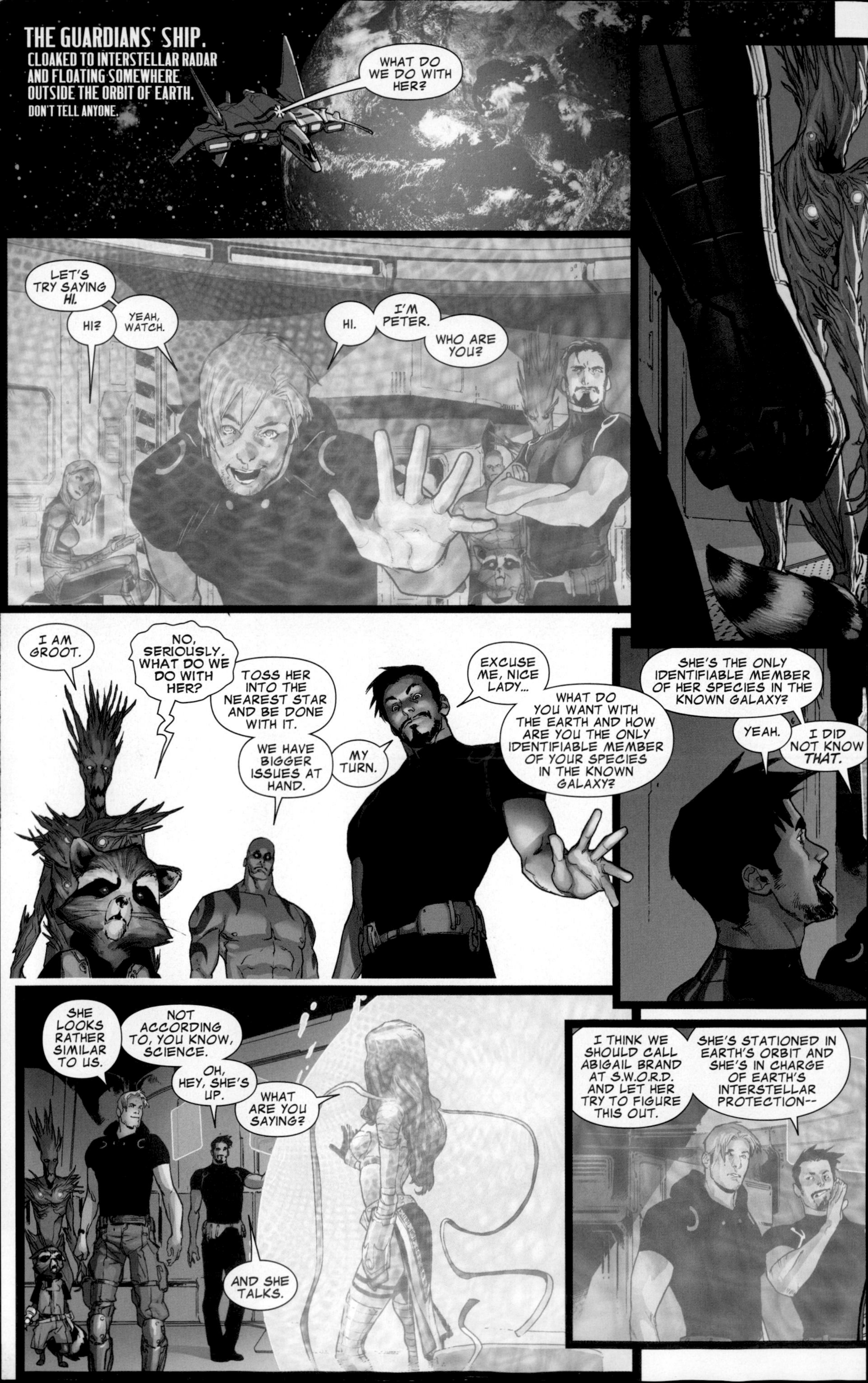
THE GUARDIANS' SHIP.
CLOAKED TO INTERSTELLAR RADAR AND FLOATING SOMEWHERE OUTSIDE THE ORBIT OF EARTH.
DON'T TELL ANYONE.
WHAT DO WE DO WITH HER?
LET'S TRY SAYING HI.
HI?
YEAH, WATCH.
HI.
I'M PETER.
WHO ARE YOU?
I AM GROOT.
NO, SERIOUSLY. WHAT DO WE DO WITH HER?
TOSS HER INTO THE NEAREST STAR AND BE DONE WITH IT.
WE HAVE BIGGER ISSUES AT HAND.
MY TURN.
EXCUSE ME, NICE LADY...
WHAT DO YOU WANT WITH THE EARTH AND HOW ARE YOU THE ONLY IDENTIFIABLE MEMBER OF YOUR SPECIES IN THE KNOWN GALAXY?
SHE'S THE ONLY IDENTIFIABLE MEMBER OF HER SPECIES IN THE KNOWN GALAXY?
YEAH.
I DID NOT KNOW THAT.
SHE LOOKS RATHER SIMILAR TO US.
NOT ACCORDING TO, YOU KNOW, SCIENCE.
OH, HEY, SHE'S UP.
WHAT ARE YOU SAYING?
AND SHE TALKS.
I THINK WE SHOULD CALL ABIGAIL BRAND AT S.W.O.R.D. AND LET HER TRY TO FIGURE THIS OUT.
SHE'S STATIONED IN EARTH'S ORBIT AND SHE'S IN CHARGE OF EARTH'S INTERSTELLAR PROTECTION--

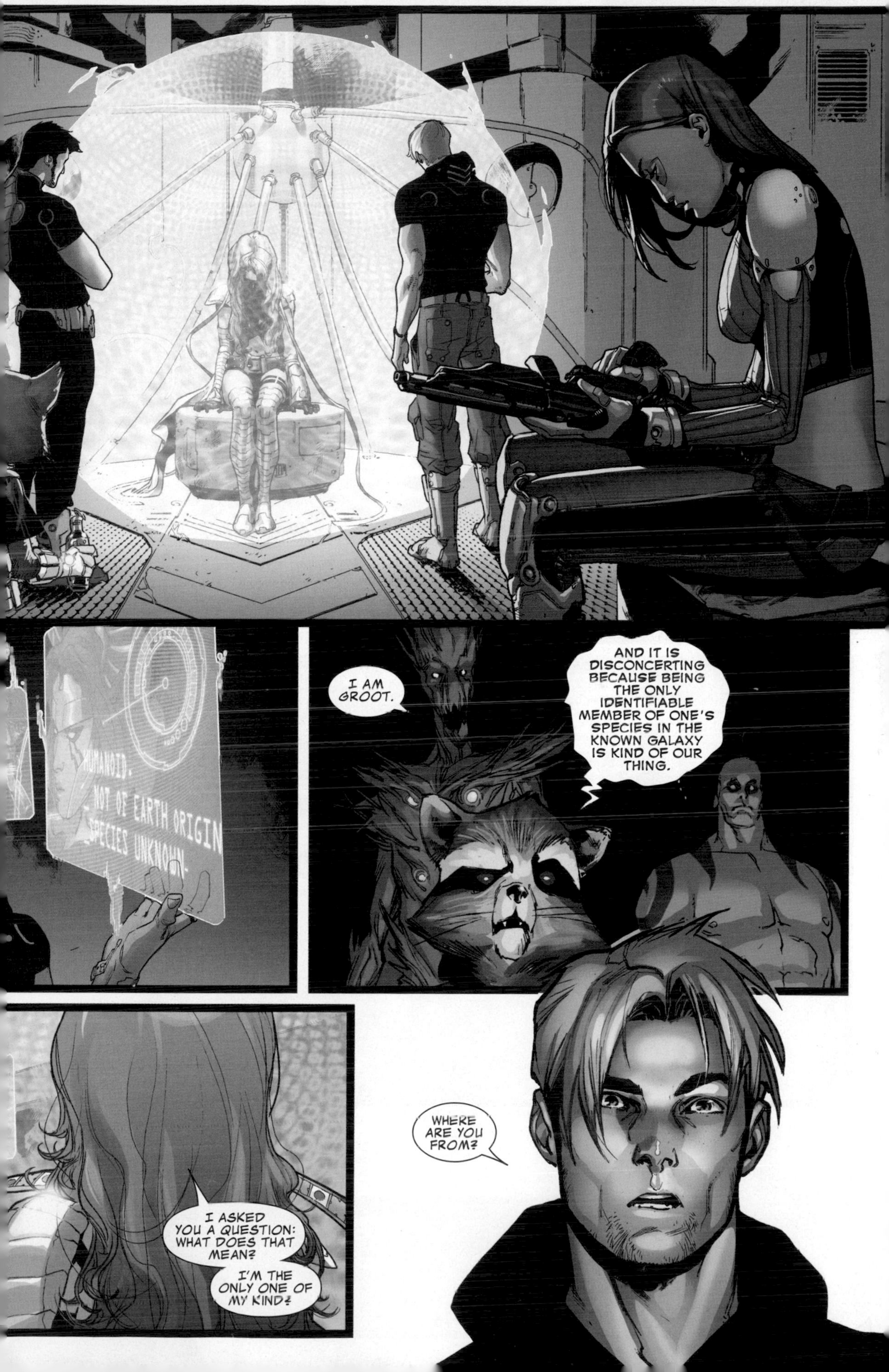
HUMANOID.
NOT OF EARTH ORIGIN
SPECIES UNKNOWN
I AM GROOT.
AND IT IS DISCONCERTING BECAUSE BEING THE ONLY IDENTIFIABLE MEMBER OF ONE'S SPECIES IN THE KNOWN GALAXY IS KIND OF OUR THING.
I ASKED YOU A QUESTION: WHAT DOES THAT MEAN?
I'M THE ONLY ONE OF MY KIND?
WHERE ARE YOU FROM?

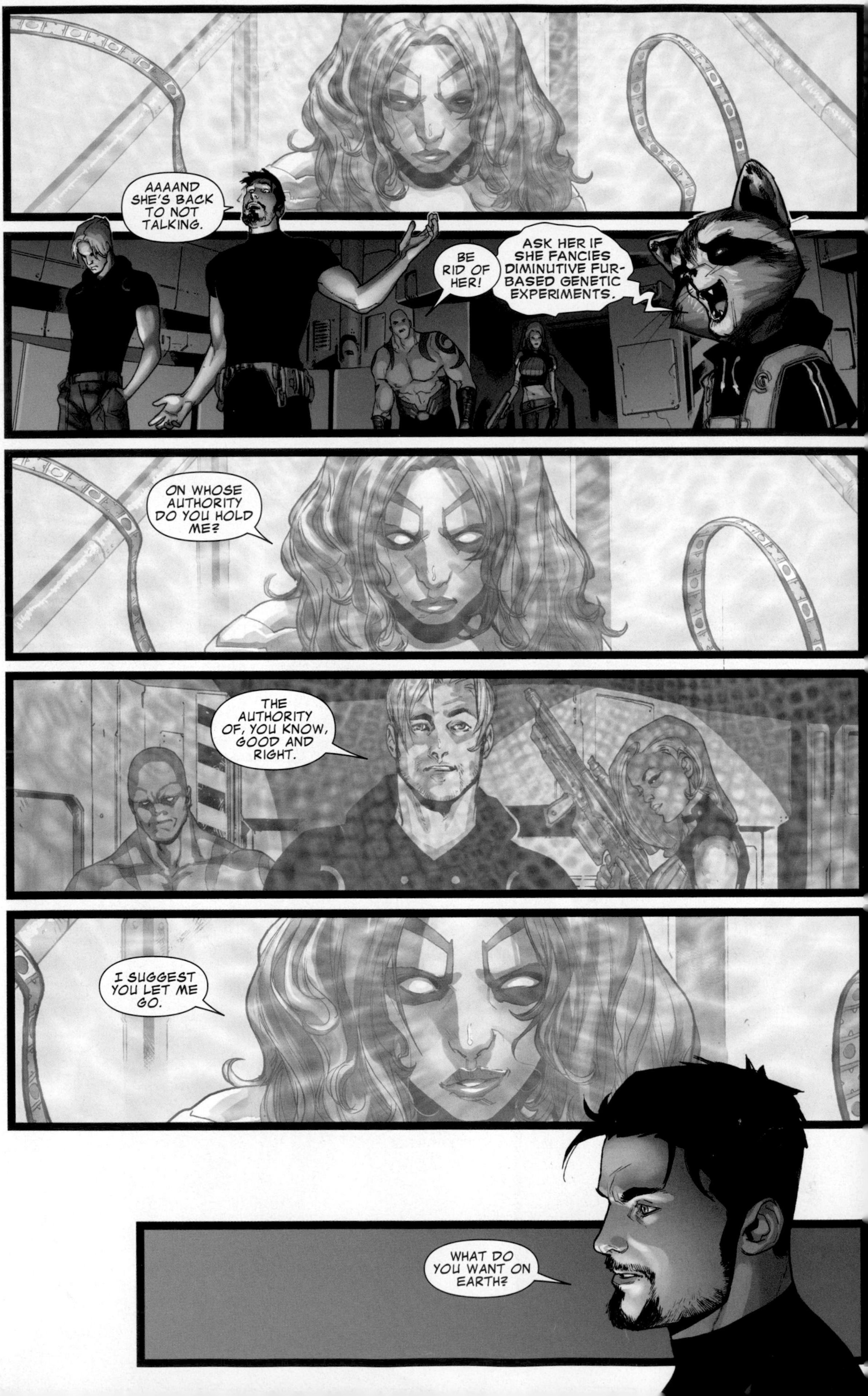
AAAAND SHE'S BACK TO NOT TALKING.
BE RID OF HER!
ASK HER IF SHE FANCIES DIMINUTIVE FUR-BASED GENETIC EXPERIMENTS.
ON WHOSE AUTHORITY DO YOU HOLD ME?
THE AUTHORITY OF, YOU KNOW, GOOD AND RIGHT.
I SUGGEST YOU LET ME GO.
WHAT DO YOU WANT ON EARTH?

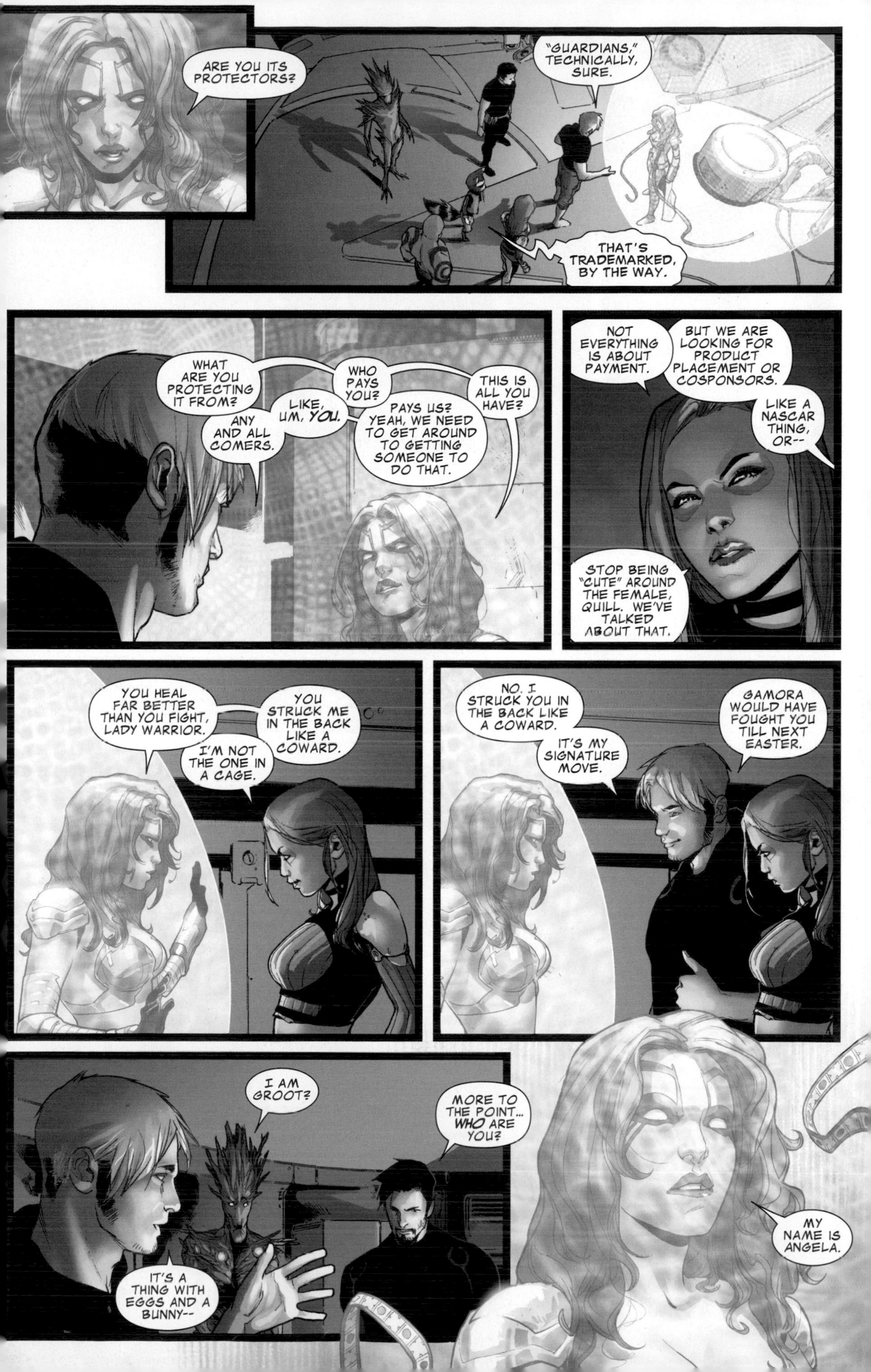
ARE YOU ITS PROTECTORS?
"GUARDIANS," TECHNICALLY, SURE.
THAT'S TRADEMARKED, BY THE WAY.
WHAT ARE YOU PROTECTING IT FROM?
ANY AND ALL COMERS.
WHO PAYS YOU?
LIKE, UM, YOU.
THIS IS ALL YOU HAVE?
PAYS US? YEAH, WE NEED TO GET AROUND TO GETTING SOMEONE TO DO THAT.
NOT EVERYTHING IS ABOUT PAYMENT.
BUT WE ARE LOOKING FOR PRODUCT PLACEMENT OR COSPONSORS.
LIKE A NASCAR THING, OR--
STOP BEING "CUTE" AROUND THE FEMALE, QUILL. WE'VE TALKED ABOUT THAT.
YOU HEAL FAR BETTER THAN YOU FIGHT, LADY WARRIOR.
YOU STRUCK ME IN THE BACK LIKE A COWARD.
I'M NOT THE ONE IN A CAGE.
NO. I STRUCK YOU IN THE BACK LIKE A COWARD.
IT'S MY SIGNATURE MOVE.
GAMORA WOULD HAVE FOUGHT YOU TILL NEXT EASTER.
I AM GROOT?
MORE TO THE POINT... WHO ARE YOU?
IT'S A THING WITH EGGS AND A BUNNY--
MY NAME IS ANGELA.

OKAY. NOW WE'RE HAVING A CONVER--

FROM "WHO'S THE BOSS" ANGELA?

ALL GROWN UP?

YOU ARE NUTTIER THAN 3 SPIDER-MEN ALL ROLLED UP INTO ONE.

NO REASON THIS CAN'T BE FUN.

WHAT DO YOU WANT FROM THE EARTH?

DO YOU KNOW OF HEVEN?

HEAVEN?

WHICH STAR SYSTEM?

I DON'T UNDERSTAND.

YOU KNOW IT'S NOT REALLY ON EARTH.

I'M SORRY.

HEAVEN. IT'S NOT ON EARTH.

THAT WAS JUST SOME CRAP BELINDA CARLISLE TRIED TO SELL US TO MAKE US FEEL BETTER ABOUT THE GO-GO'S BREAKING UP.

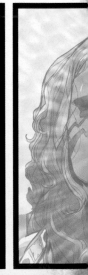

OR...

IT'S NOT?

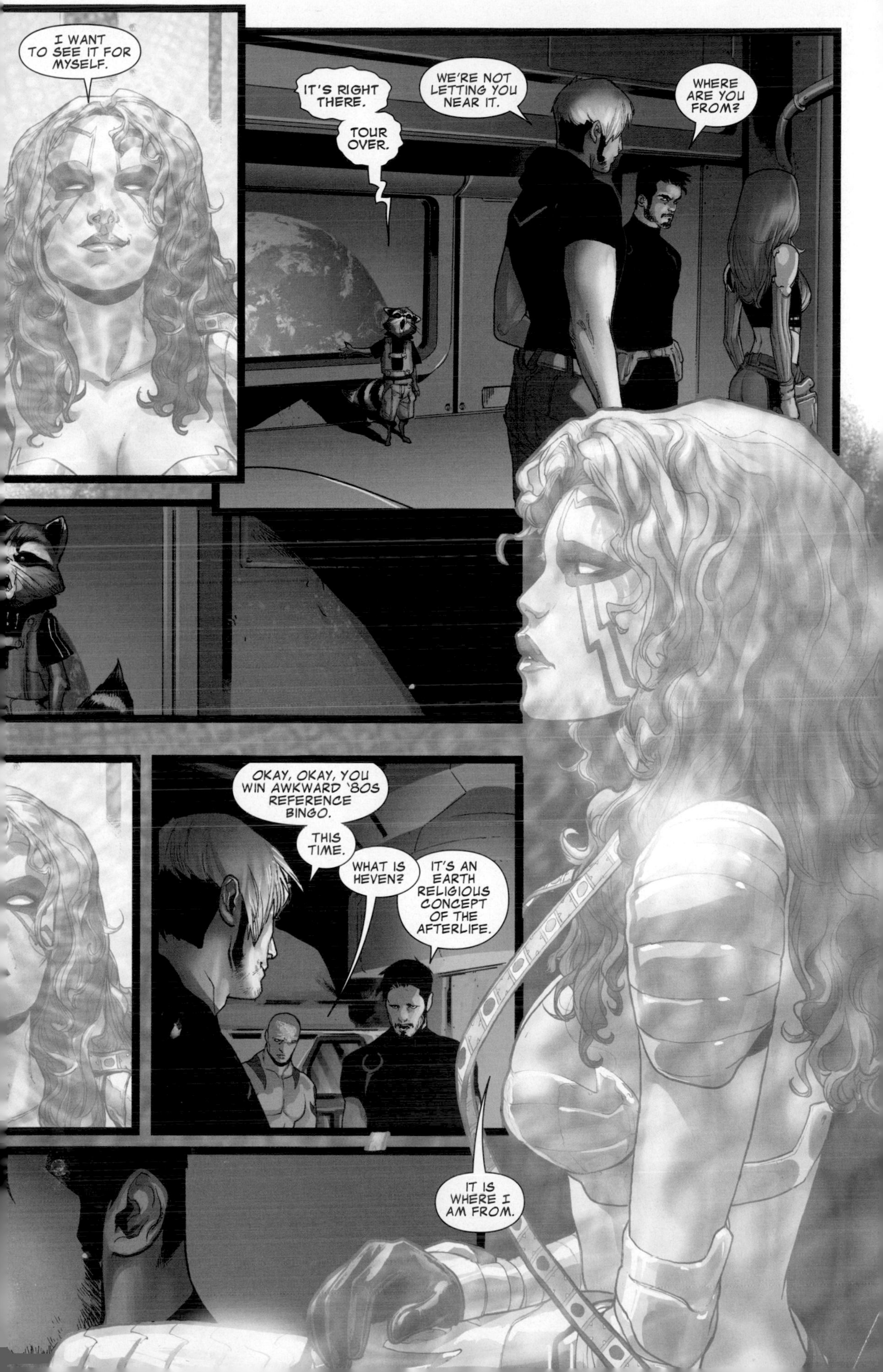
I WANT TO SEE IT FOR MYSELF.
IT'S RIGHT THERE.
TOUR OVER.
WE'RE NOT LETTING YOU NEAR IT.
WHERE ARE YOU FROM?
OKAY, OKAY, YOU WIN AWKWARD '80S REFERENCE BINGO.
THIS TIME.
WHAT IS HEVEN?
IT'S AN EARTH RELIGIOUS CONCEPT OF THE AFTERLIFE.
IT IS WHERE I AM FROM.

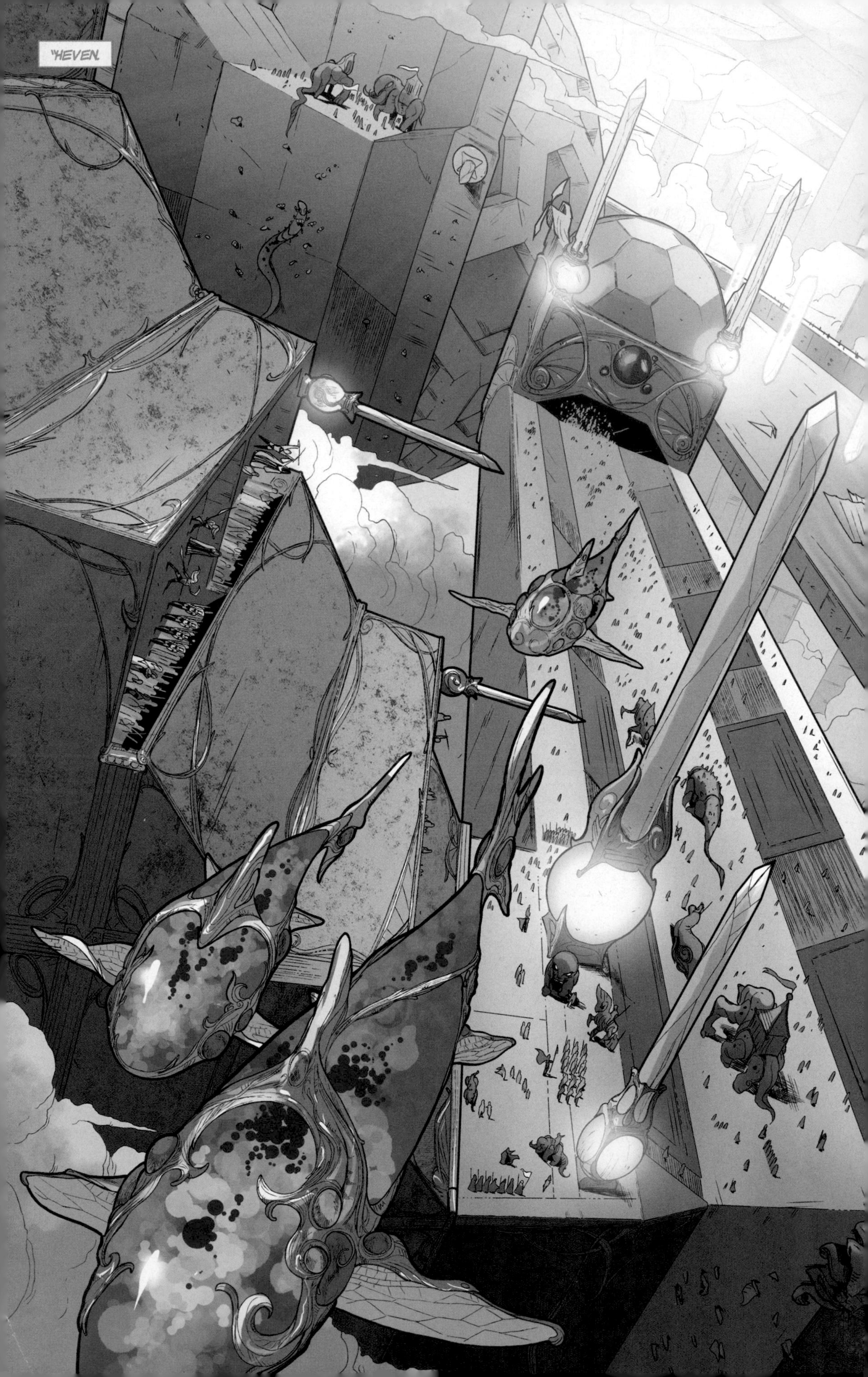
"HEVEN.

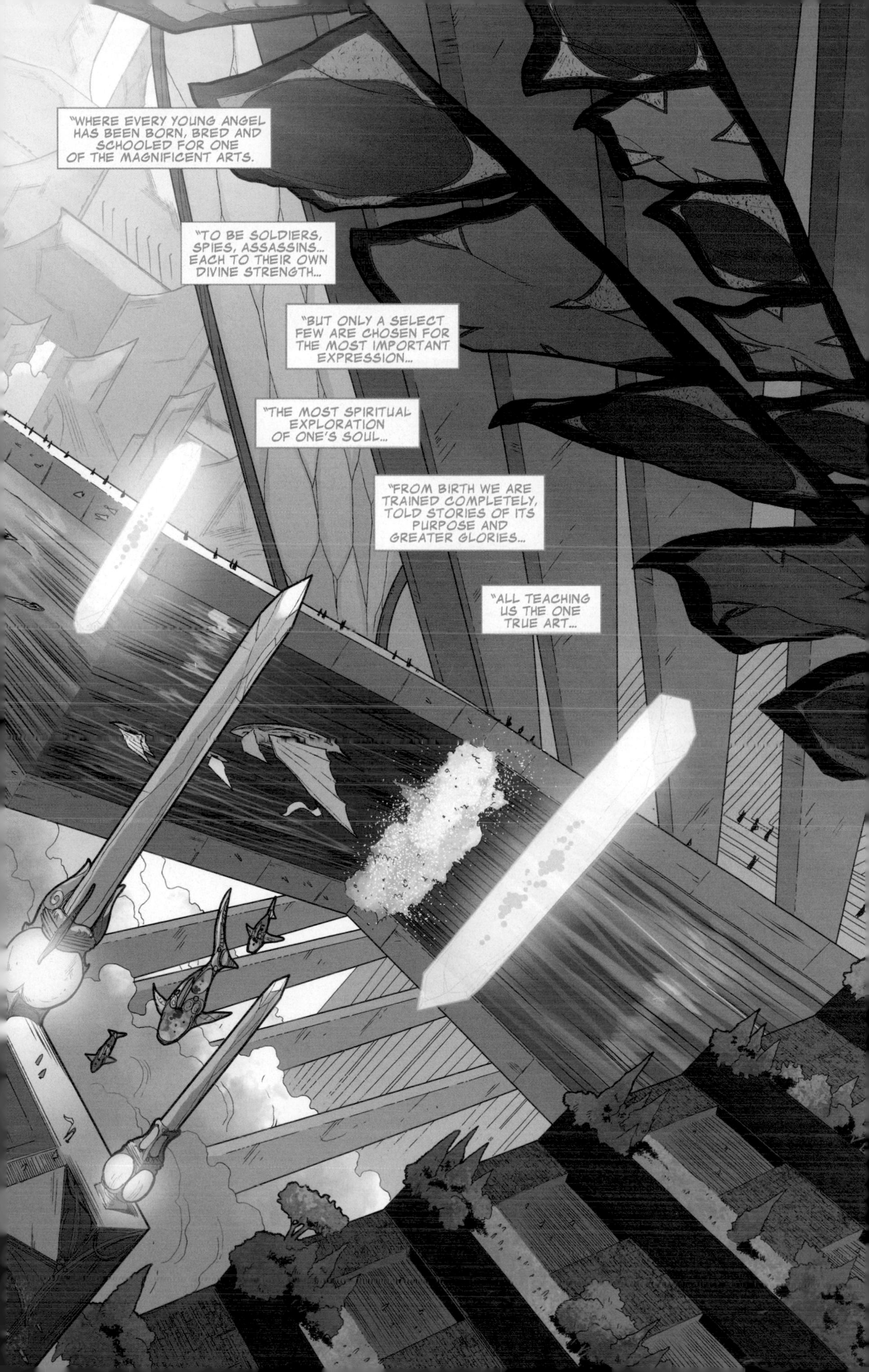
"WHERE EVERY YOUNG ANGEL HAS BEEN BORN, BRED AND SCHOOLED FOR ONE OF THE MAGNIFICENT ARTS.
"TO BE SOLDIERS, SPIES, ASSASSINS... EACH TO THEIR OWN DIVINE STRENGTH...
"BUT ONLY A SELECT FEW ARE CHOSEN FOR THE MOST IMPORTANT EXPRESSION...
"THE MOST SPIRITUAL EXPLORATION OF ONE'S SOUL...
"FROM BIRTH WE ARE TRAINED COMPLETELY, TOLD STORIES OF ITS PURPOSE AND GREATER GLORIES...
"ALL TEACHING US THE ONE TRUE ART...

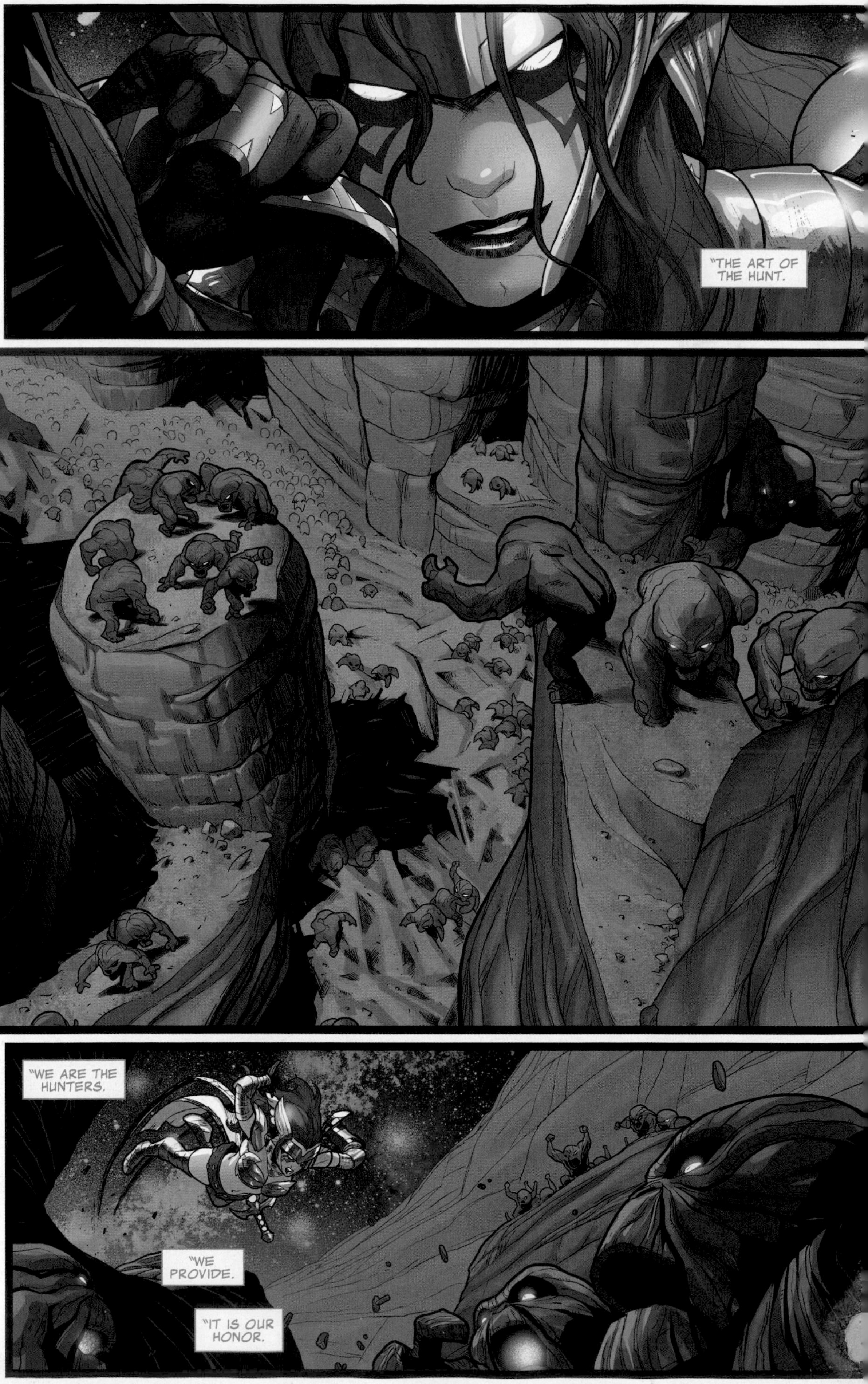
"THE ART OF THE HUNT.
"WE ARE THE HUNTERS.
"WE PROVIDE.
"IT IS OUR HONOR.

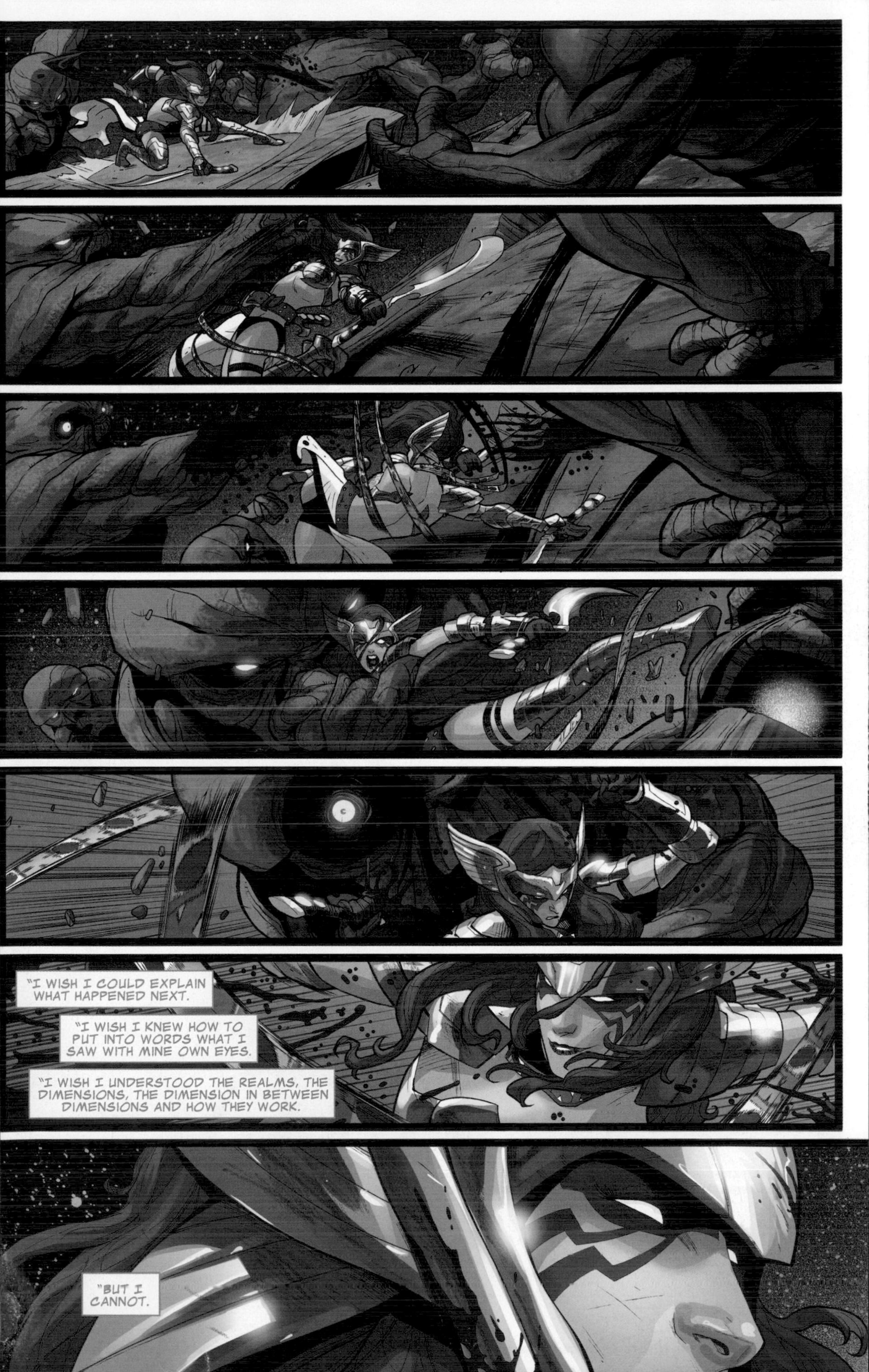
"I WISH I COULD EXPLAIN WHAT HAPPENED NEXT.
"I WISH I KNEW HOW TO PUT INTO WORDS WHAT I SAW WITH MINE OWN EYES.
"I WISH I UNDERSTOOD THE REALMS, THE DIMENSIONS, THE DIMENSION IN BETWEEN DIMENSIONS AND HOW THEY WORK.
"BUT I CANNOT.

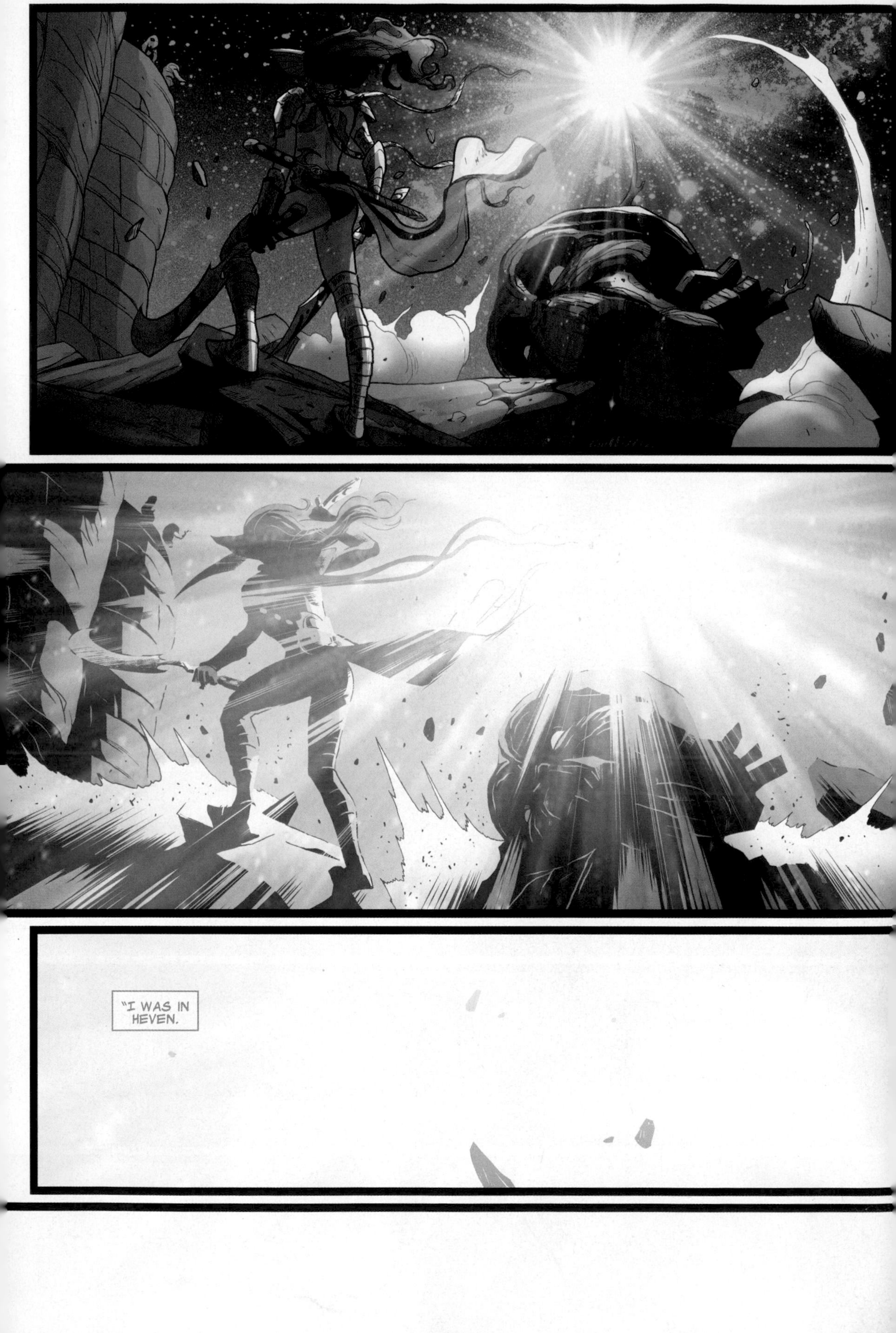
"I WAS IN HEVEN.

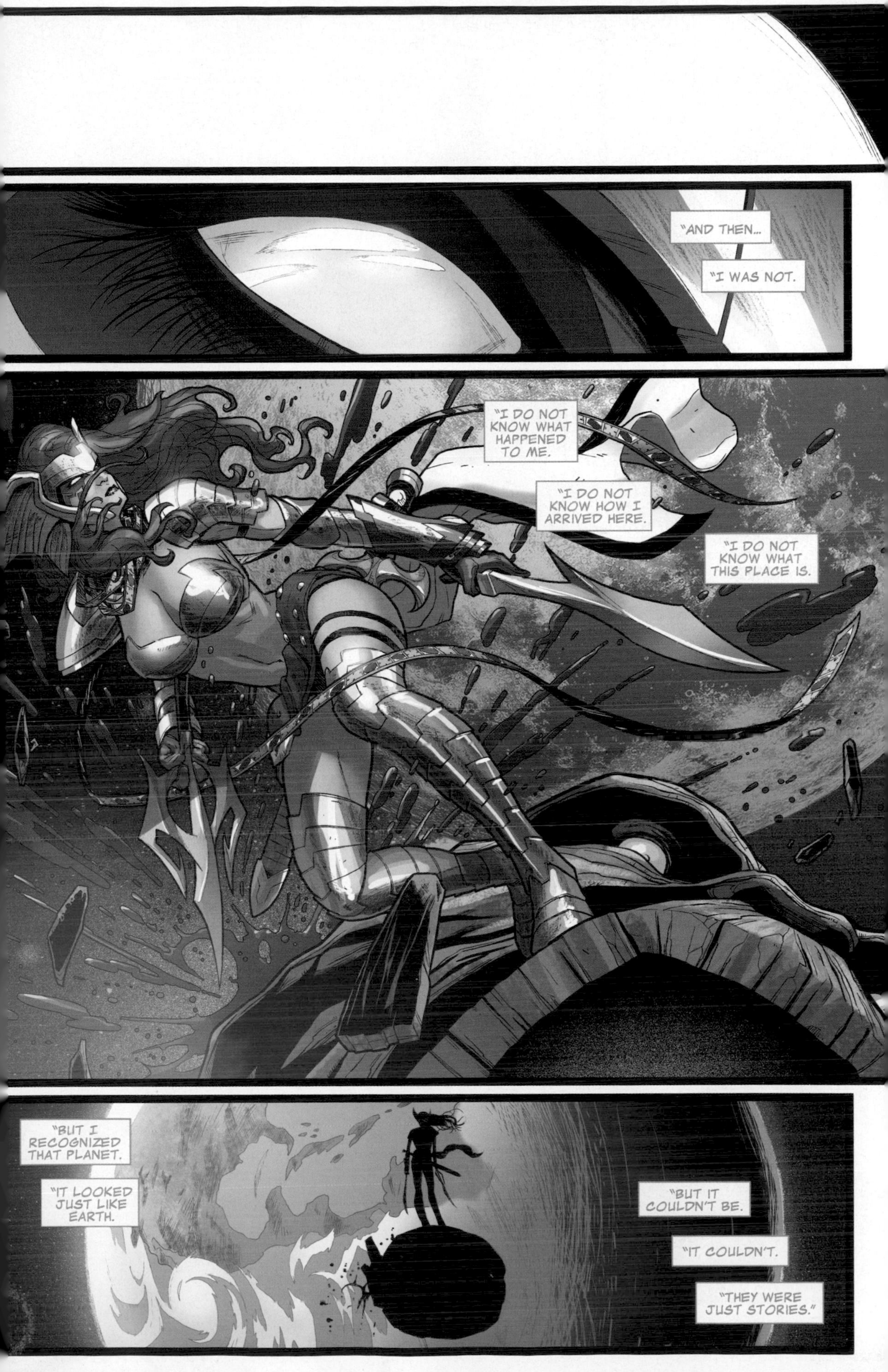
"AND THEN...
"I WAS NOT.
"I DO NOT KNOW WHAT HAPPENED TO ME.
"I DO NOT KNOW HOW I ARRIVED HERE.
"I DO NOT KNOW WHAT THIS PLACE IS.
"BUT I RECOGNIZED THAT PLANET.
"IT LOOKED JUST LIKE EARTH.
"BUT IT COULDN'T BE.
"IT COULDN'T.
"THEY WERE JUST STORIES."

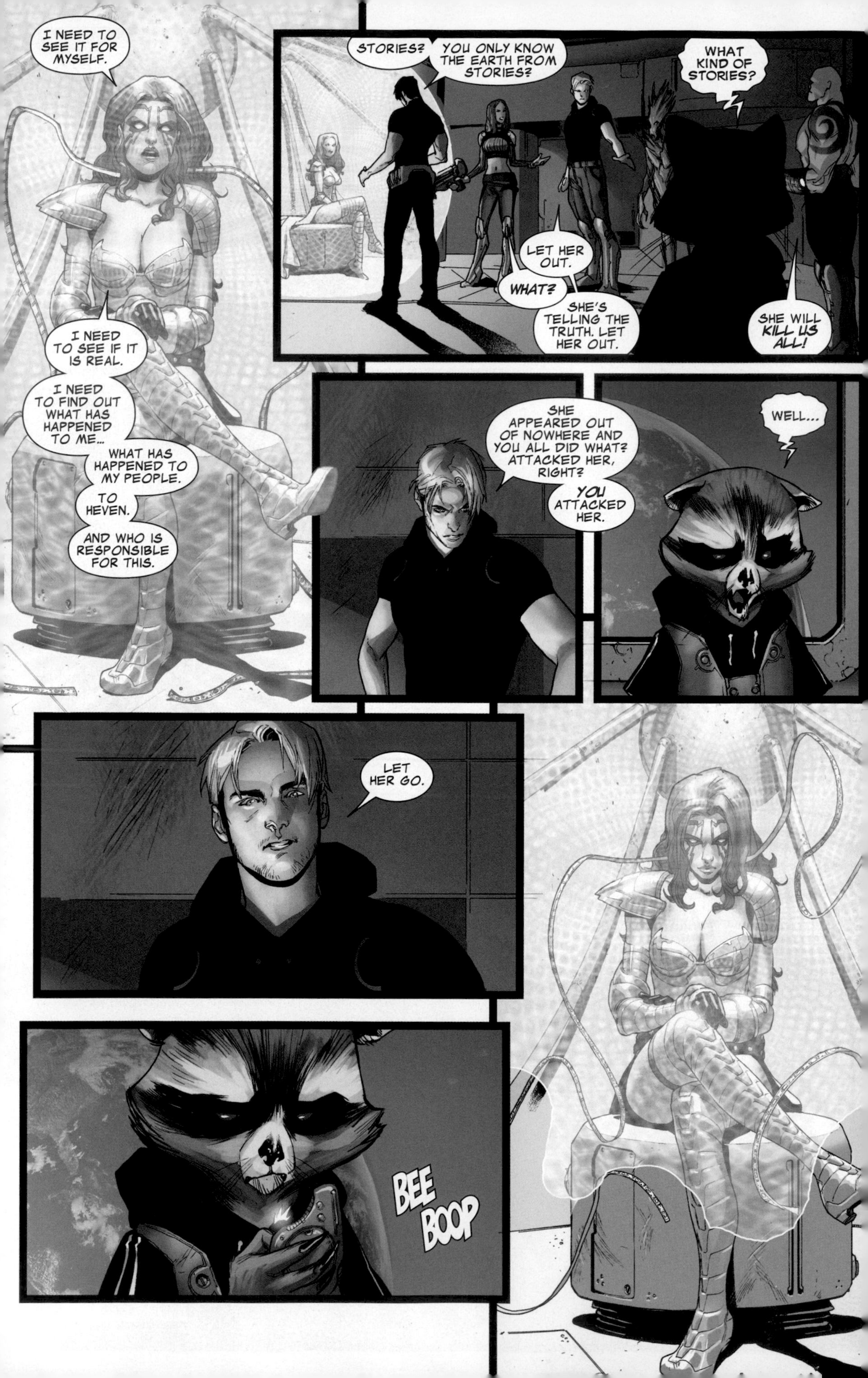

I NEED TO SEE IT FOR MYSELF.
I NEED TO SEE IF IT IS REAL.
I NEED TO FIND OUT WHAT HAS HAPPENED TO ME...
WHAT HAS HAPPENED TO MY PEOPLE.
TO HEVEN.
AND WHO IS RESPONSIBLE FOR THIS.
STORIES?
YOU ONLY KNOW THE EARTH FROM STORIES?
WHAT KIND OF STORIES?
LET HER OUT.
WHAT?
SHE'S TELLING THE TRUTH. LET HER OUT.
SHE WILL KILL US ALL!
SHE APPEARED OUT OF NOWHERE AND YOU ALL DID WHAT? ATTACKED HER, RIGHT?
YOU ATTACKED HER.
WELL...
LET HER GO.
BEE BOOP

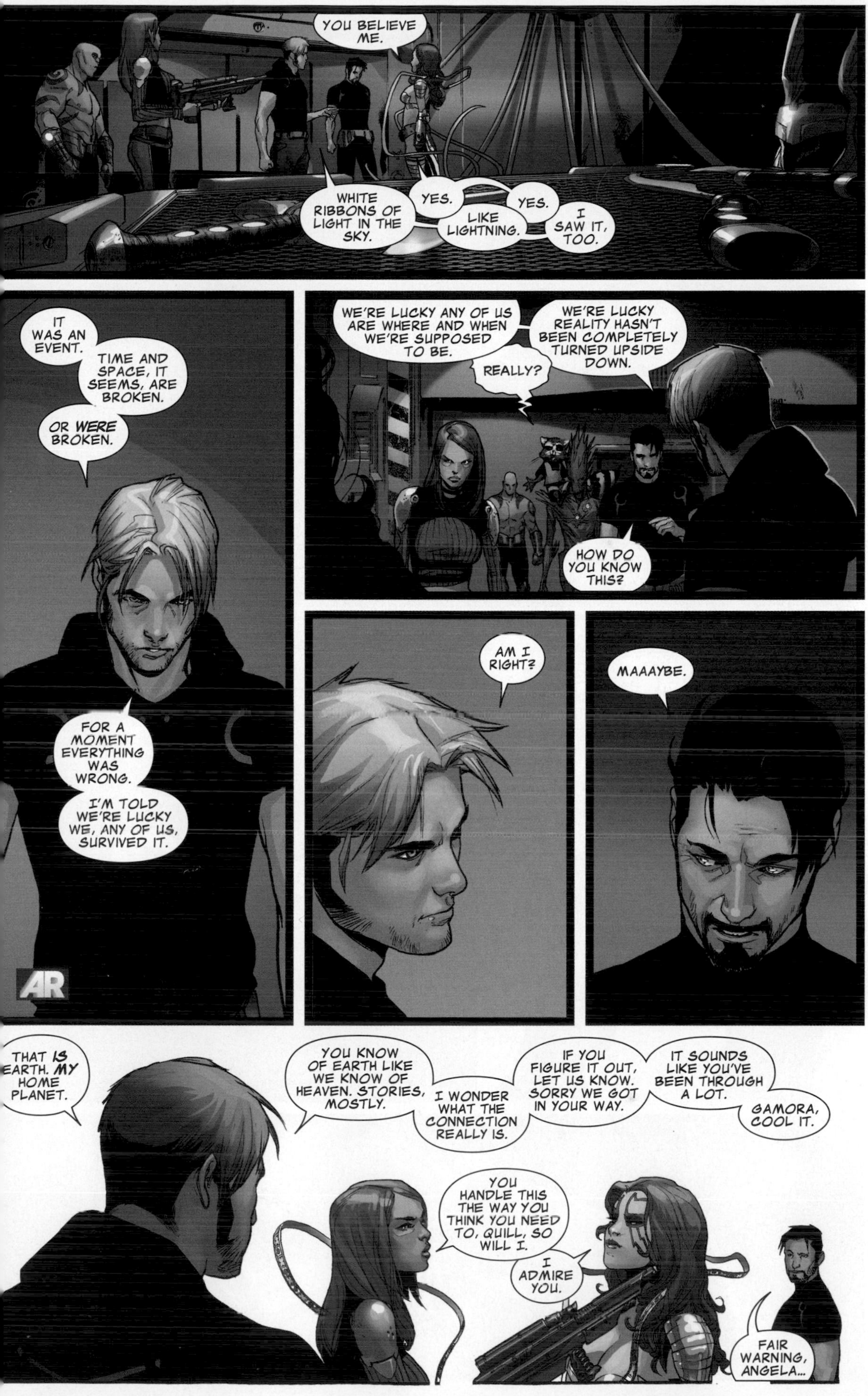
YOU BELIEVE ME.
WHITE RIBBONS OF LIGHT IN THE SKY.
YES.
LIKE LIGHTNING.
YES.
I SAW IT, TOO.
IT WAS AN EVENT.
TIME AND SPACE, IT SEEMS, ARE BROKEN.
OR WERE BROKEN.
FOR A MOMENT EVERYTHING WAS WRONG.
I'M TOLD WE'RE LUCKY WE, ANY OF US, SURVIVED IT.
WE'RE LUCKY ANY OF US ARE WHERE AND WHEN WE'RE SUPPOSED TO BE.
WE'RE LUCKY REALITY HASN'T BEEN COMPLETELY TURNED UPSIDE DOWN.
REALLY?
HOW DO YOU KNOW THIS?
AM I RIGHT?
MAAAYBE.
AR
THAT IS EARTH. MY HOME PLANET.
YOU KNOW OF EARTH LIKE WE KNOW OF HEAVEN. STORIES, MOSTLY.
I WONDER WHAT THE CONNECTION REALLY IS.
IF YOU FIGURE IT OUT, LET US KNOW. SORRY WE GOT IN YOUR WAY.
IT SOUNDS LIKE YOU'VE BEEN THROUGH A LOT.
GAMORA, COOL IT.
YOU HANDLE THIS THE WAY YOU THINK YOU NEED TO, QUILL, SO WILL I.
I ADMIRE YOU.
FAIR WARNING, ANGELA...

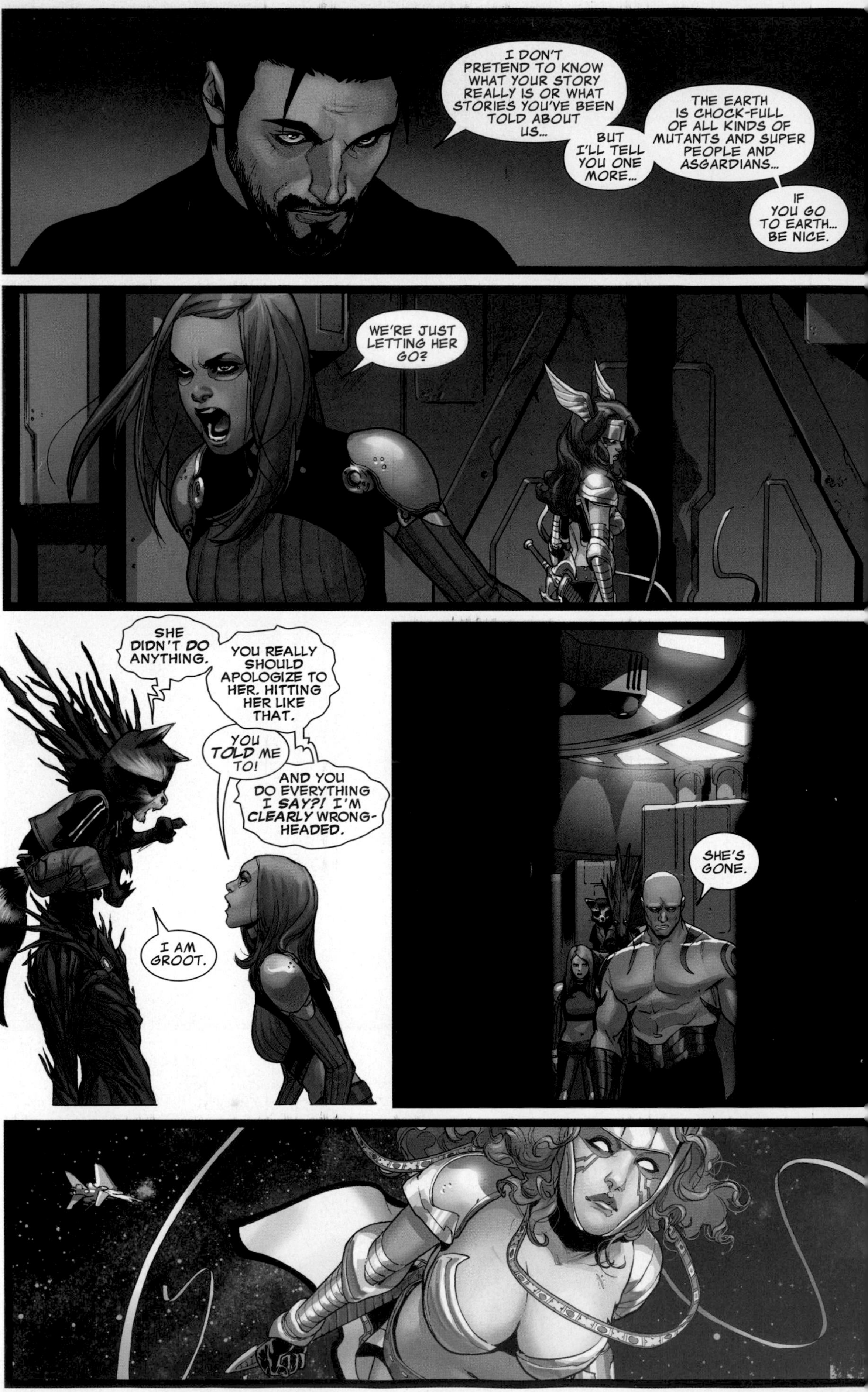
I DON'T PRETEND TO KNOW WHAT YOUR STORY REALLY IS OR WHAT STORIES YOU'VE BEEN TOLD ABOUT US...
BUT I'LL TELL YOU ONE MORE...
THE EARTH IS CHOCK-FULL OF ALL KINDS OF MUTANTS AND SUPER PEOPLE AND ASGARDIANS...
IF YOU GO TO EARTH... BE NICE.
WE'RE JUST LETTING HER GO?
SHE DIDN'T DO ANYTHING.
YOU REALLY SHOULD APOLOGIZE TO HER. HITTING HER LIKE THAT.
YOU TOLD ME TO!
AND YOU DO EVERYTHING I SAY?! I'M CLEARLY WRONG-HEADED.
I AM GROOT.
SHE'S GONE.

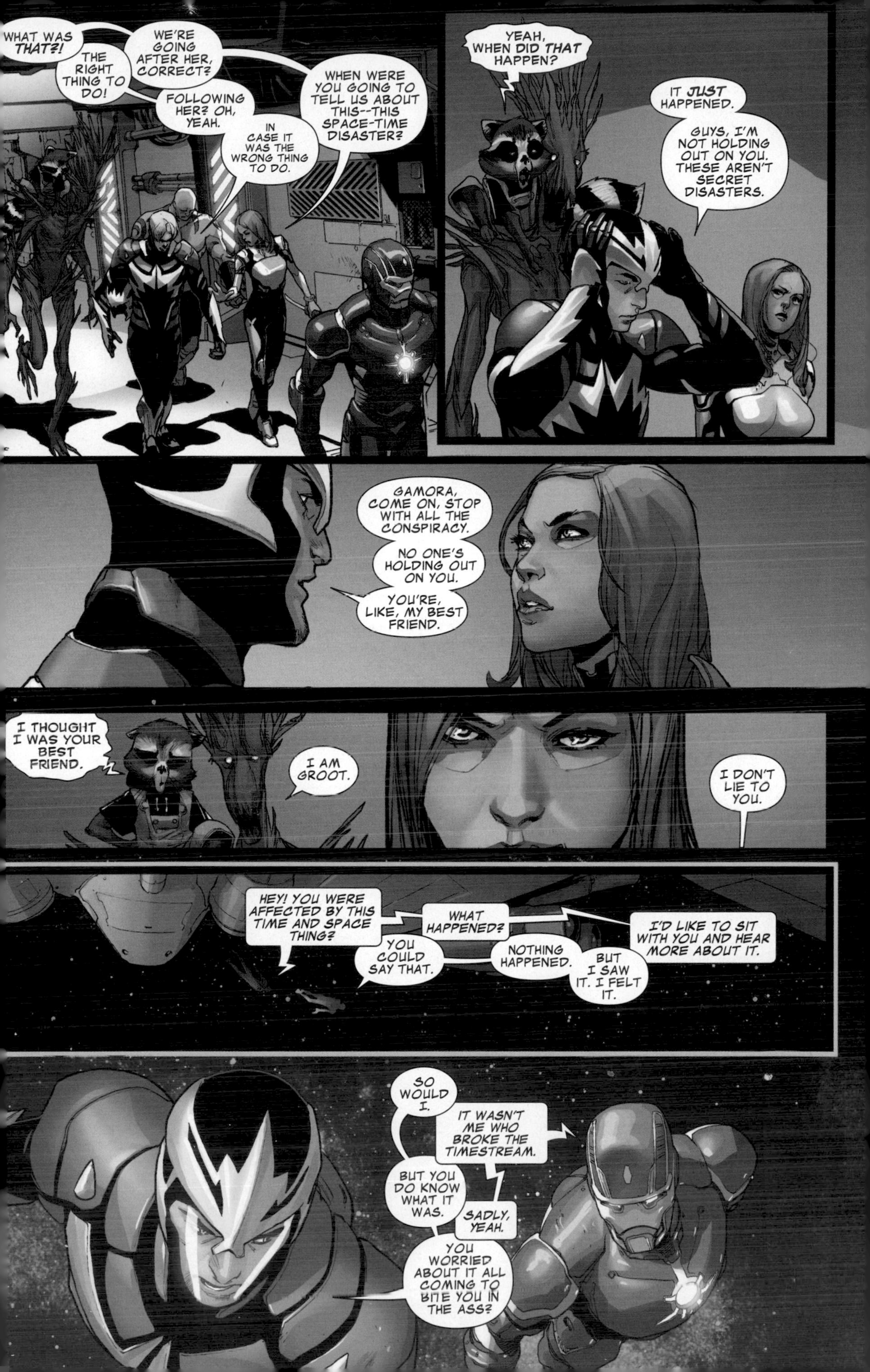
WHAT WAS THAT?!
WE'RE GOING AFTER HER, CORRECT?
THE RIGHT THING TO DO!
FOLLOWING HER? OH, YEAH.
IN CASE IT WAS THE WRONG THING TO DO.
WHEN WERE YOU GOING TO TELL US ABOUT THIS--THIS SPACE-TIME DISASTER?
YEAH, WHEN DID THAT HAPPEN?
IT JUST HAPPENED.
GUYS, I'M NOT HOLDING OUT ON YOU. THESE AREN'T SECRET DISASTERS.
GAMORA, COME ON, STOP WITH ALL THE CONSPIRACY.
NO ONE'S HOLDING OUT ON YOU.
YOU'RE, LIKE, MY BEST FRIEND.
I THOUGHT I WAS YOUR BEST FRIEND.
I AM GROOT.
I DON'T LIE TO YOU.
HEY! YOU WERE AFFECTED BY THIS TIME AND SPACE THING?
YOU COULD SAY THAT.
WHAT HAPPENED?
NOTHING HAPPENED.
BUT I SAW IT. I FELT IT.
I'D LIKE TO SIT WITH YOU AND HEAR MORE ABOUT IT.
SO WOULD I.
IT WASN'T ME WHO BROKE THE TIMESTREAM.
BUT YOU DO KNOW WHAT IT WAS.
SADLY, YEAH.
YOU WORRIED ABOUT IT ALL COMING TO BITE YOU IN THE ASS?

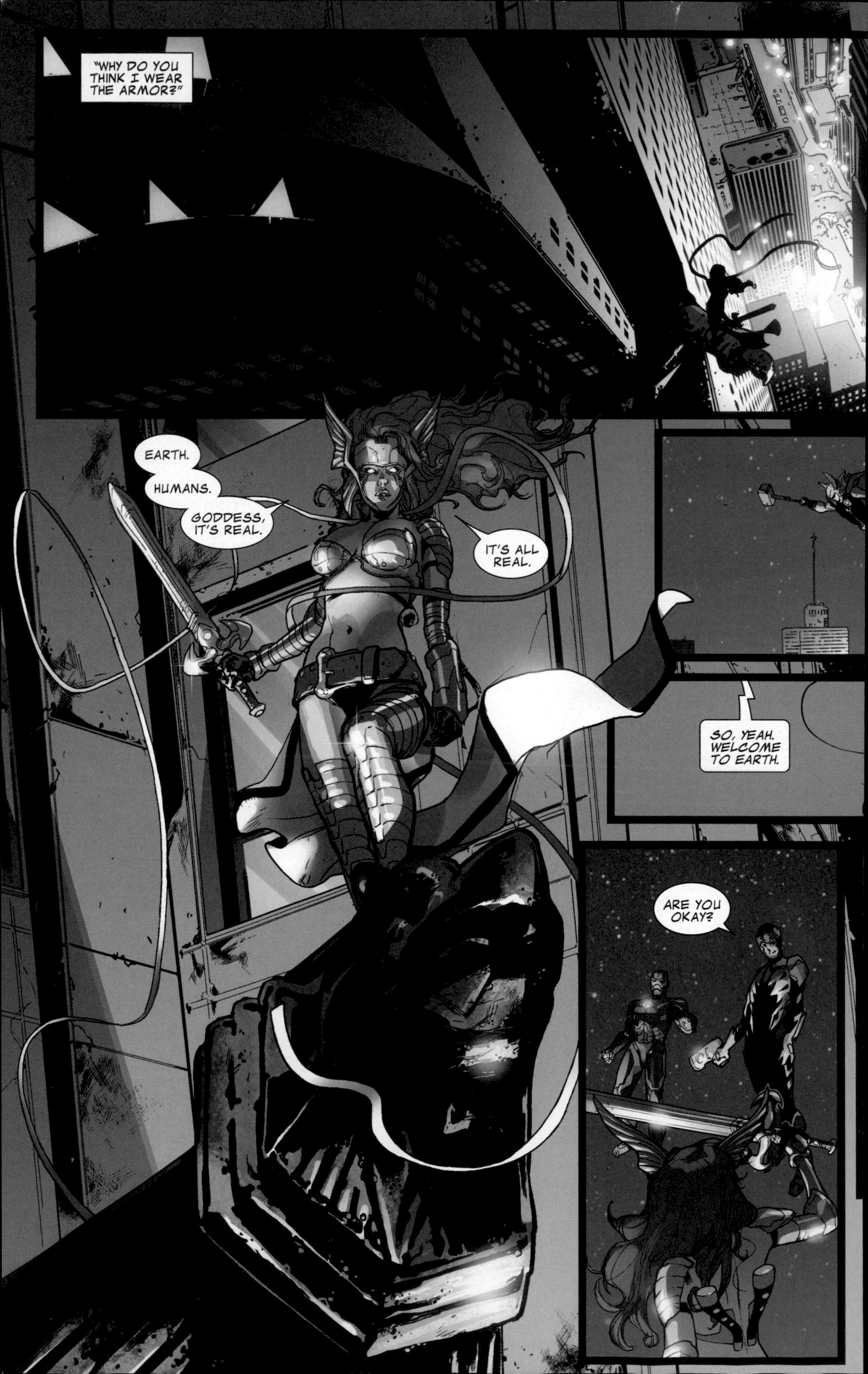
"WHY DO YOU THINK I WEAR THE ARMOR?"
EARTH.
HUMANS.
GODDESS, IT'S REAL.
IT'S ALL REAL.
SO, YEAH. WELCOME TO EARTH.
ARE YOU OKAY?

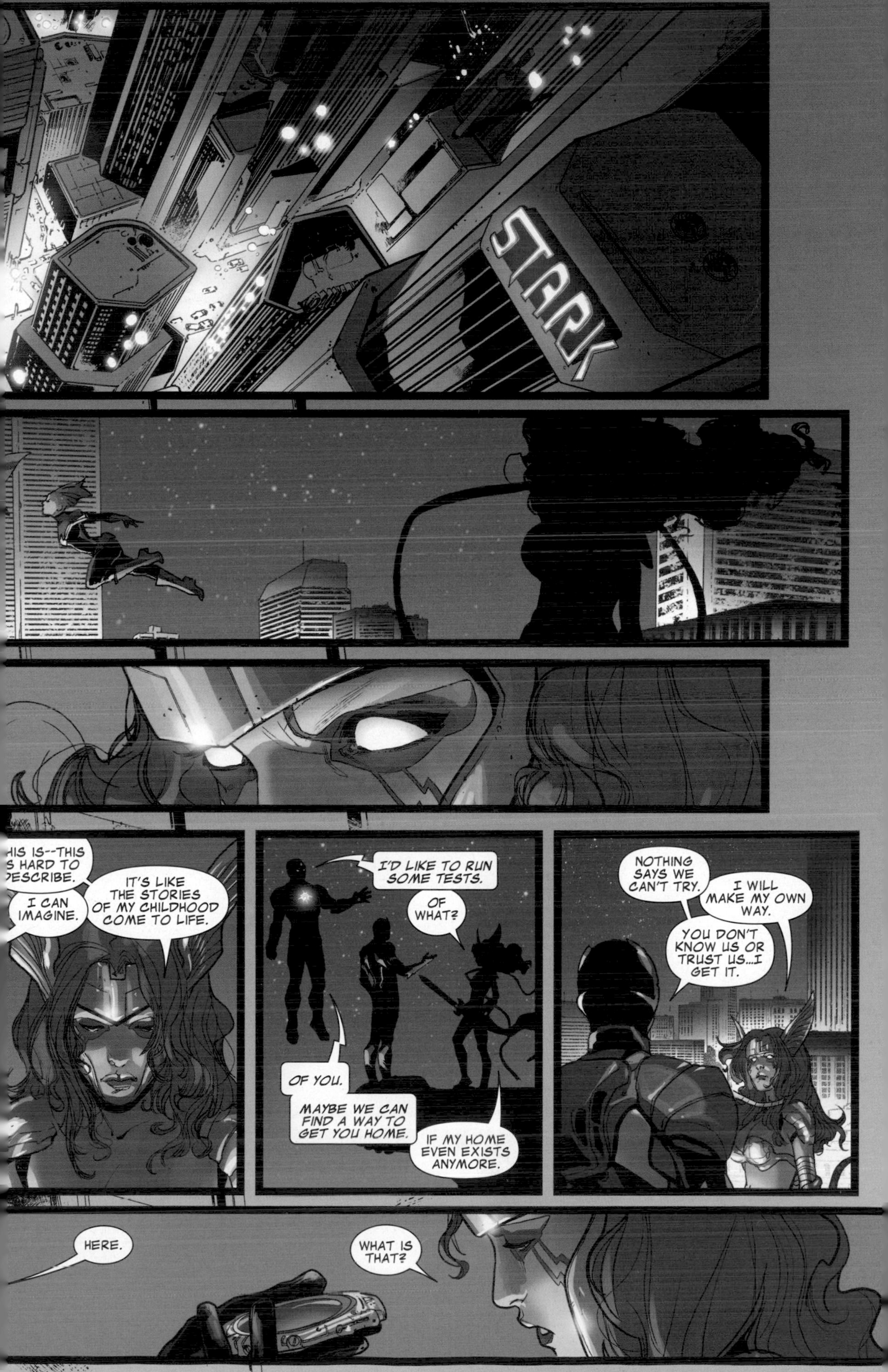
STARK
HIS IS--THIS
S HARD TO
DESCRIBE.
I CAN
IMAGINE.
IT'S LIKE
THE STORIES
OF MY CHILDHOOD
COME TO LIFE.
I'D LIKE TO RUN
SOME TESTS.
OF
WHAT?
OF YOU.
MAYBE WE CAN
FIND A WAY TO
GET YOU HOME.
IF MY HOME
EVEN EXISTS
ANYMORE.
NOTHING
SAYS WE
CAN'T TRY.
I WILL
MAKE MY OWN
WAY.
YOU DON'T
KNOW US OR
TRUST US...I
GET IT.
HERE.
WHAT IS
THAT?

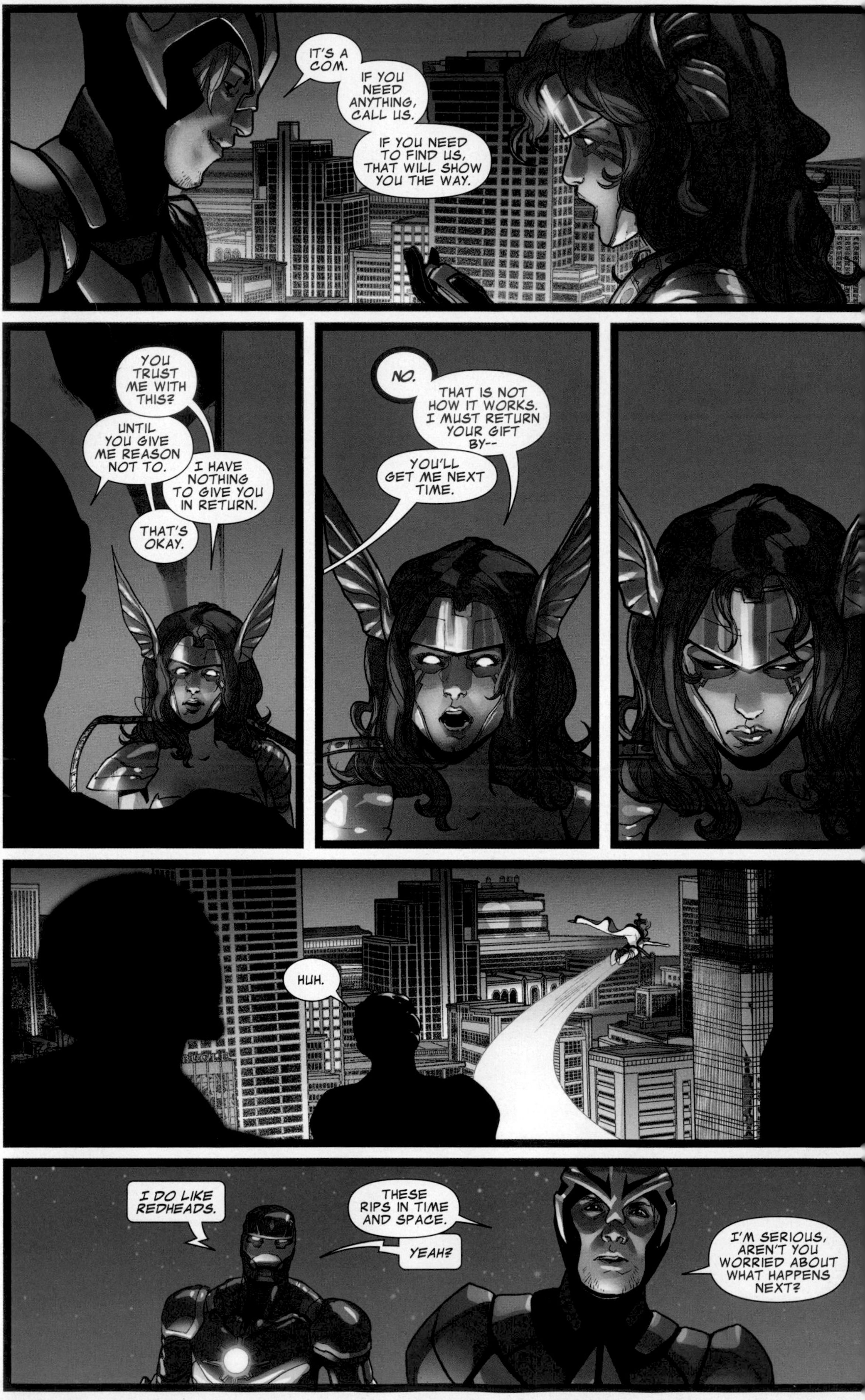
IT'S A COM.
IF YOU NEED ANYTHING, CALL US.
IF YOU NEED TO FIND US, THAT WILL SHOW YOU THE WAY.
YOU TRUST ME WITH THIS?
UNTIL YOU GIVE ME REASON NOT TO.
I HAVE NOTHING TO GIVE YOU IN RETURN.
THAT'S OKAY.
NO.
THAT IS NOT HOW IT WORKS. I MUST RETURN YOUR GIFT BY--
YOU'LL GET ME NEXT TIME.
HUH.
I DO LIKE REDHEADS.
THESE RIPS IN TIME AND SPACE.
YEAH?
I'M SERIOUS, AREN'T YOU WORRIED ABOUT WHAT HAPPENS NEXT?

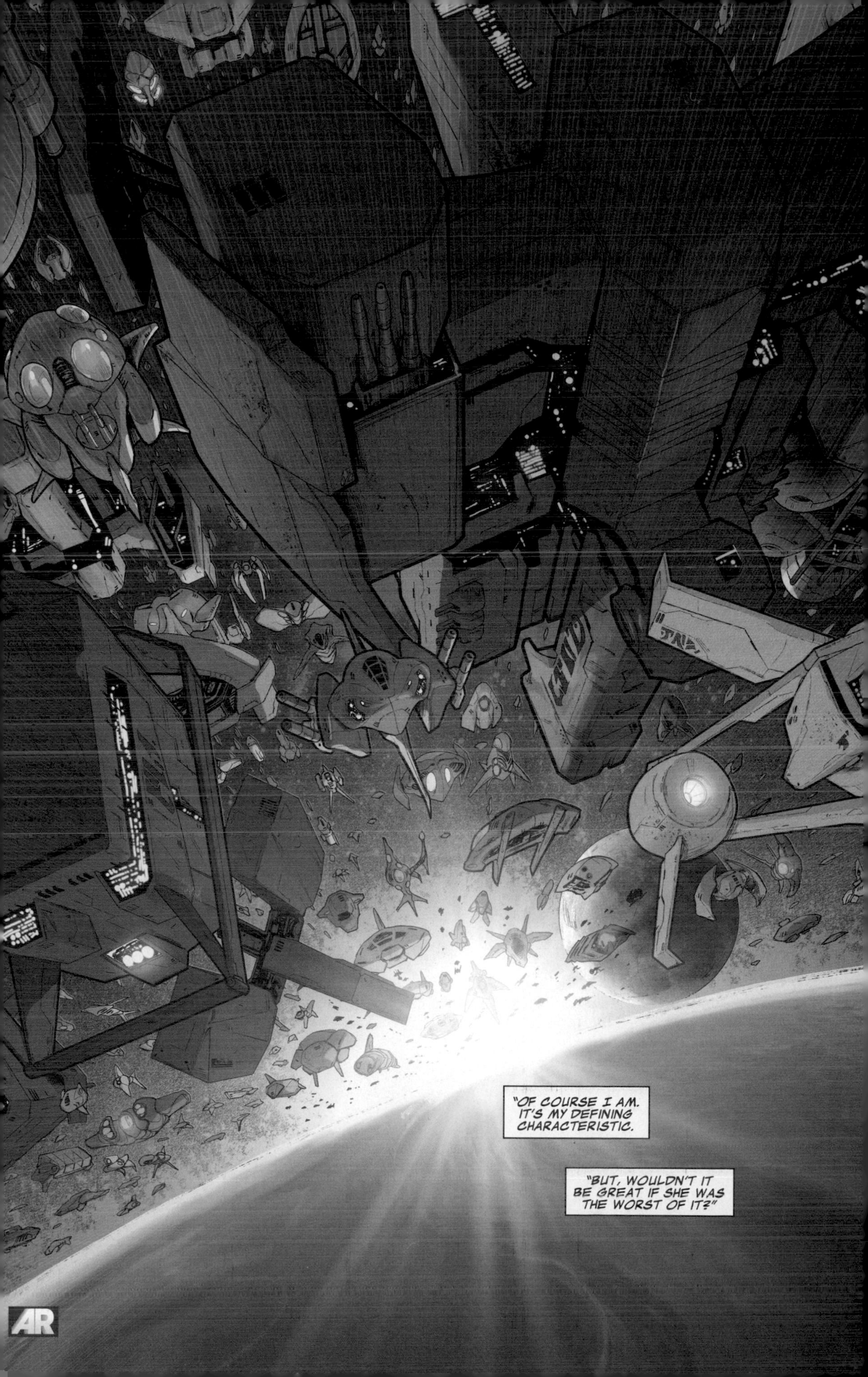
"OF COURSE I AM. IT'S MY DEFINING CHARACTERISTIC.
"BUT, WOULDN'T IT BE GREAT IF SHE WAS THE WORST OF IT?"

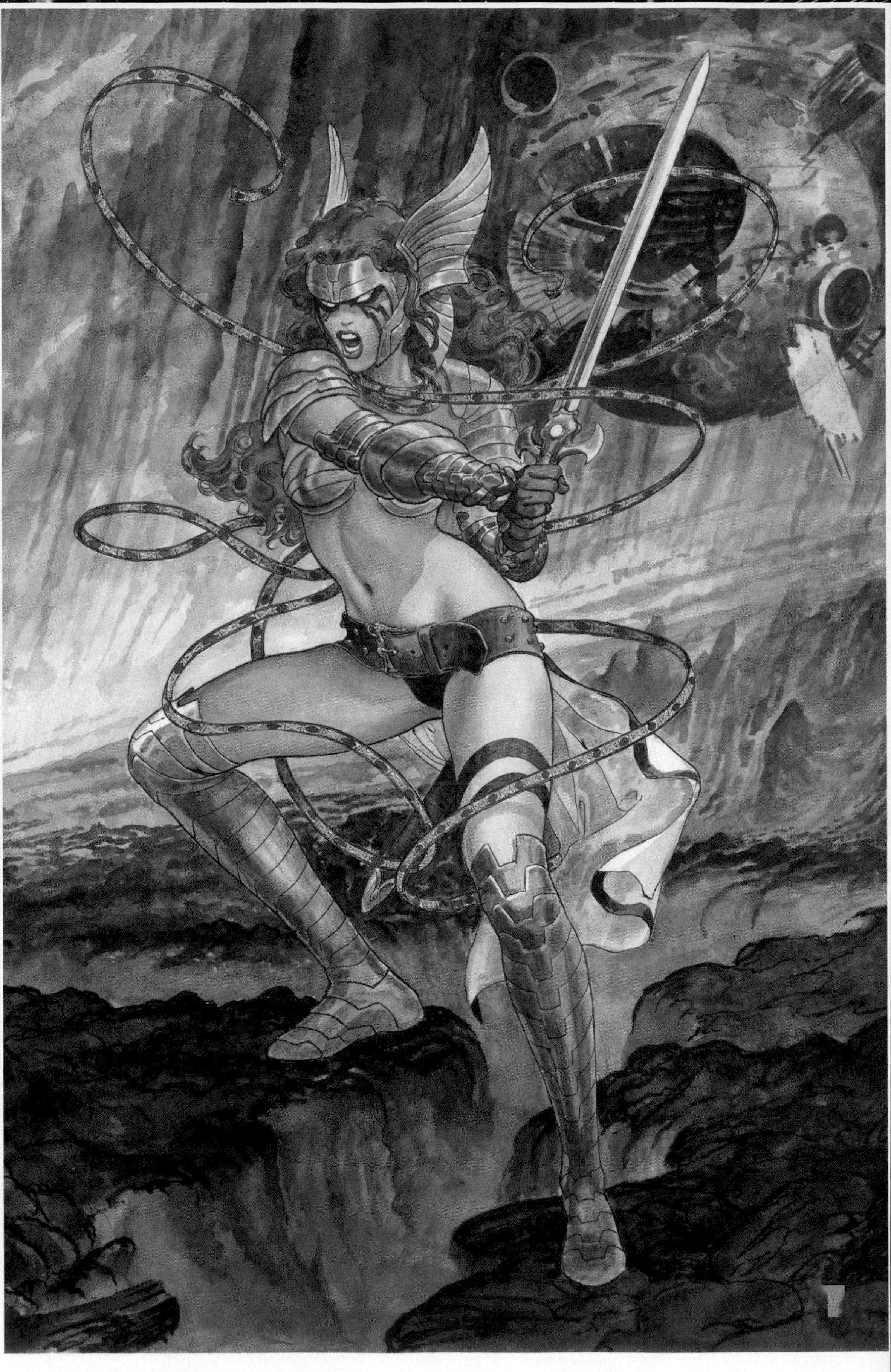

#5 VARIANT BY MILO MANARA

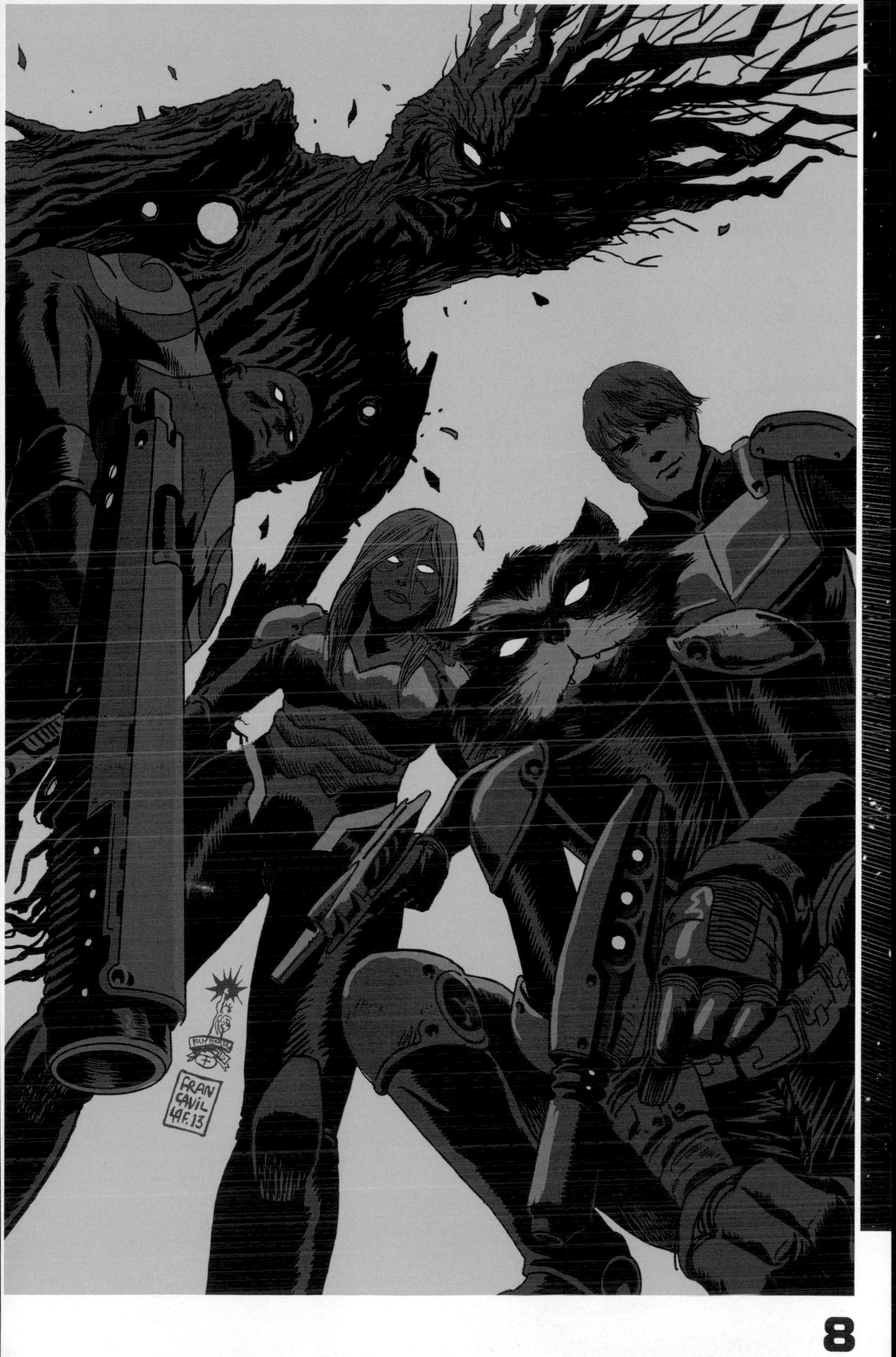

8

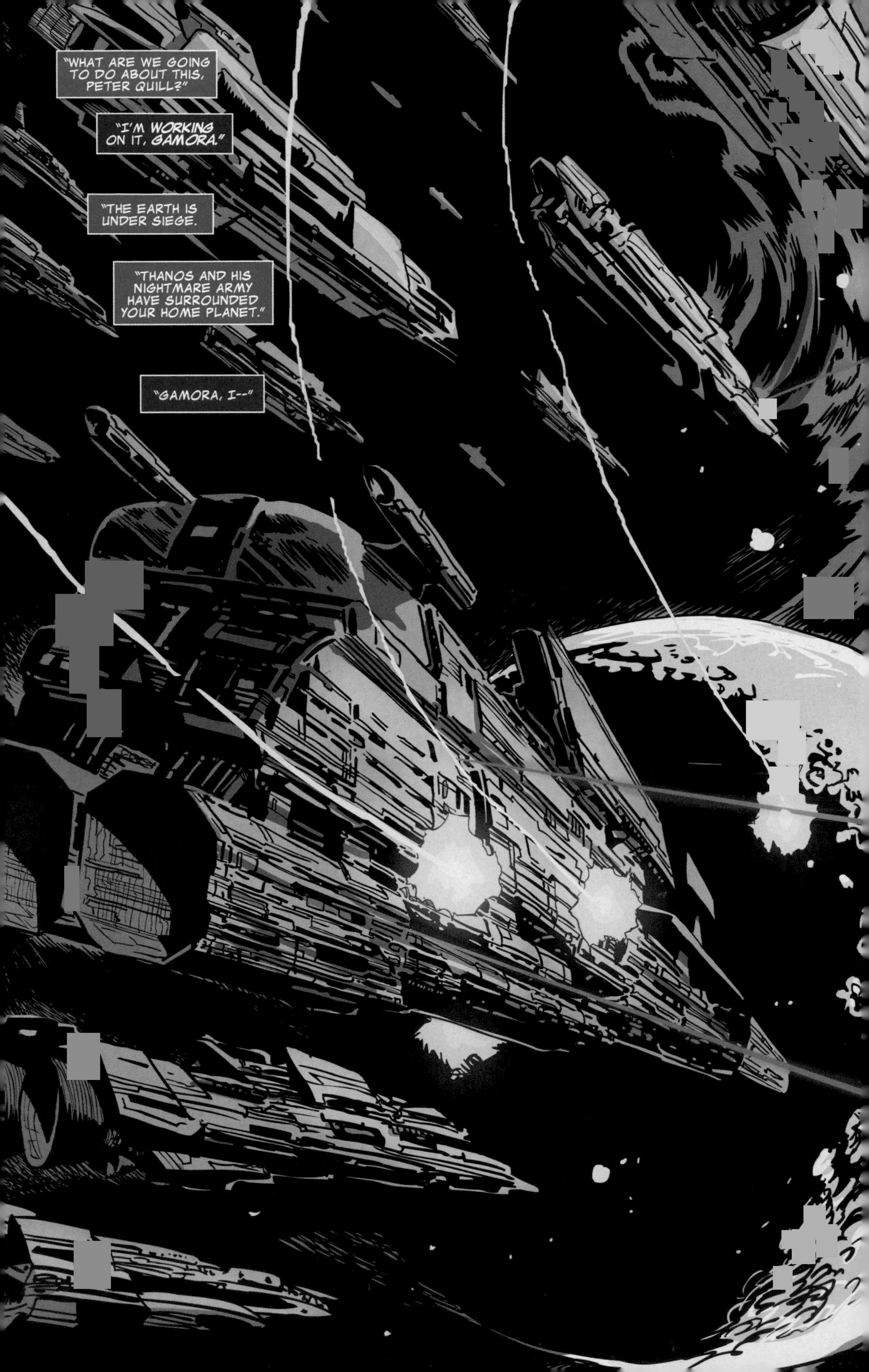
"WHAT ARE WE GOING TO DO ABOUT THIS, PETER QUILL?"
"I'M WORKING ON IT, GAMORA."
"THE EARTH IS UNDER SIEGE.
"THANOS AND HIS NIGHTMARE ARMY HAVE SURROUNDED YOUR HOME PLANET."
"GAMORA, I--"

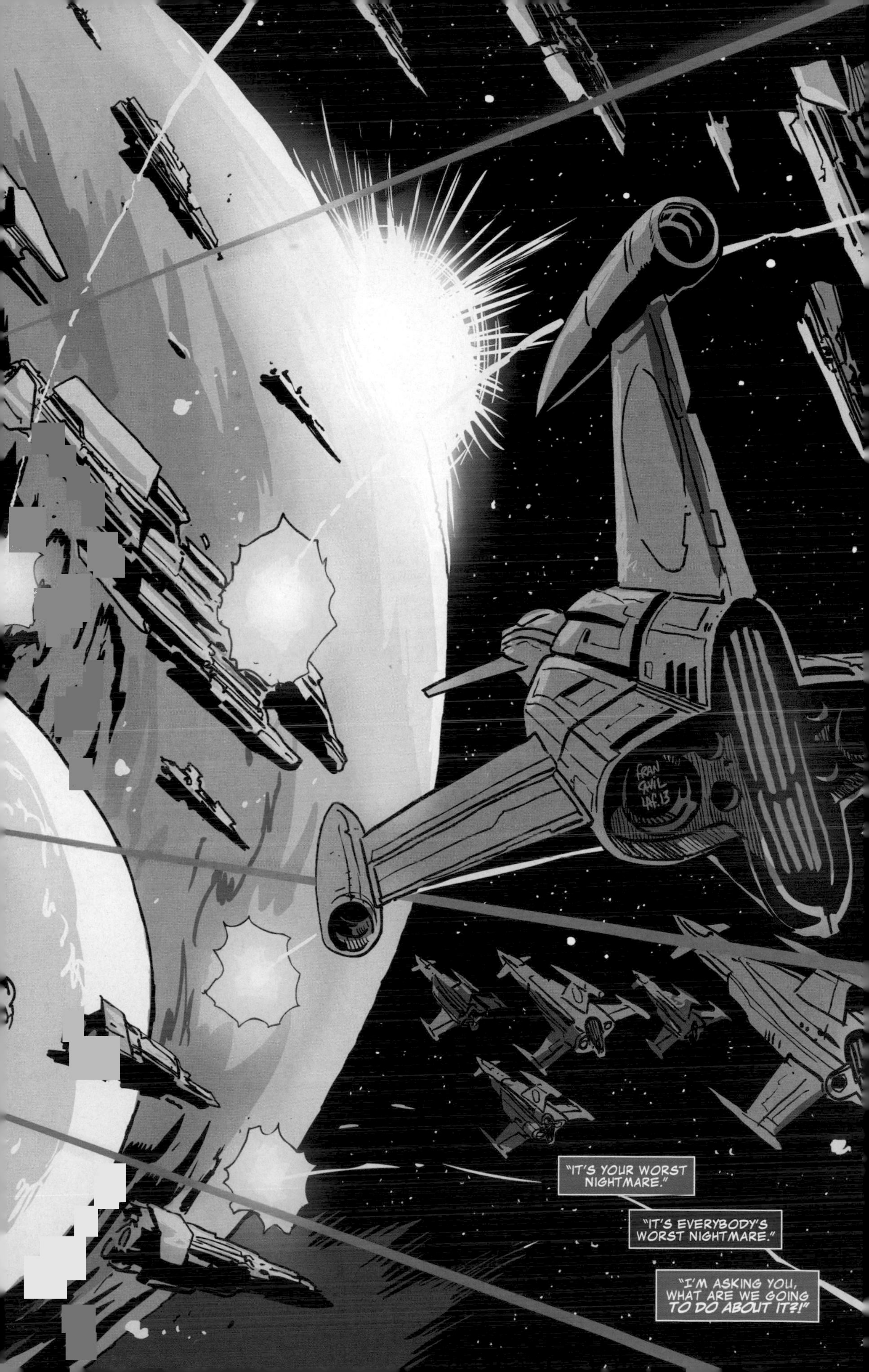
FRAN GAVIL LAF. 13
"IT'S YOUR WORST NIGHTMARE."
"IT'S EVERYBODY'S WORST NIGHTMARE."
"I'M ASKING YOU, WHAT ARE WE GOING TO DO ABOUT IT?!"

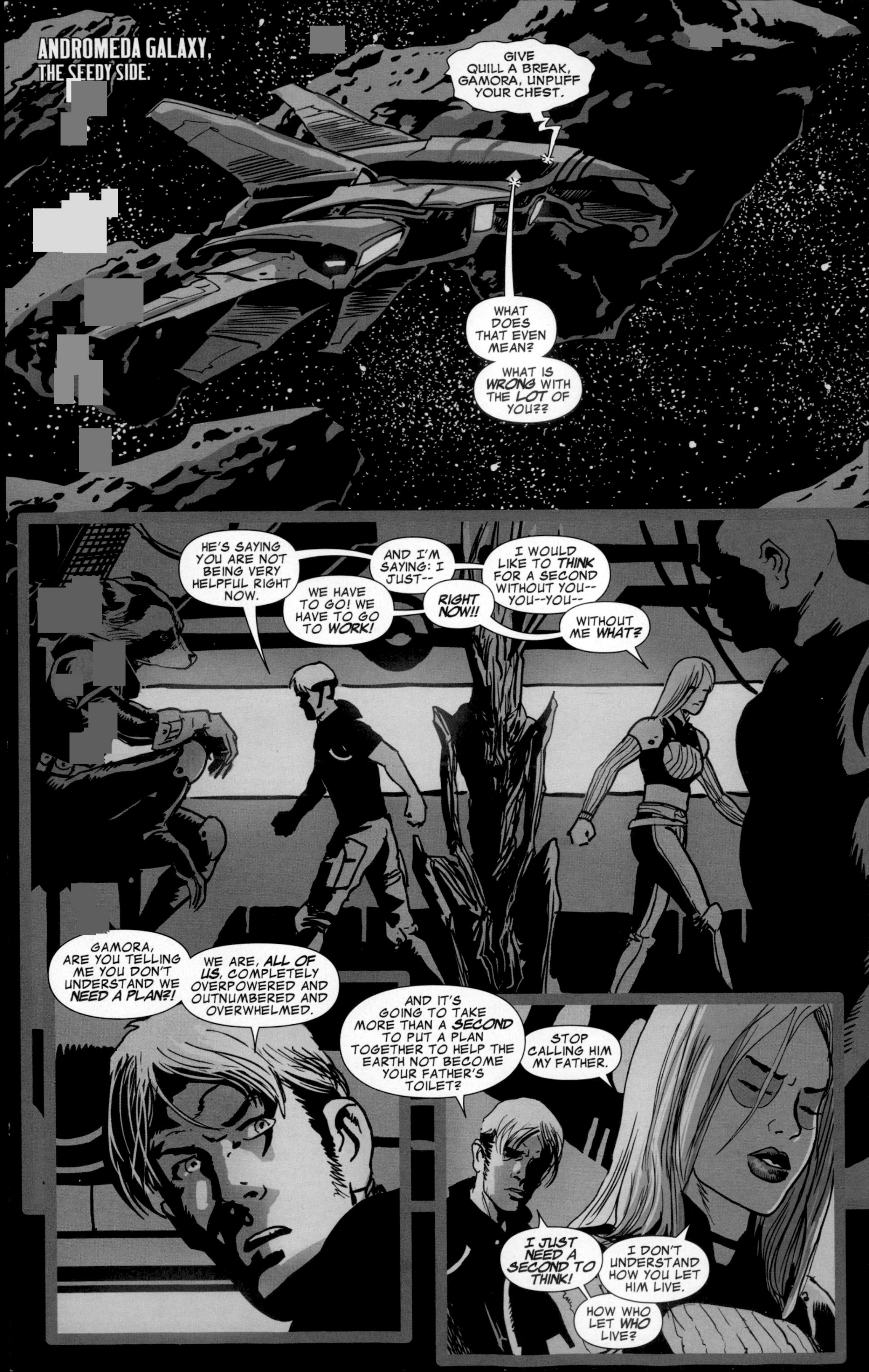
ANDROMEDA GALAXY, THE SEEDY SIDE.
GIVE QUILL A BREAK, GAMORA, UNPUFF YOUR CHEST.
WHAT DOES THAT EVEN MEAN?
WHAT IS WRONG WITH THE LOT OF YOU??
HE'S SAYING YOU ARE NOT BEING VERY HELPFUL RIGHT NOW.
AND I'M SAYING: I JUST--
I WOULD LIKE TO THINK FOR A SECOND WITHOUT YOU--YOU--YOU--
WE HAVE TO GO! WE HAVE TO GO TO WORK!
RIGHT NOW!!
WITHOUT ME WHAT?
GAMORA, ARE YOU TELLING ME YOU DON'T UNDERSTAND WE NEED A PLAN?!
WE ARE, ALL OF US, COMPLETELY OVERPOWERED AND OUTNUMBERED AND OVERWHELMED.
AND IT'S GOING TO TAKE MORE THAN A SECOND TO PUT A PLAN TOGETHER TO HELP THE EARTH NOT BECOME YOUR FATHER'S TOILET?
STOP CALLING HIM MY FATHER.
I JUST NEED A SECOND TO THINK!
I DON'T UNDERSTAND HOW YOU LET HIM LIVE.
HOW WHO LET WHO LIVE?

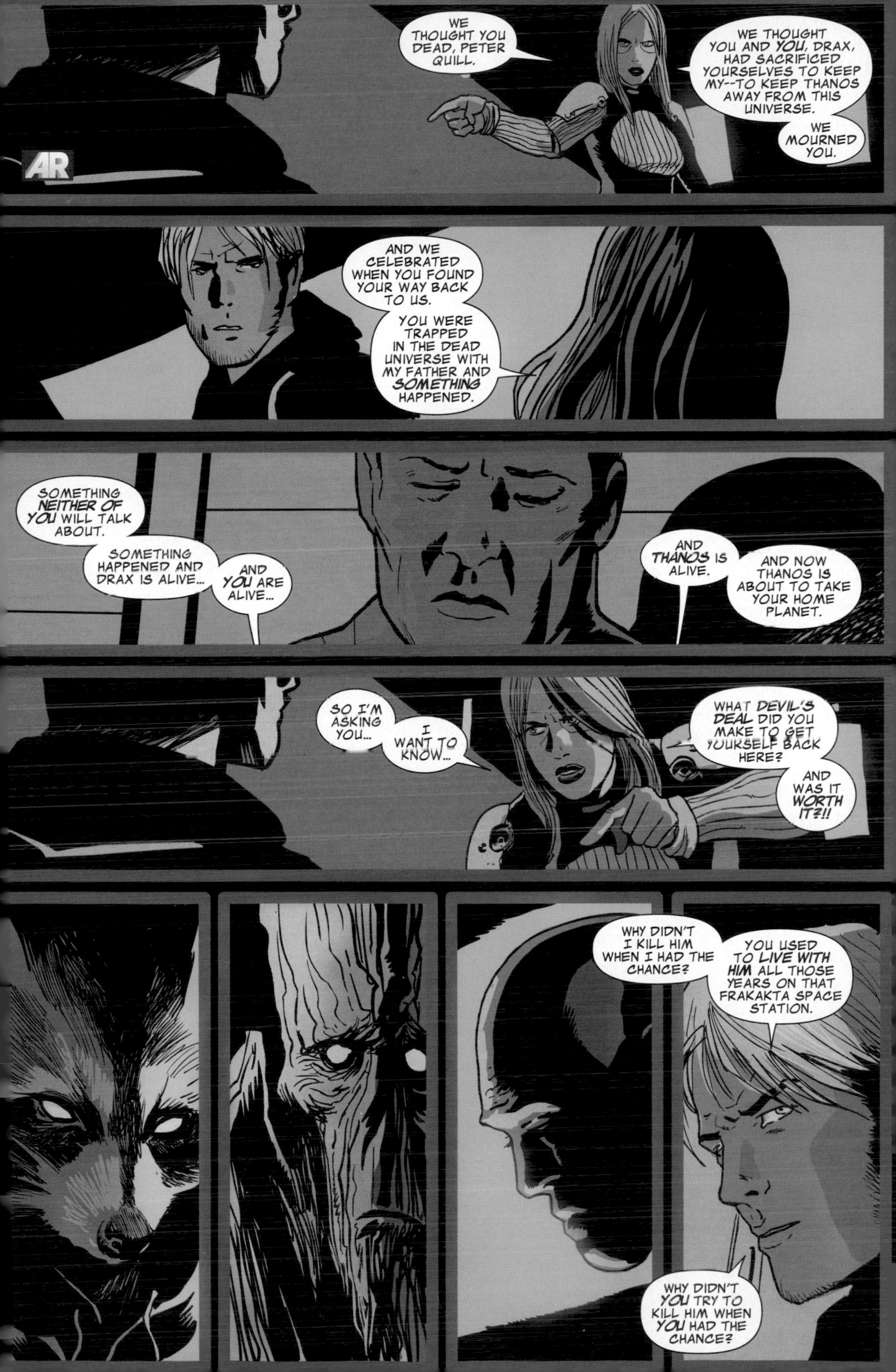

WE THOUGHT YOU DEAD, PETER QUILL.
WE THOUGHT YOU AND YOU, DRAX, HAD SACRIFICED YOURSELVES TO KEEP MY--TO KEEP THANOS AWAY FROM THIS UNIVERSE.
WE MOURNED YOU.
AND WE CELEBRATED WHEN YOU FOUND YOUR WAY BACK TO US.
YOU WERE TRAPPED IN THE DEAD UNIVERSE WITH MY FATHER AND SOMETHING HAPPENED.
SOMETHING NEITHER OF YOU WILL TALK ABOUT.
SOMETHING HAPPENED AND DRAX IS ALIVE...
AND YOU ARE ALIVE...
AND THANOS IS ALIVE.
AND NOW THANOS IS ABOUT TO TAKE YOUR HOME PLANET.
SO I'M ASKING YOU...
I WANT TO KNOW...
WHAT DEVIL'S DEAL DID YOU MAKE TO GET YOURSELF BACK HERE?
AND WAS IT WORTH IT?!!
WHY DIDN'T I KILL HIM WHEN I HAD THE CHANCE?
YOU USED TO LIVE WITH HIM ALL THOSE YEARS ON THAT FRAKAKTA SPACE STATION.
WHY DIDN'T YOU TRY TO KILL HIM WHEN YOU HAD THE CHANCE?

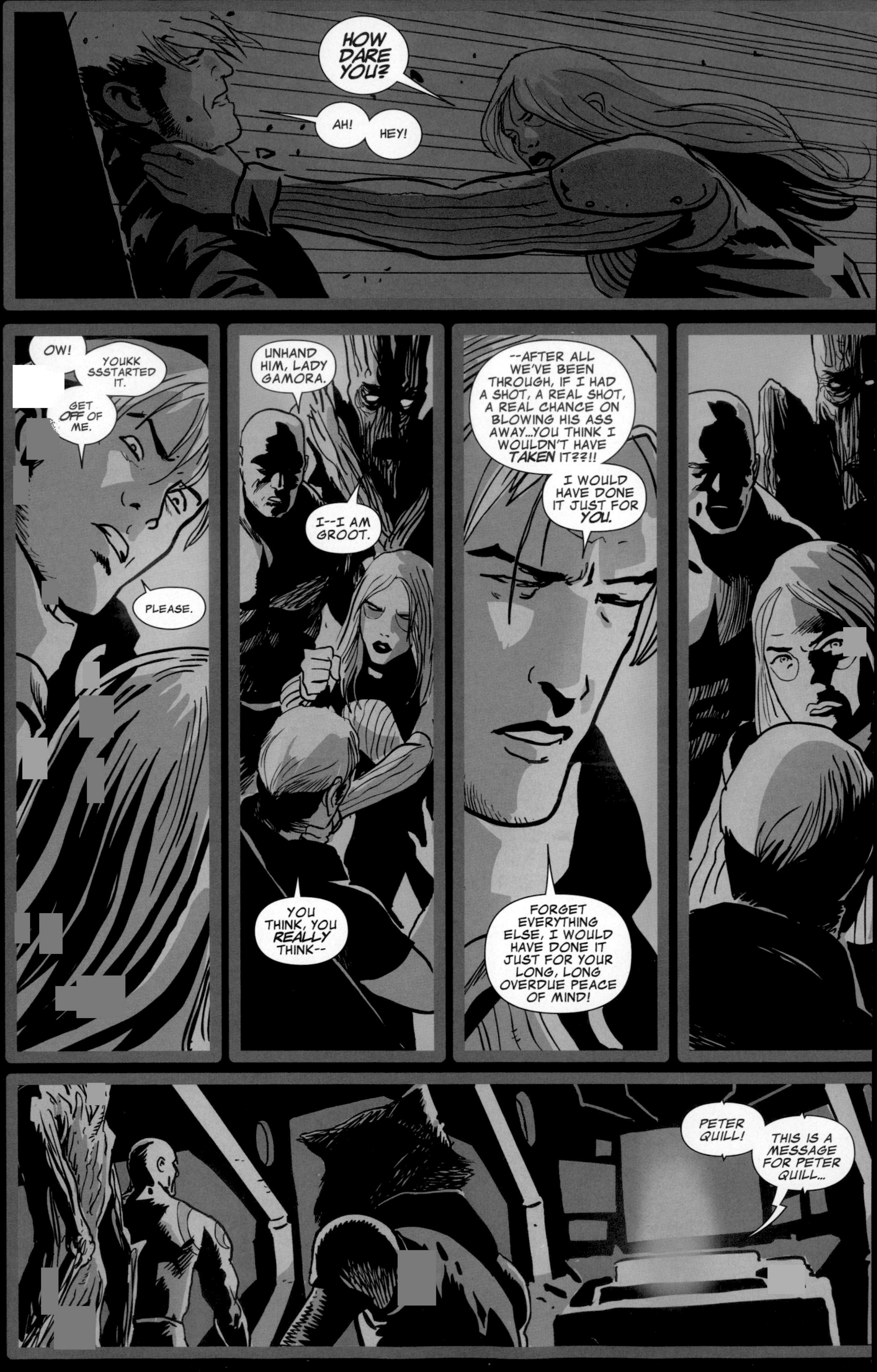
HOW DARE YOU?
AH!
HEY!
OW!
YOUKK SSSTARTED IT.
GET OFF OF ME.
PLEASE.
UNHAND HIM, LADY GAMORA.
I--I AM GROOT.
YOU THINK, YOU REALLY THINK--
--AFTER ALL WE'VE BEEN THROUGH, IF I HAD A SHOT, A REAL SHOT, A REAL CHANCE ON BLOWING HIS ASS AWAY...YOU THINK I WOULDN'T HAVE TAKEN IT??!!
I WOULD HAVE DONE IT JUST FOR YOU.
FORGET EVERYTHING ELSE, I WOULD HAVE DONE IT JUST FOR YOUR LONG, LONG OVERDUE PEACE OF MIND!
PETER QUILL!
THIS IS A MESSAGE FOR PETER QUILL...

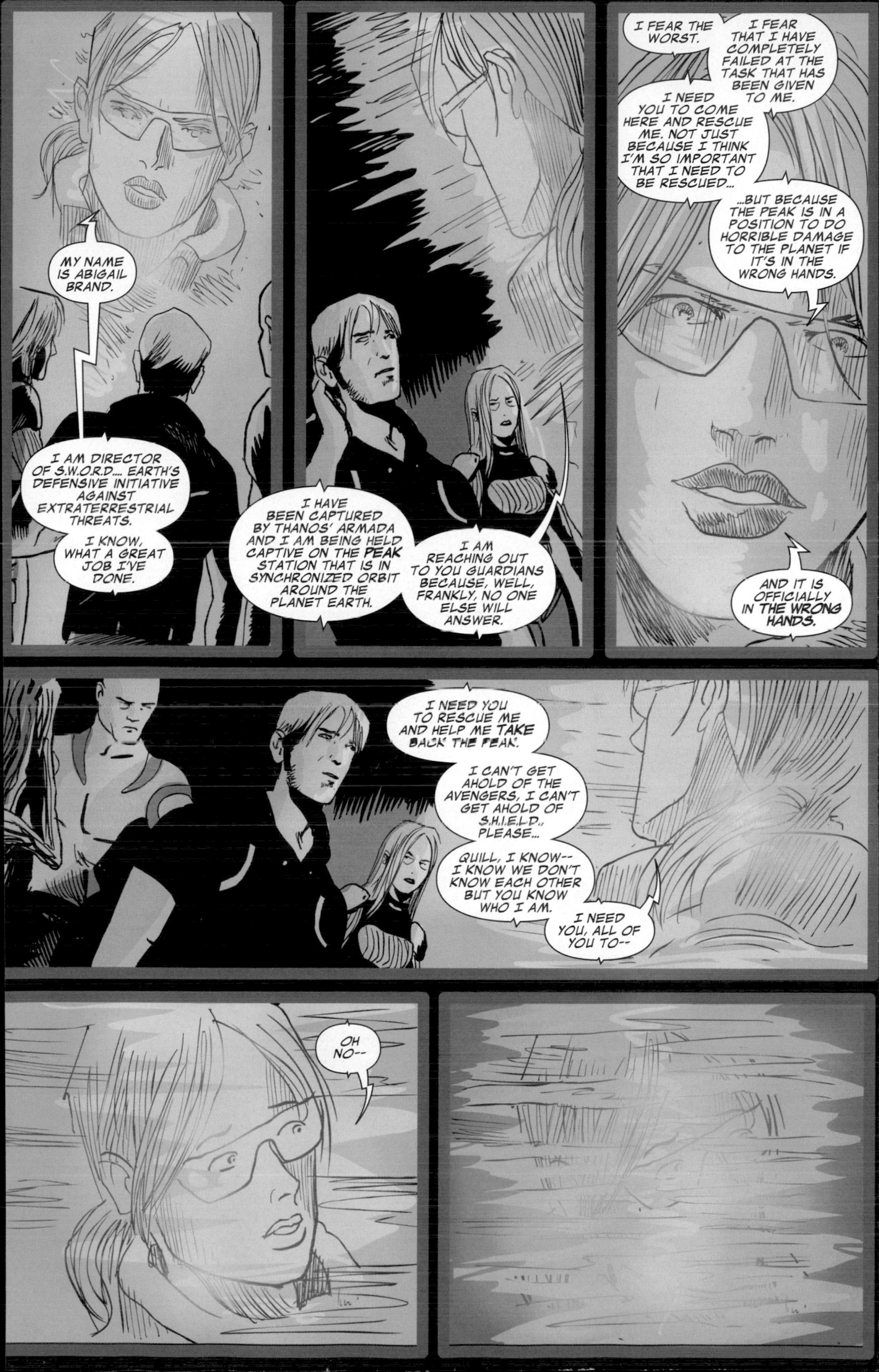
MY NAME IS ABIGAIL BRAND.
I AM DIRECTOR OF S.W.O.R.D.... EARTH'S DEFENSIVE INITIATIVE AGAINST EXTRATERRESTRIAL THREATS.
I KNOW, WHAT A GREAT JOB I'VE DONE.
I HAVE BEEN CAPTURED BY THANOS' ARMADA AND I AM BEING HELD CAPTIVE ON THE PEAK STATION THAT IS IN SYNCHRONIZED ORBIT AROUND THE PLANET EARTH.
I AM REACHING OUT TO YOU GUARDIANS BECAUSE, WELL, FRANKLY, NO ONE ELSE WILL ANSWER.
I FEAR THE WORST.
I FEAR THAT I HAVE COMPLETELY FAILED AT THE TASK THAT HAS BEEN GIVEN TO ME.
I NEED YOU TO COME HERE AND RESCUE ME. NOT JUST BECAUSE I THINK I'M SO IMPORTANT THAT I NEED TO BE RESCUED...
...BUT BECAUSE THE PEAK IS IN A POSITION TO DO HORRIBLE DAMAGE TO THE PLANET IF IT'S IN THE WRONG HANDS.
AND IT IS OFFICIALLY IN THE WRONG HANDS.
I NEED YOU TO RESCUE ME AND HELP ME TAKE BACK THE PEAK.
I CAN'T GET AHOLD OF THE AVENGERS, I CAN'T GET AHOLD OF S.H.I.E.L.D., PLEASE...
QUILL, I KNOW-- I KNOW WE DON'T KNOW EACH OTHER BUT YOU KNOW WHO I AM.
I NEED YOU, ALL OF YOU TO--
OH NO--

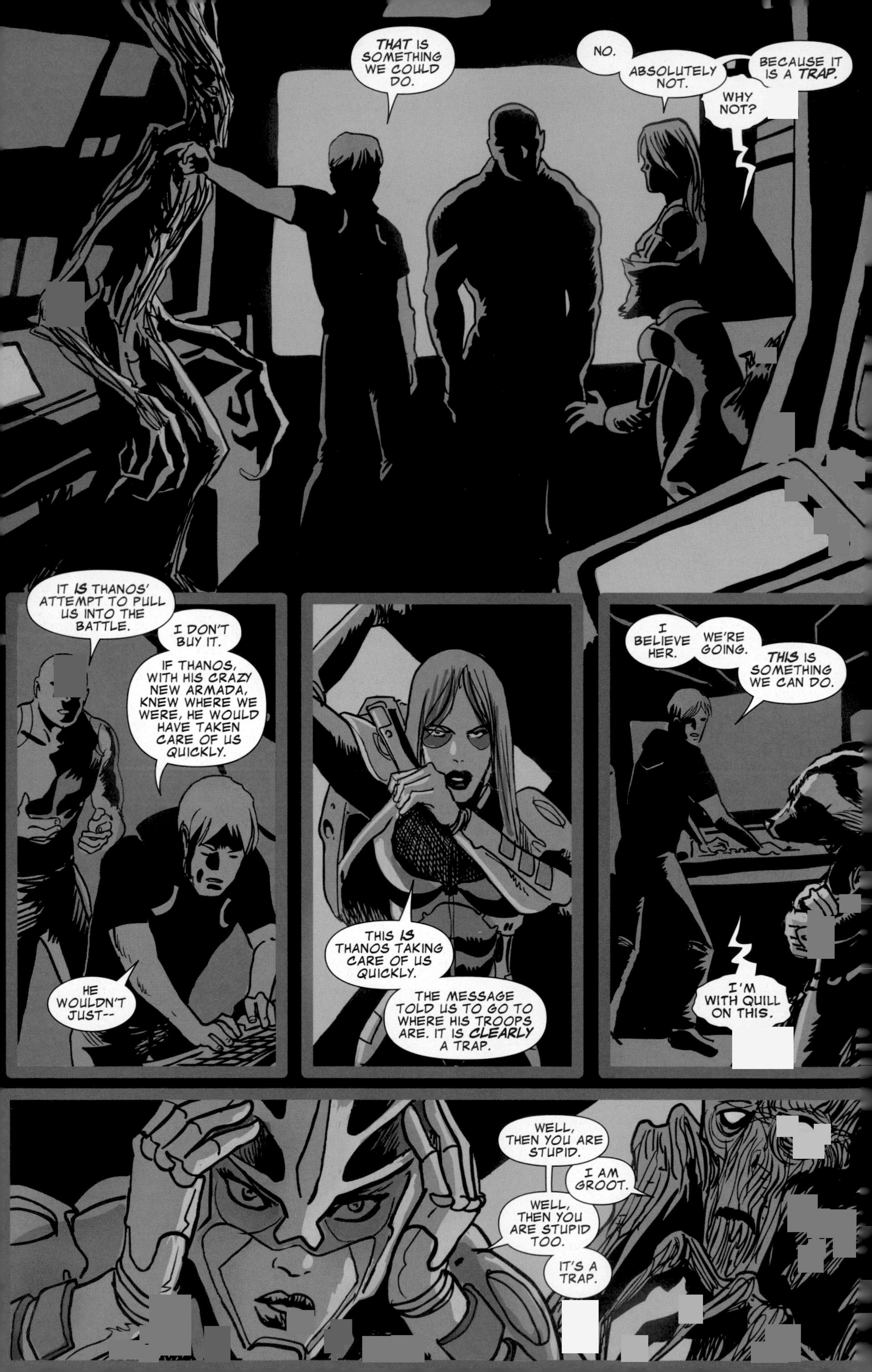
THAT IS SOMETHING WE COULD DO.
NO.
ABSOLUTELY NOT.
WHY NOT?
BECAUSE IT IS A TRAP.
IT IS THANOS' ATTEMPT TO PULL US INTO THE BATTLE.
I DON'T BUY IT.
IF THANOS, WITH HIS CRAZY NEW ARMADA, KNEW WHERE WE WERE, HE WOULD HAVE TAKEN CARE OF US QUICKLY.
HE WOULDN'T JUST--
THIS IS THANOS TAKING CARE OF US QUICKLY.
THE MESSAGE TOLD US TO GO TO WHERE HIS TROOPS ARE. IT IS CLEARLY A TRAP.
I BELIEVE HER.
WE'RE GOING.
THIS IS SOMETHING WE CAN DO.
I'M WITH QUILL ON THIS.
WELL, THEN YOU ARE STUPID.
I AM GROOT.
WELL, THEN YOU ARE STUPID TOO.
IT'S A TRAP.

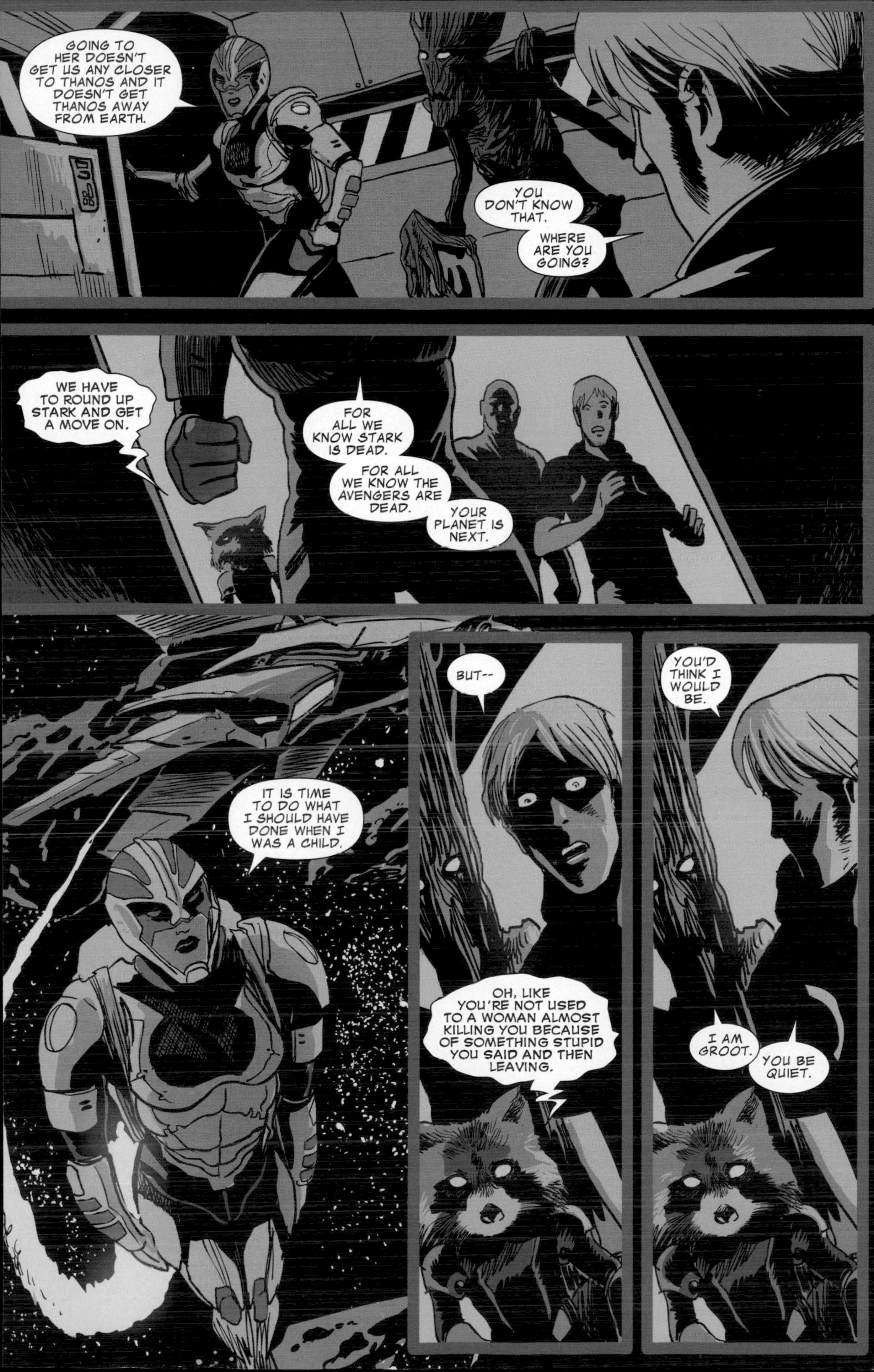
GOING TO HER DOESN'T GET US ANY CLOSER TO THANOS AND IT DOESN'T GET THANOS AWAY FROM EARTH.
YOU DON'T KNOW THAT.
WHERE ARE YOU GOING?
WE HAVE TO ROUND UP STARK AND GET A MOVE ON.
FOR ALL WE KNOW STARK IS DEAD.
FOR ALL WE KNOW THE AVENGERS ARE DEAD.
YOUR PLANET IS NEXT.
IT IS TIME TO DO WHAT I SHOULD HAVE DONE WHEN I WAS A CHILD.
BUT--
OH, LIKE YOU'RE NOT USED TO A WOMAN ALMOST KILLING YOU BECAUSE OF SOMETHING STUPID YOU SAID AND THEN LEAVING.
YOU'D THINK I WOULD BE.
I AM GROOT.
YOU BE QUIET.

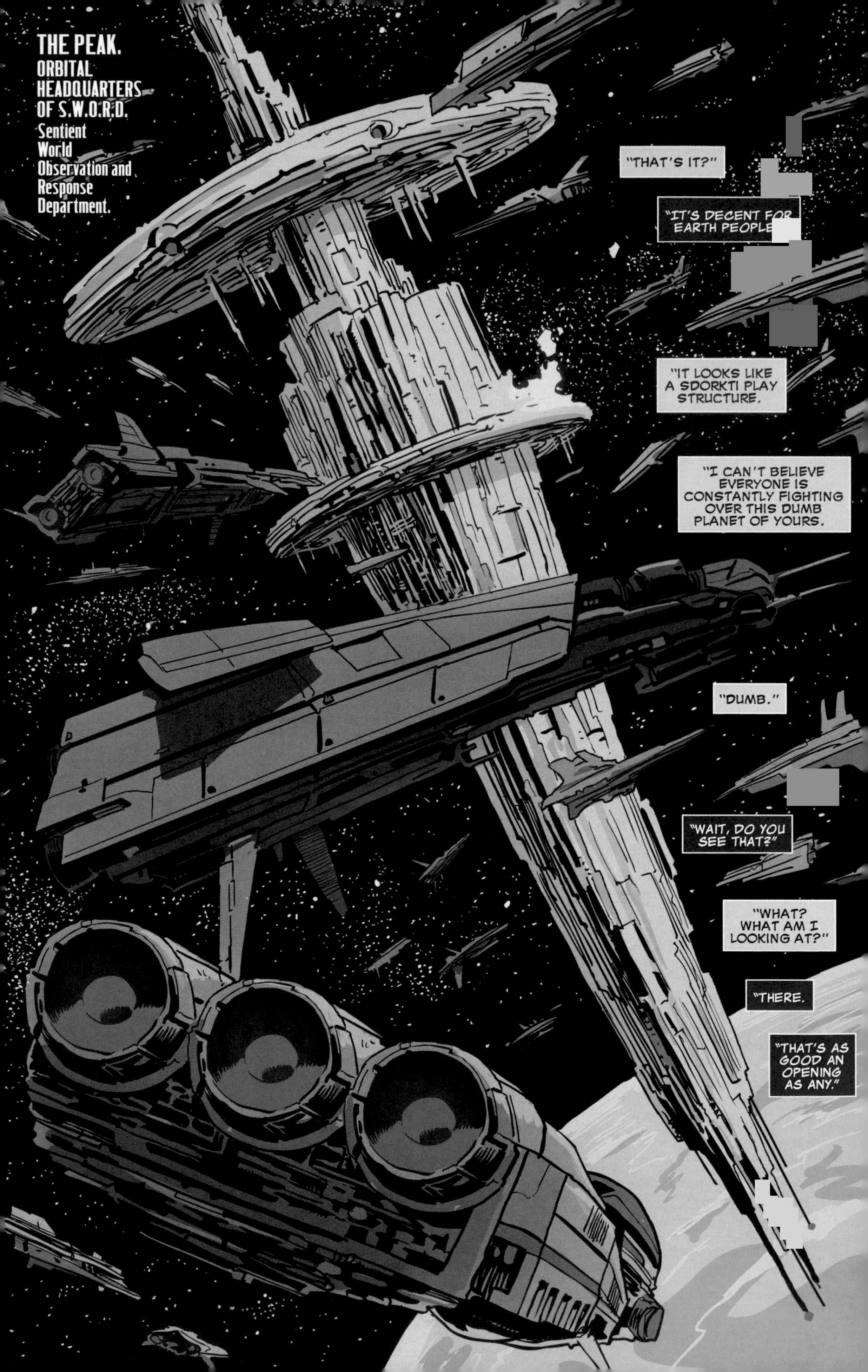
THE PEAK.
ORBITAL HEADQUARTERS OF S.W.O.R.D.
Sentient World Observation and Response Department.
"THAT'S IT?"
"IT'S DECENT FOR EARTH PEOPLE
"IT LOOKS LIKE A SDORKTI PLAY STRUCTURE.
"I CAN'T BELIEVE EVERYONE IS CONSTANTLY FIGHTING OVER THIS DUMB PLANET OF YOURS.
"DUMB."
"WAIT, DO YOU SEE THAT?"
"WHAT? WHAT AM I LOOKING AT?"
"THERE.
"THAT'S AS GOOD AN OPENING AS ANY."

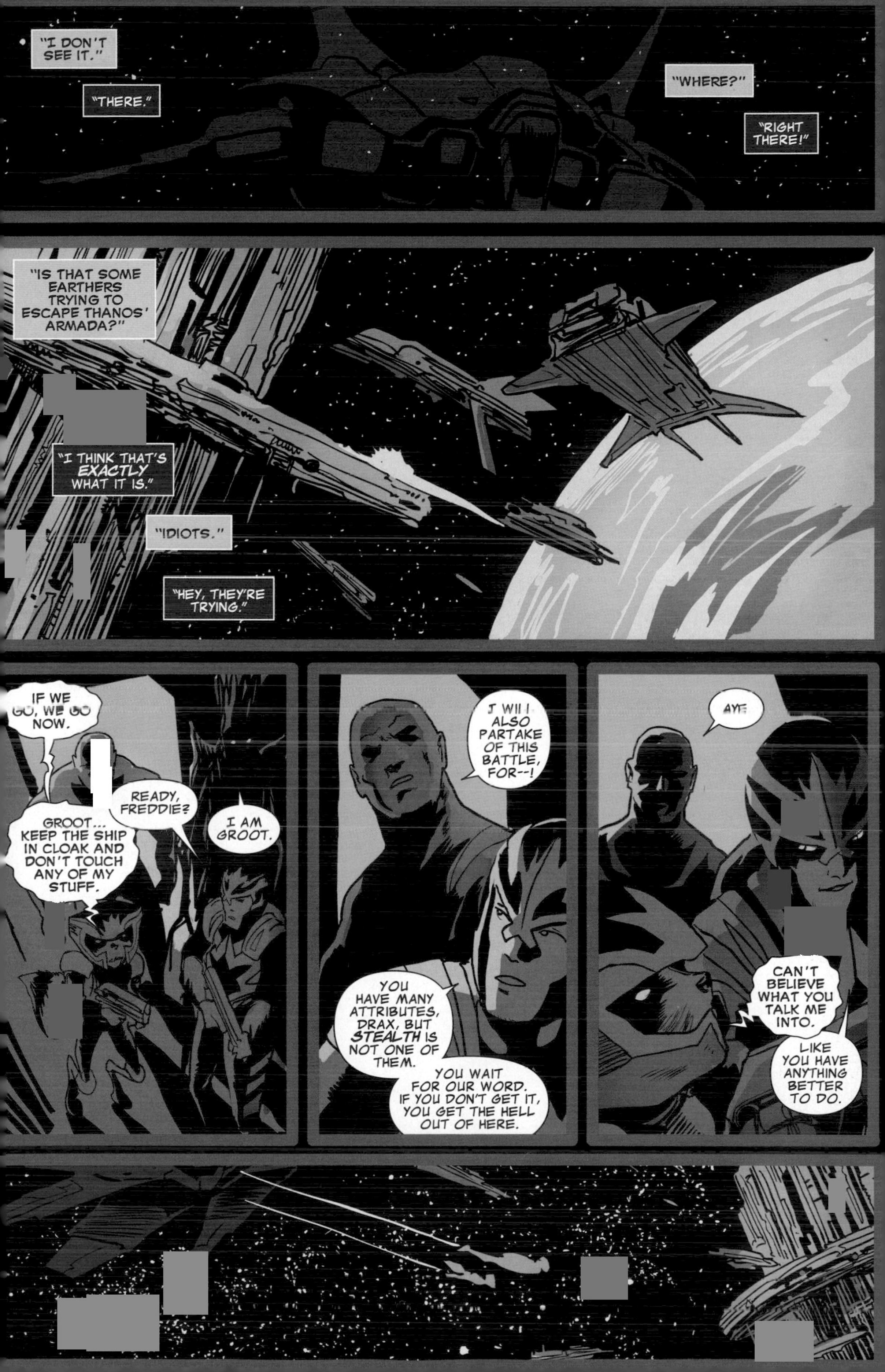
"I DON'T SEE IT."
"THERE."
"WHERE?"
"RIGHT THERE!"
"IS THAT SOME EARTHERS TRYING TO ESCAPE THANOS' ARMADA?"
"I THINK THAT'S EXACTLY WHAT IT IS."
"IDIOTS."
"HEY, THEY'RE TRYING."
IF WE GO, WE GO NOW.
READY, FREDDIE?
GROOT... KEEP THE SHIP IN CLOAK AND DON'T TOUCH ANY OF MY STUFF.
I AM GROOT.
I WILL ALSO PARTAKE OF THIS BATTLE, FOR--!
YOU HAVE MANY ATTRIBUTES, DRAX, BUT STEALTH IS NOT ONE OF THEM.
YOU WAIT FOR OUR WORD. IF YOU DON'T GET IT, YOU GET THE HELL OUT OF HERE.
AYE
CAN'T BELIEVE WHAT YOU TALK ME INTO.
LIKE YOU HAVE ANYTHING BETTER TO DO.

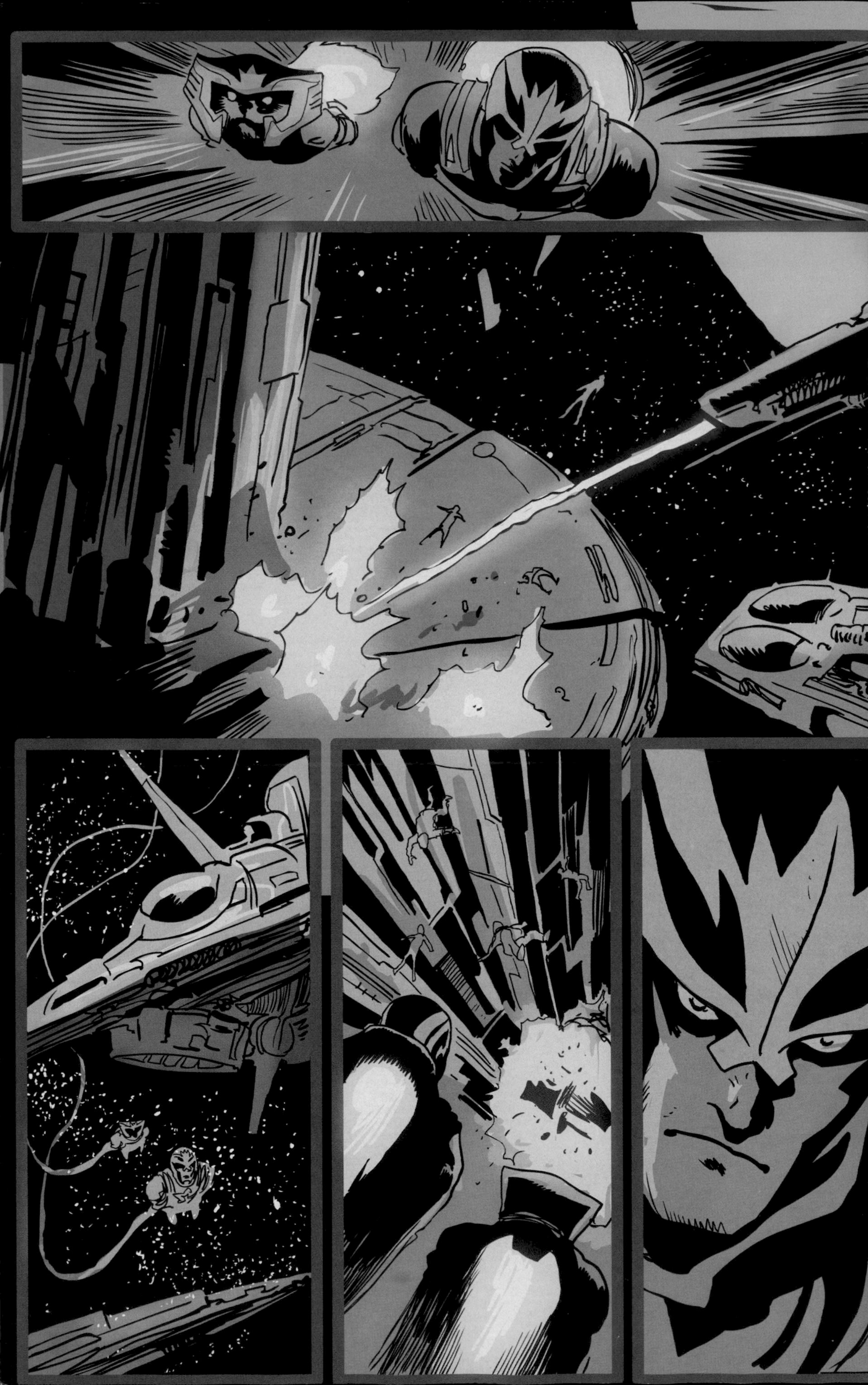

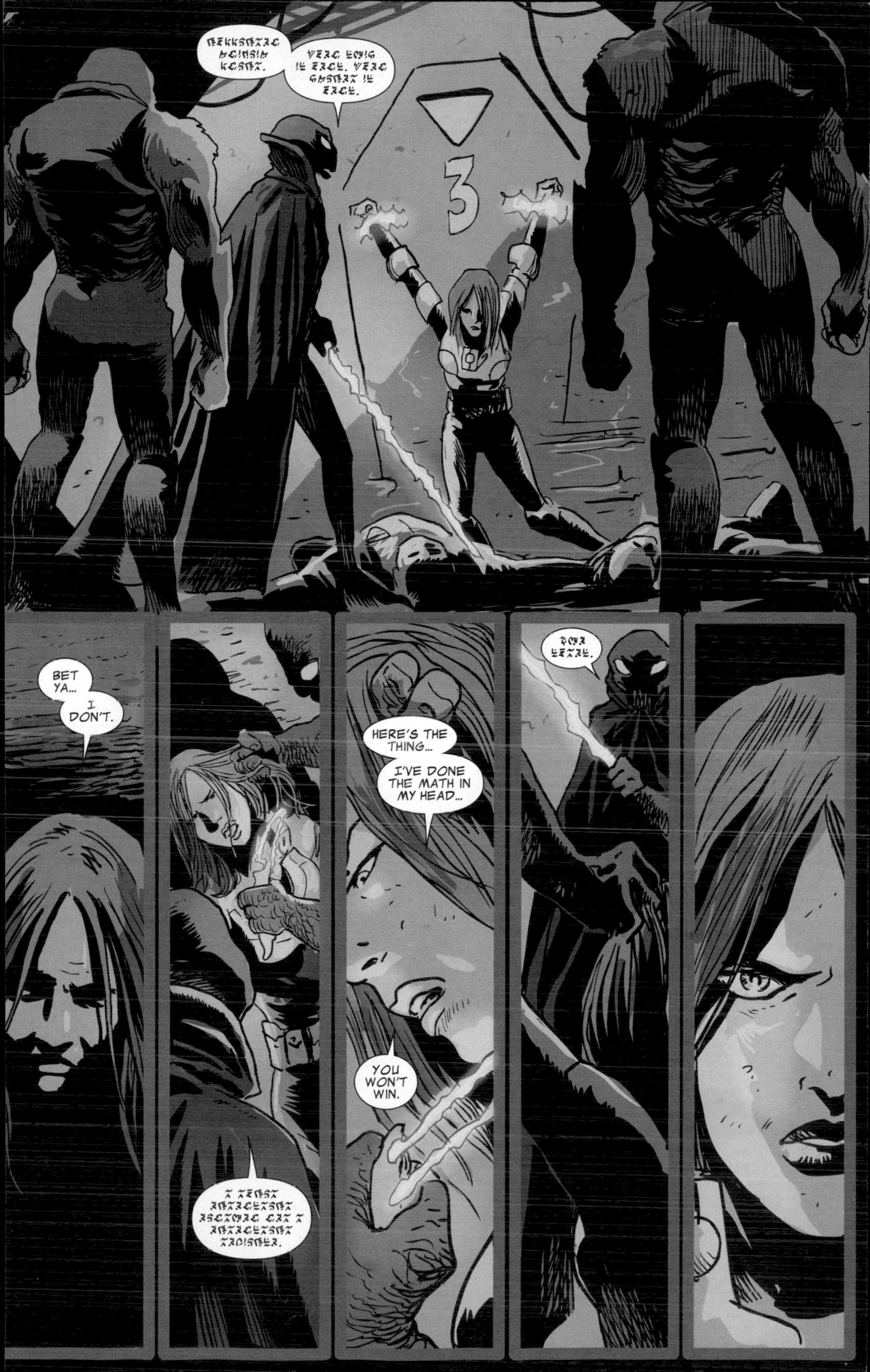
BET YA... I DON'T.
HERE'S THE THING...
I'VE DONE THE MATH IN MY HEAD...
YOU WON'T WIN.

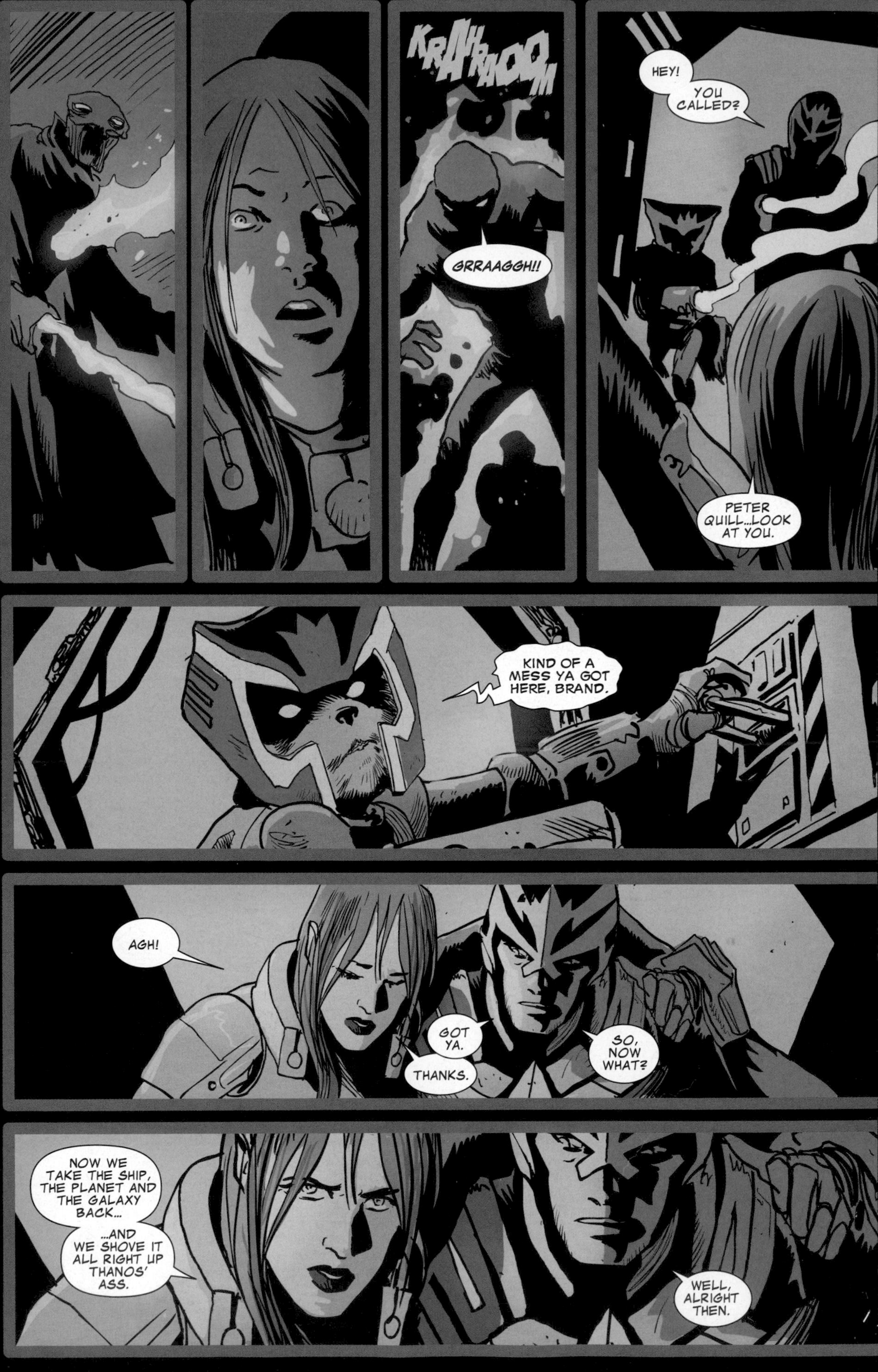
KRAHRAHOOM
GRRAAGGH!!
HEY!
YOU CALLED?
PETER QUILL...LOOK AT YOU.
KIND OF A MESS YA GOT HERE, BRAND.
AGH!
GOT YA.
THANKS.
SO, NOW WHAT?
NOW WE TAKE THE SHIP, THE PLANET AND THE GALAXY BACK...
...AND WE SHOVE IT ALL RIGHT UP THANOS' ASS.
WELL, ALRIGHT THEN.

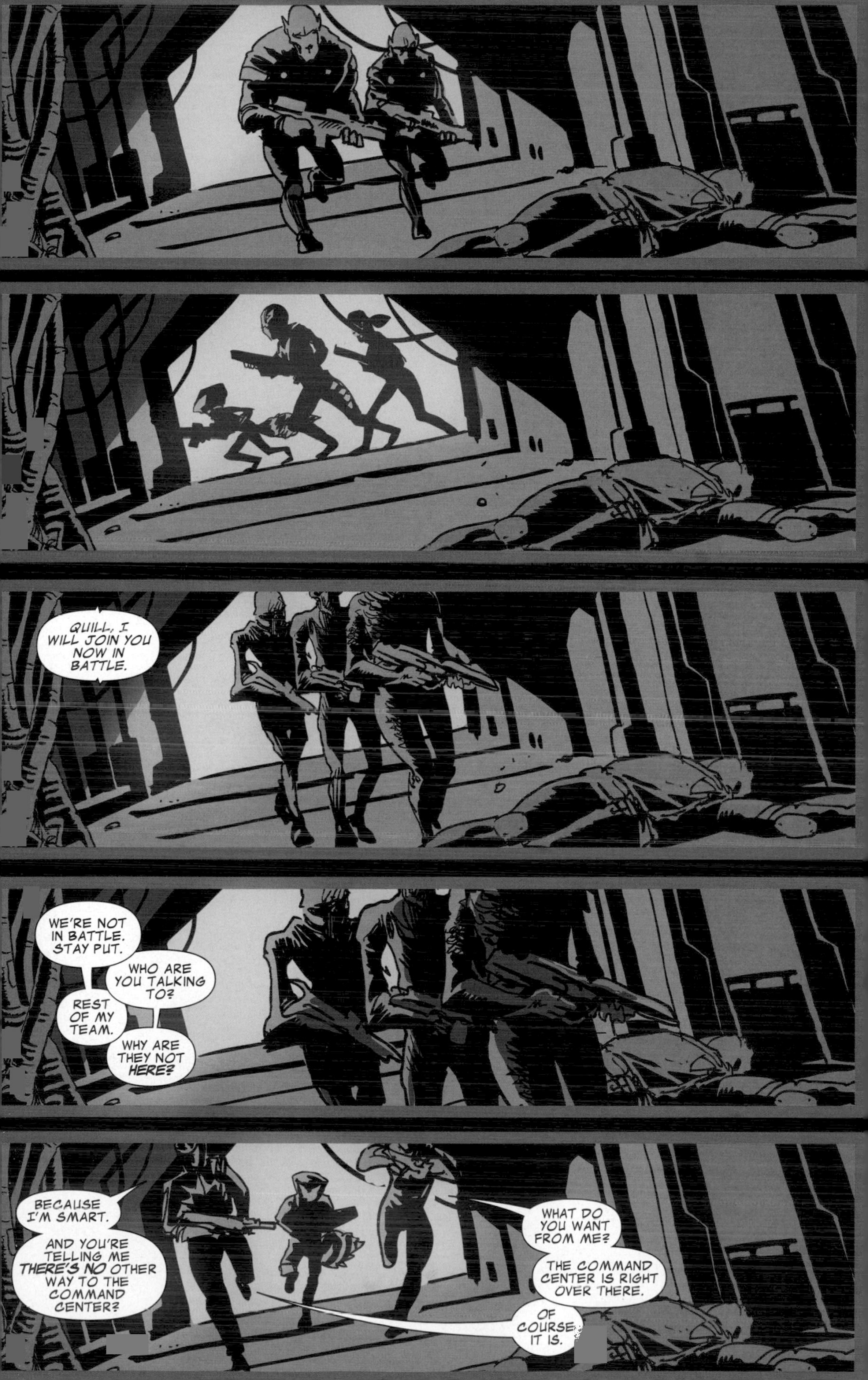
QUILL, I WILL JOIN YOU NOW IN BATTLE.
WE'RE NOT IN BATTLE. STAY PUT.
WHO ARE YOU TALKING TO?
REST OF MY TEAM.
WHY ARE THEY NOT HERE?
BECAUSE I'M SMART.
AND YOU'RE TELLING ME THERE'S NO OTHER WAY TO THE COMMAND CENTER?
WHAT DO YOU WANT FROM ME?
THE COMMAND CENTER IS RIGHT OVER THERE.
OF COURSE IT IS.

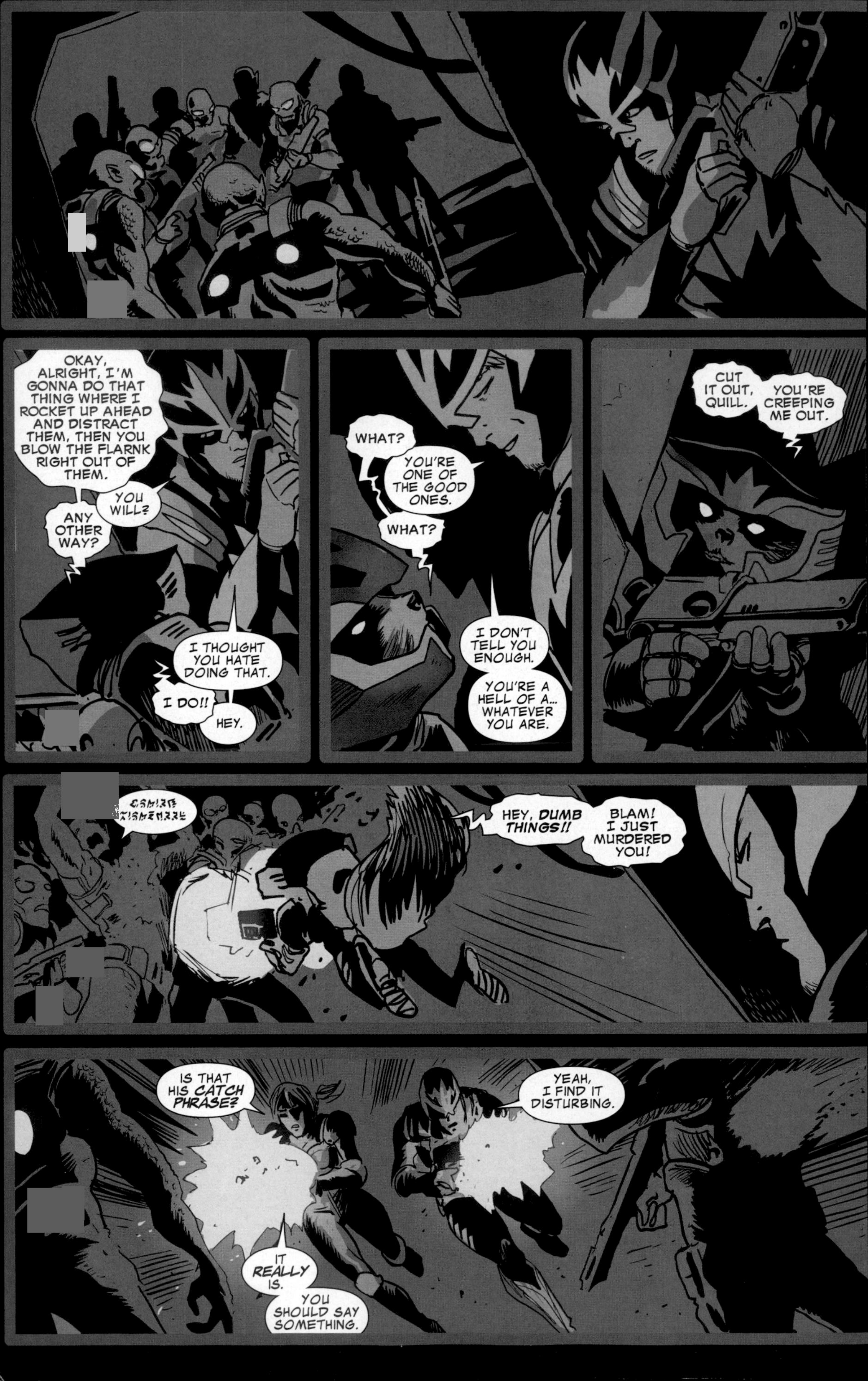
OKAY, ALRIGHT, I'M GONNA DO THAT THING WHERE I ROCKET UP AHEAD AND DISTRACT THEM, THEN YOU BLOW THE FLARNK RIGHT OUT OF THEM.
ANY OTHER WAY?
YOU WILL?
I THOUGHT YOU HATE DOING THAT.
I DO!!
HEY.
WHAT?
YOU'RE ONE OF THE GOOD ONES.
WHAT?
I DON'T TELL YOU ENOUGH.
YOU'RE A HELL OF A... WHATEVER YOU ARE.
CUT IT OUT, QUILL.
YOU'RE CREEPING ME OUT.
HEY, DUMB THINGS!!
BLAM! I JUST MURDERED YOU!
IS THAT HIS CATCH PHRASE?
YEAH, I FIND IT DISTURBING.
IT REALLY IS.
YOU SHOULD SAY SOMETHING.

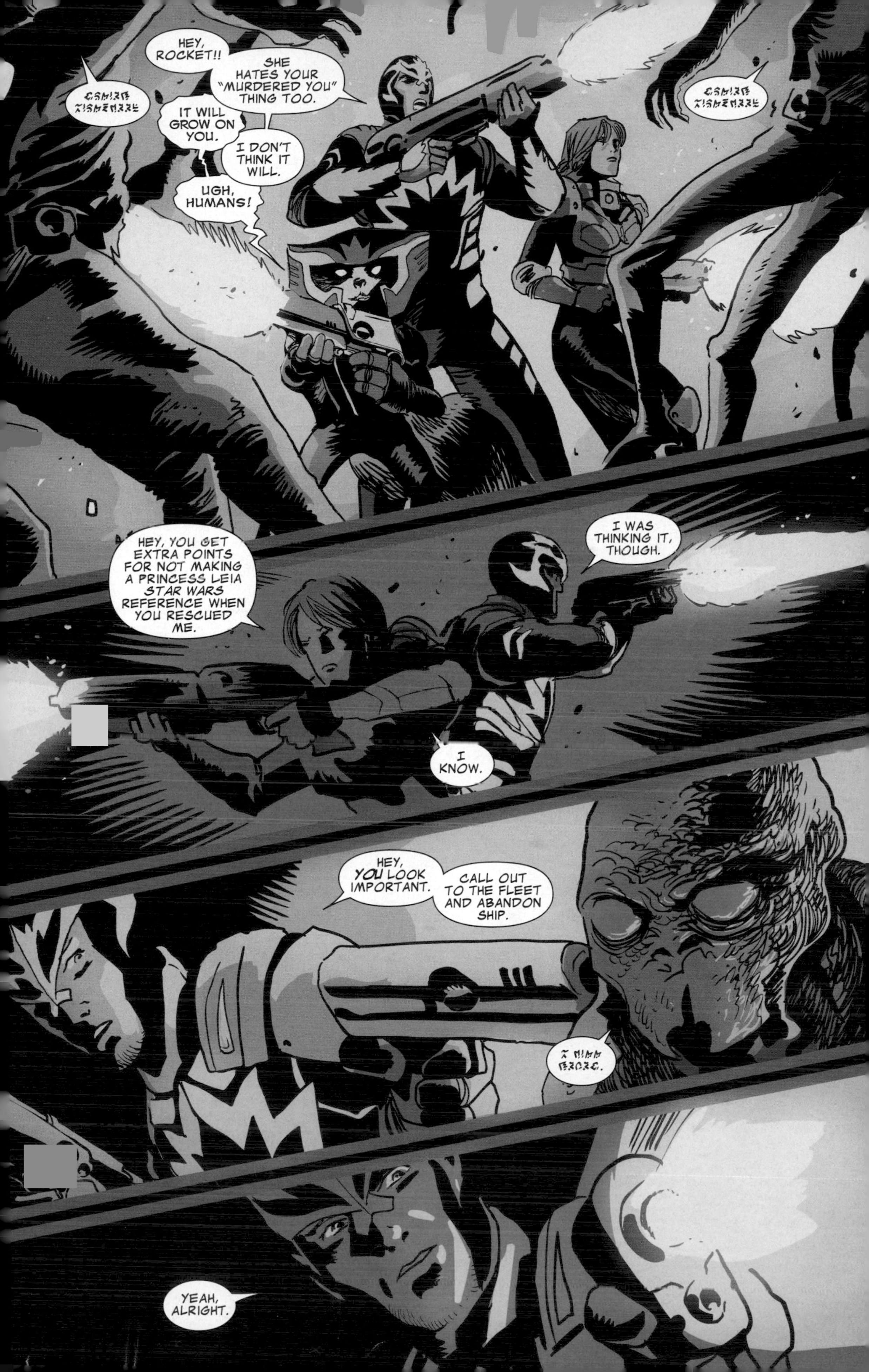
HEY, ROCKET!!
SHE HATES YOUR "MURDERED YOU" THING TOO.
IT WILL GROW ON YOU.
I DON'T THINK IT WILL.
UGH, HUMANS!
HEY, YOU GET EXTRA POINTS FOR NOT MAKING A PRINCESS LEIA STAR WARS REFERENCE WHEN YOU RESCUED ME.
I WAS THINKING IT, THOUGH.
I KNOW.
HEY, YOU LOOK IMPORTANT.
CALL OUT TO THE FLEET AND ABANDON SHIP.
YEAH, ALRIGHT.

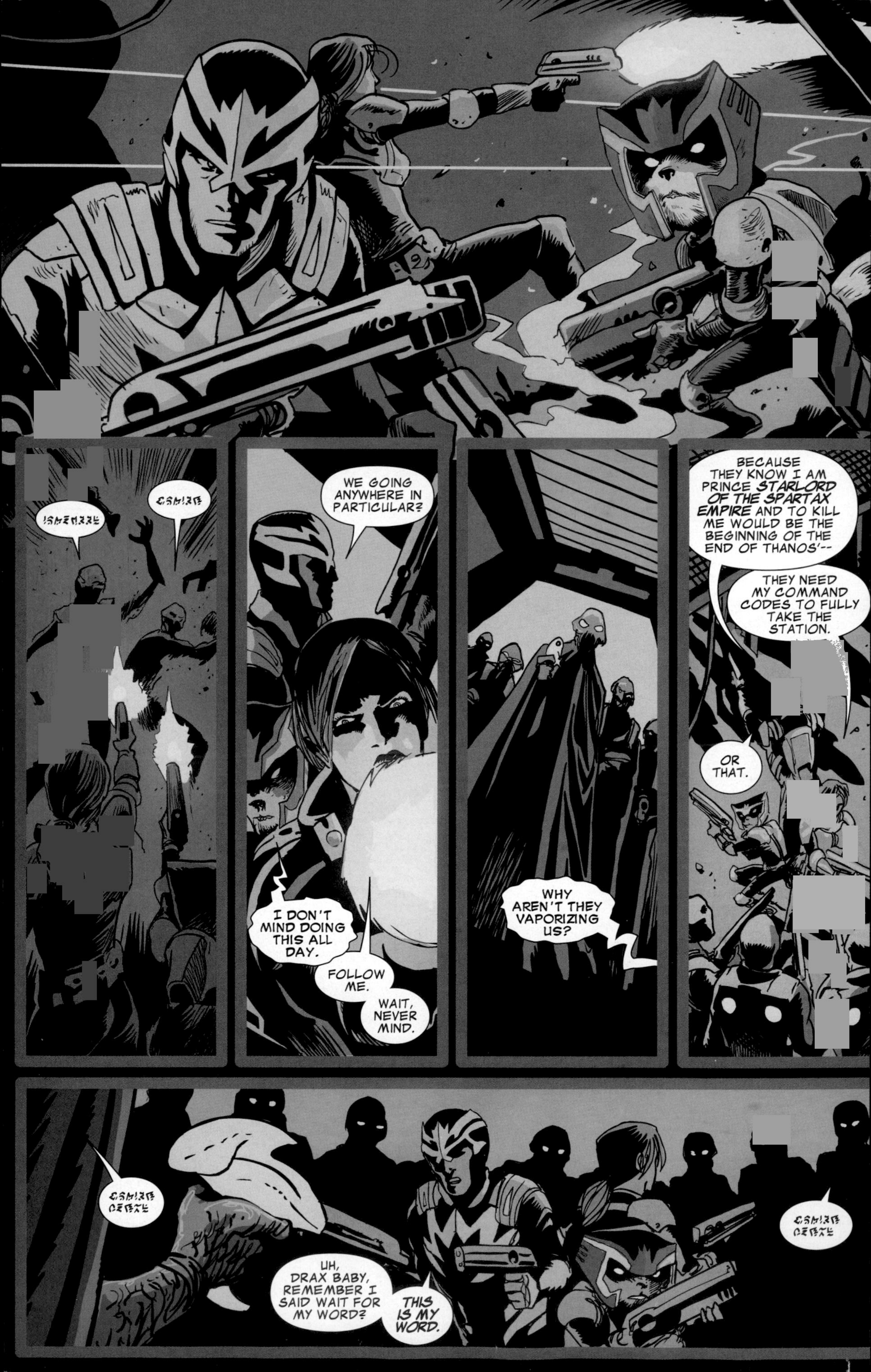
WE GOING ANYWHERE IN PARTICULAR?
I DON'T MIND DOING THIS ALL DAY.
FOLLOW ME.
WAIT, NEVER MIND.
WHY AREN'T THEY VAPORIZING US?
BECAUSE THEY KNOW I AM PRINCE STARLORD OF THE SPARTAX EMPIRE AND TO KILL ME WOULD BE THE BEGINNING OF THE END OF THANOS'--
THEY NEED MY COMMAND CODES TO FULLY TAKE THE STATION.
OR THAT.
UH, DRAX BABY, REMEMBER I SAID WAIT FOR MY WORD?
THIS IS MY WORD.

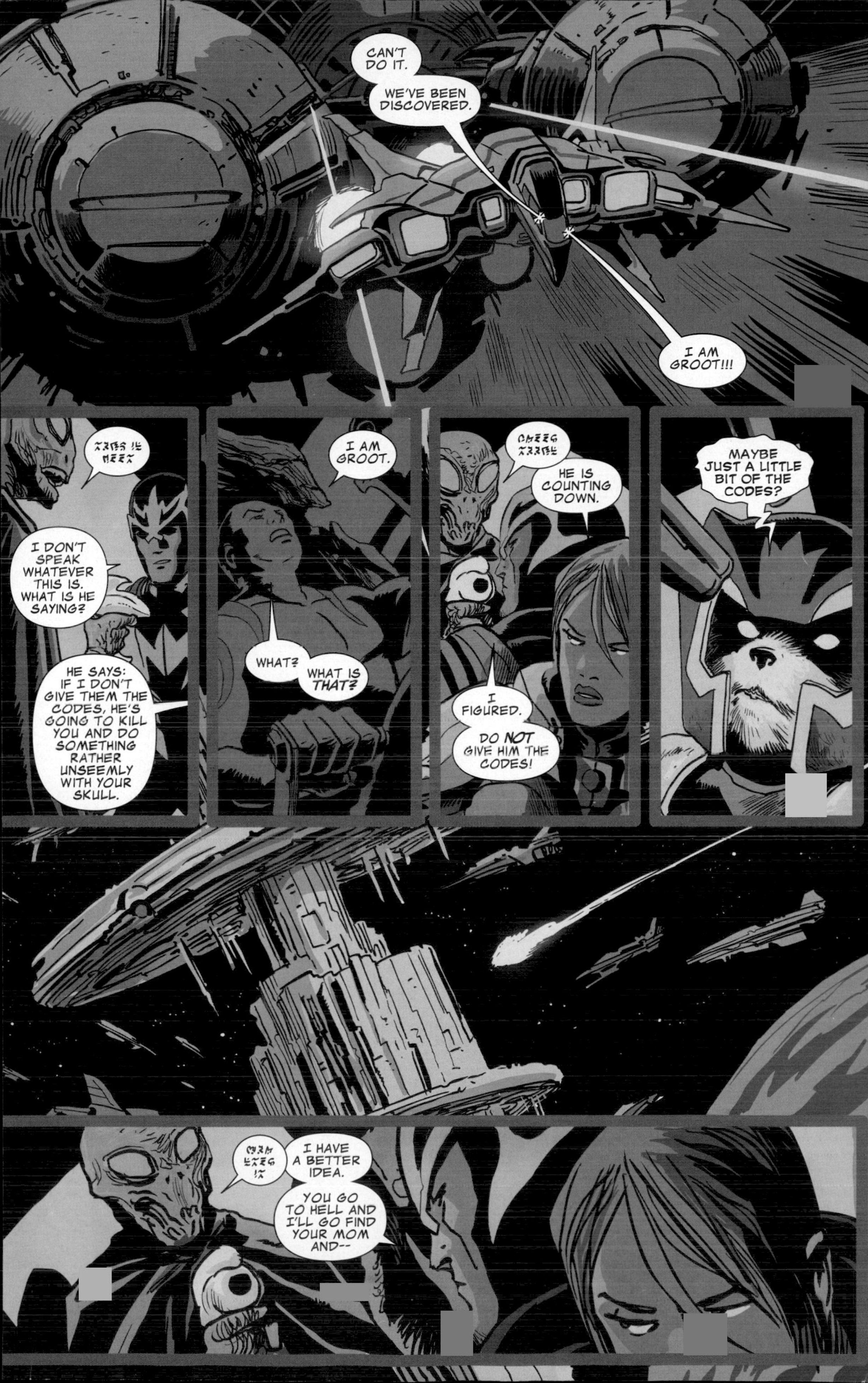

CAN'T DO IT.
WE'VE BEEN DISCOVERED.
I AM GROOT!!!
I DON'T SPEAK WHATEVER THIS IS. WHAT IS HE SAYING?
HE SAYS: IF I DON'T GIVE THEM THE CODES, HE'S GOING TO KILL YOU AND DO SOMETHING RATHER UNSEEMLY WITH YOUR SKULL.
I AM GROOT.
WHAT?
WHAT IS *THAT?*
HE IS COUNTING DOWN.
I FIGURED.
DO **NOT** GIVE HIM THE CODES!
MAYBE JUST A LITTLE BIT OF THE CODES?
I HAVE A BETTER IDEA.
YOU GO TO HELL AND I'LL GO FIND YOUR MOM AND--

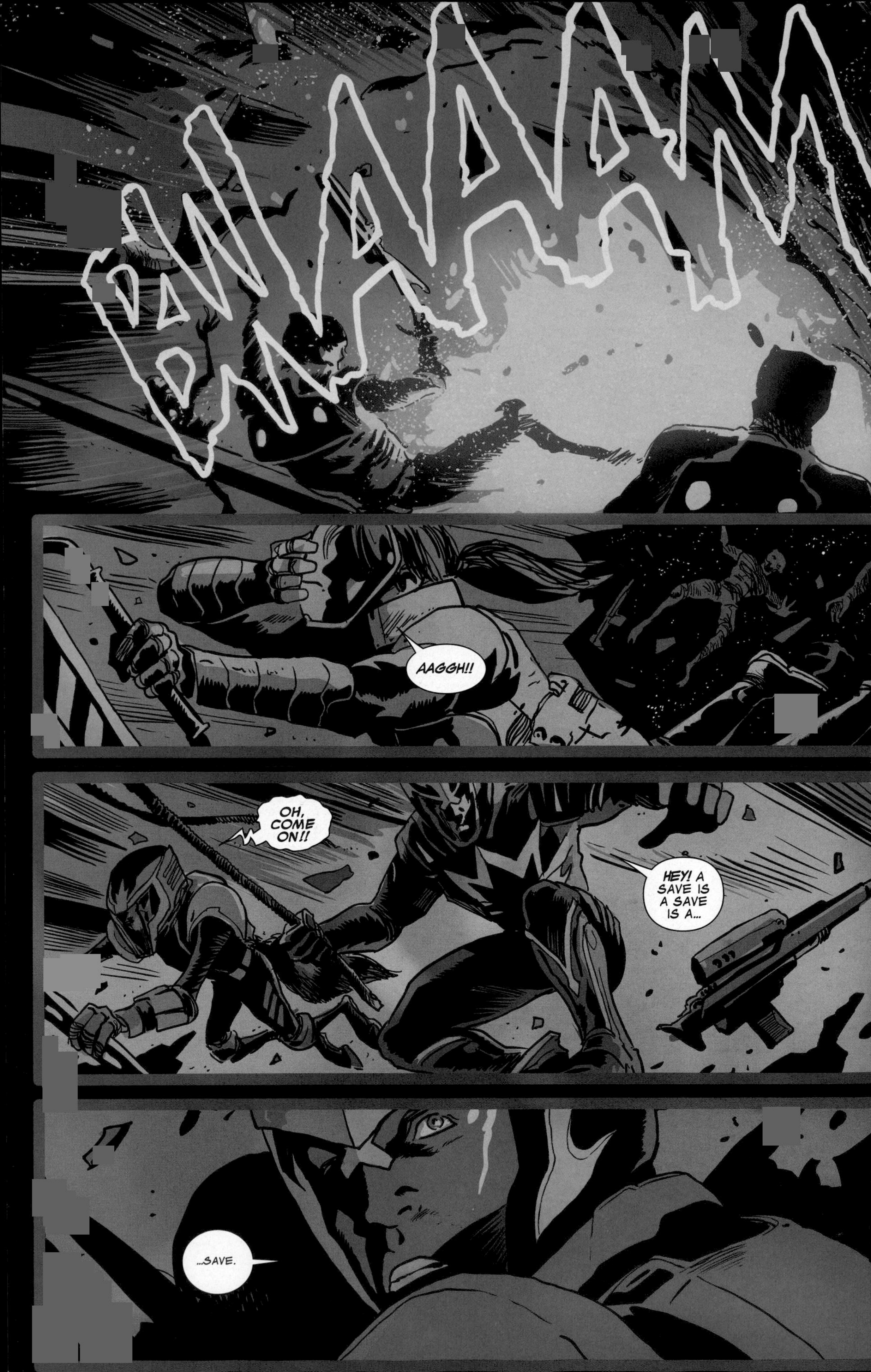
BWAAAM
AAGGH!!
OH, COME ON!!
HEY! A SAVE IS A SAVE IS A...
...SAVE.

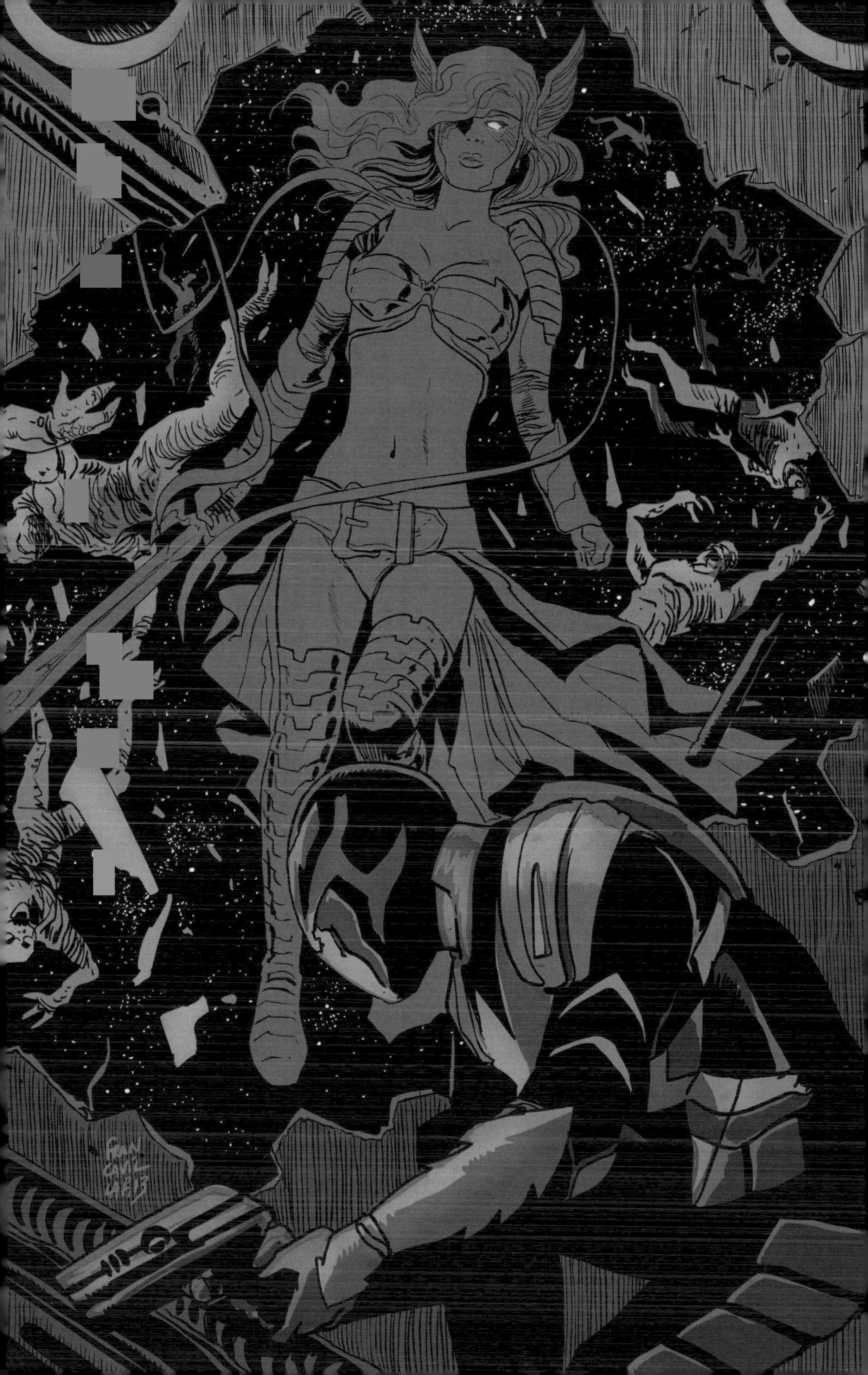

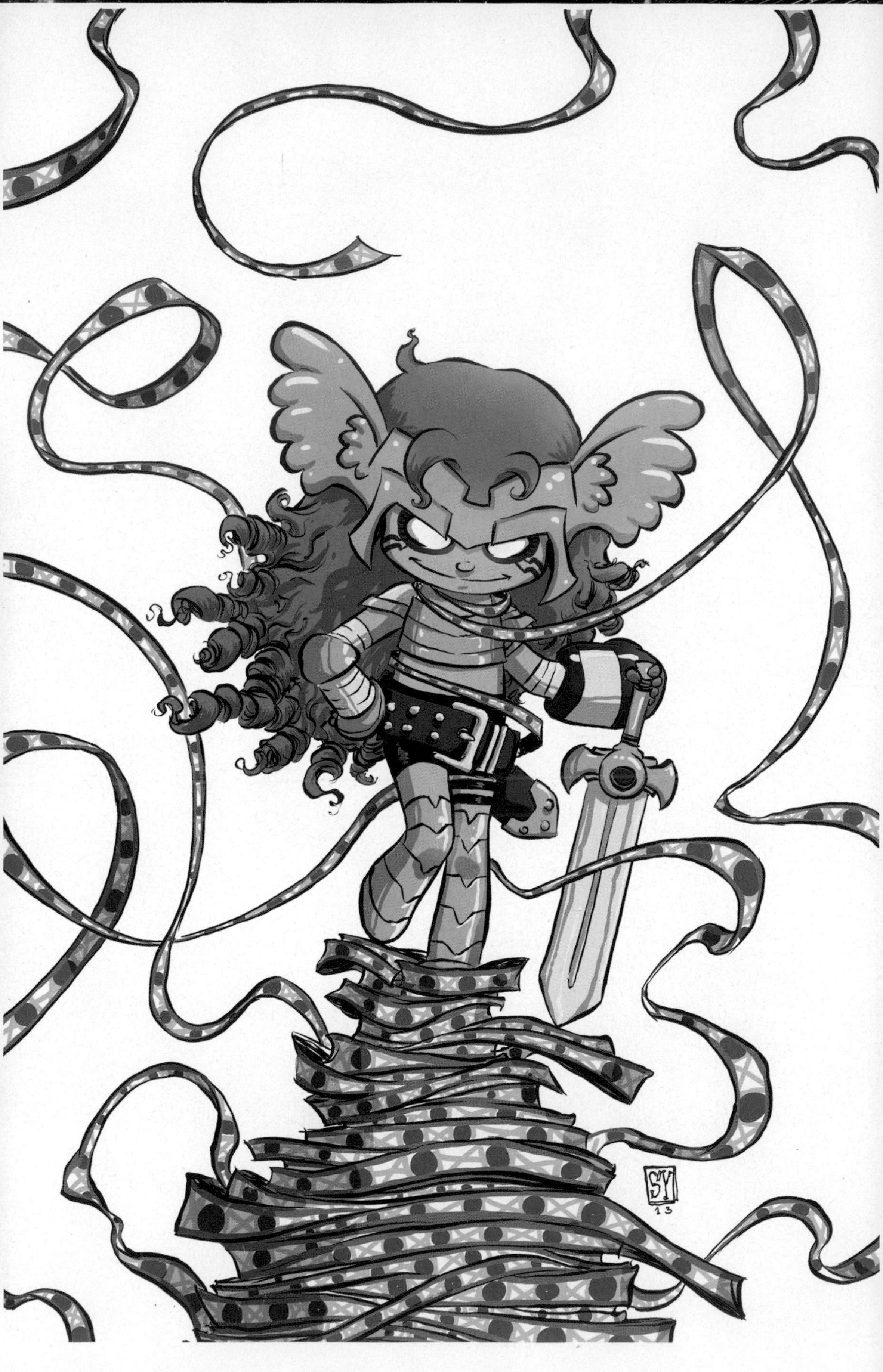
SY
13

#5 VARIANT BY SKOTTIE YOUNG

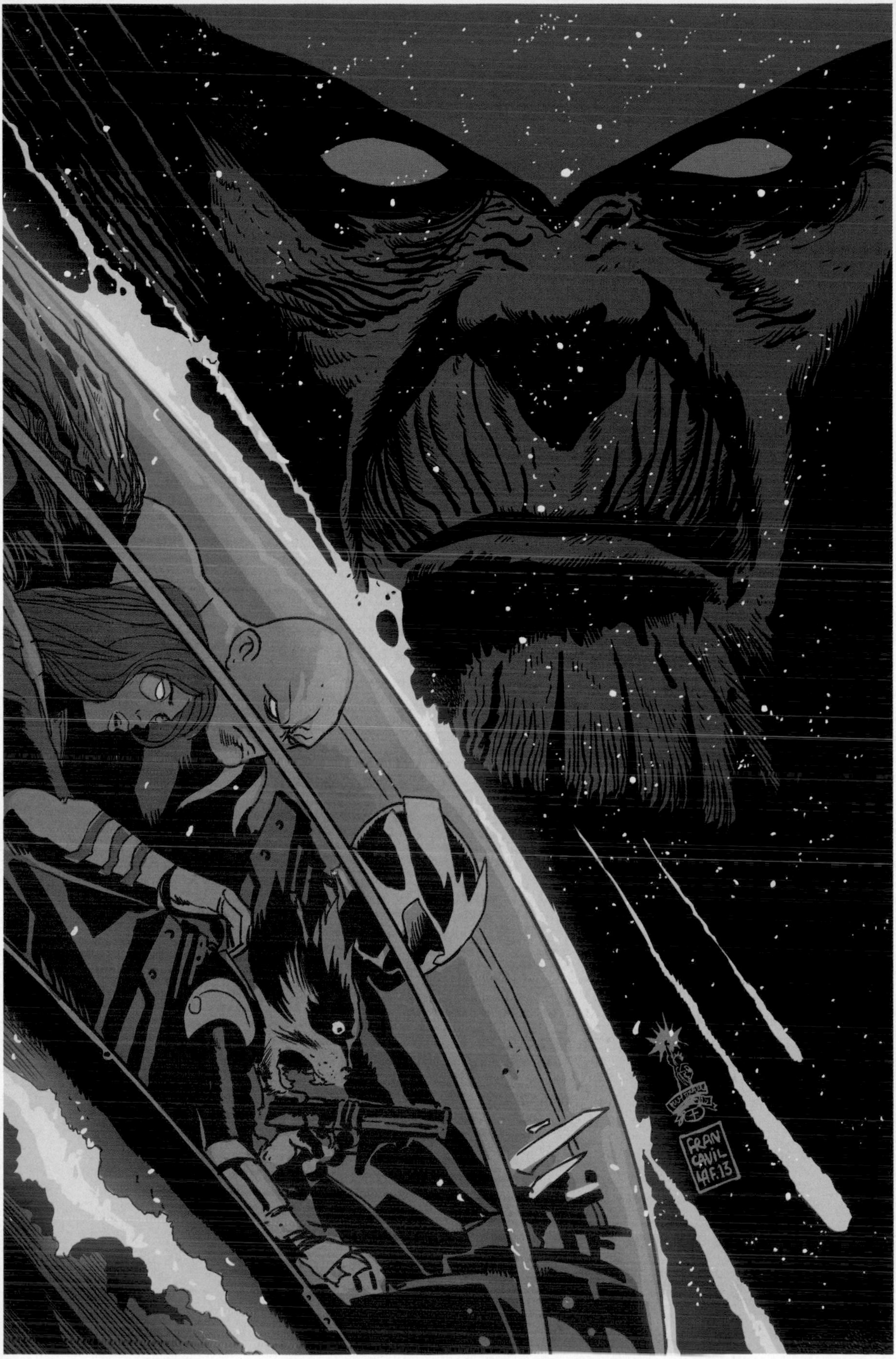

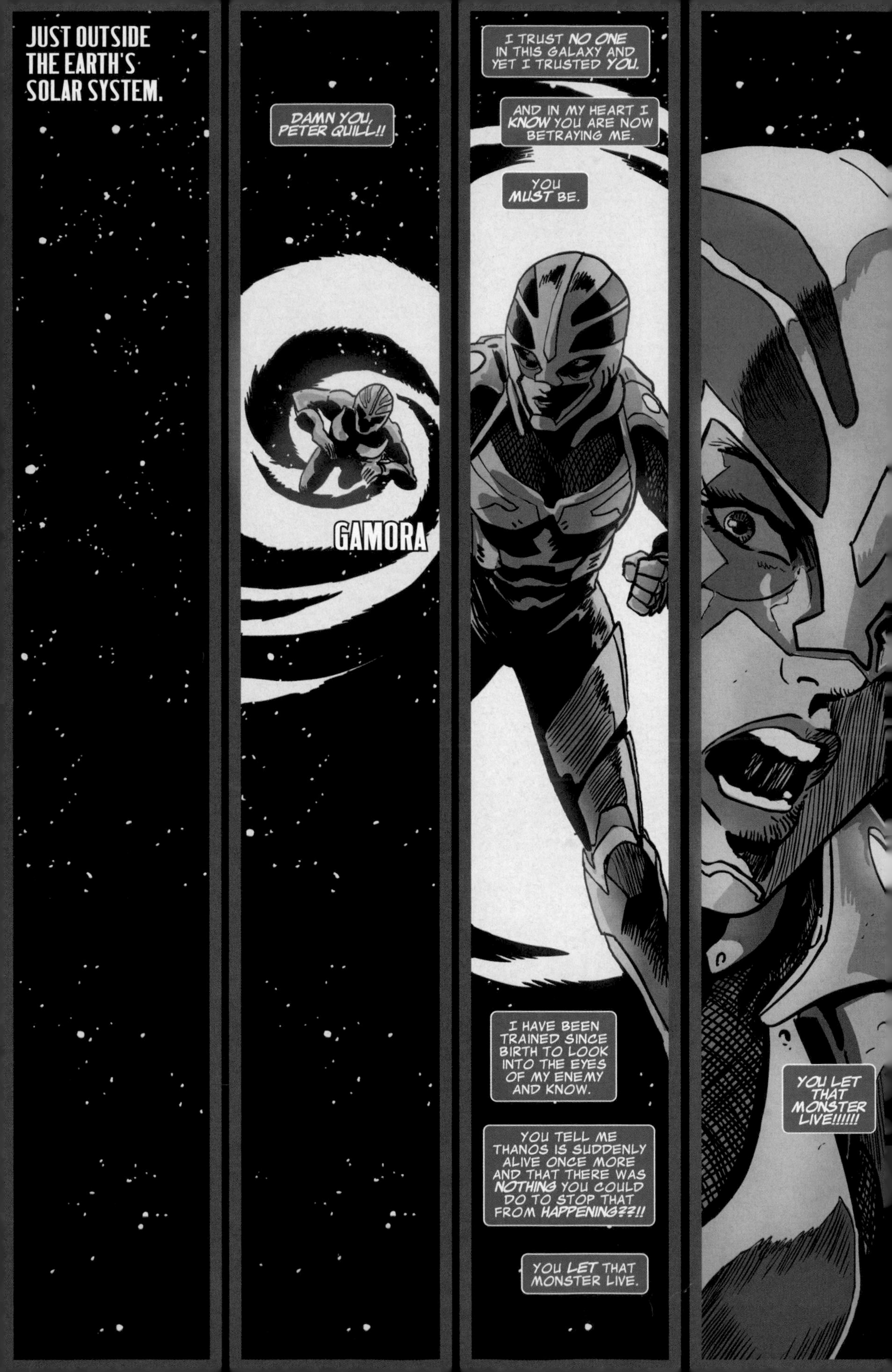
JUST OUTSIDE THE EARTH'S SOLAR SYSTEM.
DAMN YOU, PETER QUILL!!
GAMORA
I TRUST NO ONE IN THIS GALAXY AND YET I TRUSTED YOU.
AND IN MY HEART I KNOW YOU ARE NOW BETRAYING ME.
YOU MUST BE.
I HAVE BEEN TRAINED SINCE BIRTH TO LOOK INTO THE EYES OF MY ENEMY AND KNOW.
YOU TELL ME THANOS IS SUDDENLY ALIVE ONCE MORE AND THAT THERE WAS NOTHING YOU COULD DO TO STOP THAT FROM HAPPENING??!!
YOU LET THAT MONSTER LIVE.
YOU LET THAT MONSTER LIVE!!!!!!

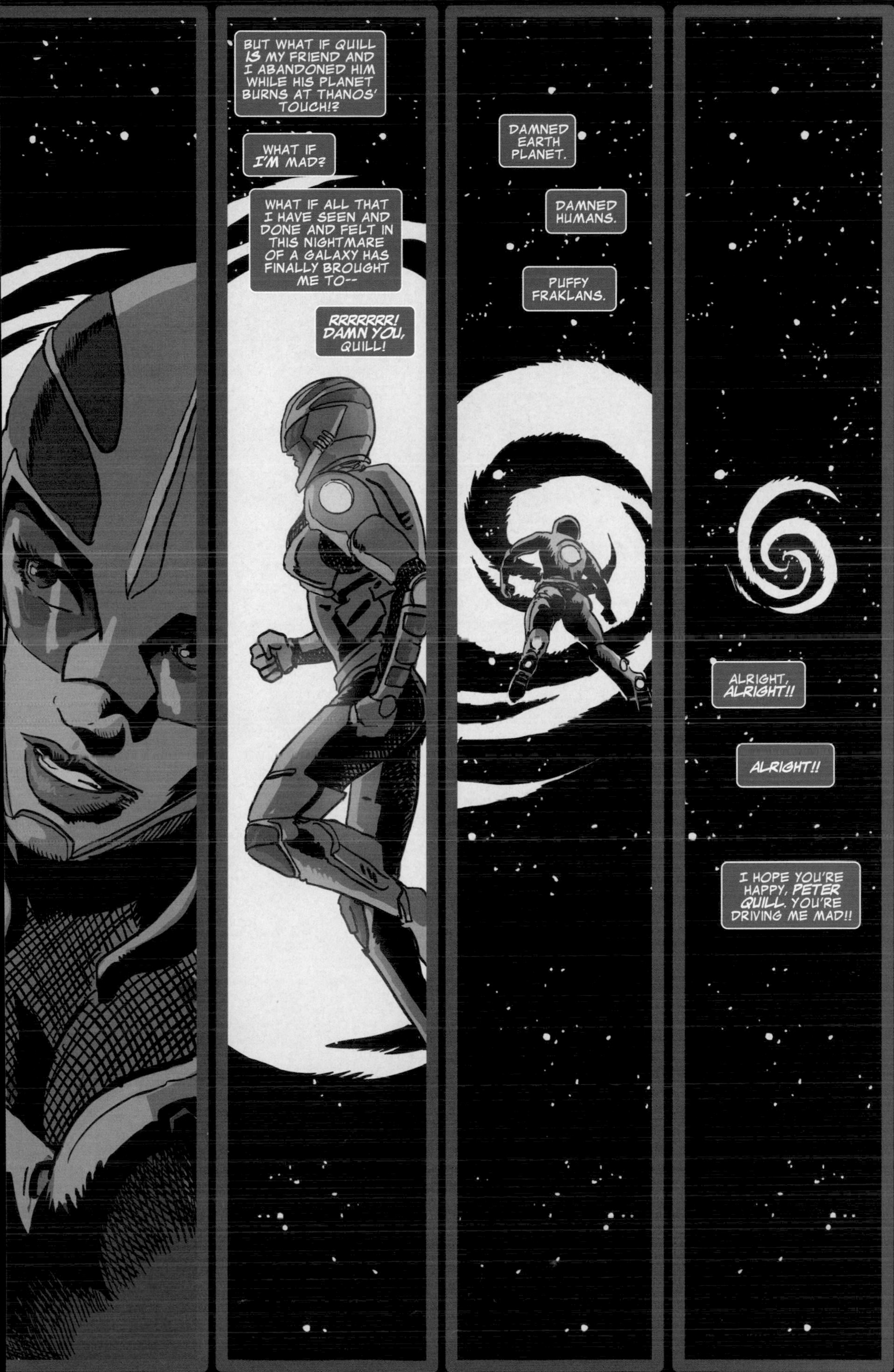

BUT WHAT IF QUILL IS MY FRIEND AND I ABANDONED HIM WHILE HIS PLANET BURNS AT THANOS' TOUCH!?
WHAT IF I'M MAD?
WHAT IF ALL THAT I HAVE SEEN AND DONE AND FELT IN THIS NIGHTMARE OF A GALAXY HAS FINALLY BROUGHT ME TO--
RRRRRRR! DAMN YOU, QUILL!
DAMNED EARTH PLANET.
DAMNED HUMANS.
PUFFY FRAKLANS.
ALRIGHT, ALRIGHT!!
ALRIGHT!!
I HOPE YOU'RE HAPPY, PETER QUILL. YOU'RE DRIVING ME MAD!!

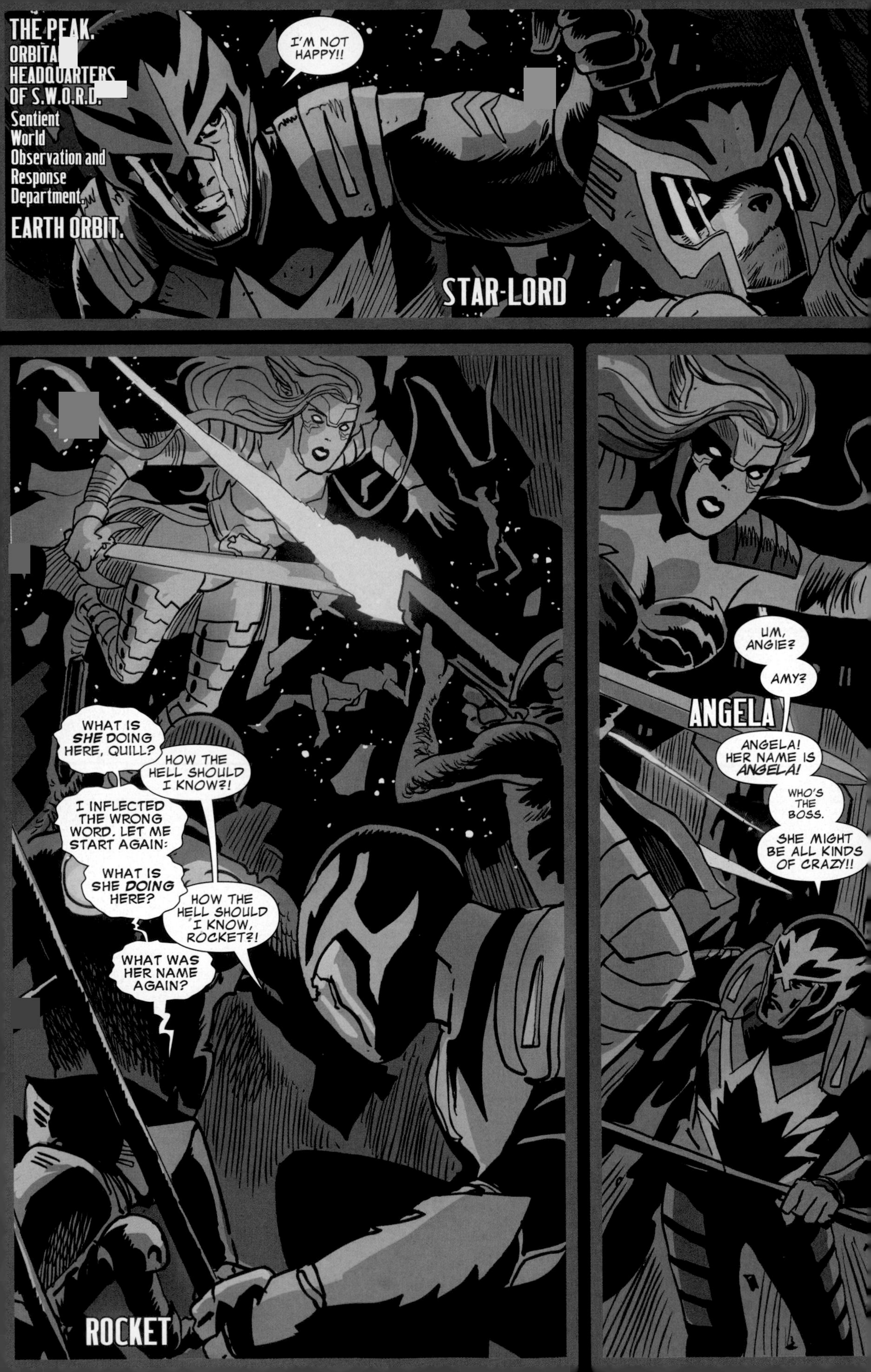

THE PEAK.
ORBITA
HEADQUARTERS
OF S.W.O.R.D.
Sentient World Observation and Response Department.
EARTH ORBIT.
I'M NOT HAPPY!!
STAR-LORD
WHAT IS SHE DOING HERE, QUILL?
HOW THE HELL SHOULD I KNOW?!
I INFLECTED THE WRONG WORD. LET ME START AGAIN:
WHAT IS SHE DOING HERE?
HOW THE HELL SHOULD I KNOW, ROCKET?!
WHAT WAS HER NAME AGAIN?
ROCKET
UM, ANGIE?
AMY?
ANGELA
ANGELA! HER NAME IS ANGELA!
WHO'S THE BOSS.
SHE MIGHT BE ALL KINDS OF CRAZY!!

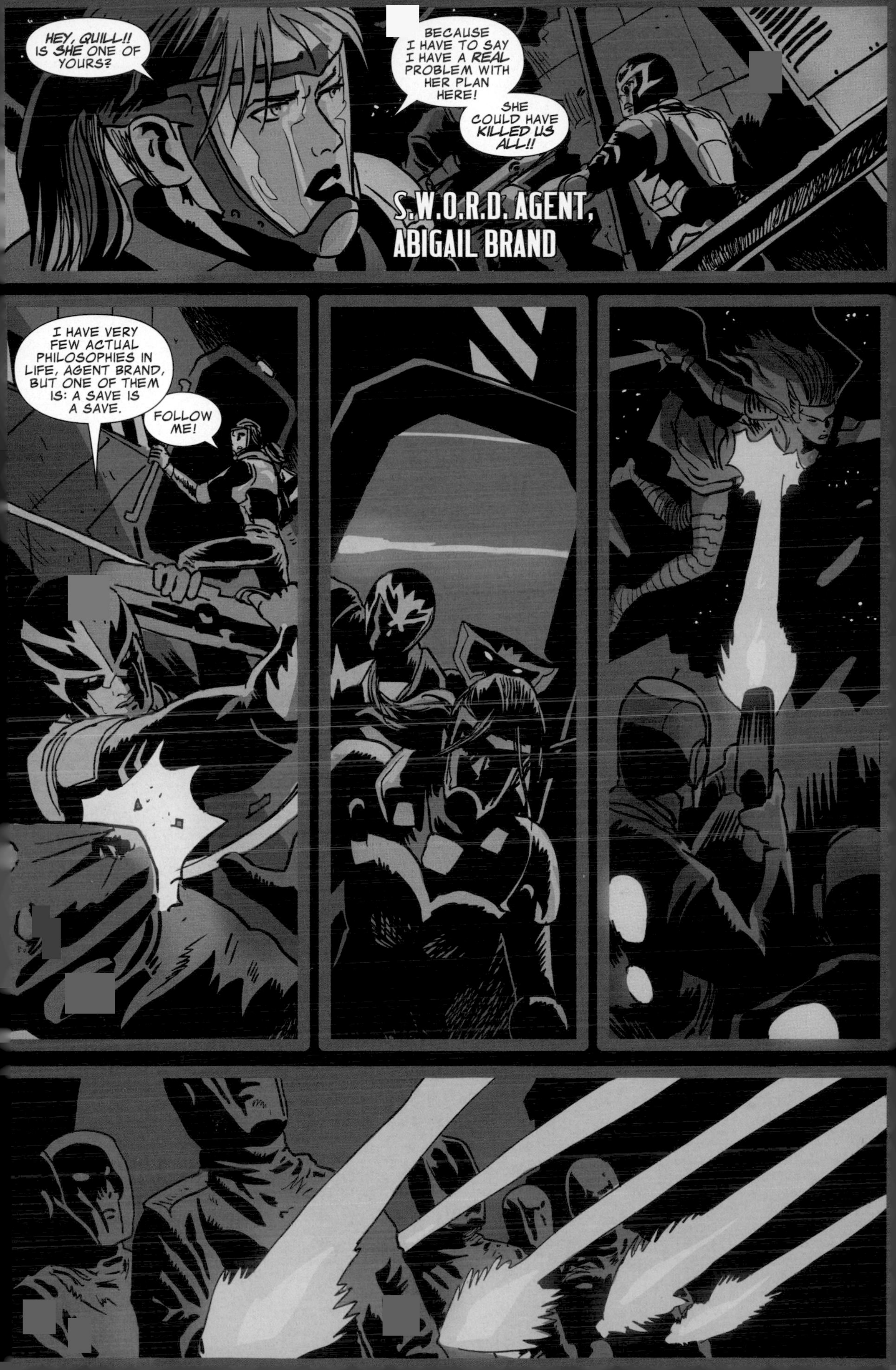
HEY, QUILL!! IS SHE ONE OF YOURS?
BECAUSE I HAVE TO SAY I HAVE A REAL PROBLEM WITH HER PLAN HERE!
SHE COULD HAVE KILLED US ALL!!
S.W.O.R.D. AGENT, ABIGAIL BRAND
I HAVE VERY FEW ACTUAL PHILOSOPHIES IN LIFE, AGENT BRAND, BUT ONE OF THEM IS: A SAVE IS A SAVE.
FOLLOW ME!

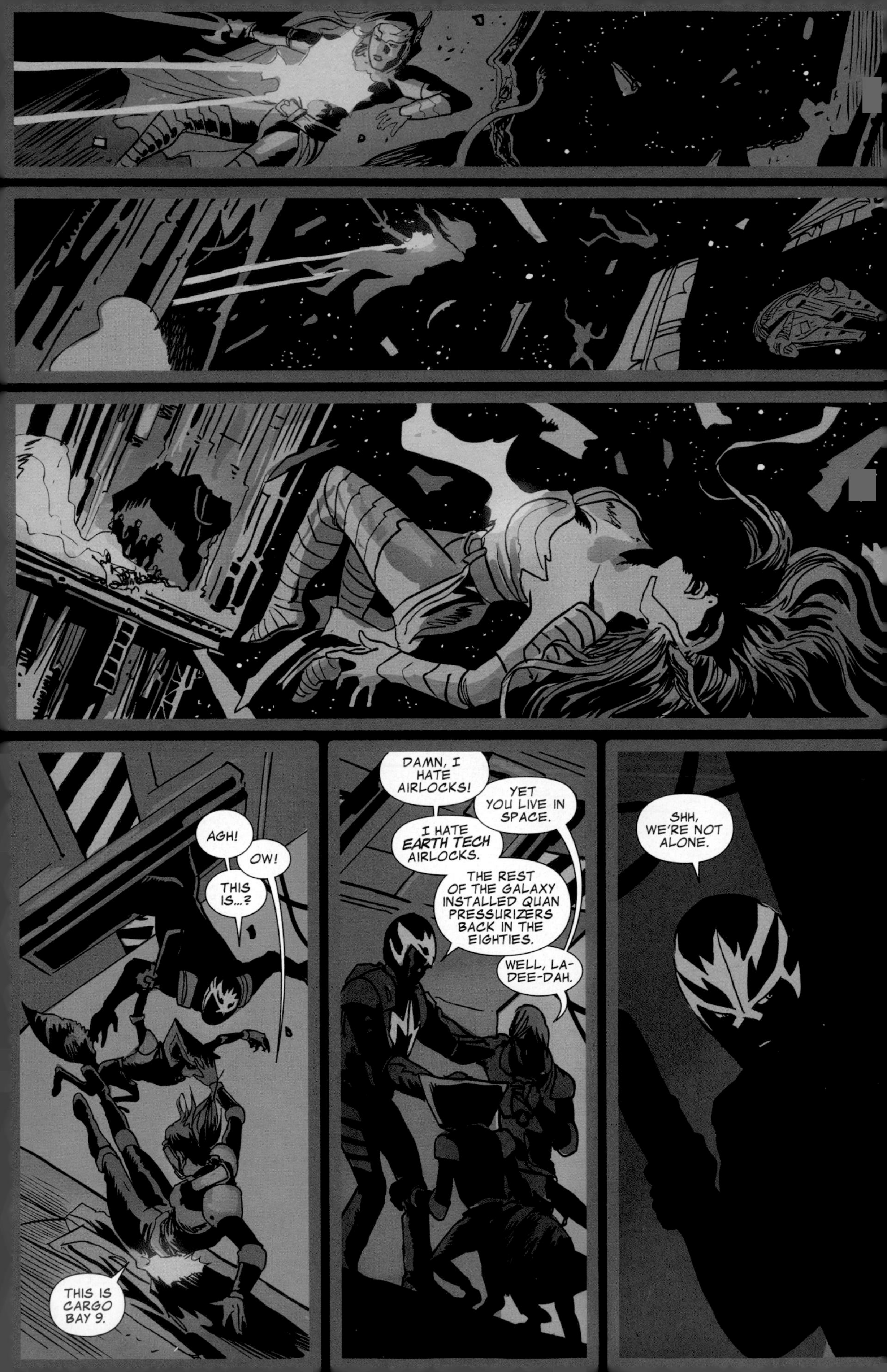

AGH!
OW!
THIS IS...?
THIS IS CARGO BAY 9.
DAMN, I HATE AIRLOCKS!
YET YOU LIVE IN SPACE.
I HATE EARTH TECH AIRLOCKS.
THE REST OF THE GALAXY INSTALLED QUAN PRESSURIZERS BACK IN THE EIGHTIES.
WELL, LA-DEE-DAH.
SHH, WE'RE NOT ALONE.

I CAN'T BELIEVE THAT CRAZY REDHEAD JUST DOVE IN OUT OF NOWHERE TO SAVE US.

THAT DOESN'T MEAN SHE'S GOING TO MARRY YOU, QUILL.

I THINK IT DOES.

SHH!! WE HAVE TO GET TO THE CONTROL ROOM.

WE HAVE TO LOWER THE EARTH DEFENSE SHIELDS SO THE AVENGERS CAN GET BACK TO EARTH.

IF THEY'RE STILL ALIVE. I HAVEN'T HEARD FROM THEM AND I'M--

ᔑᒪᓭᒷ ᔑᒲ ᓭᒷᔑ!!

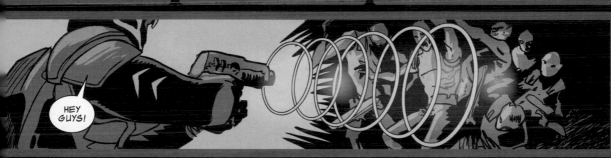

HEY GUYS!

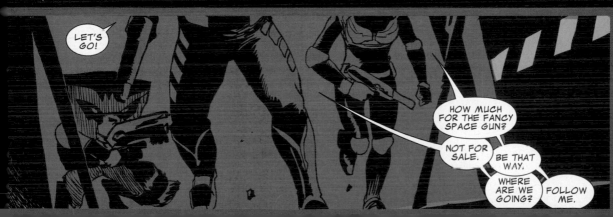

LET'S GO!

HOW MUCH FOR THE FANCY SPACE GUN?

NOT FOR SALE.

BE THAT WAY.

WHERE ARE WE GOING?

FOLLOW ME.

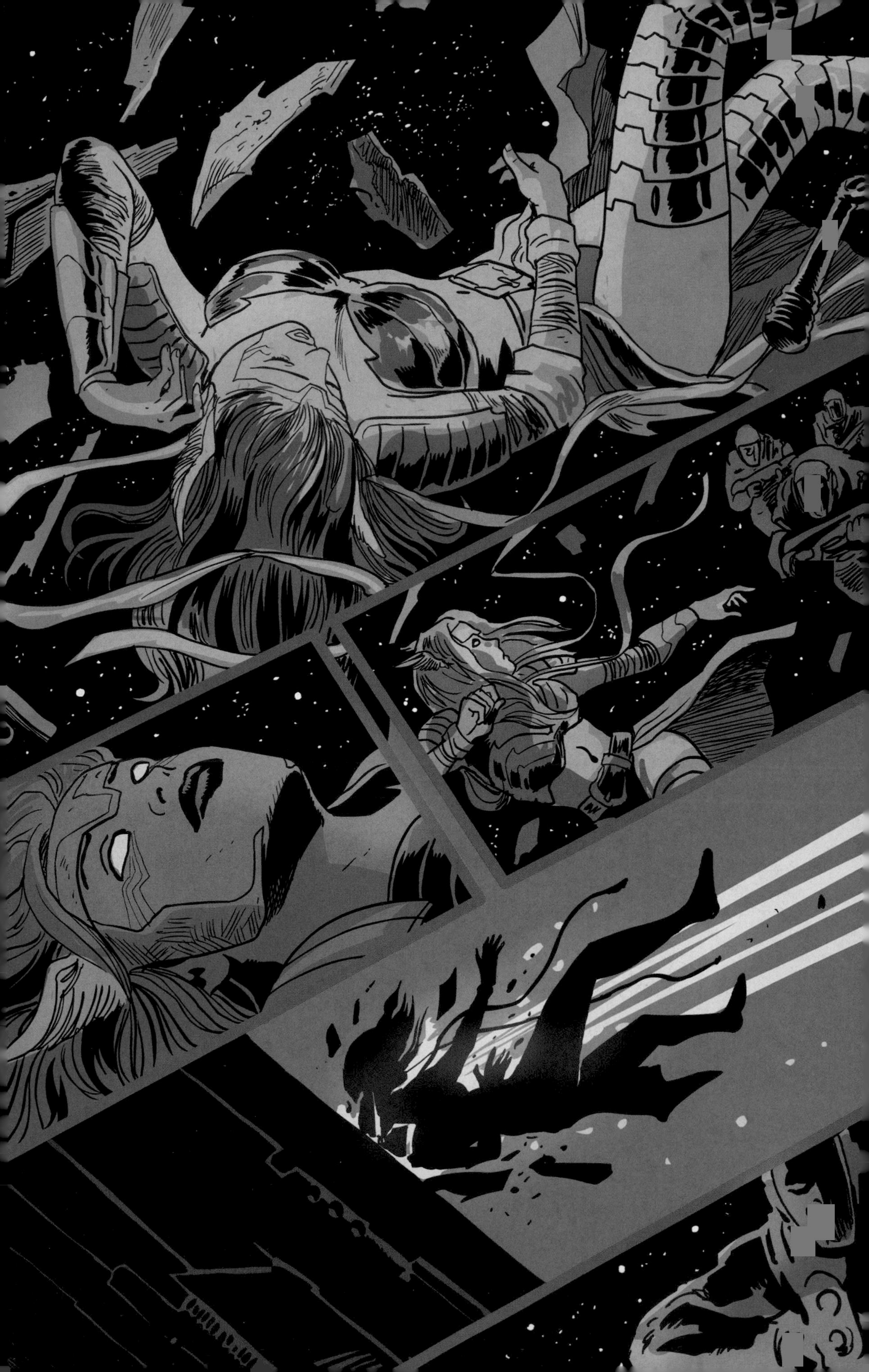

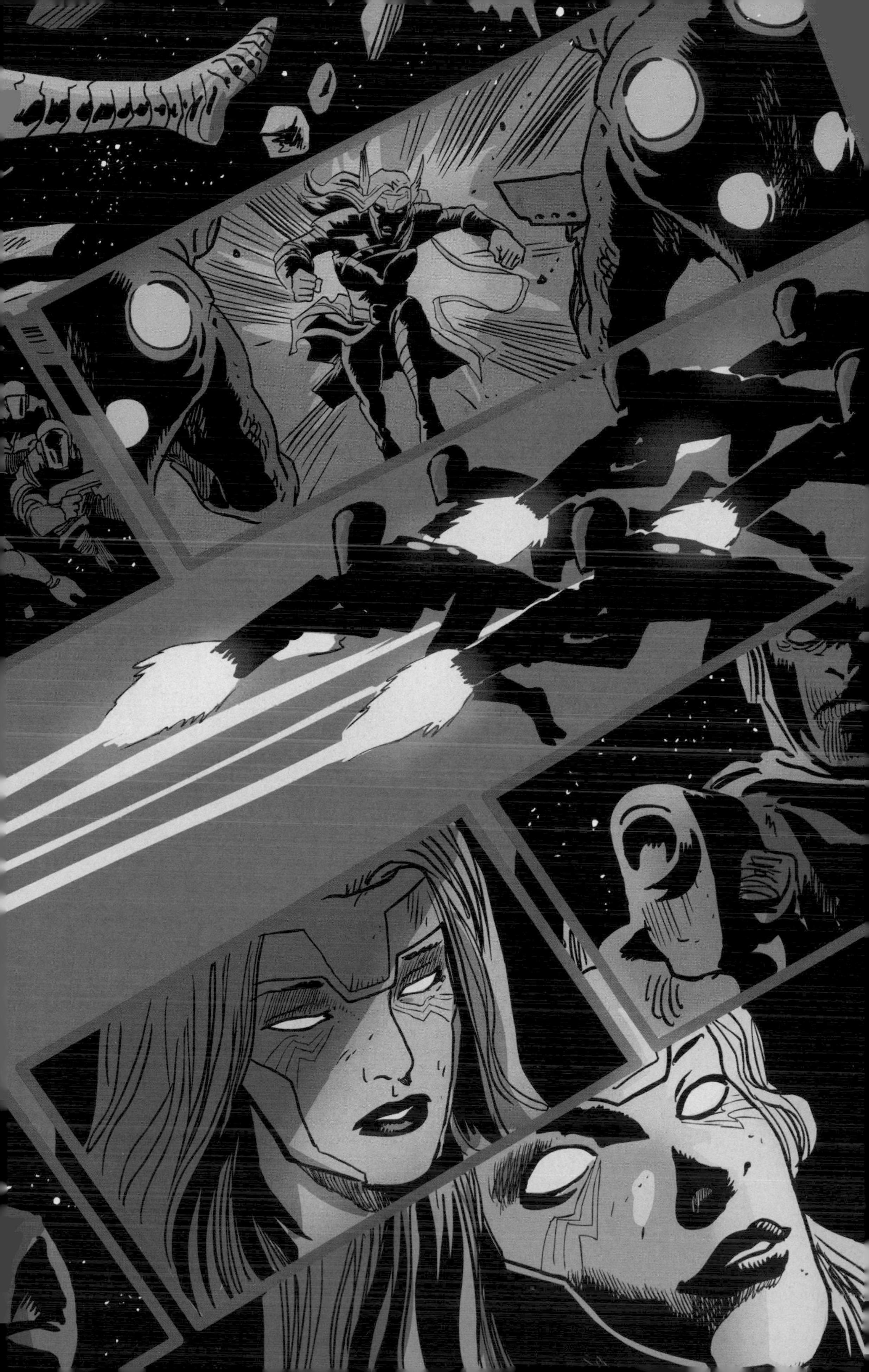

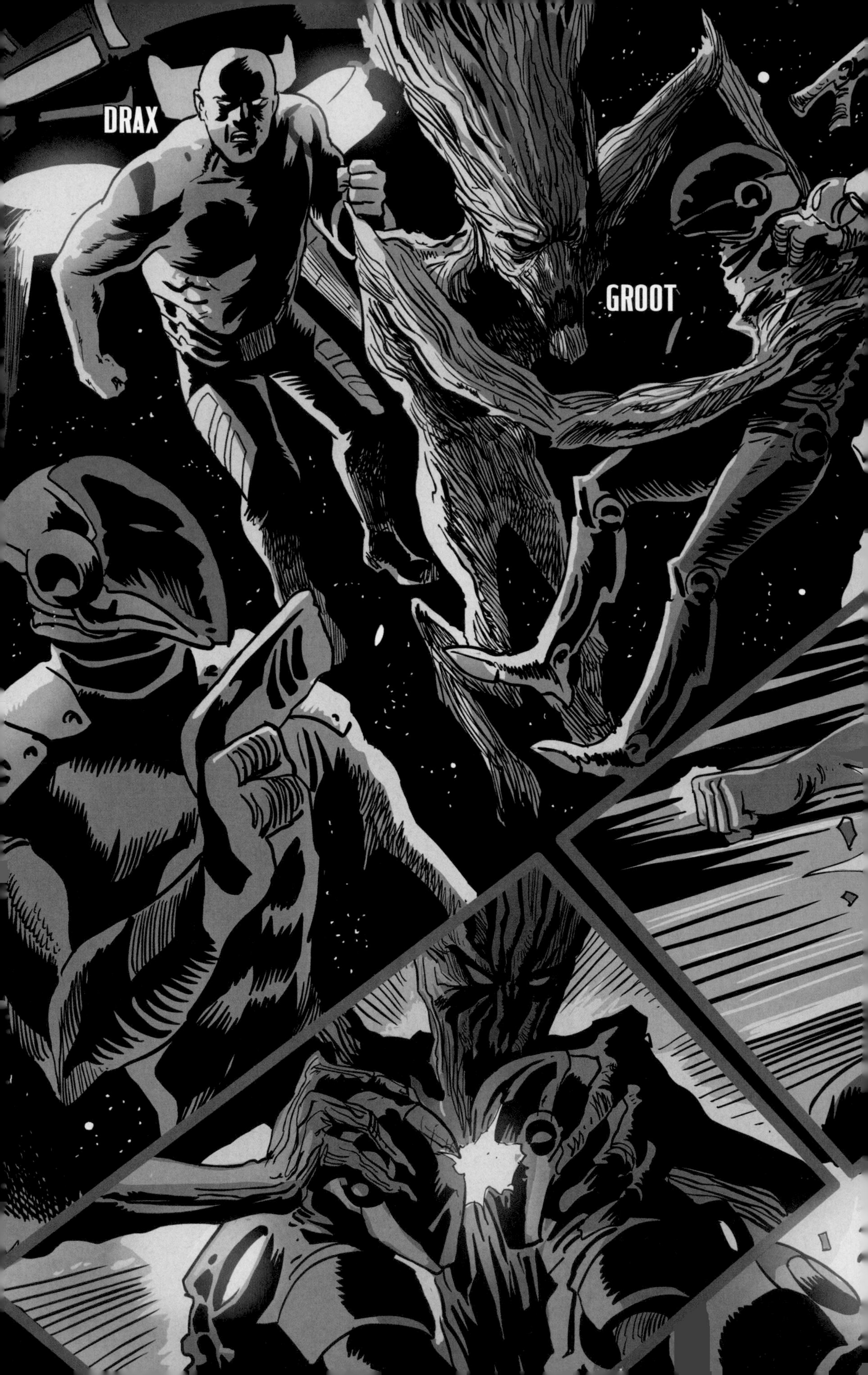
DRAX
GROOT

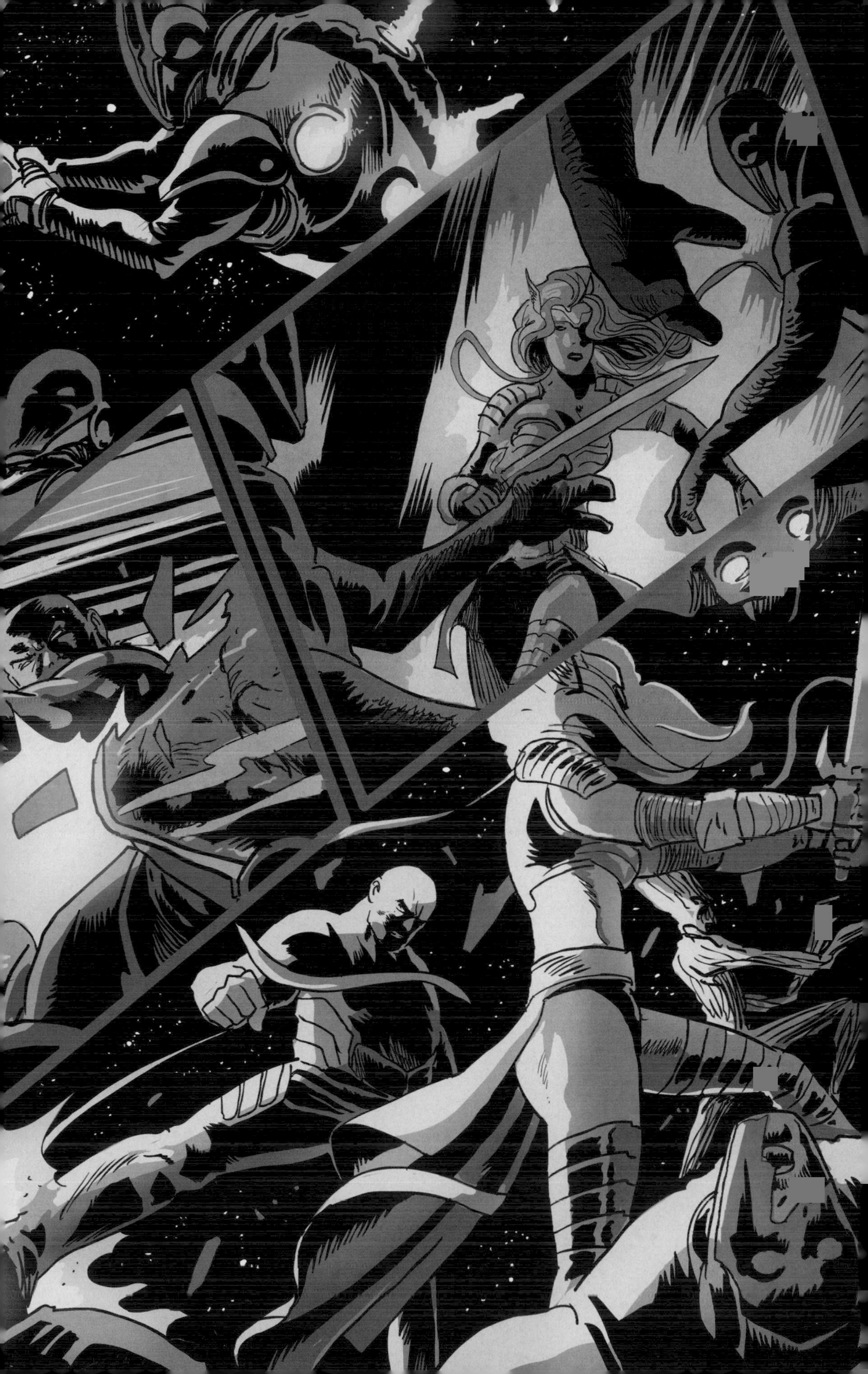

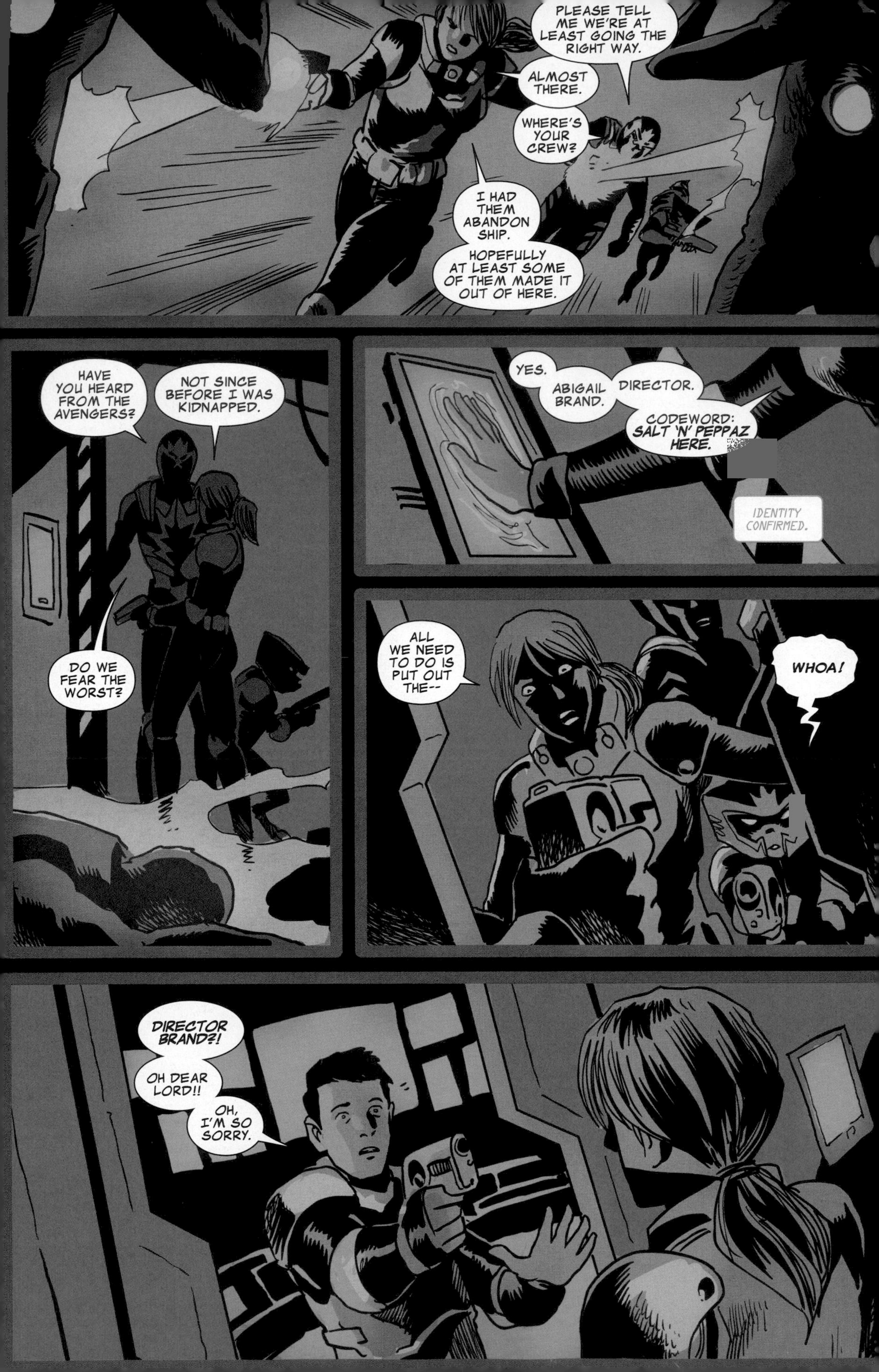
PLEASE TELL ME WE'RE AT LEAST GOING THE RIGHT WAY.
ALMOST THERE.
WHERE'S YOUR CREW?
I HAD THEM ABANDON SHIP.
HOPEFULLY AT LEAST SOME OF THEM MADE IT OUT OF HERE.
HAVE YOU HEARD FROM THE AVENGERS?
NOT SINCE BEFORE I WAS KIDNAPPED.
DO WE FEAR THE WORST?
YES.
ABIGAIL BRAND.
DIRECTOR.
CODEWORD: **SALT 'N' PEPPAZ HERE.**
IDENTITY CONFIRMED.
ALL WE NEED TO DO IS PUT OUT THE--
WHOA!
DIRECTOR BRAND?!
OH DEAR LORD!!
OH, I'M SO SORRY.

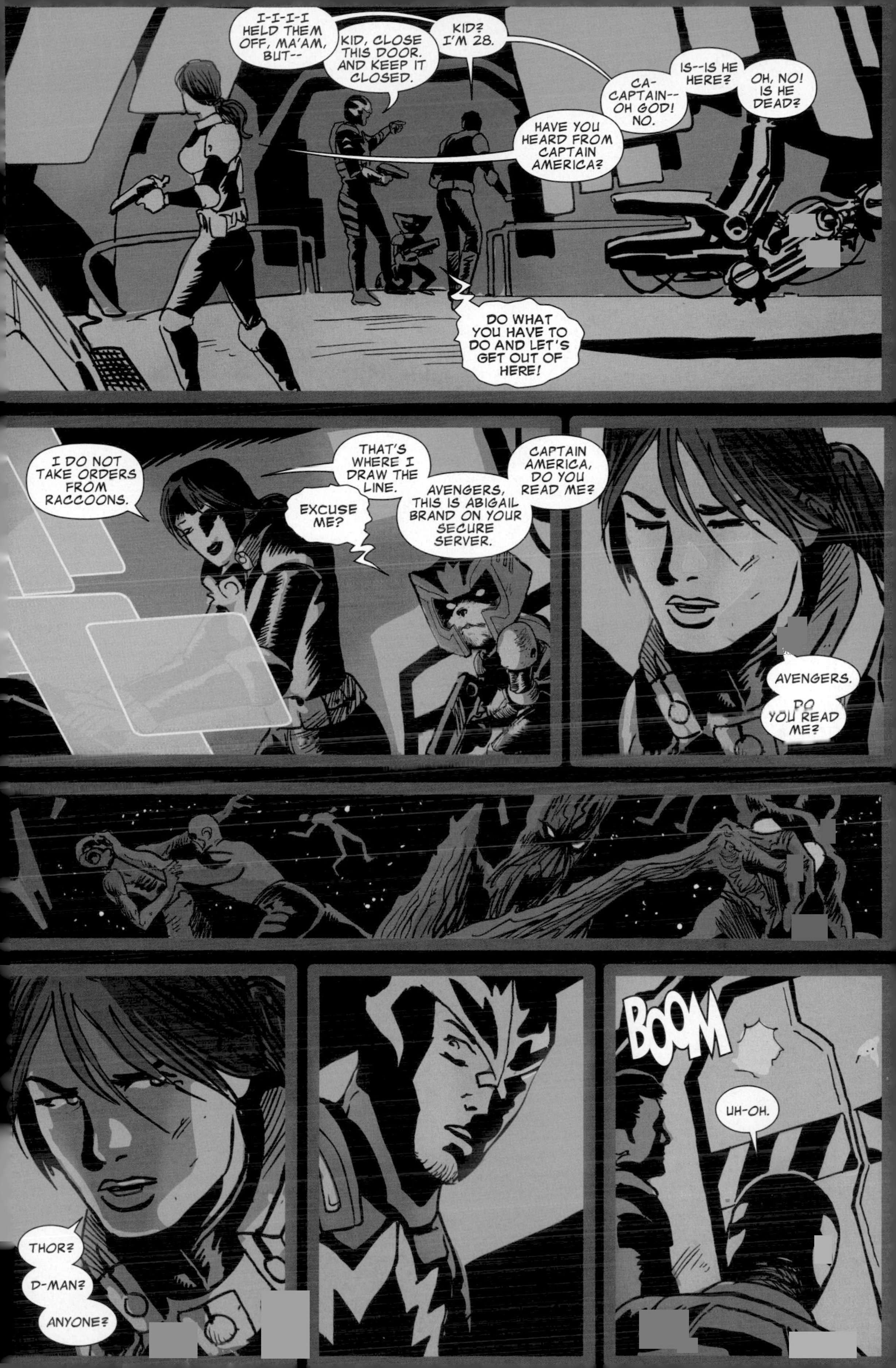
I-I-I-I HELD THEM OFF, MA'AM, BUT--
KID, CLOSE THIS DOOR. AND KEEP IT CLOSED.
KID? I'M 28.
HAVE YOU HEARD FROM CAPTAIN AMERICA?
CA-CAPTAIN-- OH GOD! NO.
IS--IS HE HERE?
OH, NO! IS HE DEAD?
DO WHAT YOU HAVE TO DO AND LET'S GET OUT OF HERE!
I DO NOT TAKE ORDERS FROM RACCOONS.
THAT'S WHERE I DRAW THE LINE.
EXCUSE ME?
AVENGERS, THIS IS ABIGAIL BRAND ON YOUR SECURE SERVER.
CAPTAIN AMERICA, DO YOU READ ME?
AVENGERS.
DO YOU READ ME?
THOR?
D-MAN?
ANYONE?
BOOM
UH-OH.

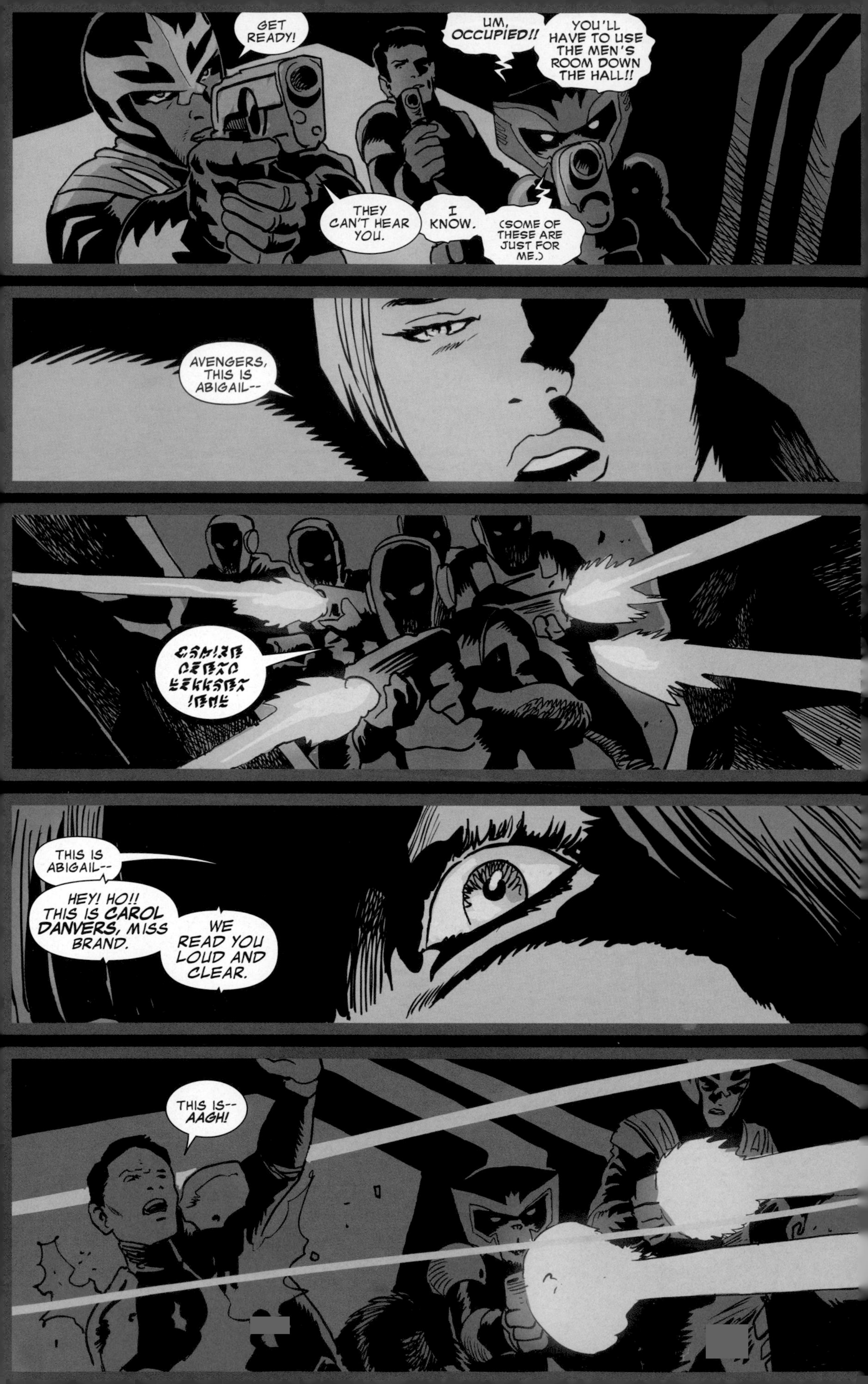
GET READY!
UM, OCCUPIED!!
YOU'LL HAVE TO USE THE MEN'S ROOM DOWN THE HALL!!
THEY CAN'T HEAR YOU.
I KNOW.
(SOME OF THESE ARE JUST FOR ME.)
AVENGERS, THIS IS ABIGAIL--
THIS IS ABIGAIL--
HEY! HO!! THIS IS CAROL DANVERS, MISS BRAND.
WE READ YOU LOUD AND CLEAR.
THIS IS-- AAGH!

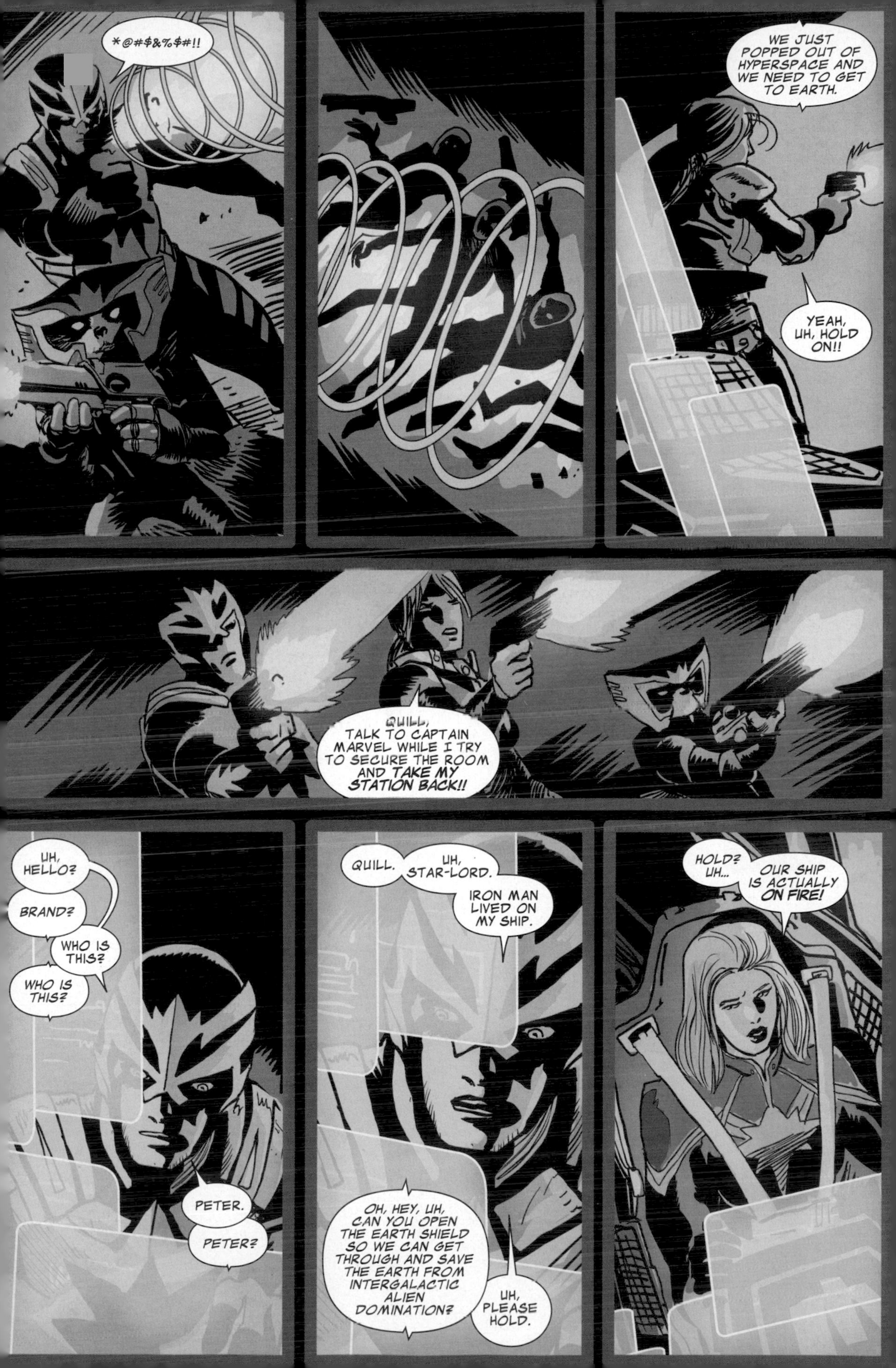
*@#$&%$#!!
WE JUST POPPED OUT OF HYPERSPACE AND WE NEED TO GET TO EARTH.
YEAH, UH, HOLD ON!!
QUILL, TALK TO CAPTAIN MARVEL WHILE I TRY TO SECURE THE ROOM AND TAKE MY STATION BACK!!
UH, HELLO?
BRAND?
WHO IS THIS?
WHO IS THIS?
PETER.
PETER?
QUILL.
UH, STAR-LORD.
IRON MAN LIVED ON MY SHIP.
OH, HEY, UH, CAN YOU OPEN THE EARTH SHIELD SO WE CAN GET THROUGH AND SAVE THE EARTH FROM INTERGALACTIC ALIEN DOMINATION?
UH, PLEASE HOLD.
HOLD? UH...
OUR SHIP IS ACTUALLY ON FIRE!

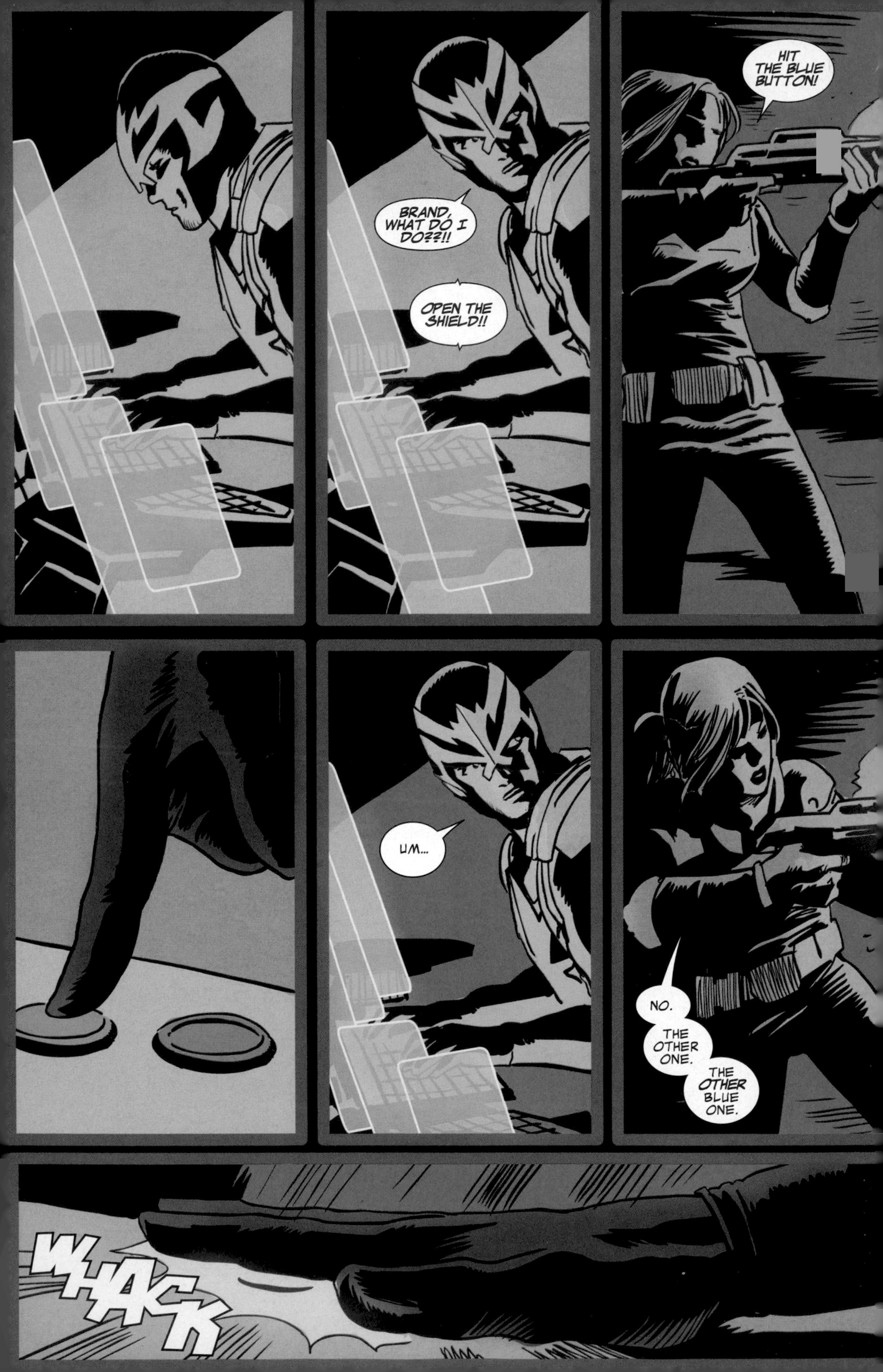
BRAND, WHAT DO I DO??!!
OPEN THE SHIELD!!
HIT THE BLUE BUTTON!
UM...
NO.
THE OTHER ONE.
THE OTHER BLUE ONE.
WHACK

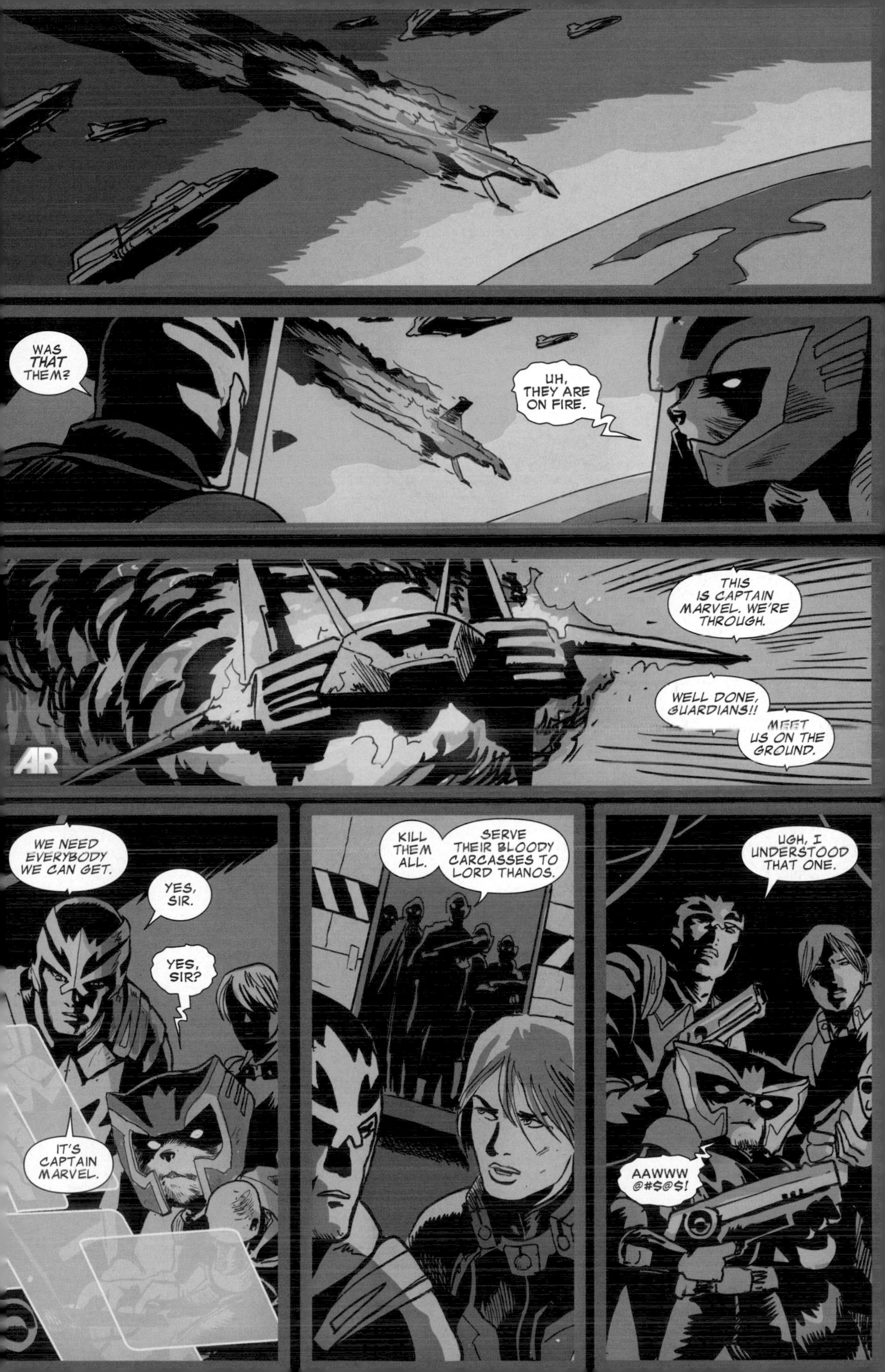
WAS THAT THEM?
UH, THEY ARE ON FIRE.
THIS IS CAPTAIN MARVEL. WE'RE THROUGH.
WELL DONE, GUARDIANS!!
MEET US ON THE GROUND.
WE NEED EVERYBODY WE CAN GET.
YES, SIR.
YES, SIR?
IT'S CAPTAIN MARVEL.
KILL THEM ALL.
SERVE THEIR BLOODY CARCASSES TO LORD THANOS.
UGH, I UNDERSTOOD THAT ONE.
AAWWW @#$@$!

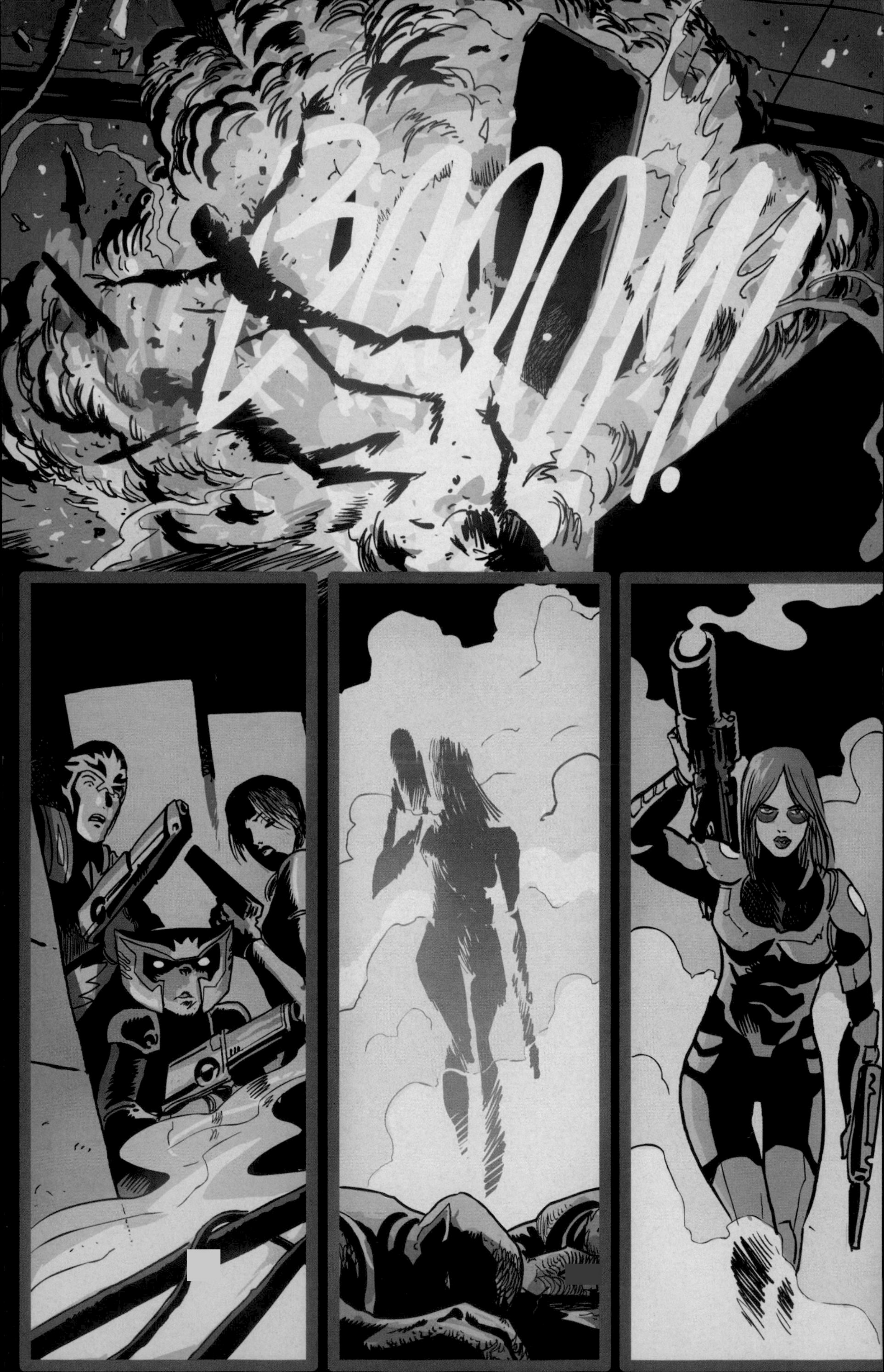
BOOM!

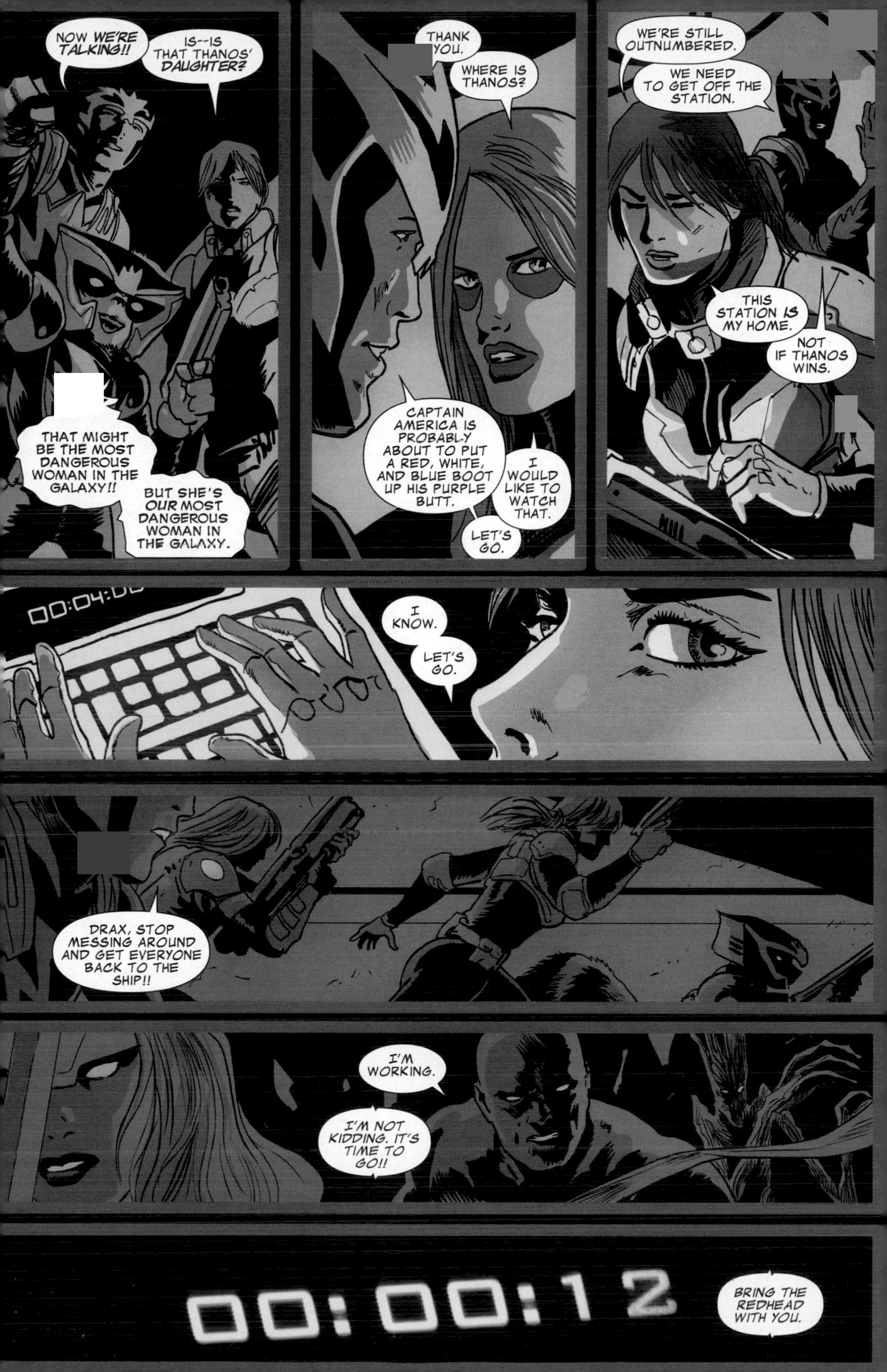
NOW WE'RE TALKING!!
IS--IS THAT THANOS' DAUGHTER?
THAT MIGHT BE THE MOST DANGEROUS WOMAN IN THE GALAXY!!
BUT SHE'S OUR MOST DANGEROUS WOMAN IN THE GALAXY.
THANK YOU.
WHERE IS THANOS?
CAPTAIN AMERICA IS PROBABLY ABOUT TO PUT A RED, WHITE, AND BLUE BOOT UP HIS PURPLE BUTT.
I WOULD LIKE TO WATCH THAT.
LET'S GO.
WE'RE STILL OUTNUMBERED.
WE NEED TO GET OFF THE STATION.
THIS STATION IS MY HOME.
NOT IF THANOS WINS.
00:04:00
I KNOW.
LET'S GO.
DRAX, STOP MESSING AROUND AND GET EVERYONE BACK TO THE SHIP!!
I'M WORKING.
I'M NOT KIDDING. IT'S TIME TO GO!!
00:00:12
BRING THE REDHEAD WITH YOU.

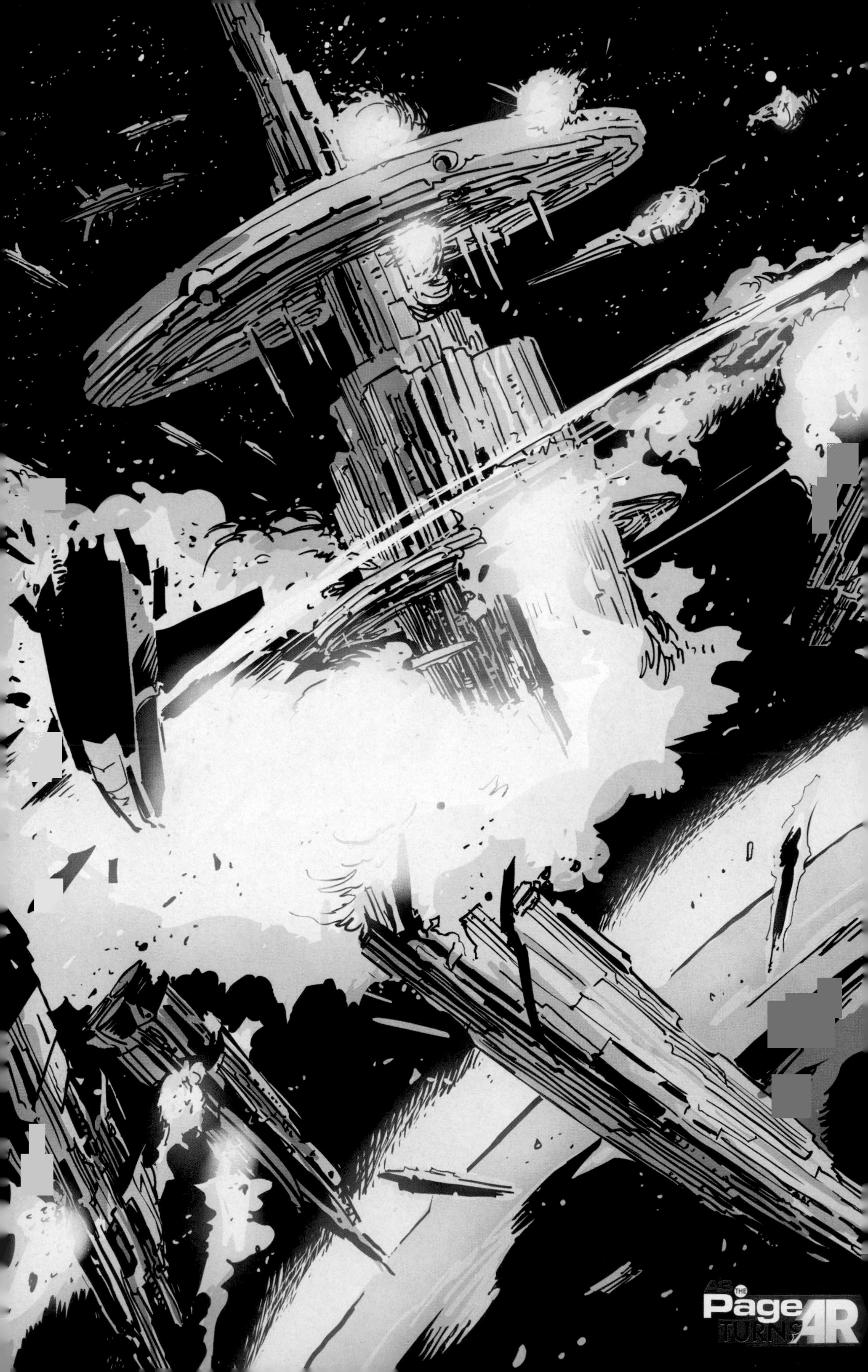

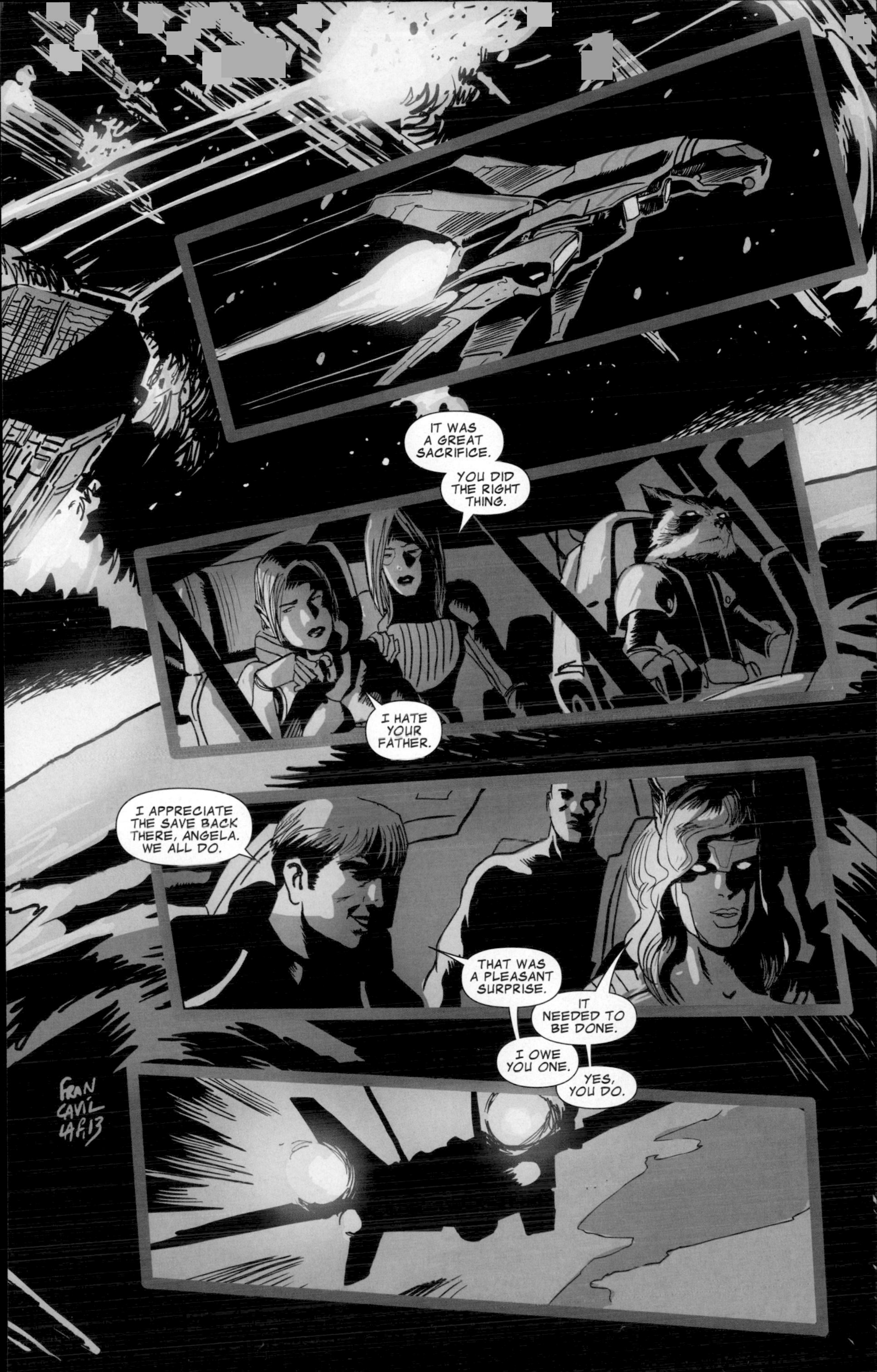

IT WAS A GREAT SACRIFICE.
YOU DID THE RIGHT THING.
I HATE YOUR FATHER.
I APPRECIATE THE SAVE BACK THERE, ANGELA. WE ALL DO.
THAT WAS A PLEASANT SURPRISE.
IT NEEDED TO BE DONE.
I OWE YOU ONE.
YES, YOU DO.

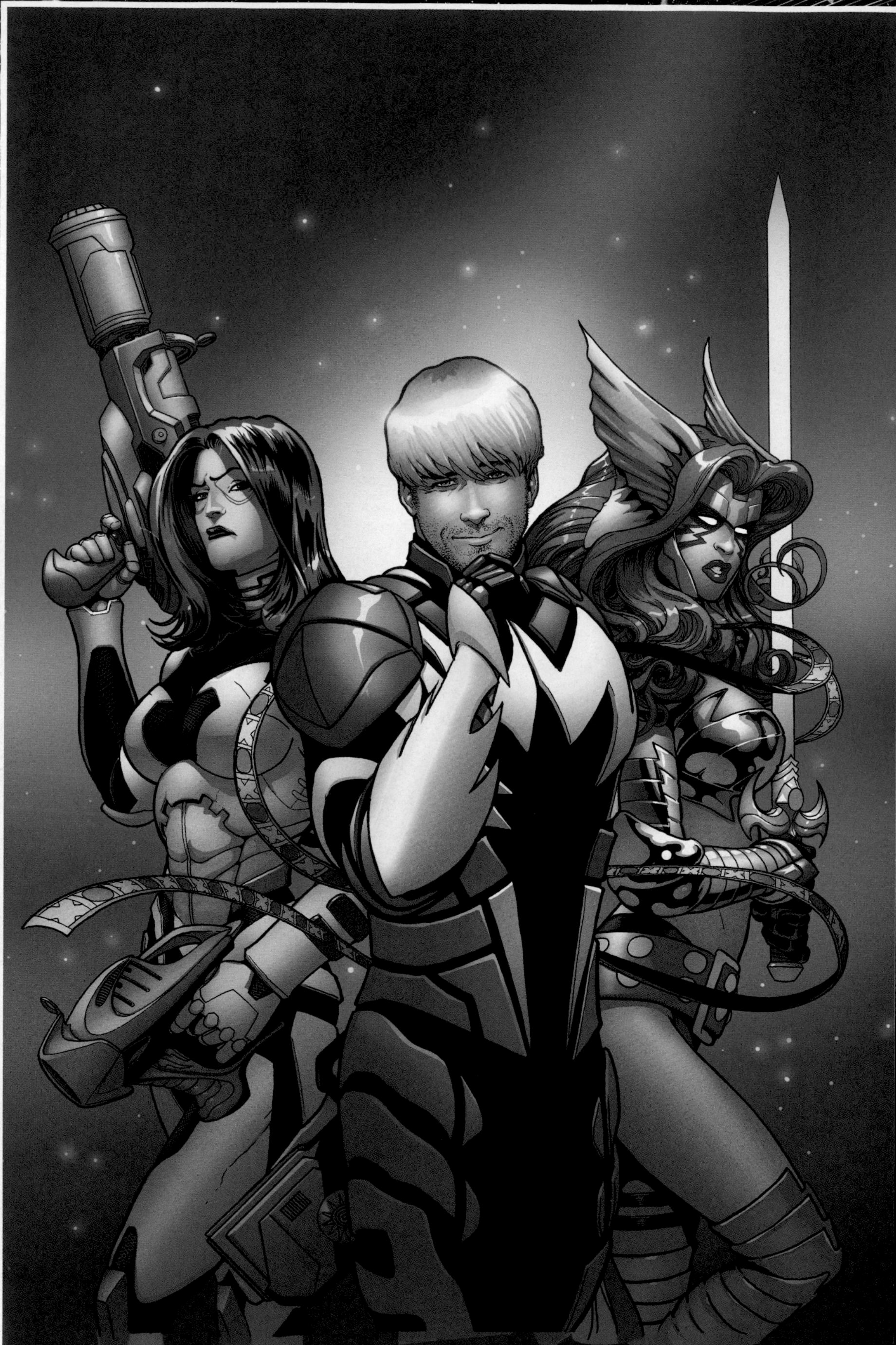

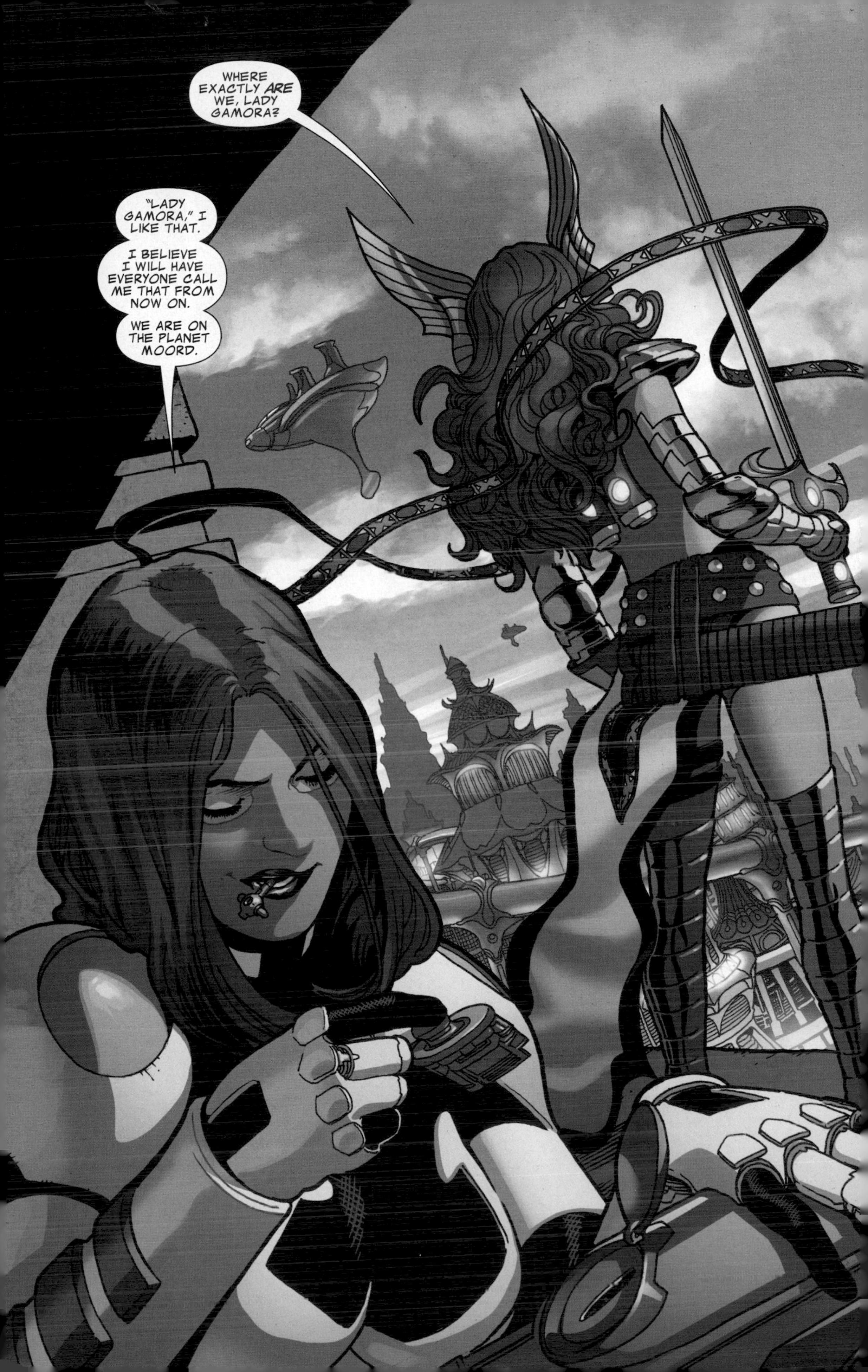
WHERE EXACTLY ARE WE, LADY GAMORA?
"LADY GAMORA," I LIKE THAT.
I BELIEVE I WILL HAVE EVERYONE CALL ME THAT FROM NOW ON.
WE ARE ON THE PLANET MOORD.

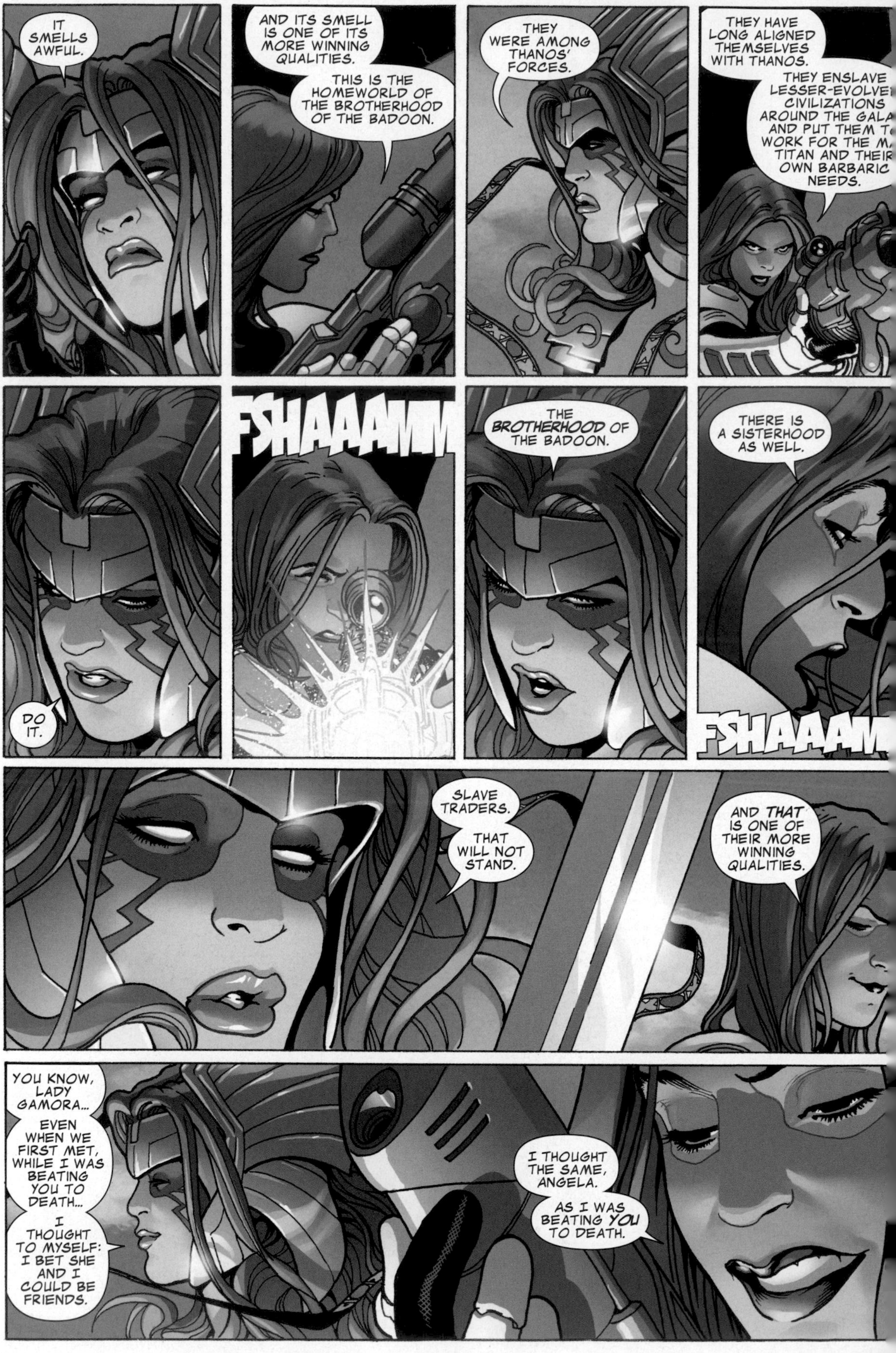

IT SMELLS AWFUL.
AND ITS SMELL IS ONE OF ITS MORE WINNING QUALITIES.
THIS IS THE HOMEWORLD OF THE BROTHERHOOD OF THE BADOON.
THEY WERE AMONG THANOS' FORCES.
THEY HAVE LONG ALIGNED THEMSELVES WITH THANOS.
THEY ENSLAVE LESSER-EVOLVE CIVILIZATIONS AROUND THE GALA AND PUT THEM T WORK FOR THE M TITAN AND THEIR OWN BARBARIC NEEDS.
DO IT.
FSHAAAMM
THE BROTHERHOOD OF THE BADOON.
THERE IS A SISTERHOOD AS WELL.
FSHAAAM
SLAVE TRADERS.
THAT WILL NOT STAND.
AND THAT IS ONE OF THEIR MORE WINNING QUALITIES.
YOU KNOW, LADY GAMORA...
EVEN WHEN WE FIRST MET, WHILE I WAS BEATING YOU TO DEATH...
I THOUGHT TO MYSELF: I BET SHE AND I COULD BE FRIENDS.
I THOUGHT THE SAME, ANGELA.
AS I WAS BEATING YOU TO DEATH.

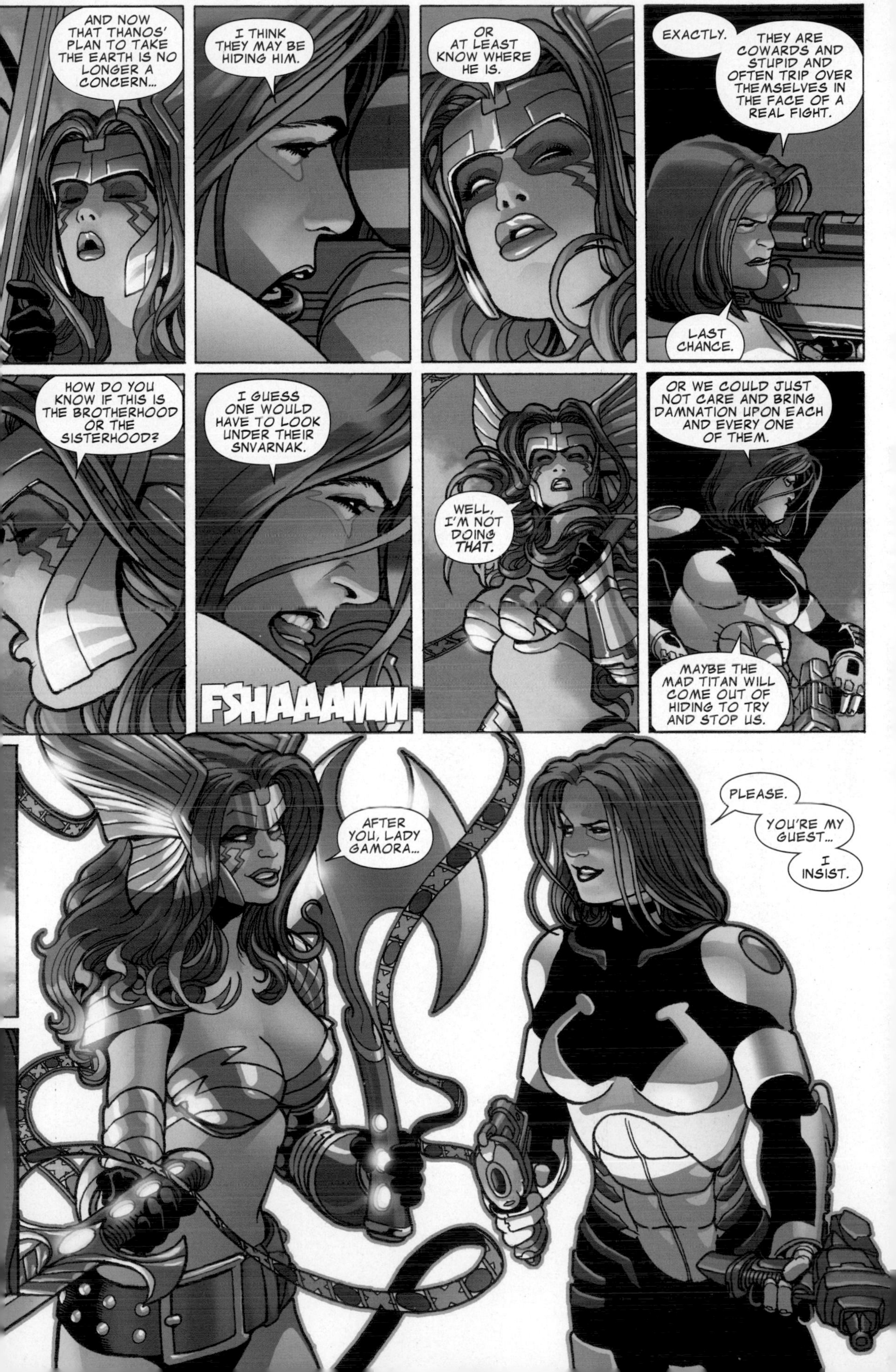
AND NOW THAT THANOS' PLAN TO TAKE THE EARTH IS NO LONGER A CONCERN...
I THINK THEY MAY BE HIDING HIM.
OR AT LEAST KNOW WHERE HE IS.
EXACTLY.
THEY ARE COWARDS AND STUPID AND OFTEN TRIP OVER THEMSELVES IN THE FACE OF A REAL FIGHT.
LAST CHANCE.
HOW DO YOU KNOW IF THIS IS THE BROTHERHOOD OR THE SISTERHOOD?
I GUESS ONE WOULD HAVE TO LOOK UNDER THEIR SNVARNAK.
FSHAAAMM
WELL, I'M NOT DOING THAT.
OR WE COULD JUST NOT CARE AND BRING DAMNATION UPON EACH AND EVERY ONE OF THEM.
MAYBE THE MAD TITAN WILL COME OUT OF HIDING TO TRY AND STOP US.
AFTER YOU, LADY GAMORA...
PLEASE.
YOU'RE MY GUEST...
I INSIST.

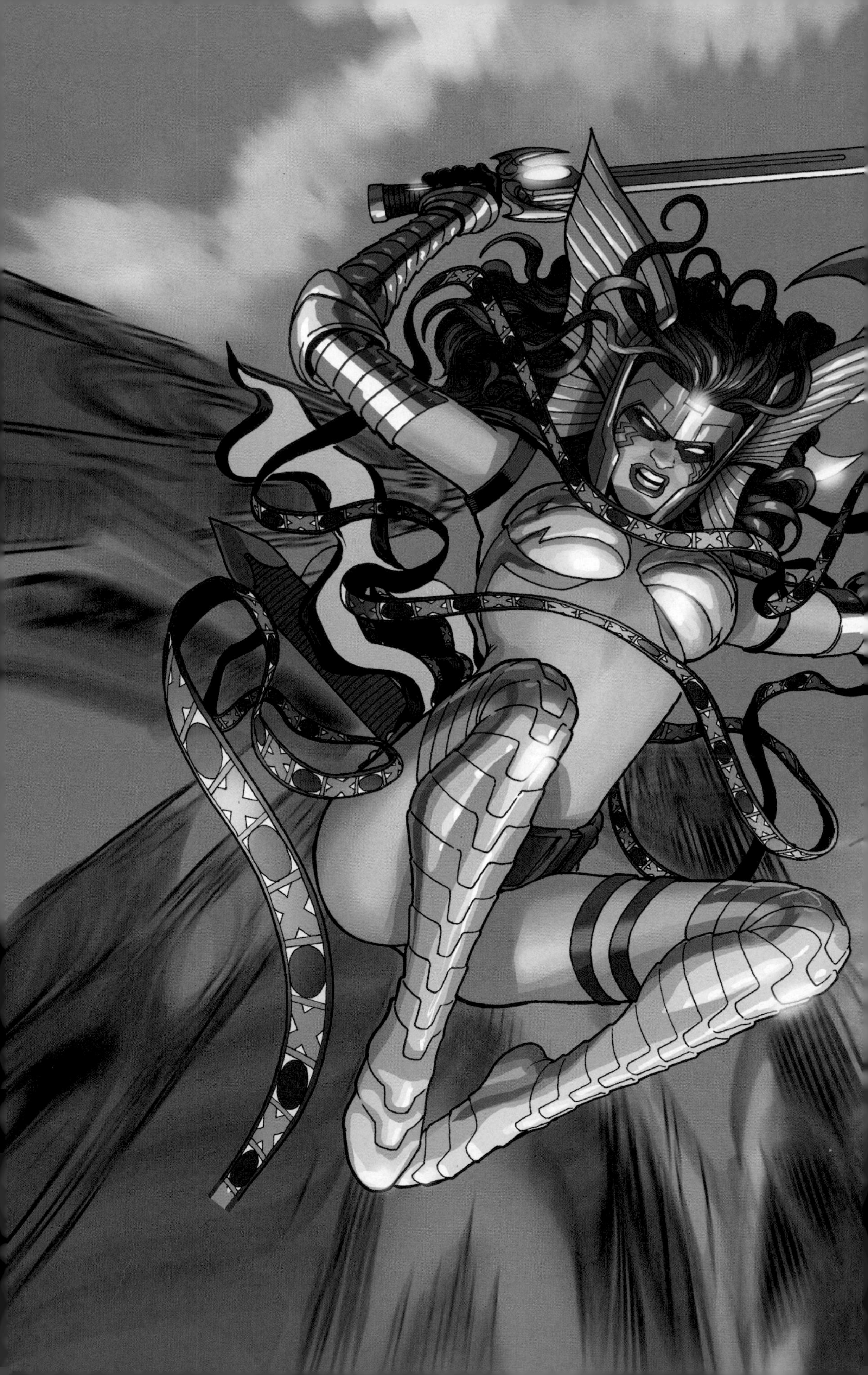

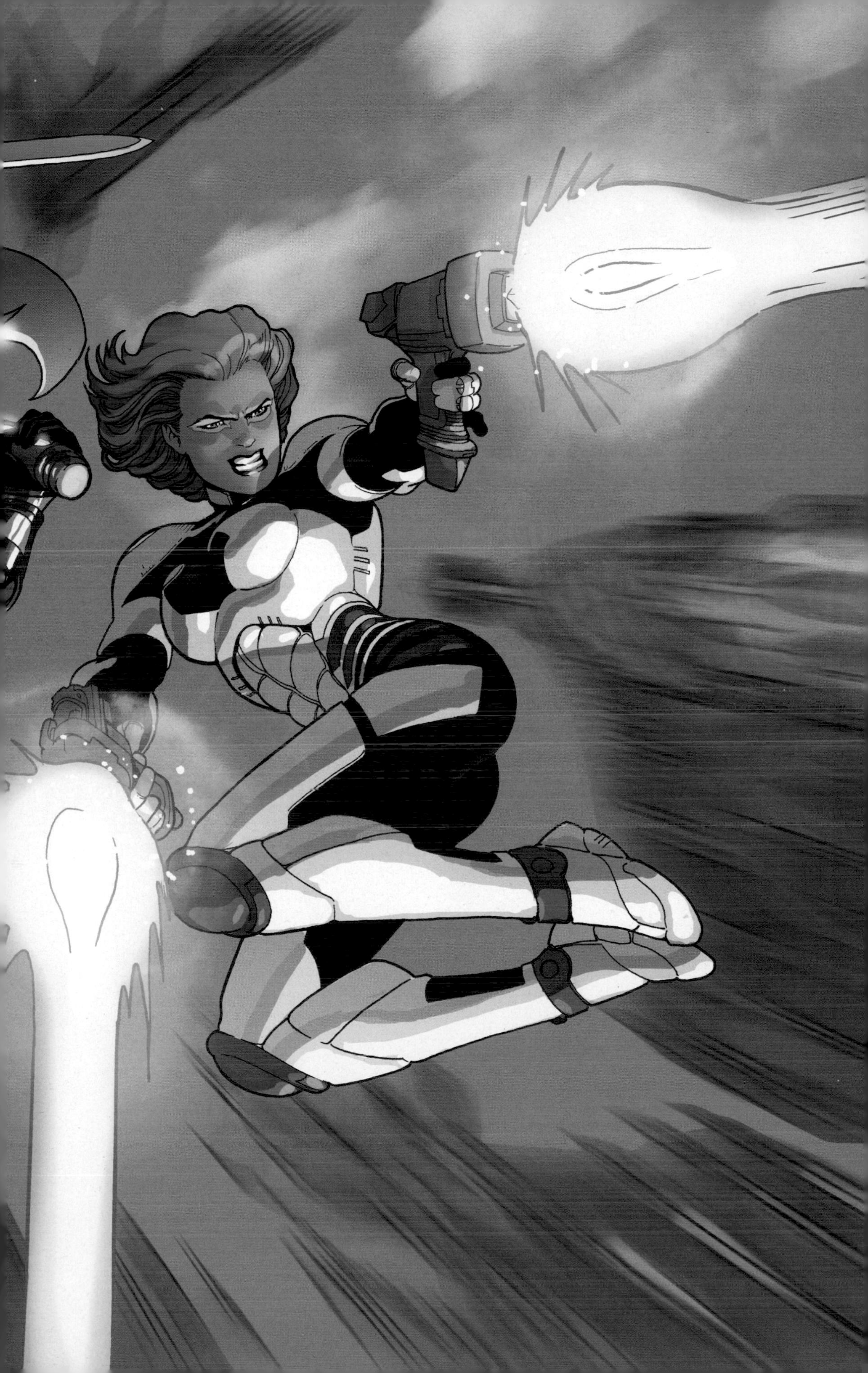

PREVIOUSLY IN *INFINITY*:
Thanos' army came very close to taking the Earth, but the Guardians helped save the planet. The Mad Titan has disappeared.

DO NOT BE AFRAID. YOU ARE NO SLAVE! WE WILL TAKE YOU FROM HERE!

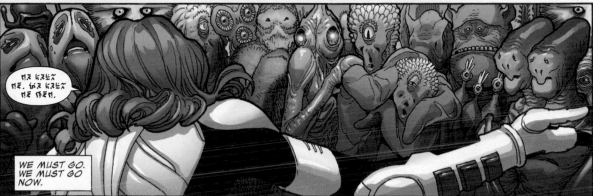

WE MUST GO. WE MUST GO NOW.

DO NOT MOVE!

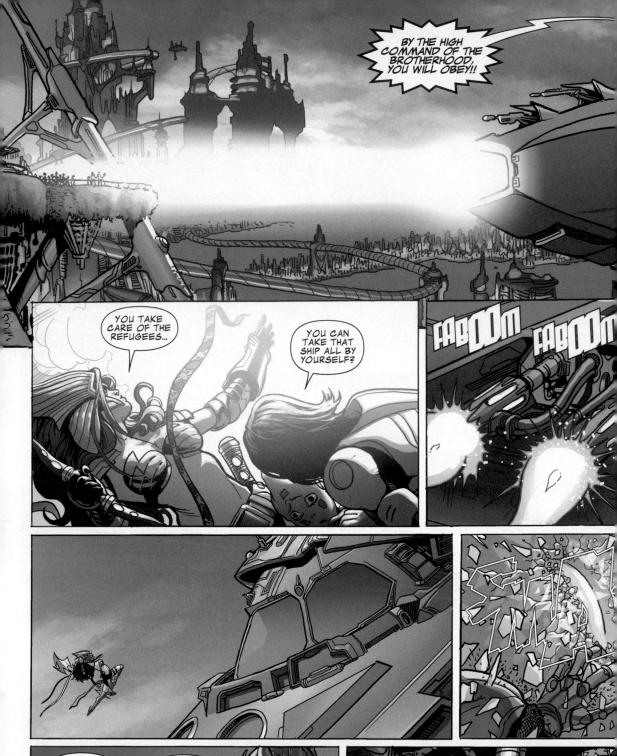

BY THE HIGH COMMAND OF THE BROTHERHOOD, YOU WILL OBEY!!

YOU TAKE CARE OF THE REFUGEES...

YOU CAN TAKE THAT SHIP ALL BY YOURSELF?

FABOOM FABOOM

IT IS ONE OF THOSE INSIPID EARTH HEROES.

WHICH ONE ARE YOU?

THERE ARE FAR TOO MANY OF YOU TO KEEP TRACK.

I AM NOT OF EARTH.

I AM ANGELA.

ONE OF YOU WILL BE SPARED SO MY NAME WILL BE REMEMBERED IN THIS HELL YOU CALL A HOMEWORLD.

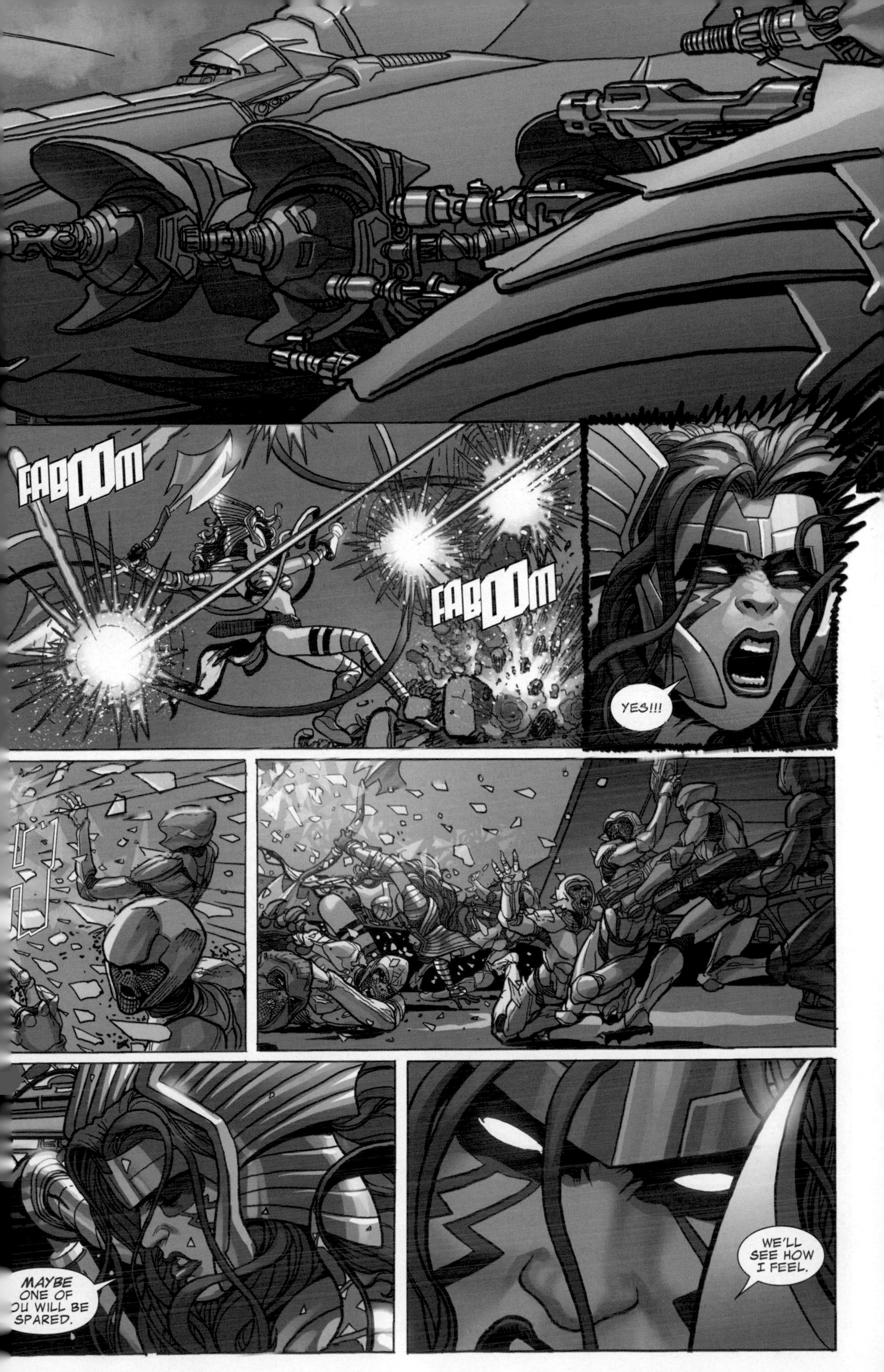
FABOOM
FABOOM
YES!!!
MAYBE ONE OF OU WILL BE SPARED.
WE'LL SEE HOW I FEEL.

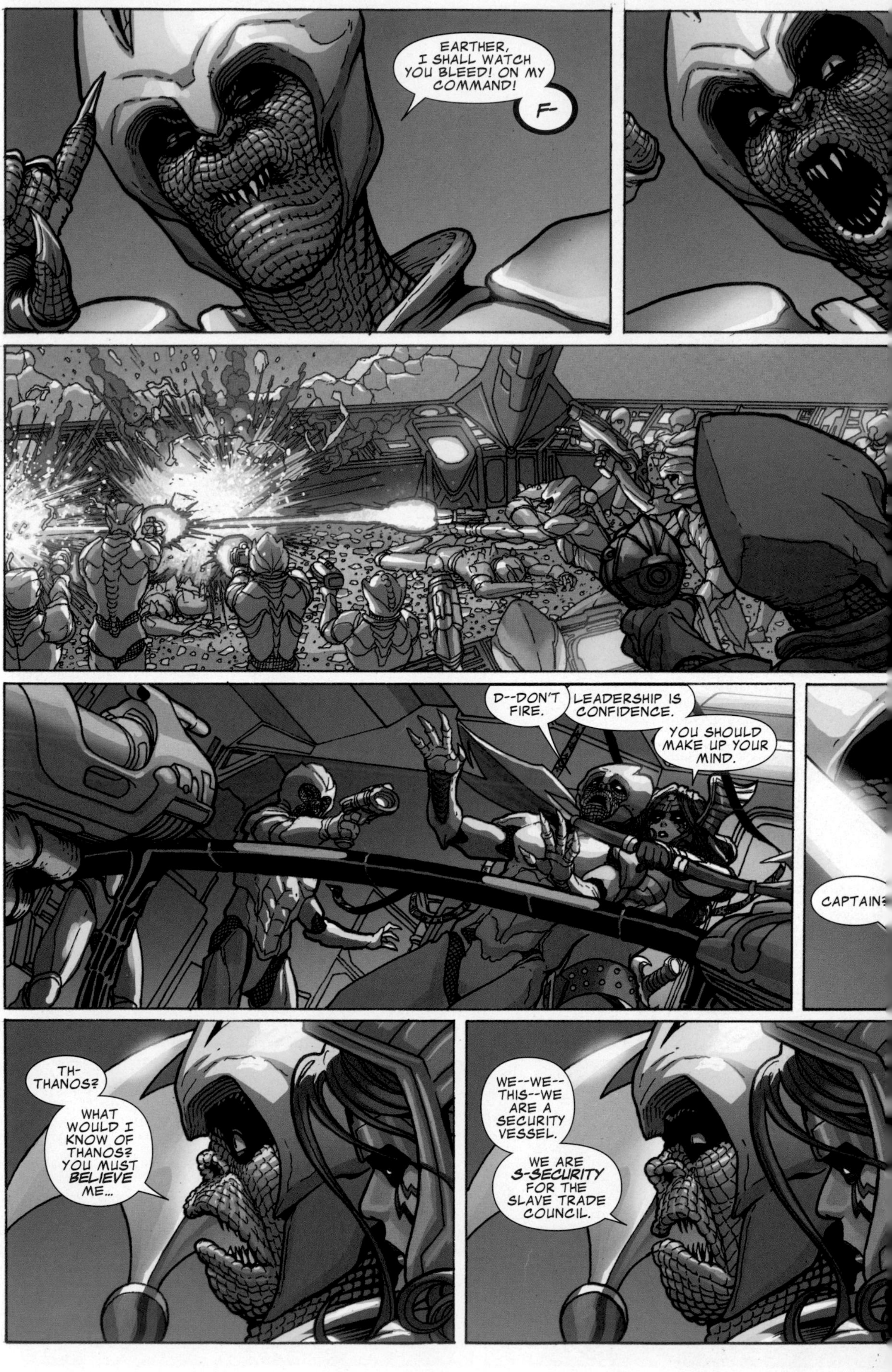
EARTHER, I SHALL WATCH YOU BLEED! ON MY COMMAND!
F-
D--DON'T FIRE.
LEADERSHIP IS CONFIDENCE.
YOU SHOULD MAKE UP YOUR MIND.
CAPTAIN?
TH-THANOS?
WHAT WOULD I KNOW OF THANOS? YOU MUST BELIEVE ME...
WE--WE--THIS--WE ARE A SECURITY VESSEL.
WE ARE S-SECURITY FOR THE SLAVE TRADE COUNCIL.

I—

-RE!

OH, NO.

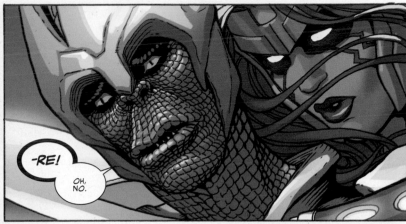

YOU ARE SOMEWHAT FASTER THAN ONE WOULD GUESS.

LET'S SEE HOW LONG IT TAKES FOR YOUR DRONES TO FIGURE IT ALL OUT.

ONLY ONE WAY OUT FOR YOU...

WHERE IS THANOS?

YOU-- YOU MUST BELIEVE ME, EARTHER.

I KNOW NOTHING-- WE--NONE OF US KNOW ANYTHING ABOUT--

I DO BELIEVE YOU.

YOU CONVINCED ME.

!CKIKIKI!

KCKCKE

CKKCK

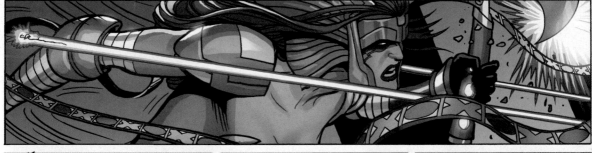

FASSOOMMM

ALL OF YOU!!
SEEK SHELTER!! RUN!!
GO!!

BKAKCZE WEZAE TE KA NEEE

WHERE? WHERE DO WE GO??

I'M NOT YOUR MOTHER!!
YOU NEED TO FIND TRANS--

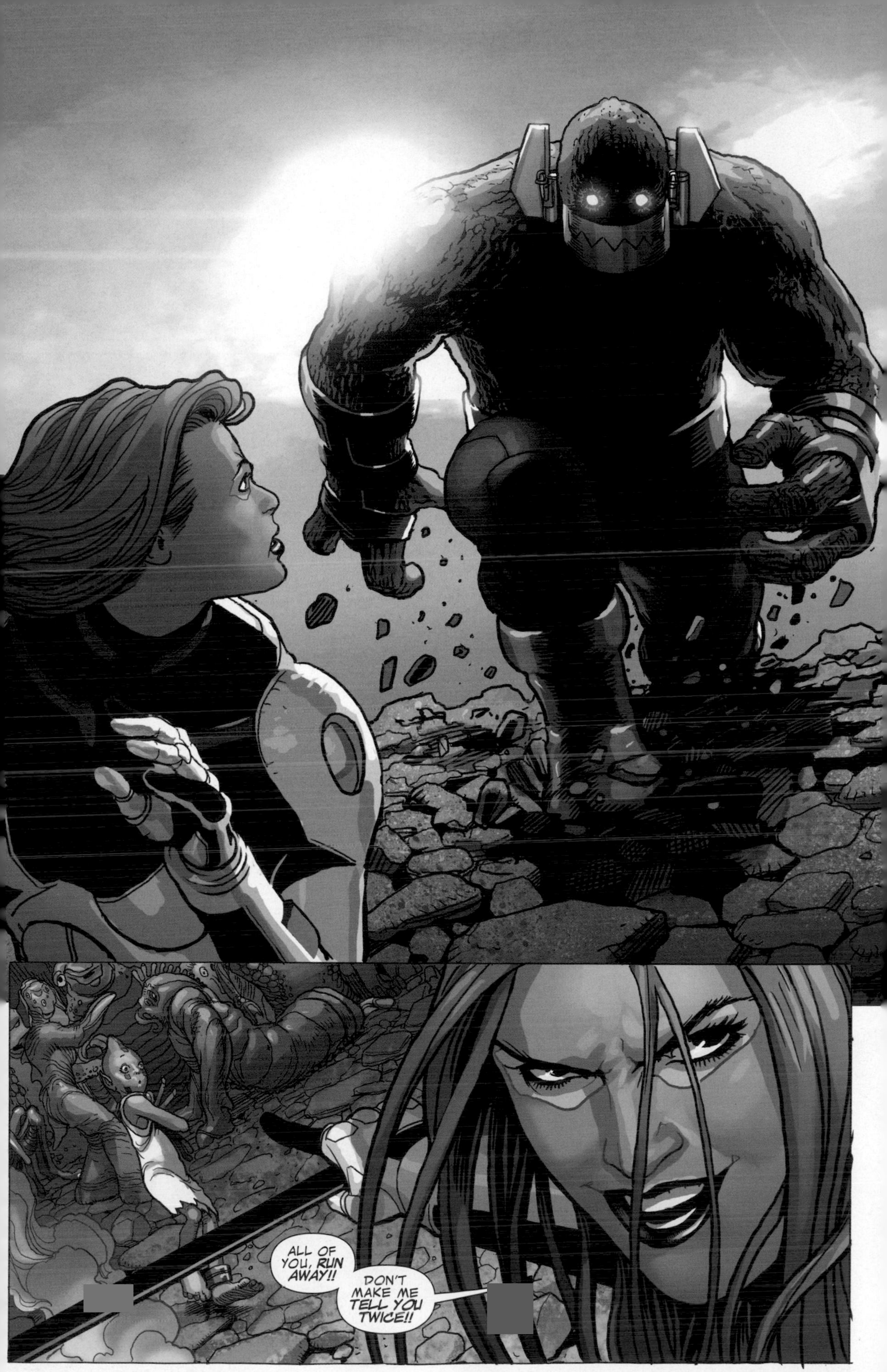
ALL OF YOU, RUN AWAY!!
DON'T MAKE ME TELL YOU TWICE!!

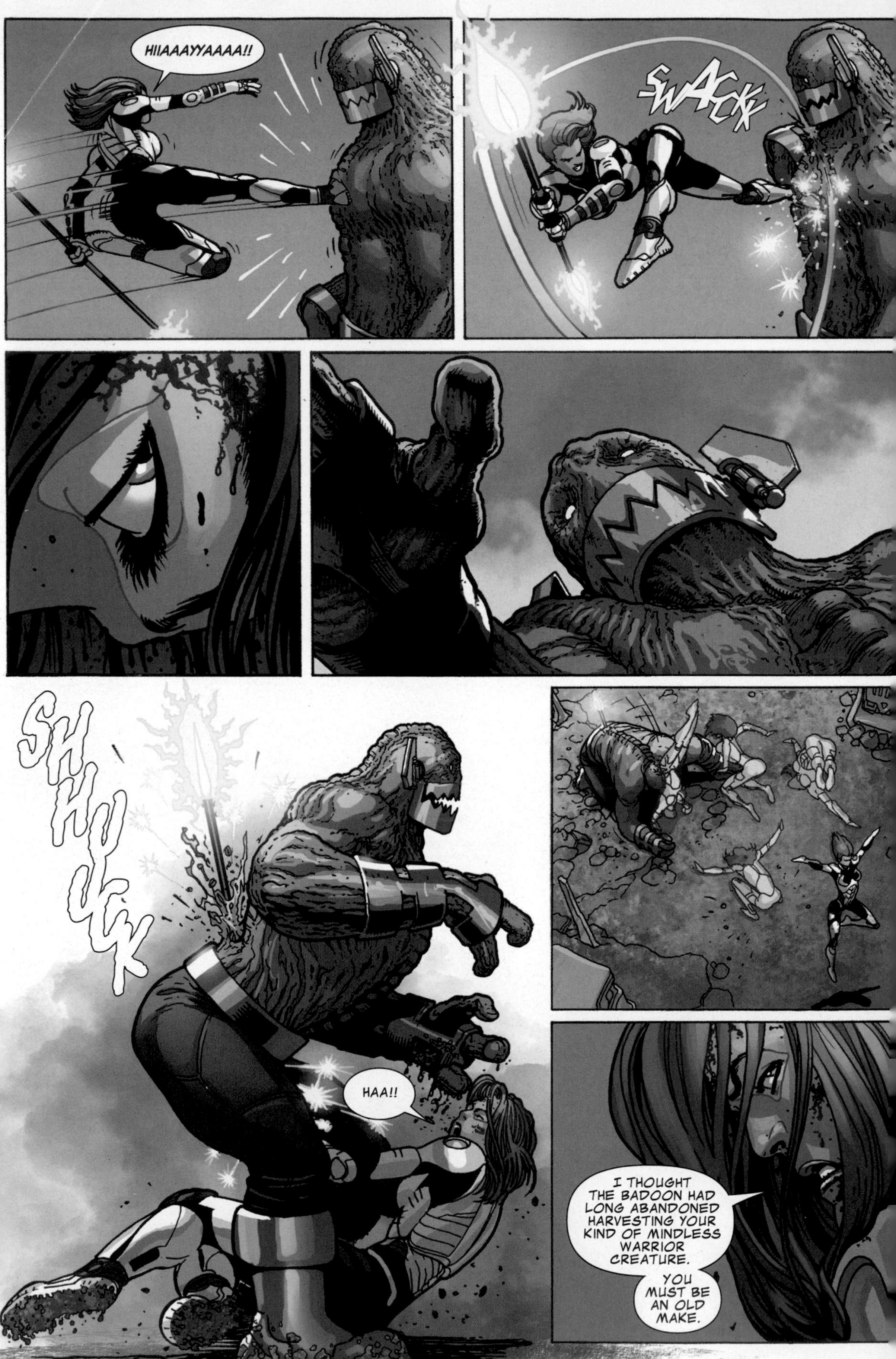
HIIAAAYYAAAA!!
SWACKK
SHHUCK
HAA!!
I THOUGHT THE BADOON HAD LONG ABANDONED HARVESTING YOUR KIND OF MINDLESS WARRIOR CREATURE.
YOU MUST BE AN OLD MAKE.

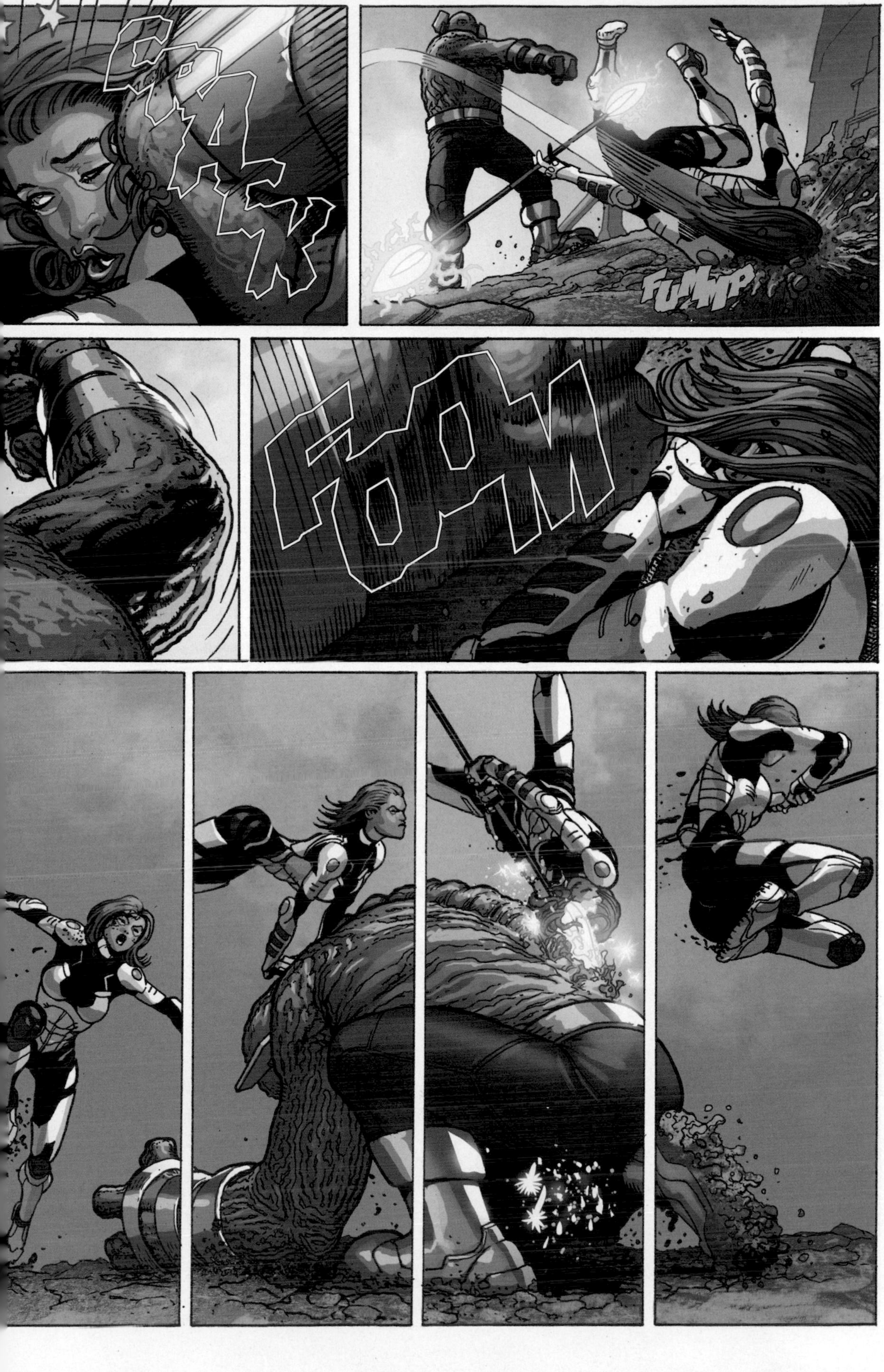
CRACK
FUMMP
FOOM

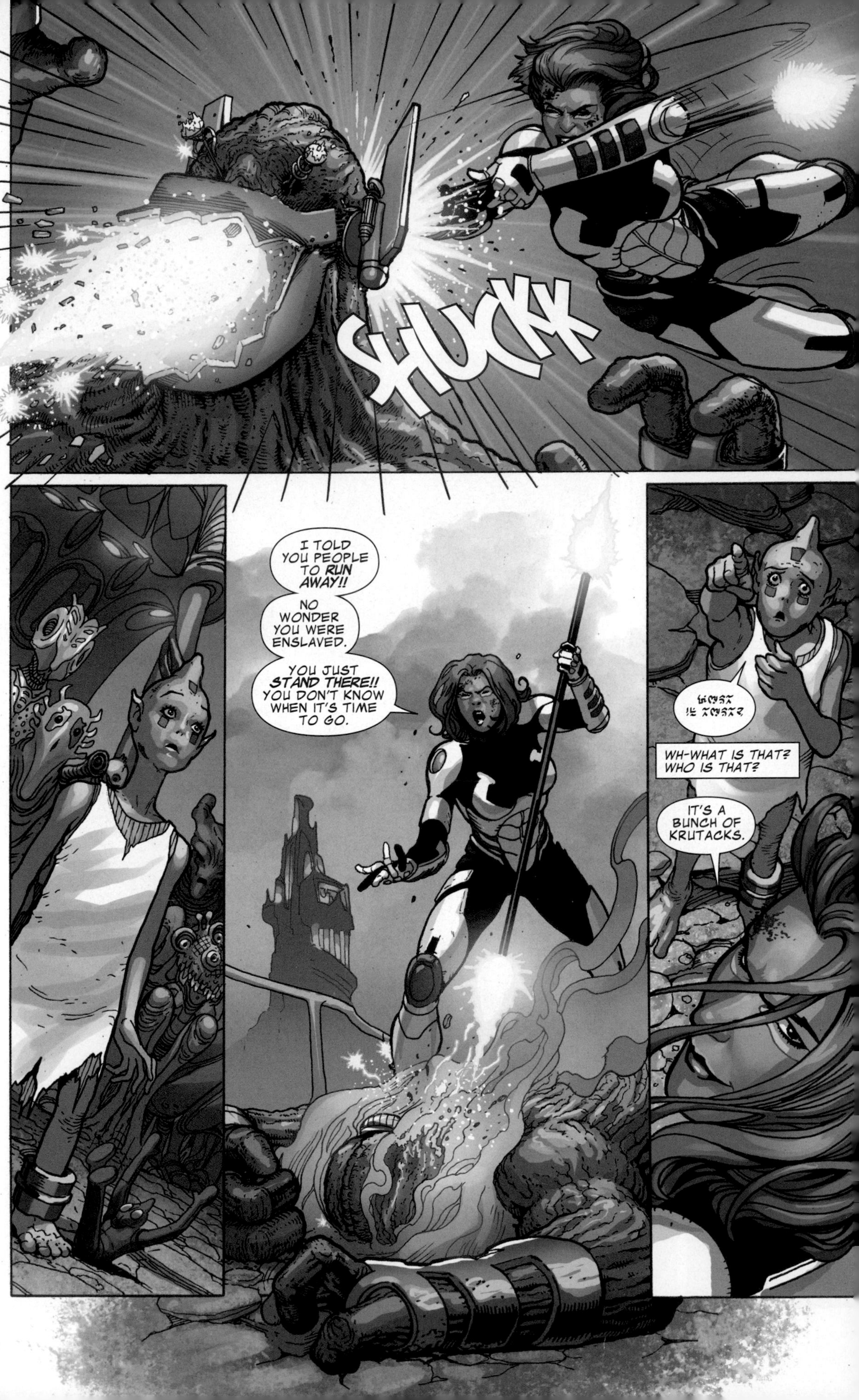
SHUCKK
I TOLD YOU PEOPLE TO RUN AWAY!!
NO WONDER YOU WERE ENSLAVED.
YOU JUST STAND THERE!! YOU DON'T KNOW WHEN IT'S TIME TO GO.
WH-WHAT IS THAT? WHO IS THAT?
IT'S A BUNCH OF KRUTACKS.

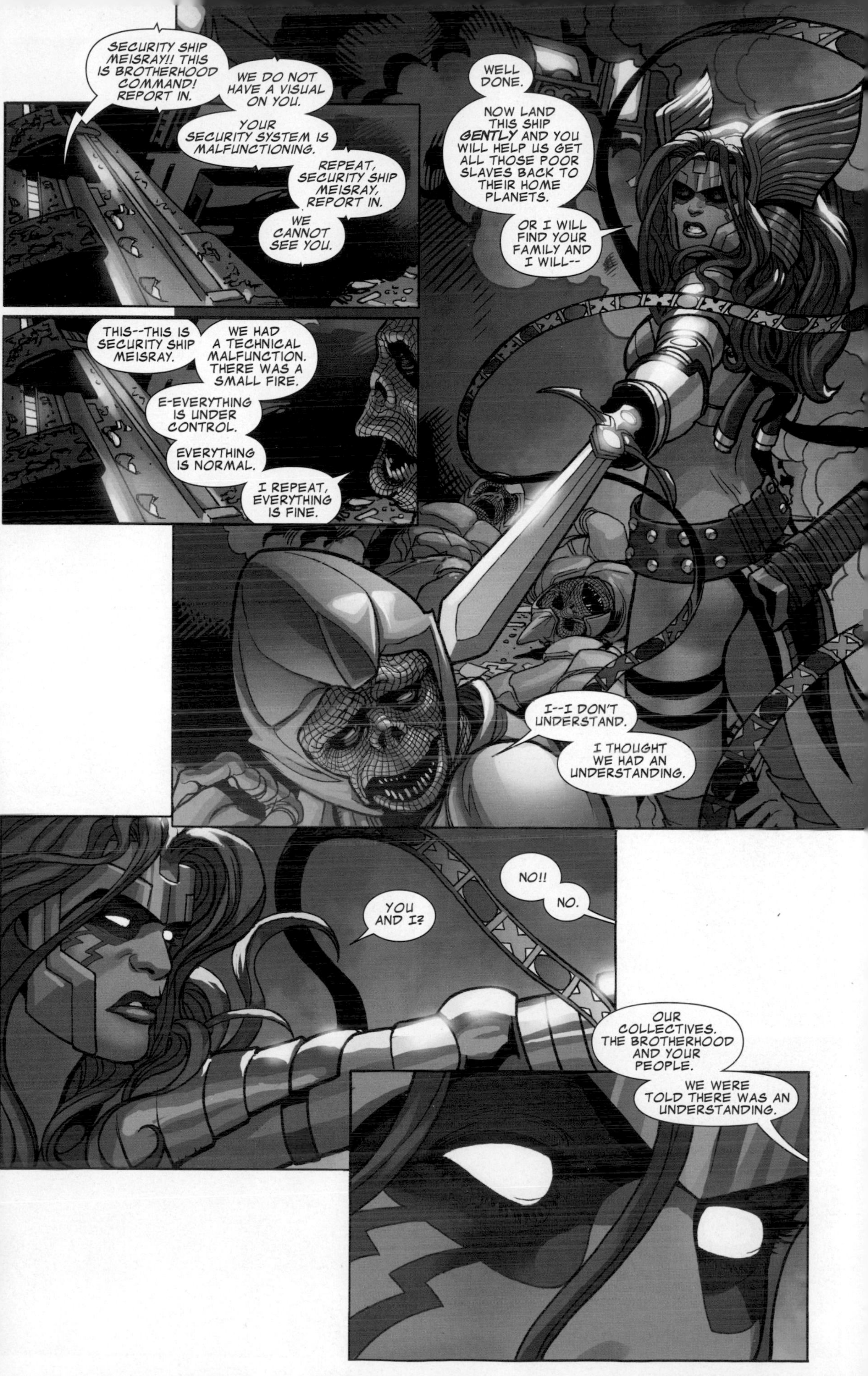
SECURITY SHIP MEISRAY!! THIS IS BROTHERHOOD COMMAND! REPORT IN.
WE DO NOT HAVE A VISUAL ON YOU.
YOUR SECURITY SYSTEM IS MALFUNCTIONING.
REPEAT, SECURITY SHIP MEISRAY, REPORT IN.
WE CANNOT SEE YOU.
THIS--THIS IS SECURITY SHIP MEISRAY.
WE HAD A TECHNICAL MALFUNCTION. THERE WAS A SMALL FIRE.
E-EVERYTHING IS UNDER CONTROL.
EVERYTHING IS NORMAL.
I REPEAT, EVERYTHING IS FINE.
WELL DONE.
NOW LAND THIS SHIP GENTLY AND YOU WILL HELP US GET ALL THOSE POOR SLAVES BACK TO THEIR HOME PLANETS.
OR I WILL FIND YOUR FAMILY AND I WILL--
I--I DON'T UNDERSTAND.
I THOUGHT WE HAD AN UNDERSTANDING.
YOU AND I?
NO!!
NO.
OUR COLLECTIVES. THE BROTHERHOOD AND YOUR PEOPLE.
WE WERE TOLD THERE WAS AN UNDERSTANDING.

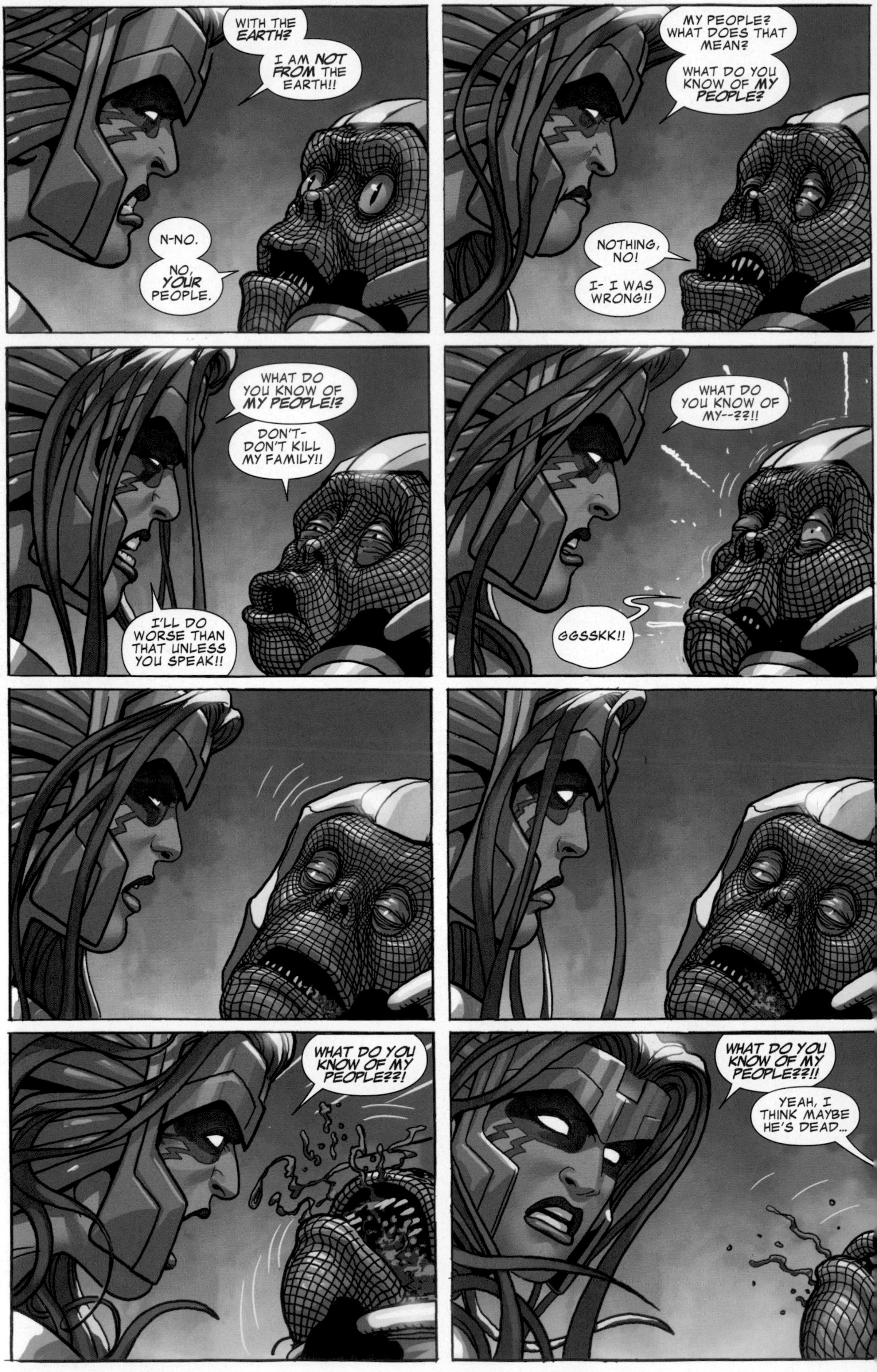

WITH THE EARTH?
I AM NOT FROM THE EARTH!!
N-NO.
NO, YOUR PEOPLE.
MY PEOPLE? WHAT DOES THAT MEAN?
WHAT DO YOU KNOW OF MY PEOPLE?
NOTHING, NO!
I- I WAS WRONG!!
WHAT DO YOU KNOW OF MY PEOPLE!?
DON'T- DON'T KILL MY FAMILY!!
I'LL DO WORSE THAN THAT UNLESS YOU SPEAK!!
WHAT DO YOU KNOW OF MY--??!!
GGSSKK!!
WHAT DO YOU KNOW OF MY PEOPLE??!
WHAT DO YOU KNOW OF MY PEOPLE??!!
YEAH, I THINK MAYBE HE'S DEAD...

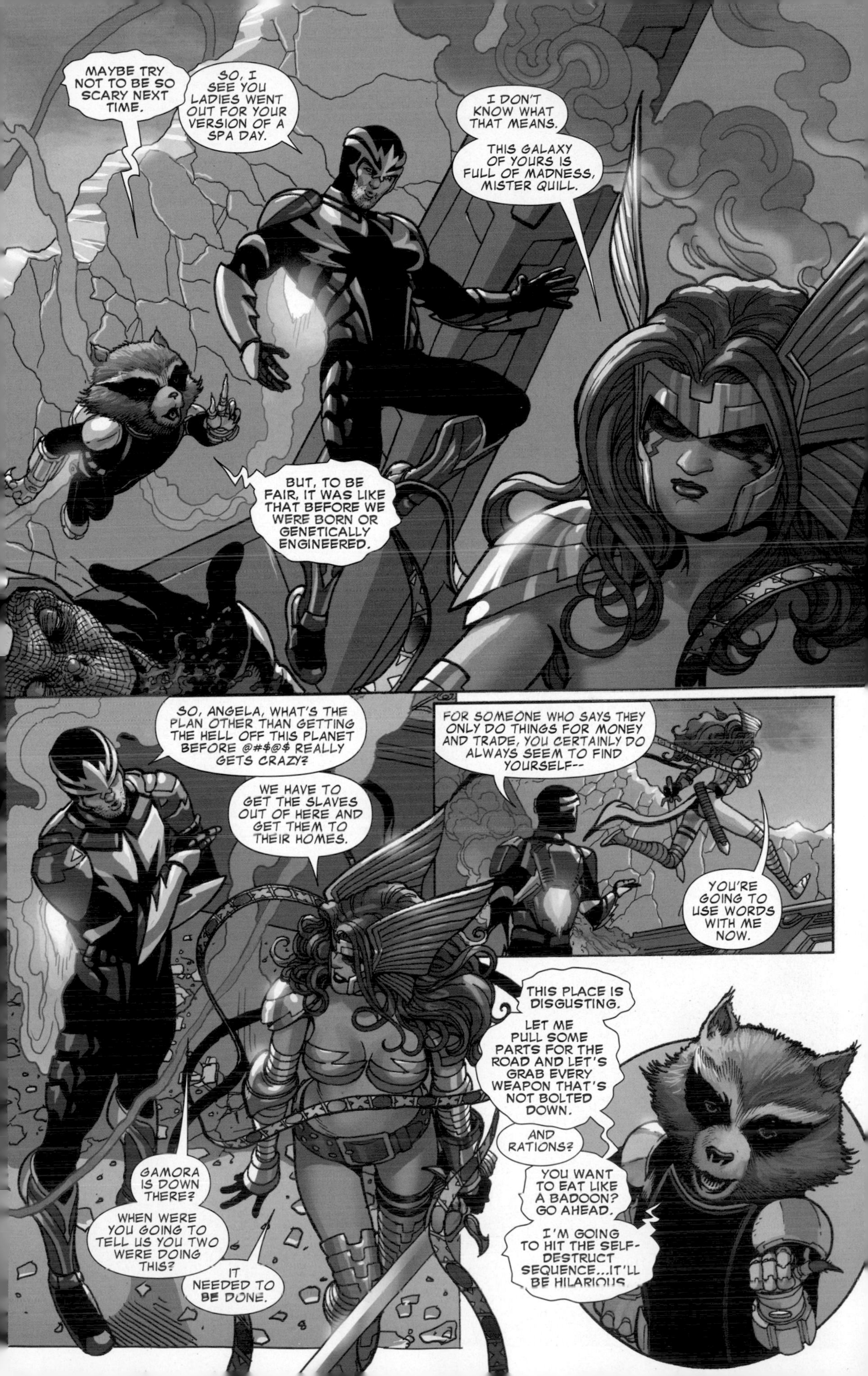
MAYBE TRY NOT TO BE SO SCARY NEXT TIME.
SO, I SEE YOU LADIES WENT OUT FOR YOUR VERSION OF A SPA DAY.
I DON'T KNOW WHAT THAT MEANS.
THIS GALAXY OF YOURS IS FULL OF MADNESS, MISTER QUILL.
BUT, TO BE FAIR, IT WAS LIKE THAT BEFORE WE WERE BORN OR GENETICALLY ENGINEERED.
SO, ANGELA, WHAT'S THE PLAN OTHER THAN GETTING THE HELL OFF THIS PLANET BEFORE @#$@$ REALLY GETS CRAZY?
WE HAVE TO GET THE SLAVES OUT OF HERE AND GET THEM TO THEIR HOMES.
FOR SOMEONE WHO SAYS THEY ONLY DO THINGS FOR MONEY AND TRADE, YOU CERTAINLY DO ALWAYS SEEM TO FIND YOURSELF--
YOU'RE GOING TO USE WORDS WITH ME NOW.
GAMORA IS DOWN THERE?
WHEN WERE YOU GOING TO TELL US YOU TWO WERE DOING THIS?
IT NEEDED TO BE DONE.
THIS PLACE IS DISGUSTING.
LET ME PULL SOME PARTS FOR THE ROAD AND LET'S GRAB EVERY WEAPON THAT'S NOT BOLTED DOWN.
AND RATIONS?
YOU WANT TO EAT LIKE A BADOON? GO AHEAD.
I'M GOING TO HIT THE SELF-DESTRUCT SEQUENCE...IT'LL BE HILARIOUS.

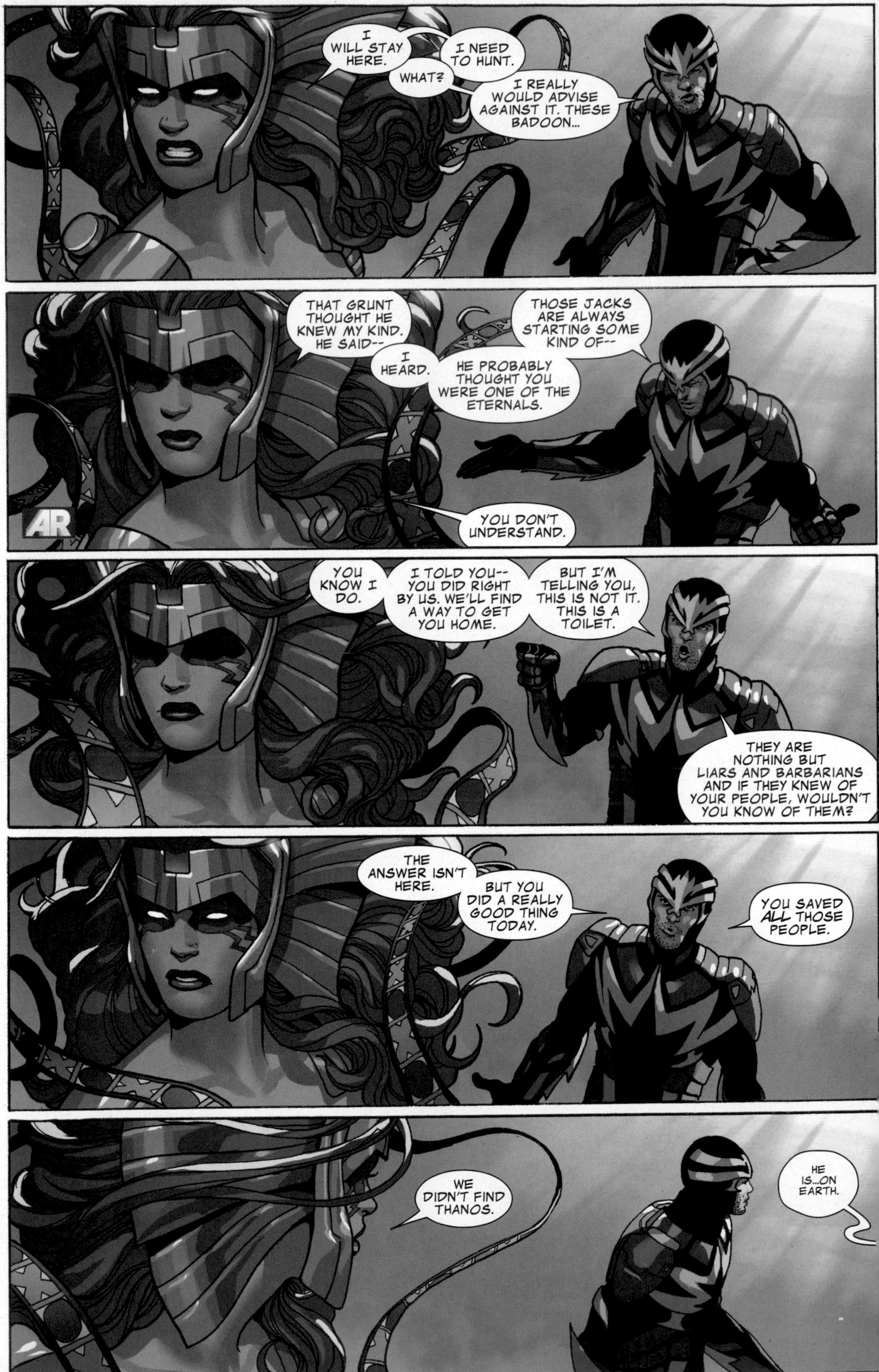
I WILL STAY HERE.
I NEED TO HUNT.
WHAT?
I REALLY WOULD ADVISE AGAINST IT. THESE BADOON...
THAT GRUNT THOUGHT HE KNEW MY KIND. HE SAID--
THOSE JACKS ARE ALWAYS STARTING SOME KIND OF--
I HEARD.
HE PROBABLY THOUGHT YOU WERE ONE OF THE ETERNALS.
YOU DON'T UNDERSTAND.
YOU KNOW I DO.
I TOLD YOU-- YOU DID RIGHT BY US. WE'LL FIND A WAY TO GET YOU HOME.
BUT I'M TELLING YOU, THIS IS NOT IT. THIS IS A TOILET.
THEY ARE NOTHING BUT LIARS AND BARBARIANS AND IF THEY KNEW OF YOUR PEOPLE, WOULDN'T YOU KNOW OF THEM?
THE ANSWER ISN'T HERE.
BUT YOU DID A REALLY GOOD THING TODAY.
YOU SAVED ALL THOSE PEOPLE.
WE DIDN'T FIND THANOS.
HE IS...ON EARTH.

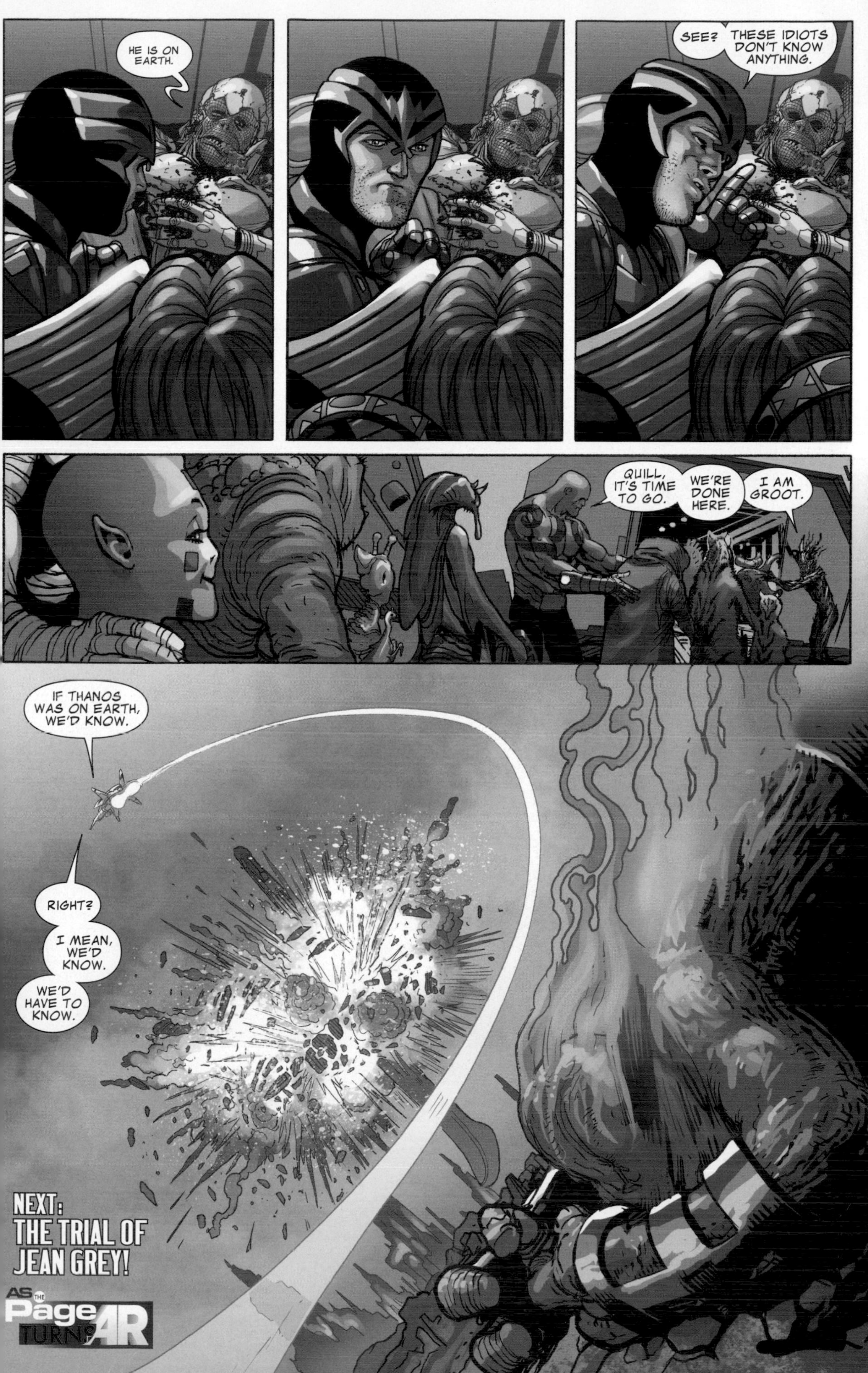
HE IS ON EARTH.
SEE?
THESE IDIOTS DON'T KNOW ANYTHING.
QUILL, IT'S TIME TO GO.
WE'RE DONE HERE.
I AM GROOT.
IF THANOS WAS ON EARTH, WE'D KNOW.
RIGHT?
I MEAN, WE'D KNOW.
WE'D HAVE TO KNOW.
NEXT: THE TRIAL OF JEAN GREY!
AS THE Page TURNS AR

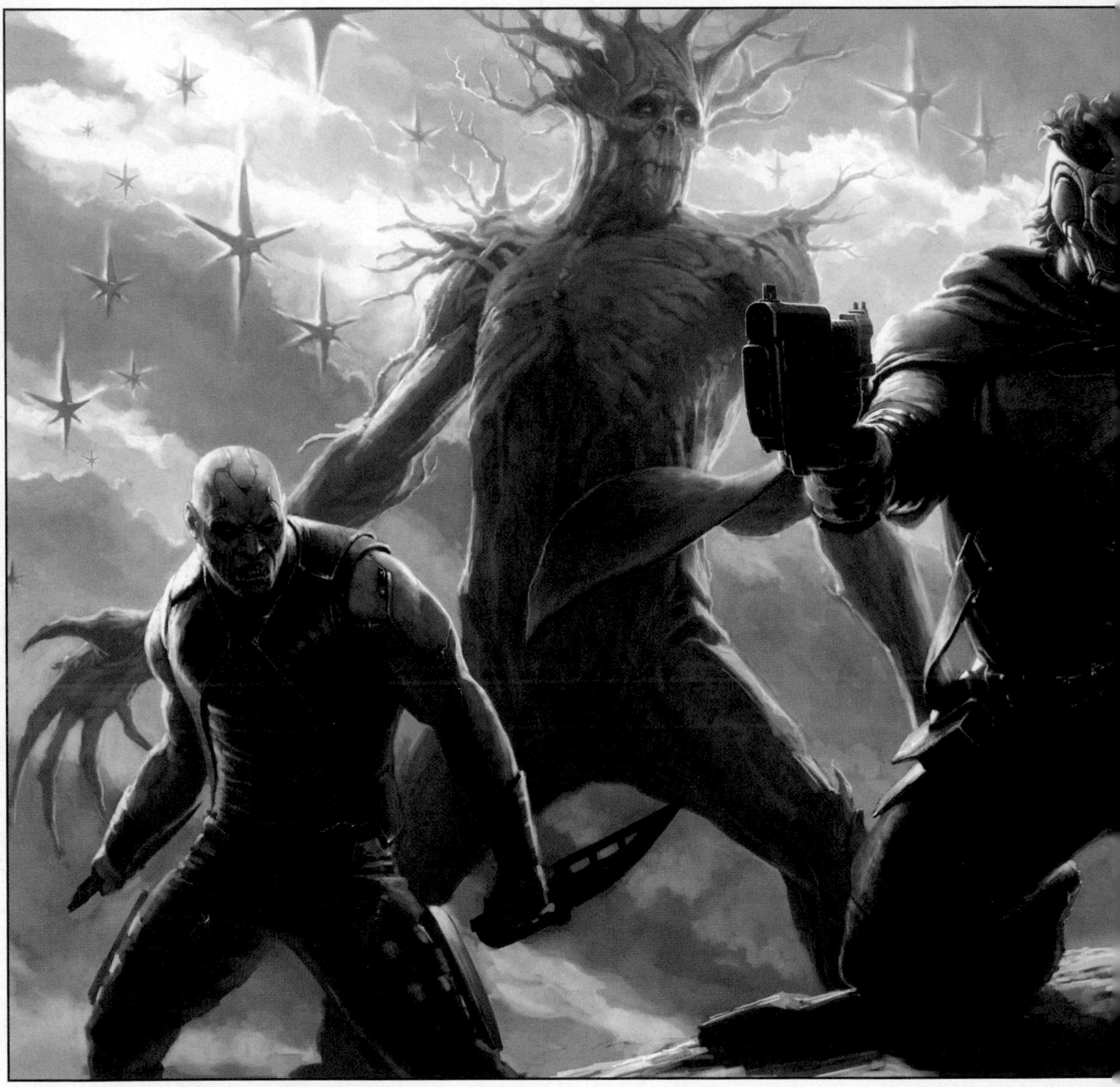

***#2-4* COMBINED VARIANTS** BY CHARLIE WEN

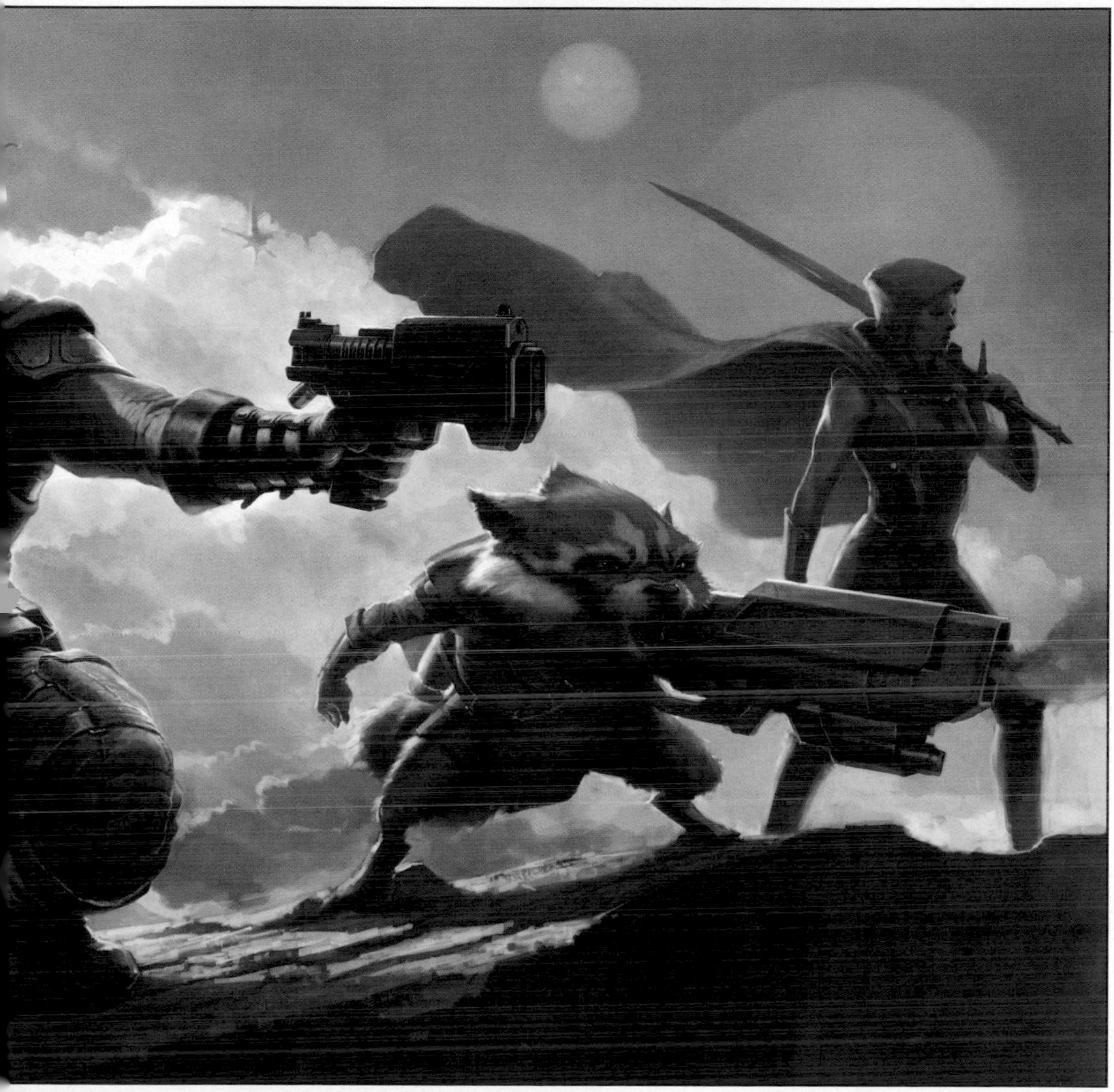

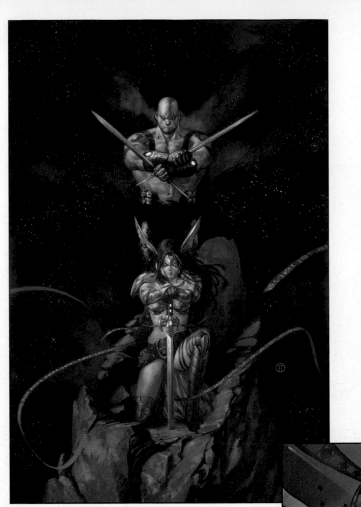

#5 DRAGON'S LAIR VARIANT
BY JULIAN TOTINO TEDESCO

#5 HASTINGS VARIANT
BY JOHN TYLER CHRISTOPHER

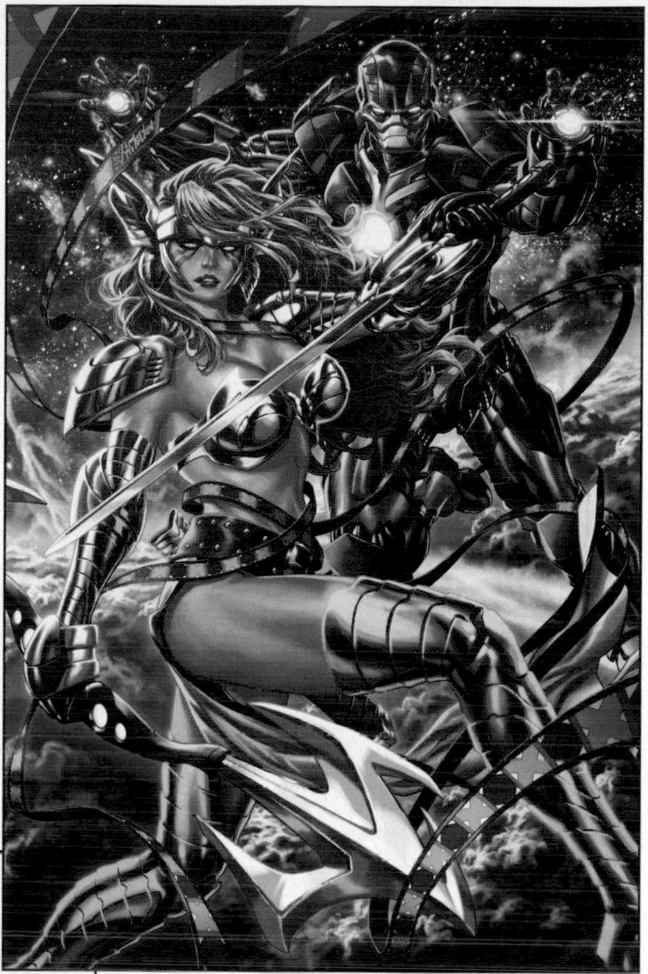

#5 MIDTOWN VARIANT
BY MARK BROOKS

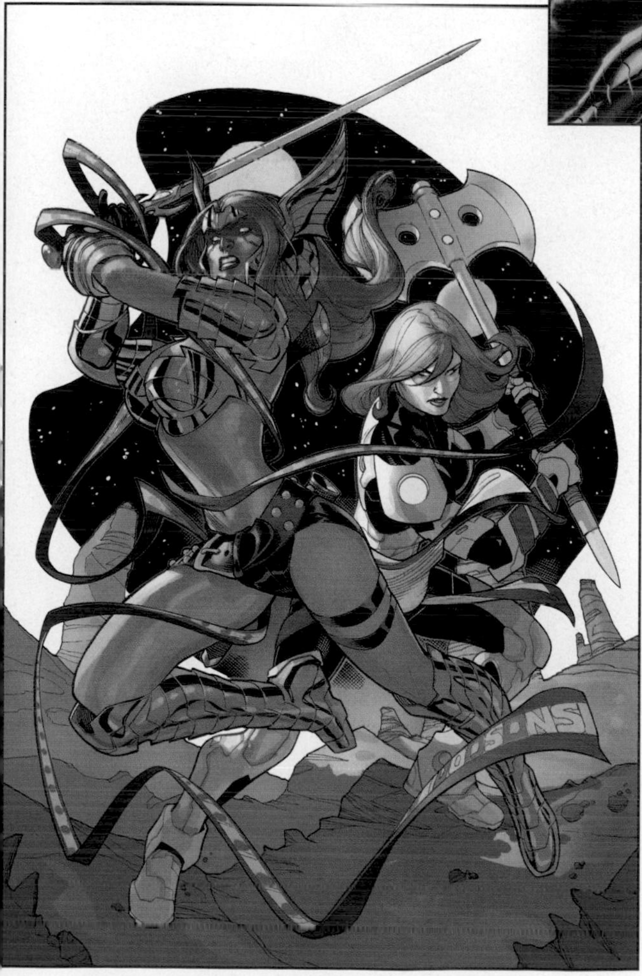

#5 MILE HIGH VARIANT
BY TERRY DODSON & RACHEL DODSON

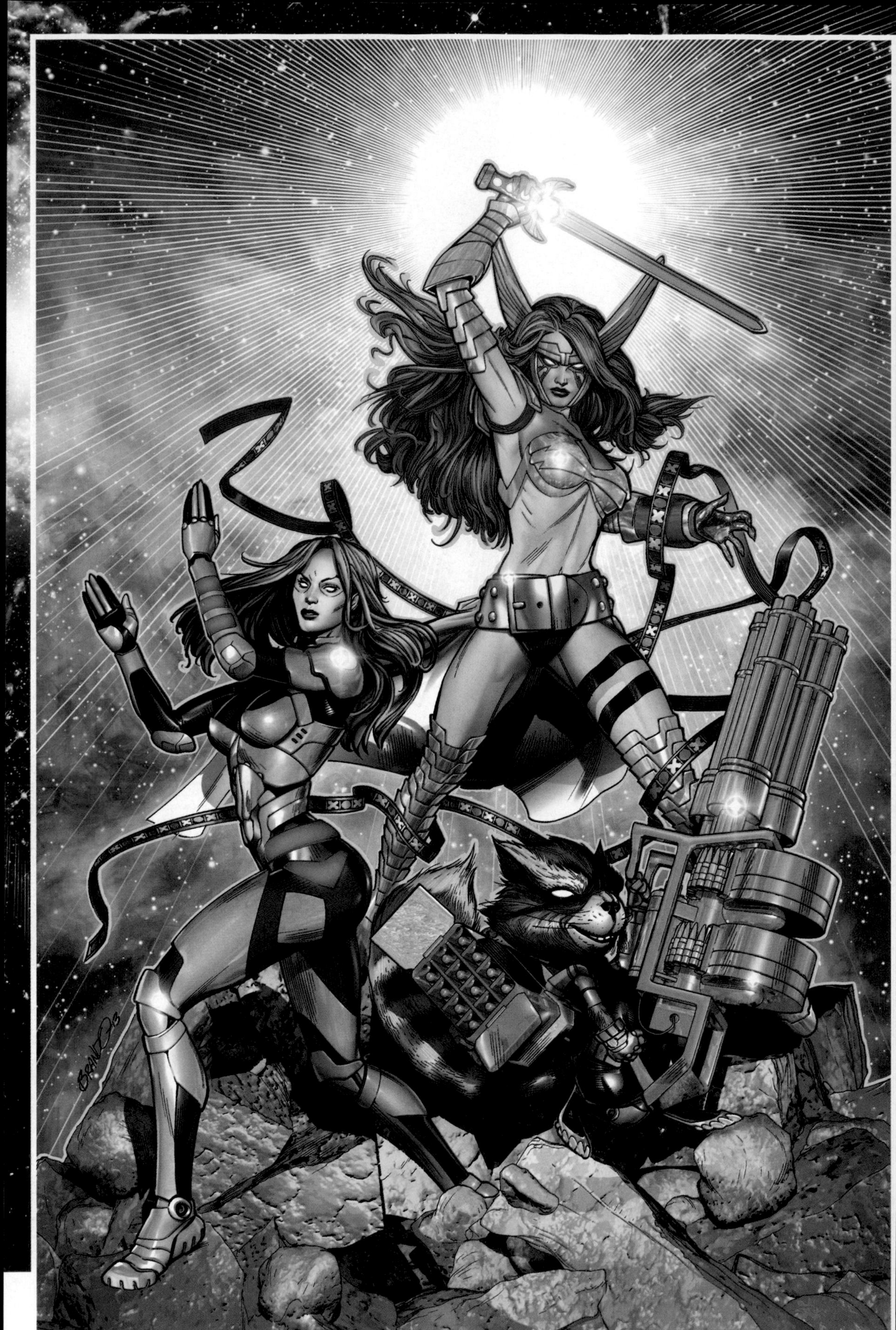

#5 FORBIDDEN PLANET VARIANT BY BRANDON PETERSON

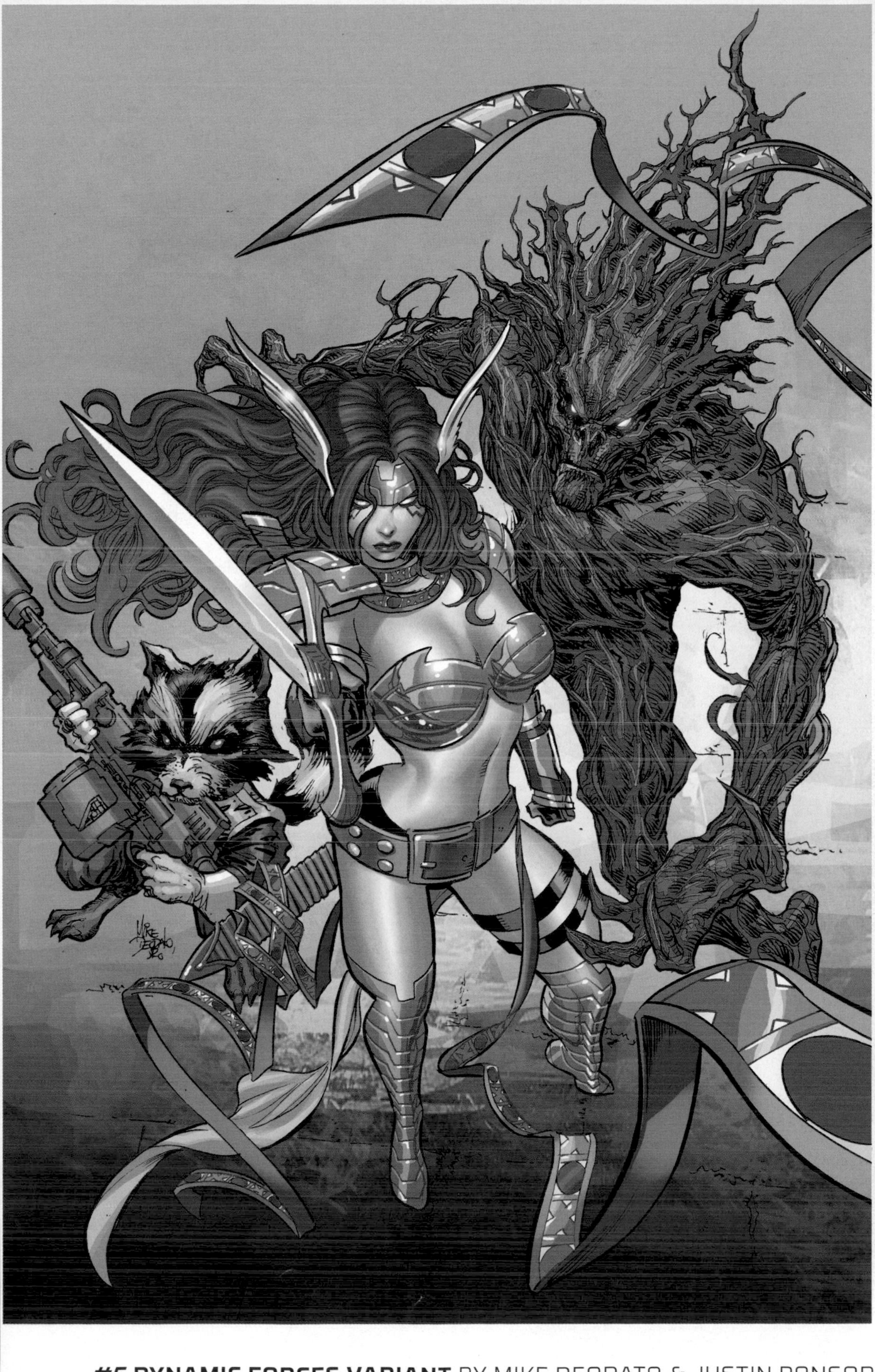

#5 DYNAMIC FORCES VARIANT BY MIKE DEODATO & JUSTIN PONSOR

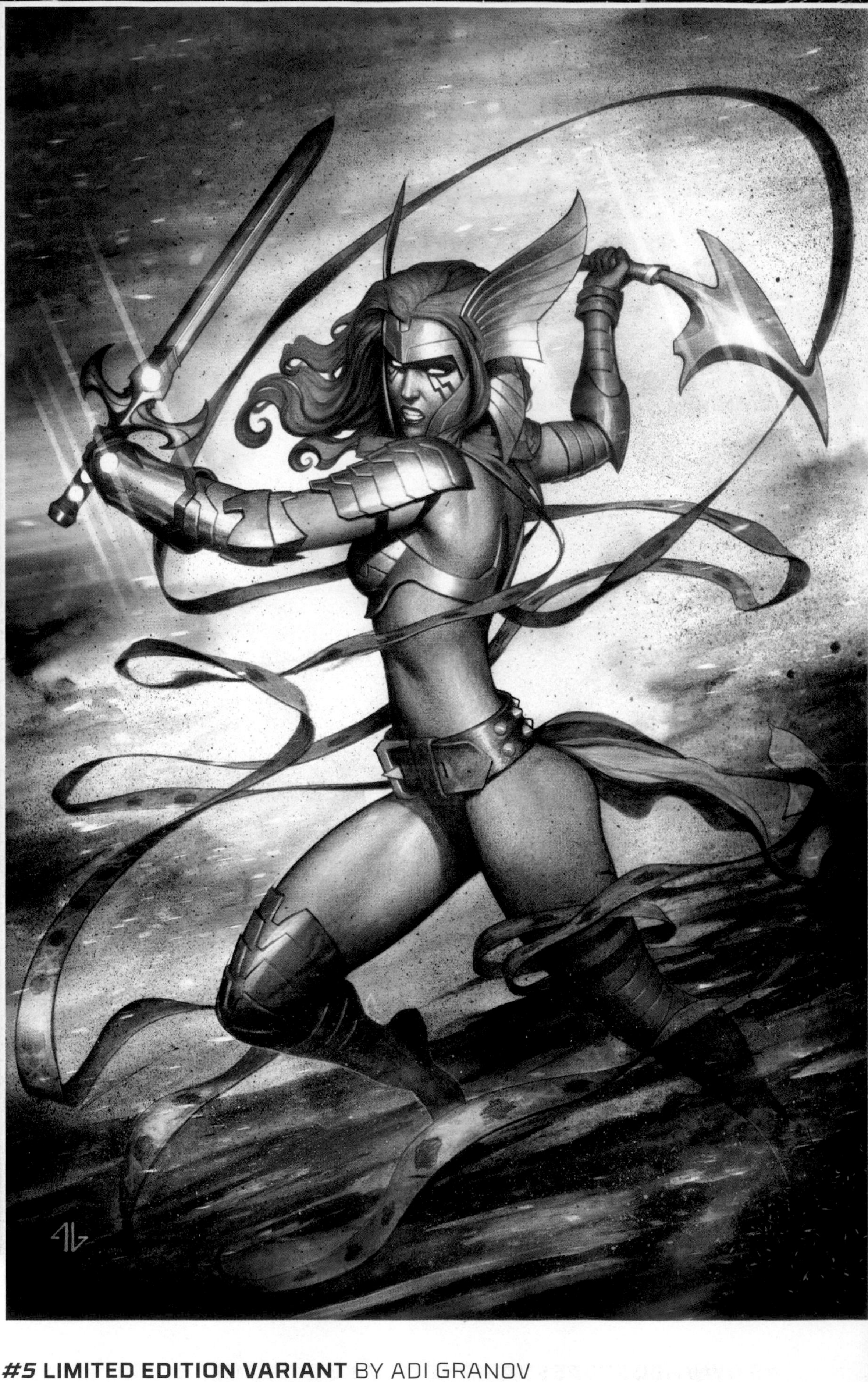

#5 LIMITED EDITION VARIANT BY ADI GRANOV

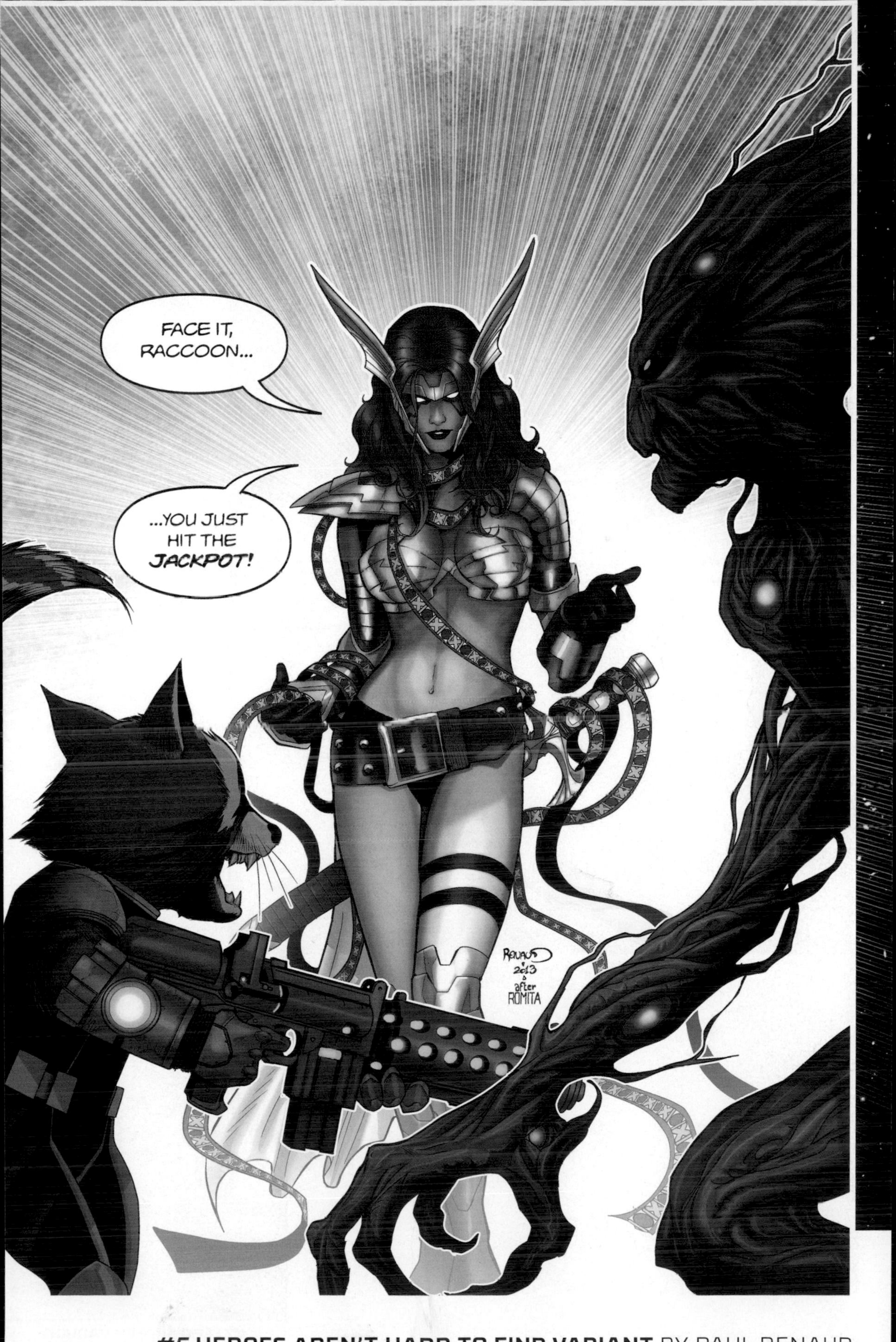
FACE IT, RACCOON...
...YOU JUST HIT THE JACKPOT!
RENAUD 2013 after ROMITA

#5 HEROES AREN'T HARD TO FIND VARIANT BY PAUL RENAUD

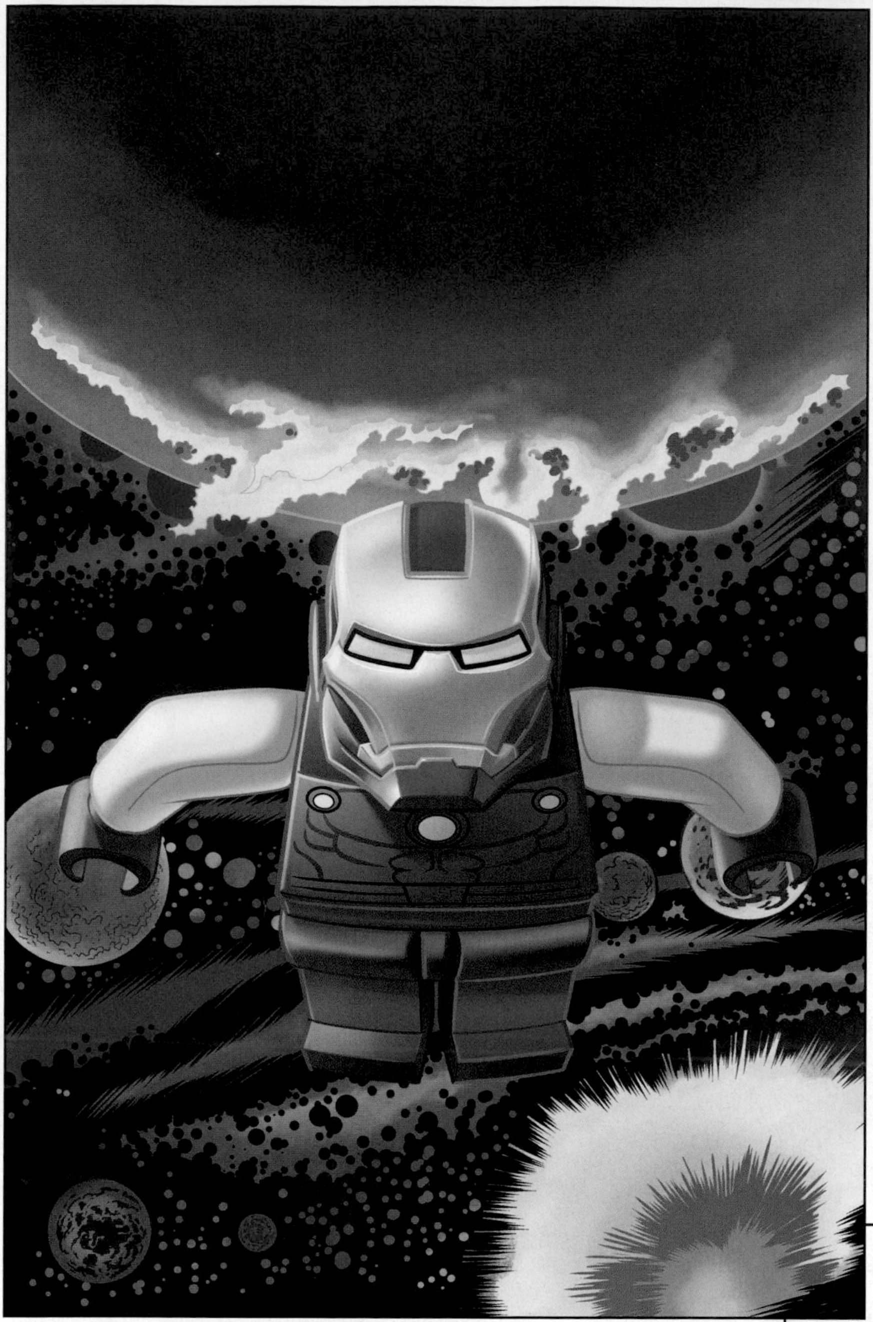

#7 LEGO VARIANT
BY LEONEL CASTELLIANI

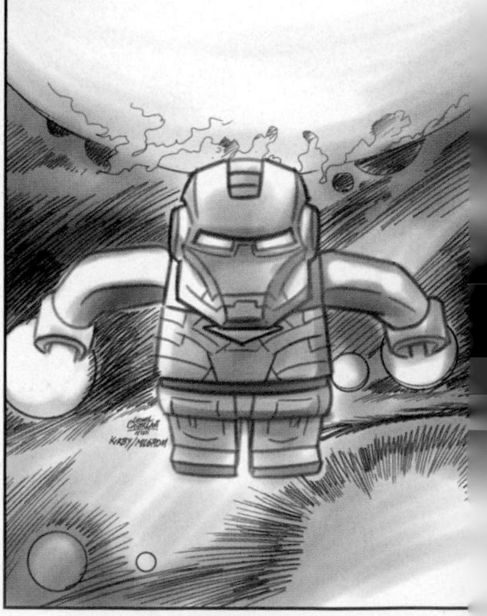

#7 LEGO SKETCH VARIANT
BY LEONEL CASTELLIANI

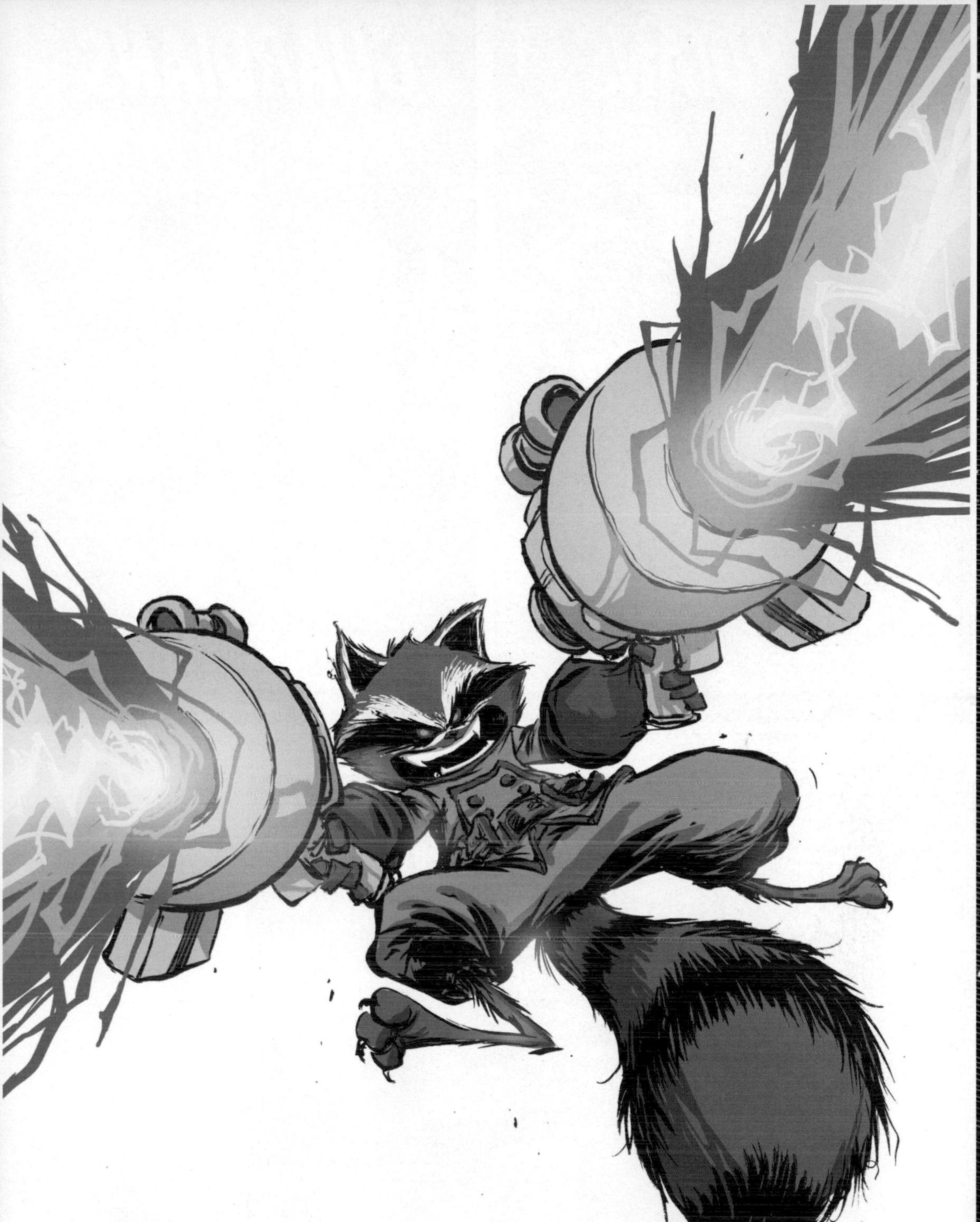
Skottie
Young
20 13

#7 VARIANT BY SKOTTIE YOUNG

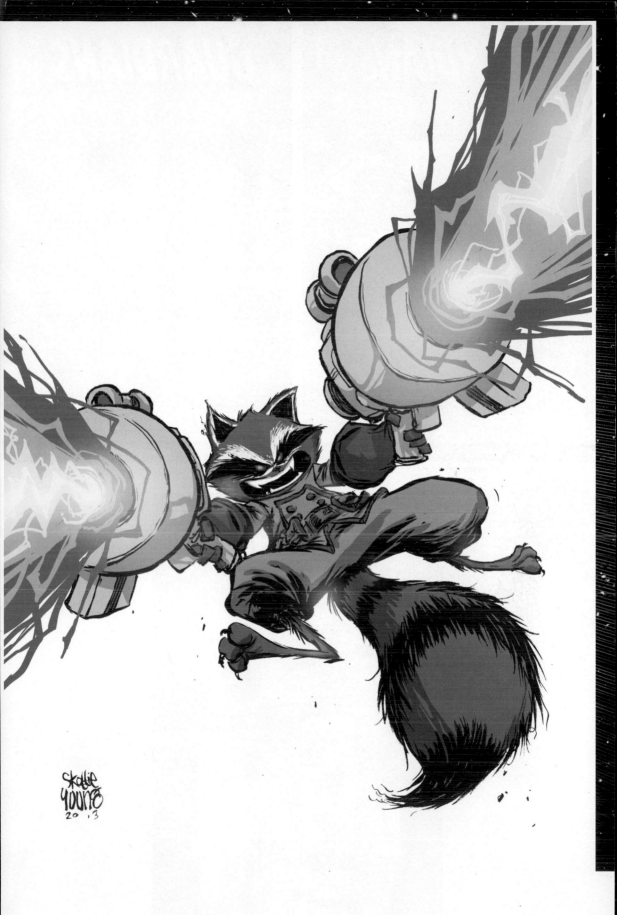

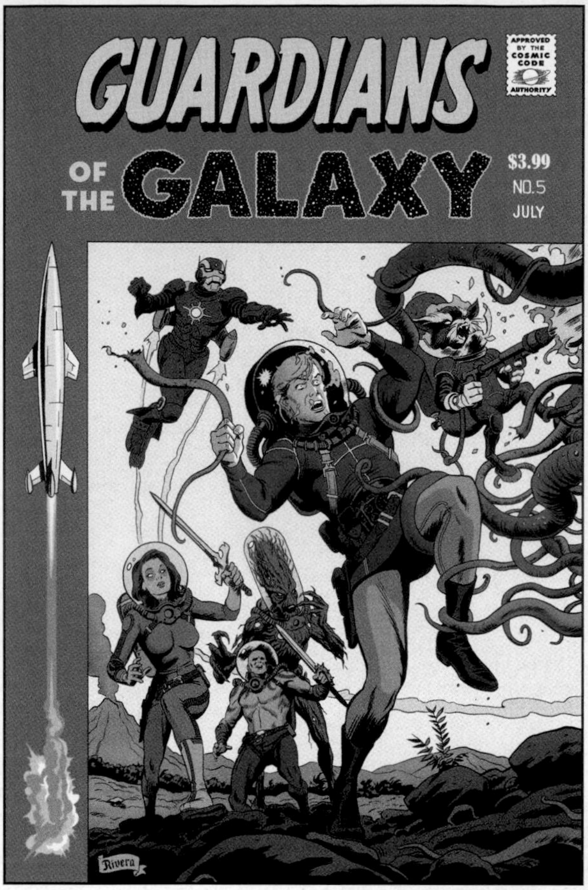
GUARDIANS
APPROVED BY THE COSMIC CODE AUTHORITY
OF THE GALAXY
$3.99
NO.5
JULY
Rivera
#5 VARIANT BY PAOLO RIVERA

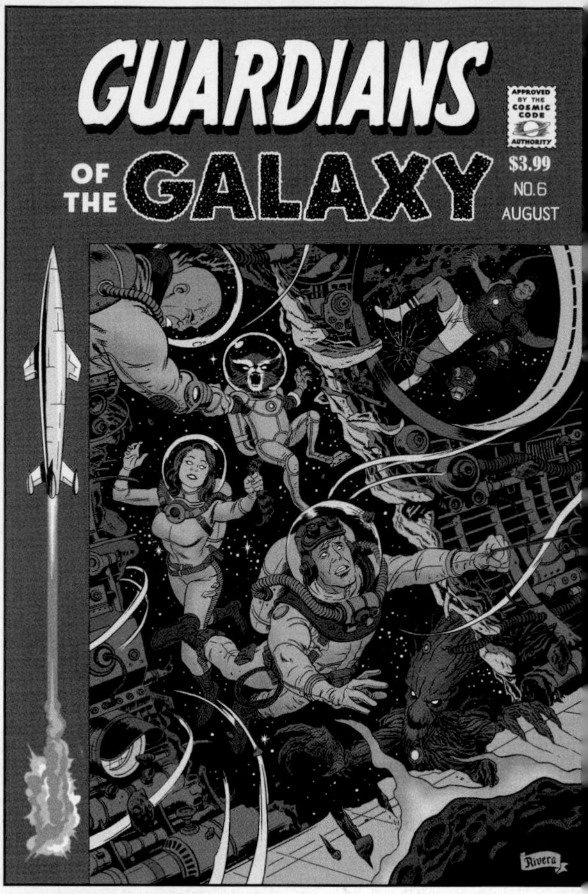
GUARDIANS
APPROVED BY THE COSMIC CODE AUTHORITY
OF THE GALAXY
$3.99
NO.6
AUGUST
Rivera
#6 VARIANT BY PAOLO RIVERA

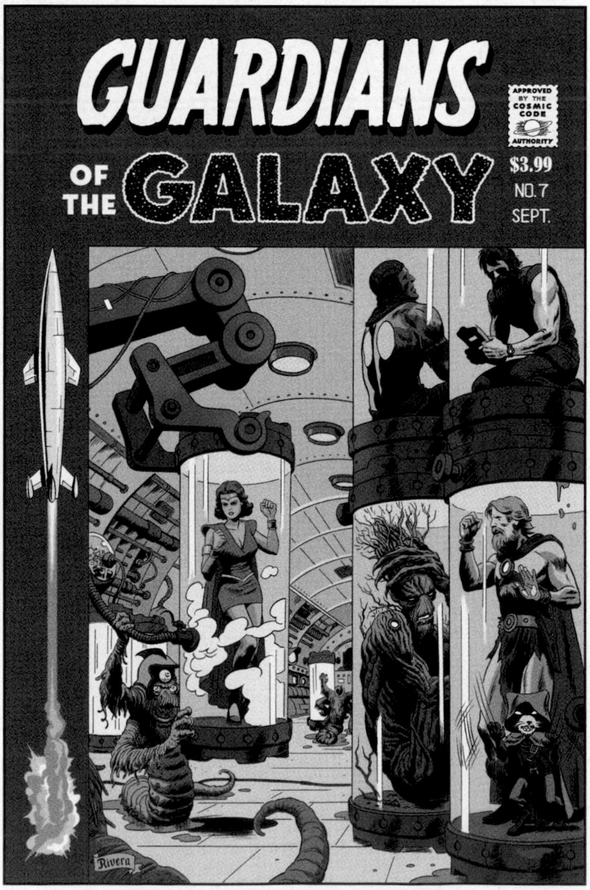
GUARDIANS
APPROVED BY THE COSMIC CODE AUTHORITY
OF THE GALAXY
$3.99
NO.7
SEPT.
Rivera
#7 VARIANT BY PAOLO RIVERA

TO ACCESS THE FREE *MARVEL AUGMENTED REALITY APP*
THAT ENHANCES AND CHANGES THE WAY YOU EXPERIENCE COMIC

1. **Download the app for free via**
   marvel.com/ARapp

2. **Launch the app on your camera-enabled Apple iOS® or Android™ device***

3. **Hold your mobile device's camera ove** any cover or panel with the **AR** grap

4. **Sit back and see the future of comics** in action!

*Available on most camera-enabled Apple iOS® and Android™ devices. Content subject to change and availability.

INDEX

Issue #4
What would you do if Tony Stark made a pass at you? .... Page 2, Panel 6
Enhancing the scene ....Page 7, Panel 5

Issue #5
AR Ambush: Brian Michael Bendis .... Pages 1-2, Panel 1
Joe Quesada on Angela in *Age of Ultron #10* .... Page 14, Panel 4

Issue #6
Enhancing the scene .... Page 10, Panel 1

Issue #7
Peter Quill's *Age of Ultron* experience .... Page 14, Panel 2
Guardians of the Galaxy cosplayers at DragonCon.................................... Page 20, Panel 1

Issue #8
Thanos flashback .... Page 4, Panel 1

Issue #9
Art evolution .... Page 16, Panel 3
As the Page Turns episode 5.. Pages 19-20, Panel 1

Issue #10
Eternals bio.. Page 20, Panel 2
As the Page Turns episode 7.. Page 21, Panel 5

TO REDEEM YOUR CODE FOR A FREE DIGITAL COPY:

1. GO TO MARVEL.COM/REDEEM. OFFER EXPIRES ON 1/29/16.

2. FOLLOW THE ON-SCREEN INSTRUCTIONS TO REDEEM YOUR DIGITAL COPY.

3. LAUNCH THE MARVEL COMICS APP TO READ YOUR COMIC NOW!

4. YOUR DIGITAL COPY WILL BE FOUND UNDER THE *MY COMICS* TAB.

5. READ & ENJOY!

YOUR FREE DIGITAL COPY WILL BE AVAILABLE O

TMA76K01HBL5

| MARVEL COMICS APP FOR APPLE® iOS DEVICES | MARVEL COMICS APP FOR ANDROID™ DEVICES |